SOUNDS OF MODER

# SOUNDS OF MODERN HISTORY

## Auditory Cultures in 19th- and 20th-Century Europe

Edited by
### Daniel Morat

berghahn
NEW YORK · OXFORD
www.berghahnbooks.com

First edition published in 2014 by
Berghahn Books
www.berghahnbooks.com

© 2014, 2017 Daniel Morat
First paperback edition published in 2017

**Library of Congress Cataloging-in-Publication Data**

Sounds of modern history: auditory cultures in 19th- and 20th-century
Europe / edited by Daniel Morat.
     pages cm
Includes bibliographical references and index.
  ISBN 978-1-78238-421-2 (hardback: alkaline paper) – ISBN 978-1-78533-
349-1 (paperback) –  ISBN 978-1-78238-422-9 (ebook)
  1.  Europe–Civilization–19th century. 2.  Europe–Civilization–20th
century. 3.  Europe–Social life and customs. 4.  Europe–Social conditions.
5.  Sound–Social aspects–Europe–History. 6.  Sound–Recording and
reproducing–Europe–History. 7.  Hearing–Social aspects–Europe–History.
8.  Noise–Social aspects–Europe–History. 9.  Social change–Europe–History.
I. Morat, Daniel, 1973-
  CB417.S68 2014
  306.09409′034–dc23

                                                              2014009648

**British Library Cataloguing in Publication Data**
A catalogue record for this book is available from the British Library

ISBN 978-1-78238-421-2 (hardback)
ISBN 978-1-78533-349-1(paperback)
E-ISBN 978-1-78238-422-9 (ebook)

# Contents

# ☙ Figures

# INTRODUCTION

*Daniel Morat*

In 2005 Michele Hilmes asked whether there was a field called "sound culture studies" and whether it mattered.[1] In 2012 the publication of the *Oxford Handbook of Sound Studies* and the *Sound Studies Reader* by Routledge was a very strong indication that there indeed is such a field and that it has already consolidated itself (that is, if handbooks and readers may generally be taken to be a sign of research consolidation in a defined field).[2] In fact, there can be no doubt that since the early 1990s, sound and auditory perception have come to play an increasingly important part in cultural studies.[3] The years after 2000 saw the publication of a number of relevant readers and collections, even before the *Oxford Handbook* and the *Sound Studies Reader* appeared.[4] Michele Hilmes's first question can therefore certainly be answered in the affirmative. But what about her second question: Does it matter?

This pertinent question can only be posed from a specific point of view. In the present collection, it will be posed from the point of view of modern history. The history of sound and of auditory perception is only a part of the larger field of sound studies, which is still dominated by media and cultural studies. Nevertheless, the subfield of sound history has also been very lively during the last few years.[5] Mark M. Smith, one of the leading proponents of the field, retraces the genealogy of scholarship on the history of sound and hearing in his essay "Futures of Hearing Pasts," which complements this introduction and which also ponders the possible future of sound history, both as a field and as a general habit of historical inquiry. But Smith has already argued in his earlier work that the aim of sound history cannot simply be to add "texture, meaning, and depth" to the history we already know. Instead, it has to open up "new storylines," that is, it has to find new explanations for historical problems and has to disclose previously unknown historical connections.[6] The central question of this collection, therefore, is whether the study of sound and of auditory cultures can open up new perspectives on the history of nineteenth- and twentieth-century Europe.

In the context of recent historiography, the scholarship on the history of sound and of hearing can be described as being part of a larger trend towards the history of the senses.[7] Within this larger trend, though, visual history is still dominant. Always comparing themselves to visual studies might, in the end, be a fruitless feature of the debates in sound studies, but it is still valid to point to the current dominance of the visual in the field of cultural and historical studies. This dominance often goes along with the thesis of a "hegemony of vision" in the modern age.[8] However, the emphasis on the "scopic regimes of modernity"[9] obscures the fact that since the mid nineteenth century the very conditions and habits of hearing and listening have also been subject to fundamental change occasioned by modern phenomena such as urbanization, industrialization, and mechanization on the one hand and the emergence of sound recording and sound transmission media on the other hand. Accordingly, it appears appropriate for historians of modernity to deal not only with visual history but also with the cultural meaning of hearing and listening, and the historical changes they have undergone. What role did sound and aurality play in the coming about of modernity? Have "auditory regimes" been equally important in the formation of modern culture and modern subjectivity as "scopic regimes"? Which dimensions of modernity have been overlooked by privileging its visual character?

In order to answer these and similar questions, the chapters in this collection focus on the period roughly between 1850 and 1950.[10] The last decades of the nineteenth century and the first two-thirds of the twentieth century have been described as the period of "high modernity," in which the most important developments of the modern age—such as industrialization and urbanization, democratization and political radicalization, the emergence of mass culture and consumer society, and the advancement of modern science and of modern media—have culminated in a maelstrom of change.[11] The emergence and distribution of new sound technologies, crucial for the transformation of auditory cultures in the modern age, fall into the same period and are part of these larger developments and changes. Many of the chapters therefore focus on the relationship between auditory cultures, sound technologies, and the development of modernity; or, to put it another way, the history of sound and of auditory cultures in the nineteenth and twentieth centuries cannot be written without taking into consideration the reproducibility of sound, which changed both the ways in which historians were, and contemporaries are, dealing with sound and sound artifacts.[12]

Many of the contributors to this collection come from the field of German history, which is why many of the historical case studies present German examples. The collection does not ask questions, though, about the specificity of national sounds.[13] Examples are also taken from the history of England, France, the Netherlands, and Austria. Rather, the chapters are based on the assumption of common developments in the industrialized nations of Europe, even if there are of course national differences and national developments that have sometimes taken different trajectories and time courses. Taken together, the chapters of this collection provide insights into the commonalities and differences of European auditory cultures in the modern age.

Finally, a comment on the concepts and semantics applied in this collection is appropriate here. It is an interesting feature of the current debates in sound studies that, despite its consolidation, the field has not yet developed a standardized terminology, let alone methodology. You can find the different notions of "sound history," "aural history," "auditory history," "history of hearing," and "history of listening," and of either "auditory," "hearing," "listening," or "audio" cultures, alongside each other without a very clear understanding of the differences between them. Accordingly, no attempts have been made to standardize the terms or concepts in the different chapters of this collection. Instead, a variety of notions and concepts have deliberately been allowed in order to present different approaches to the history of sound and of auditory cultures.

Still, there are a few basic assumptions which are shared by all contributors to this collection. The most important one can be phrased in the words of Jonathan Sterne: "Sound is an artifact of the messy and political human sphere."[14] Hearing is not simply a bodily and physical phenomenon but also a cultural capacity, and is therefore, like all sensory perception, subject to historical change. This also means that the practices of making sounds and listening to them are embedded in a wider cultural, social, and political framework, and that they are themselves being shaped by this framework at the same time as they are helping to shape it. This interplay is what the notion of "auditory culture" is intended to capture. This is why it has been chosen to function as a common denominator for this collection, even though not all of the contributors use it in their chapters.

The chapters in this collection are arranged in roughly chronological order and at the same time grouped together thematically. In Part I, as aforementioned, Mark M. Smith complements this introduction by pondering on the history and possible future of sound history. In Part II, John M. Picker and Anthony Enns trace the interplay of cultural, scientific, and technological changes of aurality in the course of the nineteenth century. In tune with Jonathan Sterne's reconstruction of the "cultural origins of sound reproduction,"[15] they both argue that the invention of sound technologies, such as the phonograph and the telephone, at the end of the nineteenth century was not the beginning of or single cause for fundamental changes in auditory cultures but rather the culmination of earlier tendencies to archive, analyze, and manipulate sound and auditory experience. Picker's chapter, "English Beat: The Stethoscopic Era's Sonic Traces," does so by dealing primarily with literary texts, which he examines for signs of a larger cultural shift toward close listening during the nineteenth century. He then analyzes several spoken word recordings of English authors made by phonograph in the 1880s and 1890s to find that the advent of sound recording simultaneously severed and deepened the relationship between speaker and speech. Anthony Enns, in his chapter "The Human Telephone: Physiology, Neurology, and Sound Technologies," retraces the ways in which the development of nineteenth-century sound technologies, such as the phonautograph, the telephone, and the audiometer, relied on scientific studies of physiology, otology, and neurology, which similarly introduced a mechanistic understanding of auditory perception. Nineteenth-century sound technologies were therefore based on the standardization, automatization, and electrification of auditory perception. That is why Enns, in his conclusion, considers them to be "inhuman."

In Part III, the chapters by Stefan Gauß and Christine Ehardt turn from the prehistory of sound technologies to the early days of their cultural adoptions and uses. They both treat the devices of early sound recording and reproduction not primarily as media of communication but as artifacts and products of industrial mass culture. Gauß, in his chapter "Listening to the Horn: On the Cultural History of the Phonograph and the Gramophone," therefore mainly speaks of "phono-objects" when referring to the devices of early sound technology. He retraces the history of their industrial manufacture and marketing, the adjustments that musicians had to make in the recording studio, the early debates about the "phonograph sound," and the cultural uses to which phono-objects were put in urban space. Christine Ehardt, in her chapter "Phones, Horns, and 'Audio Hoods' as Media of Attraction: Early Sound Histories in Vienna between 1883 and 1933," examines in particular the introduction of new sound technologies at fairs and exhibitions, theaters, and cinemas in Austria, and argues that they have initially been introduced as media of attraction—that is, as part of the amusement industry "without practical value," as one contemporary put it—before becoming mass media in the sense understood today. The same is true for early radio in the 1920s, which Ehardt treats in the second part of her chapter, thus transcending the historical caesura of World War I.

The next two chapters by Alexandra E. Hui and Sven Oliver Müller, which compose Part IV, deal with music listening and musical expertise. In her chapter, "From the Piano Pestilence to the Phonograph Solo: Four Case Studies of Musical Expertise in the Laboratory and on the City Street," Hui argues that in the years around 1900 the multiple and evolving forms of musical expertise changed in relation to the simultaneously shifting listening culture. By juxtaposing debates about musical expertise and scientific knowledge between German and Austrian musicologists, physiologists, and psychologists, such as Eduard Hanslick, Carl Stumpf, Wilhelm Wundt, and Erich von Hornbostel, with Edison's demonstration recitals of his phonograph, she shows that both scientific techniques of listening and techniques of listening inflicted by the phonograph changed the sounds that could be heard and the ones that could not be heard. In contrast to that, Sven Oliver Müller's chapter, "The Invention of Silence: Audience Behavior in Berlin and London in the Nineteenth Century," turns to the study of audience behavior in concert halls and opera houses. Müller shows that changes in listening habits do not necessarily have to be explained with the advent of sound technologies. They can also be traced back to social changes in the urban middle classes and, furthermore, to cultural transfers between different European cities and nations—in Müller's case between Berlin (where concerts audiences first fell silent) and London.

Part V deals with listening habits and the politics of sound during World War I. Daniel Morat's chapter, "Cheers, Songs, and Marching Sounds: Acoustic Mobilization and Collective Affects at the Beginning of World War I," starts by giving close attention to the outbreak of the war in Berlin in the summer of 1914. By analyzing the political dynamics of the shouting and singing in the streets of Berlin during the July crisis and the first days of the war, the chapter dissolves the clear distinction between producers and audiences of sound. Rather the cheering crowds appear to be both senders and recipients of their own acoustic message, boosting themselves into new forms of acoustic mass mobilization that point ahead to the subsequent history of the twentieth century. Hansjakob Ziemer in his chapter, "Listening on the Home Front: Music and the Production of Social Meaning in German Concert Halls during World War I," picks up Müller's question about the connection between listening practices and social interactions in concerts halls, and adds to it the political dimension of wartime nationalism. He describes how listeners used symphonic music as a projection space through which the national community could be imagined, and how individuals turned to musical experiences in order to cope with the hardships of the war on the home front.

The three chapters in Part VI, by Axel Volmar, Carolyn Birdsall, and James Mansell, then turn to the interwar period and scrutinize the impact of wartime sounds on the auditory cultures of the 1920s and 1930s. Volmar's chapter, "In Storms of Steel: The Soundscape of World War I and its Impact on Auditory Media Culture during the Weimar Period," does so by analyzing the new listening techniques developed in trench warfare and on the industrialized battlefields of World War I. Volmar then argues that the collective listening experiences of the war prepared the cultural background for the large-scale distribution of acoustic media during the Weimar Republic. He shows this, for instance, by analyzing in detail how military listening techniques transformed into civilian practices such as amateur radio. Carolyn Birdsall's chapter, "Sound Aesthetics and the Global Imagination in German Media Culture around 1930," takes up this interest in the acoustic media of the Weimar Republic. Using the concept of "auditory imagination," Birdsall asks how modern (urban) sound and auditory experience were imagined and creatively rendered in the interwar period in Germany. By more closely analyzing Fritz Walter Bischoff's 1928 radio play *Hallo! Hier Welle Erdball!*, and Walther Ruttmann's 1929 sound film *Melodie der Welt*, Birdsall shows how a global soundscape was conceived in relation to montage aesthetics, sound film techniques, and technological tropes about modern urban perception.

In contrast to Axel Volmar's emphasis on the newness of the listening techniques emerging from World War I and the transformative character of its auditory experience, James Mansell relativizes the importance of the war as a caesura in auditory cultures in his chapter, "Neurasthenia, Civilization and the Sounds of Modern Life: Narratives of Nervous Illness in the Interwar Campaign against Noise." Instead he stresses the continuities between late nineteenth-century and interwar noise abatement campaigns. He finds them especially in the ways in which French and British noise abatement activists of the interwar period still used the theories and narratives of nervousness developed before World War I to underpin their crusade against noise. In its intermingling of medical and literary accounts of nervousness, Mansell argues, interwar noise abatement built discursive bridges between the late nineteenth-century's fin-de-siècle moment and the renewed cultural pessimism of the 1930s.

The last chapter by Annelies Jacobs, "The Silence of Amsterdam before and during World War II: Ecology, Semiotics, and Politics of Urban Sound," which comprises Part VII, finally takes us into World War II. Before analyzing the silences and sounds of Amsterdam from 1918 to 1945, though, Jacobs distinguishes three different approaches to soundscapes of the past—the ecology, semiotics, and politics of sound—and advocates their combination. In her analysis of newspaper articles, diaries, and memoirs of Amsterdam residents, Jacobs then shows how the ecology, semiotics, and politics of urban sounds changed with the beginning of World War II and how, for instance, silence or the noise of an airplane could take on completely different meanings under the conditions of German occupation.

Taken together, the chapters of this collection do not offer a single narrative of the development of auditory cultures in nineteenth- and twentieth-century Europe. Instead they present different approaches and possible ways in which the study of sound and of auditory perception can contribute to a broader understanding of modern history. By doing so, they all show that, to answer Michele Hilmes's second question, sound does indeed matter and that examining how sound and auditory perception are interwoven into the fabric of modern experience helps us to get a better understanding of the past two centuries.

## Acknowledgements

In addition to all the contributors, I would like to thank Madeleine Brook and Balázs Jádi for their indispensable help with preparing the manuscript of this collection for publication. Madeleine Brook has also translated the chapter by Axel Volmar into English. Alastair Matthews has provided the translation of my chapter. Jackie Brind has created the index. Thomas Blanck and Helen Wagner have helped with proofreading. The Fritz Thyssen Stiftung has provided financial support for all of this. Martin Garstecki of the Wissenschaftskolleg zu Berlin (Institute for Advanced Study) has been a great help in bringing the authors of this collection together. At Berghahn Books, I would especially like to thank Adam Capitanio, Elizabeth Berg, Charlotte Mosedale, and Nigel Smith for turning the manuscript into a book.

# Notes

1. Michele Hilmes, "Is There a Field Called Sound Culture Studies? And Does It Matter?," *American Quarterly* 57, no. 1 (2005): 249–59.
2. Trevor Pinch and Karin Bijsterveld, eds., *The Oxford Handbook of Sound Studies* (Oxford, 2012); Jonathan Sterne, ed., *The Sound Studies Reader* (Abingdon, UK, 2012).
3. See, for instance, Rick Altman, ed., *Sound Theory, Sound Practice* (New York, 1992); Douglas Kahn and Gregory Whitehead, eds., *Wireless Imagination: Sound, Radio, and the Avant-Garde* (Cambridge, MA, 1992).
4. See Nora M. Alter and Lutz Koepenick, eds., *Sound Matters: Essays on the Acoustics of Modern German Culture* (New York, 2004); Michael Bull and Les Back, eds., *The Auditory Culture Reader* (Oxford, 2003); Jim Drobnick, ed., *Aural Cultures* (Toronto, 2004); Veit Erlmann, ed., *Hearing Cultures: Essays on Sound, Listening, and Modernity* (Oxford, 2005).
5. See, for instance, Mark M. Smith, ed., *Hearing History: A Reader* (Athens, GA, 2004).
6. Mark M. Smith, *Listening to Nineteenth-Century America* (Chapel Hill, NC, 2001), 262.
7. See Martin Jay, "In the Realm of the Senses: An Introduction," *The American Historical Review* 116 (2011): 307–15; Mark M. Smith, *Sensing the Past: Seeing, Hearing, Smelling, Tasting, and Touching in History* (Berkeley, 2007).
8. David Michael Levin, ed., *Modernity and the Hegemony of Vision* (Berkeley, 1993).
9. Martin Jay, "Scopic Regimes of Modernity," in *Vision and Visuality*, ed. Hal Foster (Seattle, 1988), 3–27.
10. Interestingly, the chapters on "Sounds European" in Mark M. Smith's collection *Hearing History* cover the Middle Ages and the early modern period up to the eighteenth century but stop at the middle of the nineteenth century; see Smith, *Hearing History*, 69–220.
11. Ulrich Herbert, "Europe in High Modernity: Reflections on a Theory of the 20th Century," *Journal of Modern European History* 5 (2007): 5–20.
12. See David Suisman and Susan Strasser, eds., *Sound in the Age of Mechanical Reproduction* (Philadelphia, 2010).
13. As other collections do; see, for instance, Alter/Koepenick, *Sound Matters*; Florence Feiereisen and Alexandra Merley Hill, eds., *Germany in the Loud Twentieth Century: An Introduction* (Oxford, 2012).
14. Jonathan Sterne, *The Audible Past: Cultural Origins of Sound Reproduction* (Durham, NC, 2003), 13.
15. Ibid.

# Bibliography

Alter, Nora M., and Lutz Koepenick, eds. *Sound Matters: Essays on the Acoustics of Modern German Culture*. New York, 2004.

Altman, Rick, ed. *Sound Theory, Sound Practice*. New York, 1992.

Bull, Michael, and Les Back, eds. *The Auditory Culture Reader*. Oxford, 2003.

Drobnick, Jim, ed. *Aural Cultures*. Toronto, 2004.

Erlmann, Veit, ed. *Hearing Cultures: Essays on Sound, Listening, and Modernity*. Oxford, 2005.

Feiereisen, Florence, and Alexandra Merley Hill, eds. *Germany in the Loud Twentieth Century: An Introduction*. Oxford, 2012.

Herbert, Ulrich. "Europe in High Modernity: Reflections on a Theory of the 20th Century," *Journal of Modern European History* 5 (2007): 5–20.

Hilmes, Michele. "Is There a Field Called Sound Culture Studies? And Does It Matter?," *American Quarterly* 57, no. 1 (2005): 249–59.

Jay, Martin. "Scopic Regimes of Modernity," in *Vision and Visuality*. Ed. Hal Foster. Seattle, 1988, 3–27.

———. "In the Realm of the Senses: An Introduction," *The American Historical Review* 116, vol. 2 (2011): 307–15.

Kahn, Douglas, and Gregory Whitehead, eds. *Wireless Imagination: Sound, Radio, and the Avant-Garde*. Cambridge, MA, 1992.

Levin, David Michael, ed. *Modernity and the Hegemony of Vision*. Berkeley, 1993.

Pinch, Trevor, and Karin Bijsterveld, eds. *The Oxford Handbook of Sound Studies*. Oxford, 2012.

Smith, Mark M. *Listening to Nineteenth-Century America*. Chapel Hill, NC, 2001.

———. *Sensing the Past: Seeing, Hearing, Smelling, Tasting, and Touching in History*. Berkeley, 2007.

———, ed. *Hearing History: A Reader*. Athens, GA, 2004.

Sterne, Jonathan. *The Audible Past: Cultural Origins of Sound Reproduction*. Durham, NC, 2003.

———, ed. *The Sound Studies Reader*. Abingdon, UK, 2012.

Suisman, David, and Susan Strasser, eds. *Sound in the Age of Mechanical Reproduction*. Philadelphia, 2010.

# PART I

# SOUND HISTORY IN PERSPECTIVE

1

# FUTURES OF HEARING PASTS

*Mark M. Smith*

Consider this chapter as a meditation of sorts, one that ponders the future of sound studies. I could take the additive, enumerative approach and simply list specific topics that I suspect will emerge in the field in the next decade. And, to be sure, I will do a little of that. But I have opted to think about something a little broader, with reach, traction, and interpretive purchase—and, frankly, with much greater fidelity to the actual history and historiography of sound studies that goes beyond mere prognostication and enumeration. I would like, in short, to consider how sound studies, both as a field and as an intellectual habit, will serve the discipline of history.[1]

To do this, I need to attend to a couple of matters first. For reasons that will become clear, this chapter needs to reflect, albeit briefly, on the genealogy of the writing on the history of sound, sound studies, and historical acoustemology. It also considers the current state of the "field" in an effort to suggest what writing on sound studies might look, and sound, like a decade or more from now. In the process, I stress the largely underappreciated "deep" origins of the field, trace its growth in the 1990s, and try to account for the veritable explosion of studies in the past decade. I will then argue that the "field" of sound studies is also helpfully and profitably understood as a desirable "habit" of historical inquiry. The chapter ends by considering the best metrics for evaluating the success of sound studies in future years.

The differences between sound studies as a "field" and sound studies as a "habit" are important, and warrant brief definition. By "field" I mean, simply, a fairly delimited and professionally communicable and digestible area of scholarly inquiry, replete with its own consciousness as a field and its own imperatives. Hence, the field of sound studies is not unlike the field of, say, women's studies or visual studies, albeit less well developed at the moment. By "habit" I mean methodological, epistemological, and even ontological embeddedness—a way of examining the past that becomes second nature so that evidence is read, consciously and even subconsciously, for tidbits of the acoustic, smatterings of the auditory, gestures of silence, noise, listening, and sound. Habit is apparent when scholars who are not self-identified sound studies practitioners begin to think like sound studies practitioners, or when colleagues in, say, women's studies or visual studies begin to excavate evidence of acoustemology and incorporate that evidence into their own work, thereby adding texture, meaning, and interpretive purchase to that work. The habit of sound studies is far less developed than the field, but I strongly suspect that a decade or so from now, scholars interested in the study of sound, especially those in the humanities, will be talking about not only the maturation of the field, but the maturation of the habit beyond their own disciplinary imperatives and inquiries.

My operative questions, the ones I will try to answer throughout, are these: How will we know when the "field" is no longer "new"? How do our colleagues working in other areas of historical inquiry use, perceive, and understand sound studies? What are the particular intellectual and interpretive dividends of a matured historiography? And what are the barriers to that maturation? Briefly, my answers to these questions are as follows: The origins of sound studies, at least as understood and practiced by historians, were to some extent, even if unwittingly, a product of a shift toward a brand of social history that stressed intersensoriality—or, at least, the importance of multisensory understanding, in which sound, silence, noise, and acoustemology generally, were framed within the larger coordinates of the senses generally. To be sure, these early efforts were modest, bereft of much interpretive power, and less than robust. But they were important not least because they tended, again perhaps inadvertently, to treat the study of the senses generally as less than a discrete "field" and more as a desirable intellectual habit of historical inquiry.

My second point, and one we might profitably think of as the second stage in the growth of sound studies, details the way in which sound studies evolved and is, in fact, still evolving. This is perhaps best characterized as a moment in which historians trained in traditional evidentiary categories began to write about sound within those same categories—those at once veining their "fields" with a habit of sound consciousness and, simultaneously, paying less attention to intersensoriality. Rather, they began profiling sound more conspicuously and almost exclusively. This trend, one that is welcome and fruitful for reasons explained below, began in the 1990s and continues now.

My last point—and the most conjectural of the arguments presented here—asks what sound studies might look and sound like a decade or two from now. This is, of course, an audacious, even silly question, one begging contradiction. But I tentatively argue that sound studies might well follow two, simultaneous tracks. The first will be the continued emphasis on what I consider dedicated sound works: works that frame their historical inquiries explicitly and unapologetically within the rubrics of acoustemology. This will constitute the continued development of the field of historical sound studies. The second track will be the related and, in fact, braided relationship between historical sound studies as a field and historical sound studies as a scholarly and increasingly public habit. Sound studies will, I venture, not only percolate into the public realm and become embedded in textbook narratives and various forms of public history (most likely in museums), but will also, ironically and perhaps poetically, return to intersensoriality, but on a much more enhanced, robust basis than was apparent in the work of early social, sensory-minded historians. And there will be significant benefits from such a course of action, if it is done properly. Perhaps the greatest challenge facing the popularization of sound studies, and applied sensory history generally, will be the continued and appropriate historicization of the topic and efforts to resist offering up a digestible, communicable, usable, but ultimately deeply misleading application of the sensate past.

In 2000, Douglas Kahn, arguably one of the pioneers of sound studies, wrote in *The Australian Review of Books* that sound studies were now "awake," courtesy of the work of a host of historians from different countries in multiple disciplines. Many of them were working in relative isolation, seemingly unaware that their colleagues in different sub-specialties were also beginning to study field-specific historical problems from the perspective of acoustemology. For most of the 1990s, this was indeed the case, and, in fact, had been so since the first toe-dipping into sensory history a couple of decades earlier. Up until quite recently, sound studies had been practiced by historians (myself included) who were trained in conventional fields—such as early modern English history, modern French history, environmental history, U.S. nineteenth-century history—and they had found their way to acoustemology by applying auditory insights in an effort to better understand the particular interpretive imperatives facing their specific fields.[2]

One reason for this coming or "awakening," as Kahn called it, to historical sound studies was because of the emergence of social history, beginning mainly in the 1970s. I have elaborated this argument elsewhere, but it is worth emphasizing that social history's tendency to consider the breadth, depth, and interlaced aspects of the human experience helped create a frame of mind and nurse an investigative temper and way of understanding that helped a variety of historians go beyond an unwittingly visualist representation of the past.[3]

We might profitably summarize the evolution of the history of the senses, from the early work of the Annales school and social history through to the early 2000s, by highlighting four main points. First, it seems clear that early social history's interest in what we might consider deep excavation had the effect of alerting historians to the senses generally. Second, from there, we witnessed the growth of subfield specific sound studies, works that in part grew out of social history inspired subfields, such as environmental history, that cleaved towards a history of sound in an effort to answer subfield specific questions. Third, it seems that most of the post-Annales work tended to frame itself in oppositional terms, principally in the form of reacting against what writers understood as an occularcentric way of understanding the past. Lastly, most of the work written in this period was framed within the histories of specific nation states, most notably France, England, and the United States.

Parallel to, and related to, these trends was the emergence of a way of understanding the field of sound studies that was indebted to Science and Technology Studies (STS). STS signaled an early maturation in the field by attending to sound in a nonoppositional way, by making firmer gestures toward the importance of intersensoriality, and by increasingly moving away from the study of single nation states. The first two points are apparent in, for example, Emily Thompson's superb study, *The Soundscape of Modernity: Architectural Acoustics and the Culture of Listening in America, 1900–1933*. Thompson describes her book as "a history of aural culture," one charting "dramatic transformations in what people heard" and "equally significant changes in the ways that people listened." Thompson's study uses listening to give depth beyond the eye, "to recover more fully the texture of an era known as 'The Machine Age,'" and to "comprehend more completely the experience of change." Thompson follows Alain Corbin and the Annales school, and conceives of a soundscape as "simultaneously a physical environment and a way of perceiving that environment; it is both a world and a culture constructed to make sense of that world."[4]

Thompson claims that a "soundscape's cultural aspects incorporate scientific and aesthetic ways of listening, a listener's relationship to their environment, and the social circumstances that dictate who gets to hear what." Rather than focusing exclusively on how "social circumstances" dictated cultural norms of listening, Thompson is also alert to the interplay between subjectivity and experience and changes in structure and society, thus braiding the important work of social and cultural historians with emerging work by historians of the environment.[5] She locates the shifts in how people listened to changes in sound, themselves "the result of technological mediation" in which "[s]cientists and engineers discovered ways to manipulate traditional materials of architectural construction in order to control the behavior of sound in space." Some of these changes in sound were incidental to the rise of industrial and urban modernity, while others were a product of technological and architectural advances. Contingent on these material changes were "new trends in the culture of listening," and Thompson uses shifts and advances in both to trace the emergence of modernity in twentieth-century America.[6]

While Thompson tends to focus on the work of scientists in their production of sound and manipulation of acoustical spaces, she remains sensitive to the public implications of the anti-noise crusades of the early twentieth century, the timing and significance of the creation of quiet zones, and municipal authorities' reconfiguration of noise ordinances. Like the early work of environmental historian Raymond Smilor, she also situates her work within the broader understanding of how noise, and its regulation and meaning, was contested by different constituencies and social groups. Following Douglas Kahn's admonition, Thompson tries to show that modernity must be heard as well as seen, and she does not see vision and aurality in necessary tension. Her aim, instead, is to insert listening and hearing into future investigations into the rise of modernity, and Thompson sees the interaction between materialism and consciousness as critical to investigations of the historical process.[7]

Recent work, especially work rooted in STS (though not exclusively so), suggests two new directions: first, work is increasingly sensitive to all of the senses and the relationships between them, even as it remains framed within the coordinates of historical acoustemology; and second, newer work ventures, quite deliberately, to go beyond the treatment of discreet national experiences. This tendency, one that does not preclude examination of nationally framed acoustemological histories, is apparent in the work of several historians. Witness, for example, the work of John Picker, whose superb *Victorian Soundscapes* gestures toward an explicitly transnational history. James Mansell is also doing similar work. Perhaps the best example of the move toward transnational historical acoustemology is Karin Bijsterveld's 2008 study, *Mechanical Sound: Technology, Culture, and Public Problems of Noise in the*

*Twentieth Century*, which examines the history of noise and anti-noise campaigns in France, Britain, the United States, Germany, and the Netherlands.[8] This tendency toward transnational, comparative sound studies is all to the good for two main reasons. First, and preeminently, sound studies, like the history of the senses generally, has always been rooted in a thoroughly historicized understanding of its subject and has aggressively and rightly eschewed universalist conceits which offer bland and unpersuasive claims about the transcendental nature of the senses. Historical sound studies offer little by way of "is," but rather, and properly, stress the highly contingent "was." Almost without exception, sound studies situates its subject historically and, in the process, highlights the way that history, time, place, and context shaped changing, and sometimes competing, meanings of sound, noise, and silence. There is no better way to profile this understanding than to compare and contrast those meanings, not only over time but through space. This is most likely one of the motivating factors behind this shift to the transnational. The shift is also clearly indebted to larger forces in our profession, which have been pushing for more and better transnational histories generally for a long time. And yet sound studies is not simply reactive; rather, and as I recently argued, sensory history also functions in an inspirational fashion, pushing colleagues to think more expansively—not just about space and time, but about the full senate texture of the past.[9]

These tendencies are also apparent in the recent *Oxford Handbook of Sound Studies*, edited by Karin Bijsterveld and Trevor Pinch. It brings together dozens of scholars of sound, some conventional social historians (such as myself), others keenly interested in the cultural representation and meaning of sound, noise, and silence, and still others working on various aspects of the history, biology, and epistemologies of hearing. Certainly, the essays in the collection (my own included) are frequently and very helpfully anchored in national histories, but a good number of them offer transnational comparisons and are deliberately and refreshingly geographically fugitive. The collection is also interdisciplinary, and the authors refuse to be contained by conventional categories of analysis. They examine the material production and consumption of sound and silence, noise and music; they focus on the materiality of sound, stressing that sound is not only embedded in history, society, and culture, but also in science, technology, and medicine—their instruments, machines, and ways of knowing and interacting. Most of the essays are not written in deliberate opposition to vision, and many of them gesture, sometimes quietly, sometimes loudly, toward the importance of intersensoriality. Work on the acoustemology of the automobile, for example, often points toward the probable relevance of the sense of touch (through vibration), and the likely importance of smell as an additional sense that helped reinscribe the cultural aesthetics guiding the acoustics of automobile design. So, too, with the collection's treatment of the acoustemology of medicine, a topic that inevitably touches on the history of the tactile, olfactory, visual, and tasting body.[10]

This sort of conceptual and empirical work will invite, and already is inviting, a reconfiguration of sound studies as a field into sound studies as an investigative habit. The field of sound studies is alive and kicking, and will continue to grow. Like other fields, it is being taught as such in universities, and university presses are increasingly publishing and treating it as a field of historical and scholarly inquiry. But more than that, sound studies is also entering into the habits of scholarly and public consciousness, becoming increasingly apparent not only in college textbooks, but also in the public realm, especially in museums. Although such endeavors are not new, they are becoming more common, presumably because museums believe that sensory installments in their spaces are appealing and meaningful to visitors.

To their credit, museum curators and curators of historical homes are, increasingly it seems, turning to historians of the senses for advice about how best to incorporate the senses into their spaces. The most thoughtful curators are anxious to historicize the senses so that visitors get a sense not only of, say, the sounds of late nineteenth-century Chicago (as is the case, for example, at the Jane Addams Hull House), but, critically, what those sounds meant to people who lived in Chicago at that time. In other words, the best historical sites seek to distinguish between the reproduction of a sound from the past and how the meaning of that sound or noise or silence has changed over time. At play here is a question—one that museum curators have not always asked—about the historicity of the senses, their reproducibility, and whether or not we can (or ought to) try to reexperience the sensate past.[11] The problem is not a new one. In his seminal commentary on how best to approach a history of the senses, Alain Corbin expressed similar concerns in his discussion of Guy Thuillier's "positivist" effort to "trace the evolution of the sensory environment." Thuillier, explained Corbin, "has attempted to compile a catalogue and measure the relative intensity of the noises which might reach the ear of a villager in the Nivernais in the middle of the nineteenth century." Indeed, there is something alluring about the apparent innocence of mere cataloging, and good minds can be fooled. Even Corbin had some nice, if perhaps too charitable, things to say about this approach. He thinks that reading Thuiller's catalogue "you can almost hear … the ringing of the hammer on the anvil, the heavy thud of the wooden mallet wielded by the [c]artwright, the insistent presence of bells and the whinny of horses in an aural environment where the noise of the amplifier was unknown." There are other reasons Corbin believes this approach "is by no means negligible": "[i]t aids immersion in the village of the past; [and] it encourages the adoption of a comprehensive viewpoint." But Corbin also says that such an approach "is based on a questionable postulate, it implies the non-historicity of the modalities of attention, thresholds of perception, significance of noises, and configuration of the tolerable and the intolerable." Without a dedicated and careful attempt to attach meaning to those noises, cataloging is not only of very modest heuristic worth, but is, in fact, quite dangerous in its ability to inspire unwitting faith that these are the "real" and unchanging sounds of the past.[12]

Keeping Corbin's counsel in mind will be important as we help curators think about not only which sounds to deploy (either newly recorded or archivally reproduced), but also how to deploy them. Here, we need to stress the preeminent importance of contextualizing the sounds that museum visitors hear. Rather than simply feeding sounds to ears, we need to help visitors understand the context in which those sounds were produced, and how their reproduction can tell us not only about the nature of the past, but about our own intellectual preferences and prejudices.

The migration of sound studies as a field into the public realm will, I suspect, continue, and it holds implications. It will continue in several ways, not just into museums, but also, and increasingly, into textbooks for teaching introductory history courses. Already, we are beginning to see the introduction of the sensate, especially the auditory, into textbook narratives, and, in that process, we are seeing the emergence of the habit of sound studies. Textbook writers are braiding the sounds of the past, borrowing liberally from our field, and, in the process, habituating themselves to the sort of auditory and sensate evidence usually excluded from such narratives. And as sound studies becomes increasingly transnational and comparative it will also become increasingly intersensorial, so that we will begin to write more expansively about the relationship between sound and vision, sound and touch, and especially sound and smell.

To put it pithily but, I hope, meaningfully: it is not the case that sound studies "the field" will become subsumed by sound studies "the habit"; rather, sound studies will become ever more vibrant precisely because it has the capacity to inform the habit of historical research and consciousness in many other fields and venues.

## Notes

1. See also Richard Cullen Rath, "Hearing American History," *Journal of American History* 95 (2008): 417–31; Sophia Rosenfeld, "A Case for Paying Attention to the Historical Ear," *American Historical Review* 116 (2011), 316–34.
2. Douglas Kahn, "Sound Awake," *Australian Review of Books* (2000), 21–22.
3. See Mark M. Smith, "Making Sense of Social History," *Journal of Social History* 37 (2003), 165–86.
4. Emily Thompson, *The Soundscape of Modernity: Architectural Acoustics and the Culture of Listening in America, 1900–1933* (Cambridge, 2002), 1.
5. For recent work on environmental history, sound, and the senses generally, see Peter A. Coates, "The Strange Stillness of the Past: Toward an Environmental History of Sound and Noise," *Environmental History* 10 (October 2005), 1–33; Joy Parr, *Sensing Changes* (Vancouver, 2010). See, too, Sarah Keyes, "'Like a Roaring Lion': The Overland Trail as a Sonic Conquest," *Journal of American History* 96 (2009), 19–43.
6. Thompson, *Soundscape of Modernity*, ch. 5, 1–4.
7. Ibid., ch. 4, 9–11. Douglas Kahn, "Introduction: Histories of Sound Once Removed," in *Wireless Imagination: Sound, Radio, and the Avant-Garde*, eds. Douglas Kahn and Gregory Whitehead (Cambridge, 1992), 1–29. See also Hillel Schwartz, "Beyond Tone and Decibel: The History of Noise," *Chronicle of Higher Education* (9 January 1998), B8.
8. John M. Picker, *Victorian Soundscapes* (Oxford, 2003); James Mansell, *Sound and Selfhood in Early Twentieth-Century Britain* (Urbana, forthcoming); Karin Bijsterveld, *Mechanical Sound: Technology, Culture, and Public Problems of Noise in the Twentieth Century* (Cambridge, 2008).
9. Mark M. Smith, "Still Coming to 'Our' Senses," *Journal of American History* 95 (September 2008), 378–80.
10. Trevor Pinch and Karin Bijsterveld, eds., *The Oxford Handbook of Sound Studies* (Oxford, 2012).
11. These are points I raised in my keynote address, "Looking to Make Sense: Perils and Prospects in Applied Sensory History," *Historic House Luncheon, Annual Meeting of the American Association of Museums* (Los Angeles, 24 May 2010).
12. Alain Corbin, *Time, Desire and Horror: Towards a History of the Senses* (Cambridge, 1995), 183. Note also Joy Parr, "Notes for a More Sensuous History of Twentieth-Century Canada: The Timely, the Tacit, and the Material Body," *Canadian Historical Review* 82 (December 2001), 720–45; and Richard M. Carp, "Perception and Material Culture: Historical and Cross-Cultural Perspectives," *Historical Reflections/Réflexions Historiques* 23 (1997), 269–300.

# Bibliography

Bijsterveld, Karin. *Mechanical Sound: Technology, Culture, and Public Problems of Noise in the Twentieth Century*. Cambridge, 2008.

Carp, Richard M. "Perception and Material Culture: Historical and Cross-Cultural Perspectives." *Historical Reflections/Reflexions Historiques* 23 (1997): 269–300.

Coates, Peter A. "The Strange Stillness of the Past: Toward an Environmental History of Sound and Noise." *Environmental History* 10 (October 2005): 1–33.

Corbin, Alain. *Time, Desire and Horror: Towards a History of the Senses*. Cambridge, 1995.

Kahn, Douglas. "Sound Awake." *Australian Review of Books* (July 2000): 21–22.

———. "Introduction: Histories of Sound Once Removed." In *Wireless Imagination: Sound, Radio, and the Avant-Garde*. Eds. Douglas Kahn and Gregory Whitehead. Cambridge, 1992, 1–29.

Keyes, Sarah. "'Like a Roaring Lion': The Overland Trail as a Sonic Conquest." *Journal of American History* 96 (June 2009): 19–43.

Mansell, James. *Sound and Selfhood in Early Twentieth-Century Britain*. Urbana, IL, forthcoming.

Parr, Joy. "Notes for a More Sensuous History of Twentieth-Century Canada: The Timely, the Tacit, and the Material Body." *Canadian Historical Review* 82 (December 2001): 720–45.

———. *Sensing Changes*. Vancouver, 2010.

Picker, John M. *Victorian Soundscapes*. Oxford, 2003.

Pinch, Trevor, and Karin Bijsterveld, eds. *The Oxford Handbook of Sound Studies*. Oxford, 2012.

Rath, Richard Cullen. "Hearing American History," *Journal of American History* 95 (September 2008): 417–31.

Rosenfeld, Sophia. "A Case for Paying Attention to the Historical Ear." *American Historical Review* 116 (April 2011): 316–34.

Schwartz, Hillel. "Beyond Tone and Decibel: The History of Noise." *Chronicle of Higher Education* (9 January 1998): B8.

Smith, Mark M. "Making Sense of Social History." *Journal of Social History* 37 (September 2003): 165–86.

———. "Still Coming to 'Our' Senses." *Journal of American History* 95 (September 2008): 378–80.

———. "Looking to Make Sense: Perils and Prospects in Applied Sensory History." *Historic House Luncheon, Annual Meeting of the American Association of Museums*. Los Angeles, 24 May 2010.

Thompson, Emily. *The Soundscape of Modernity: Architectural Acoustics and the Culture of Listening in America, 1900–1933*. Cambridge, 2002.

# PART II

# LITERATURE, SCIENCE, AND SOUND TECHNOLOGIES IN THE NINETEENTH CENTURY

2

# ENGLISH BEAT
## The Stethoscopic Era's Sonic Traces
*John M. Picker*

May 2010 saw the publication in the United States of three books on noise: Garret Keizer's *The Unwanted Sound of Everything We Want: A Book About Noise*; George Foy's *Zero Decibels: The Quest for Absolute Silence*; and George Prochnik's *In Pursuit of Silence: Listening for Meaning in a World of Noise*. It is safe to say that the appearance of just one of these titles would have attracted the attention of scholars of aural history and culture. But the simultaneous appearance of all three, written by journalists, published by trade presses (PublicAffairs, Scribner, and Doubleday, respectively), and reviewed in the likes of the *New York Times*, suggests that this may be something of a watershed moment for students of sound, especially those of us in literary studies, accustomed to feeling marginalized by the visually oriented masses in the academy and outside it.[1]

Keizer's, Foy's, and Prochnik's books have many similarities. Chief among these is their concern about the significance of silence in the contemporary world. They are all anxious products of industrial modernity, worrying over the loss of quiet spaces and trying to find, as one of the subtitles puts it, "meaning in a world of noise." To bring this closer to bear on what many of us try to do in our scholarship, and indeed what we are doing in this book, we might amend that phrase slightly: what I am trying to find is the meaning, or meanings, *of* a world of noise.

In this chapter, I seek to trace nineteenth-century aurality as it became newly urbanized, industrialized, and commercialized—that is to say, newly modern. Overviews of the later nineteenth century typically have been deaf to the ways that sound shaped individuals and communities, and how responses to it articulated concerns over identity and self-definition. The invention of the phonograph in 1877 was in a sense the culmination of the impulse to archive, analyze, and manipulate the sonic experiences that this era was making richer and more complex. My argument begins with a consideration of nineteenth-century literary texts that capture the larger cultural shift toward close listening during the period. I move on to perform my own close listening of several spoken word recordings made by phonograph in the 1880s and 1890s. My analysis of these records suggests the ways that the advent of sound recording simultaneously severed and deepened the relationship between speaker and speech—in particular, the dynamics between two Victorian poets and their literal and figurative disembodied voices.

## Mediate Auscultation and the Close Listener

If the phonograph is an end point, then modern aurality begins with the stethoscope. The stethoscope was the Enlightenment's response to the mystification of sound and the body. By rendering corporeal listening into the basis of medical diagnoses, and by establishing in its basic design a clinical distance between doctor and patient, the stethoscope represented, on the one hand, the rational conquest of previously undetected sound and led to the rise of the clinically skilled listener. On the other hand, such a development had a more problematic aspect, creating an environment in which newly amplified sound demanded attention and could become impossible to ignore. "Mediate auscultation," the technical term for the sounding of the body with the stethoscope, had an obvious impact, of course, on trained medical professionals: as Stanley Joel Reiser has written, "The effects of the stethoscope on physicians were analogous to the effects of printing on Western culture."[2] But in broader cultural terms, the use of the stethoscope can be taken as a valorization of the activity of intense close listening. Nineteenth-century literary sources reveal the ways that this condition created in Britain and America new kinds of hypersensitive hearers and new manifestations of anxiety concerning Victorian identity. Echoes of the stethoscope's social effects can be detected in the quests of Keizer, Foy, Prochnik, and their fellow twenty-first-century silence seekers.

Although the stethoscope was invented by Laennec in 1816, it only gradually gained acceptance in Britain and the United States over the second quarter of the nineteenth century. The controversy that it generated is suggested by the skeptical comments of the later physician to Queen Victoria, John Forbes, in the preface to his English translation (1821) of Laennec's treatise *De l'auscultation médiate*:

It must be confessed that there is something even ludicrous in the picture of a grave physician formally listening through a long tube applied to the patient's thorax, as if the disease within were a living being that could communicate its condition to the sense without. Besides, there is in this method a sort of bold claim and pretension to certainty and precision of diagnosis, which cannot, at first sight, but be somewhat startling to a mind deeply versed in the knowledge and uncertainties of our art, and to the calm and cautious habits of philosophising to which the English Physician is accustomed. On all these accounts, and others that might be mentioned, I conclude, that the new method will only in a few cases be speedily adopted, and never generally.[3]

For all Forbes's discomfort with mediate auscultation, his translation went through four editions through 1834 and was critical in facilitating the general adoption of Laennec's stethoscope and technique across the English-speaking world. Forbes hints here at the kinds of professional and corporeal anxieties that the stethoscope provoked, but for a perspective on the greater implications of this new form of close listening on the individual psyche and the culture at large, we might turn to the works of two masters of nineteenth-century fiction who admittedly make for an unlikely pair: Edgar Allan Poe and George Eliot.

## "That Roar which Lies on the Other Side of Silence": Poe and Eliot

Poe's story, "The Man of the Crowd" (1840), with its emphasis on physiognomy and problematic vision, has often been read as a commentary on the new sensory anxieties brought about by the age of photography, although, as James Lastra observes, the story also less obviously registers the soundtrack of the modern city.[4] I suggest that Poe's "The Tell-Tale Heart," published three years later, is the louder double of "The Man of the Crowd" in its obsession with the inescapable aurality of modernity, and forms a parallel commentary on the troubling repercussions of what also should be called the age of stethoscopy. "The Tell-Tale Heart" is, simply put, a remarkably noisy story. Indeed, in his first try at publishing it, Poe received a rejection that in more senses than one recommended turning it down: "If Mr. Poe would condescend to furnish more quiet articles," it read, "he would be a most desirable correspondent."[5] Needless to say, Poe ignored the advice.

The narrator of "The Tell-Tale Heart" is, of course, a homicidal maniac who murders an old man and buries the corpse beneath the floor of his room. The narrator's "disease," he tells us, "had sharpened my senses—not destroyed—not dulled them. Above all was the sense of hearing acute. I heard all things in the heaven and in the earth. I heard many things in hell."[6] Significantly, the murder is instigated by the narrator's desire to escape the stare of the old man's "pale blue eye, with a film over it": "[w]henever it fell upon me, my blood ran cold; and so, by degrees—very gradually—I made up my mind to take the life of the old man, and thus rid myself of the eye forever" (792). Poe highlights the anxiety produced by both the photographic "film" and eye that leads to the murder, and the stethoscopic beating that leads to his narrator's undoing. The police arrive, and as he talks to them, the narrator hears *"a low, dull, quick sound—much such a sound as a watch makes when enveloped in cotton"* (indeed, it may even *be* a watch, as some critics have speculated, though the story does not say). The sound persists ("It grew louder—louder—louder! ... hark! louder! louder! louder! *louder!*—") until it forces his admission of guilt: "I admit the deed!—tear up the planks!—here, here!—it is the beating of his hideous heart!" (797).

The punning imperative at the end to "hear! hear!" the heartbeats that are amplified for the narrator alone suggests that the "disease" he suffers from is an auscultative pathology, a telltale symptom of stethoscopic modernity. Not content merely to dramatize this condition, Poe mocks the newfound power of the amplification of hidden bodily sound: in the story, the one who hears so acutely is a murderer, and his "patient" is his victim. For a more sustained, less gothic, but in some ways equally worried consideration of the sociocultural impact of the stethoscope, however, we could hardly do better than to turn our ear to George Eliot.

Eliot uses an acute sense of hearing as her governing metaphor for the sympathetic connections among people that it is her work's central project to encourage. A stethoscope appears very early on, in "Janet's Repentance," one of the stories in her first published book of fiction, *Scenes of Clerical Life*, from 1857. In this story, set in the early 1830s, the instrument reveals Edgar Tryan's internal deterioration from overwork as an evangelical preacher: "It was not necessary or desirable to tell Mr Tryan what was revealed by the stethoscope, but Janet knew the worst."[7] Throughout her subsequent novels, and in the wake of Laennec's medical revolution, Eliot will elaborate upon the kind of stethoscopic perception that permits the attentive individual to access the invisible lives of others. Indeed, this is already articulated in "Janet's Repentance": "surely, surely the only true knowledge of our fellow-man is that which enables us to feel with him—which gives us a fine ear for the heart-pulses that are beating under the mere clothes of circumstance and opinion" (257).

Eliot's fiction is full of hidden hearts beating for those perceptive men and women who would hear them. As she memorably put it in *Middlemarch* (1871–72), in which a stethoscope also makes an appearance, "if we had a keen vision and feeling of all ordinary human life, it would be like hearing the grass grow and the squirrel's heart beat, and we should die of that roar which lies on the other side of silence."[8] This is not an empty metaphor (few in Eliot are), but one rich with sonic associations. Behind it stand not only Eliot's familiarity with Laennec (who is mentioned in *Middlemarch* as a potential model for the ambitious physician Tertius Lydgate), but also her knowledge of the writings of Helmholtz. Helmholtz began his work on sound in 1856, the year Eliot began writing fiction, and he delivered his important lecture "The Physiological Causes of Harmony in Music," in which he explicated his resonance theory of hearing, in 1857, the year *Scenes of Clerical Life* was serialized in *Blackwood's Magazine*. Eliot and her common-law husband George Henry Lewes owned German and French editions of Helmholtz's acoustics magnum opus *Die Lehre von den Tonempfindungen als physiologische Grundlage für die Theorie der Musik* (1863), and shortly before beginning *Middlemarch*, Eliot noted that she was reading Helmholtz on music. Helmholtz's theory of sympathetic resonance, which explained how the ear as a kind of "nervous piano," was able to perceive musical notes, itself sympathetically resonated with Eliot's aesthetic project to dramatize the varieties of close listening through which her characters, and by extension her readers, develop compassion and affinity.

The anxiety in Eliot's final novel, however, is the burden of the stethoscopic age: that of hearing too much and too well. Written on the other side of *Middlemarch*, the novel *Daniel Deronda* (1876) is, among other things, about choice: in this era of close listening, when there is so much new to hear, to what and to whom should one listen? This is the year of the telephone, after all, and Eliot's most challenging, experimental book, like Alexander Graham Bell's device, is about learning how to answer the call, and indeed, which call to answer. Eliot's eponymous hero discovers his calling in the words of Mordecai, the consumptive visionary who guides Deronda toward a proto-Zionist quest for a Jewish homeland that in turn denies him the more conventional expectation of a future with the widowed Gwendolen Harleth Grandcourt, with whom he has a powerful psychological relationship. Bell and Eliot shared an interest in Helmholtzian acoustics: the technology of the telephone is premised, as is Eliot's fiction, on a broad application of the principle of sympathetic resonance. Two years after *Deronda*, Eliot attended a private demonstration of the telephone during its debut in

England, marveled at its utility, and went on to incorporate the new terminology into her prose. In the opening of a late historical novel left unfinished at her death, Eliot aligns her writing endeavor with the new mode of communications she called "telephonic converse": "It is a telescope you may look through a telephone you may put your ear to."[9] For the author who for so long had urged closer listening to others, how apposite, then, that her fictional enterprise reached an endpoint suspended on a telephone line.

## An "Unprotected Man": Carlyle at Home

For Eliot, the lesson of stethoscopic modernity is that to live the most outwardly attuned life her protagonist has to make choices about where to direct his attention—that is, he must learn to listen selectively. Such a solution eluded many of her contemporaries who could not help but hear too much of their increasingly distracting urban soundscapes. George Augustus Sala leads off the tenth volume of Charles Dickens's *Household Words* with a passage that expounds upon the noisy soundtrack of mid-Victorian London streets:

> Still must I hear! Shall the hoarse peripatetic ballad-singer bawl the creaking couplets of The Low-backed Car beneath my window; shall the summer breeze waft the strains of Pop Goes the Weasel upon my ears, and drive me to confusion, while I am endeavouring to master the difficulties of the Turkish alphabet; shall the passing butcherboy rattle his bones, and the theological beggar-man torture a psalm tune into dolorous cadences; shall the young lady in the apartment next to mine string my nerves into the rigours, while she is practising Les Souvenirs de Cracovie, with that ceaseless verbal accompaniment of one, and two, and three; one, and two, and three! Shall music in some shape or other resound from the distant costermonger and the proximate street boy; the brooding swallows sitting upon the eaves, and showing me their sunny backs; the ill-ground organ in the next street; and the beaten tom-tom and execrable caterwauling of Howadjee Lall from Bombay! To say nothing of the deep-mouthed dog next door; the parrot at number eight which is always endeavouring to whistle Il Segreto, and always trying back, and never succeeds in accomplishing more of the air than the first three-quarters of a bar; and Colonel Chumpfist's man servant over the way, who sings valorously while he cleans his master's boots in the area! Shall all these things be, and I not sing, lest haply my readers think they have already had enough and to spare, of my musical reminiscences![10]

Sala's anxious ear takes in many of the "musical" disturbances that posed a special threat to the segment of middle-class Victorian professionals, including Dickens, whose living and working spaces overlapped. How could this emerging class of brain-workers support themselves and their families if their efforts were constantly interrupted by the sounds of the streets?

One answer was provided by Thomas Carlyle, whose stethoscopic language as early as *Sartor Resartus* (1833–34) predicted Eliot's in *Middlemarch*: as he wrote in *Sartor*, "O thou philosophic Teufelsdröckh, that listenest while others only gabble, and with thy quick tympanum hearest the grass grow!"[11] Carlyle was known to hold forth loudly on the value of silence: "SILENCE, SILENCE: in a thousand senses I proclaim the indispensable worth of Silence, our only safe dwelling-place often," he wrote (to Geraldine Jewsbury, 15 June 1840).[12] In 1853, after years of infuriation by city noises of all kinds, especially the "demon fowls" of neighbors, Carlyle resolved to create a space for silence at the top of his house. He confessed to Ralph Waldo Emerson:

> I had for 12 years had such a soundproof inaccessible Apartment schemed out in my head; and last year, under a poor helpless builder, had finally given it up: but Chelsea, as London generally, swelling out as if it were mad, grows every year noisier; a *good* builder turned up, and with a last paroxysm of enthusiasm, I set him to. My notion is, he will succeed; in which case, it will be a great possession to me for the rest of my life. (9 September 1853)

Carlyle's soundproof study in part grew out of his insecurity over his ambiguously gendered professional status as a home-based mental, as opposed to physical, laborer—or as he put it, an "unprotected man" (letter to Jane Welsh Carlyle, 29 July 1853). The silent room was a way for the author to claim territory domestically and sonically for a kind of "strenuously idle" masculinity. Carlyle's complicated relationship with Victorian notions of gender and professionalism was fundamentally irresolvable, and it should not be a surprise that his silent fantasy could not be realized. As he put it, "The room considered as a *soundless* apartment may be safely pronounced an evident *failure*: I do hear all manner of sharp noises,—much reduced in intensity, but still perfectly audible" (to Jean Carlyle Aitken, 16 May 1854). The anxieties Carlyle experienced would reach their apex a decade later, when he, Dickens, and their peers petitioned in support of the Street Music Act. This legislation attempted (as with Carlyle's soundproof study, with limited success) to crack down on organ grinders and the other working poor, mostly foreign musicians whose unpredictable soundings clashed with the quiet on which middle-class English male literary and artistic labor depended.

## Mr. Browning Forgets: Close Listening to a Lapse

With the invention of the phonograph in the last quarter of the century, however, new forms of mechanical music and stethoscopic practice would fully enter the Victorian home and provoke new anxieties. To the extent that the sound of the voice was identified with a speaking body, to listen to the phonograph was a further application of the Victorian invention of binaural stethoscopy, by which I mean listening with both ears to the sounds of the body. Yet in this case, the "body," fixed on cylinder as voice, had become a new kind of remnant and a reminder of the physical presence of the speaker. If Helmholtz had managed to disenchant the sound of the voice by delineating the components of tone and the elements of hearing, users of the fin-de-siècle phonograph succeeded in re-enchanting the voice as a mystical sound from beyond the grave.

The earliest recording of a major literary figure, Robert Browning, testifies to the anxious self-consciousness the phonograph often provoked. The record originated during an 1889 dinner party attended by him and Edison's London agent, George Gouraud, after which Gouraud directed Browning, who was known to object to public speaking, to talk into the phonograph.[13] Browning began to recite his "'How They Brought the Good News from Ghent to Aix,'" but did not get very far:

> [*Gouraud*:] My dear Edison, my dear Edison. I have sent you by the means of the phonograph several interesting souvenirs of its brief residence in London. Nothing that I have sent you will be more welcome to you than the words which will follow now—words that are none other than those of one of England's—I may say, of one of England and *America's* most distinguished poets: those of Robert Browning. Now listen to his voice.

> [*Browning*:]
> I sprang to the saddle, and Joris, and he;
> I galloped, Dirck galloped, we galloped all three;
> "Speed!" echoed the wall to us galloping through;
> "Speed!" echoed the —er—[*pause*]
> Then the gates shut behind us, the lights sank to rest [*pause*]

> I'm terribly sorry, but I don't remember my own verses; but one thing which I shall remember all my life is, the astonishing sensation produced upon me by your wonderful invention.
> Robert Browning!

> [*Gouraud*:] Bravo bravo bravo! Hip hip hooray…[14]

In his introduction, which is omitted from most commercial versions of this recording, Gouraud makes a point of situating Browning within a transatlantic literary context, which Browning discreetly takes up with his choice of a poem about a distantly traveling message. The driving meter of "'How They Brought the Good News,'" that iamb followed by three anapests, produces the rhythmic gallop that acts as an aid to memory; it is no accident that variations on "gallop" appear five times in the opening stanza (as published) alone:

> I sprang to the stirrup, and Joris, and he;
> I galloped, Dirck galloped, we galloped all three;
> "'Good speed!'" cried the watch, as the gate-bolts undrew;
> "'Speed!'" echoed the wall to us galloping through;
> Behind shut the postern, the lights sank to rest,
> And into the midnight we galloped abreast.[15]

The actor James Mason recorded a masterful collection of Browning's poetry for the Caedmon label in the 1960s.[16] Mason's reading of "'How They Brought the Good News'" makes palpably clear the breathless effects of the anapestic rhythm. The range of his tone, from the hushed "Yet there is time" and "So we were left galloping, Joris and I" to the more ebullient "How they'll greet us" works alongside, or rather on top of, the meter; and his deliberate pauses, as at "Galloped … and stood," draw listeners in, playing ever so slightly with our rhythmic expectations. In his definitive renditions of Browning's dramatic monologues, Mason shows how much of an acoustic experience Browning's poetry really is. To return to Browning's own recitation, however, is to experience not the virtuous mettle of meter, which would have enabled him to better remember the lines, but the limitations of metrical effects for the too-human mind and mouth.

If Browning's breakdown mid-stanza seems to parallel those of the poem's two of three horses that falter on their way to Aix, that is because the work itself is an antiquated transportation poem, and of a fabricated event, at that. Published in the midst of the Railway Boom of the 1840s, Browning's poem creates a horse-powered history that never happened in order to reflect on the bewildering rhythms of a steam-powered present. Browning most likely wrote the poem in August 1844, on his second Italian journey. In May of that year, the opening of the Royal Academy Exhibition featured one of the most iconic of Victorian paintings, Turner's *Rain, Steam, and Speed—The Great Western Railway*.[17] William Makepeace Thackeray, reviewing the show for *Fraser's Magazine*, famously wrote about the painting:

As for Mr. Turner, he has out-prodigied almost all former prodigies. He has made a picture with real rain, behind which is real sunshine, and you expect a rainbow every minute. Meanwhile, there comes a train down upon you, really moving at the rate of fifty miles an hour, and which the reader had best make haste to see, lest it should dash out of the picture, and be away up Charing Cross through the wall opposite. All these wonders are performed with a means not less wonderful than the effects are. The rain, in the astounding picture called "'Rain—Steam—Speed,'" is composed of dabs of dirty putty *slapped* on to the canvass with a trowel; the sunshine scintillates out of very thick, smeary lumps of chrome yellow. The shadows are produced by cool tones of crimson lake, and quiet glazings of vermilion, although the fire in the steam-engine *looks* as if it were red. I am not prepared to say that it is not painted with cobalt and pea-green. And as for the manner in which the "'*Speed*'" is done, of that the less said the better,—only it is a positive fact that there is a steam-coach going fifty miles an hour. The world has never seen anything like this picture.[18]

I have not found any evidence to confirm that Browning saw this exhibition, although his passion for the visual arts suggests he would have had a tendency to take this kind of thing in. Still, for my purposes, one of the most remarkable things about the painting is its self-consciousness about its place in the history of English painting, the way it seems as if an eighteenth-century landscape painting on the left half of the canvas, like something out of Constable, is spliced together with the radically modern right half featuring the speeding railway. That is to say, Turner in *Rain, Steam, and Speed* makes aesthetically explicit the kind of social and environmental transition he was witnessing. Browning characteristically does not so much juxtapose the past and present in plain sight, as it were, as leave it to his readers to recognize the implicit contrast.

The "iron horse" of the railway was remaking not only the English landscape in the period of the poem's composition, but also the Belgian one, where the newly created kingdom had, from the mid-1830s, a "primary objective" in its railway building "to establish international lines of communication across the borders."[19] As the *Handbook for Travellers on the Continent*, first published in the 1830s, would go on to note some years later, "Belgium, from the level surface of the country, is peculiarly well suited for railroads, which can be constructed at much less cost here than in England, and have in consequence extended their ramifications through all parts of the kingdom."[20] "'How They Brought the Good News from Ghent to Aix'" indirectly acknowledges this contemporaneous technological breakthrough in communications and international travel: the "good news" of the 1843–44 completion of the costly and complicated railway line linking Ghent and Belgium with Aix-la-Chapelle and Prussia.

It ultimately makes sense for Browning to etch by phonograph needle, or at least start to, his covert railway verse on Edison's communications breakthrough in 1888 with the knowledge that his message will be carried back to the United States. Yet the poem never makes the "good news" (whatever that apparently vital message turns out to be) known to the reader—or to the listener, especially the listener to the Browning recording. Browning stops short in the delivery of a poem that stops short of what might be called full media disclosure. The "good news" is delivered to Aix, but it is never delivered to *us*. We are left to wonder if Browning's forgetfulness is telling after he chooses such an appropriate poem to break off delivering.[21]

After Browning's death in December 1889, the wax cylinder recording was used in an unprecedented form of poet worship. In December 1890, for the first anniversary of the poet's funeral, F. J. Furnivall, President of the London Browning Society, brought together Gouraud and others for what Browning's sister called an "indecent séance": "Poor Robert's dead voice to be made interesting amusement," she wrote; "God forgive them all. I find it difficult."[22] The event was illustrated in W. T. Stead's *Review of Reviews*, where it was titled "A Voice from the Dead" (see figure 2.1).[23] (It is no coincidence that Stead was a noted spiritualist.) The thumbnail image in the upper-right corner is based on an actual photo of Browning, but by the way it is positioned, he appears to be looking down on the proceedings somewhat chagrined. It is not clear if that is because he is depressed by the number of apparently respectable people who are listening to, as the caption puts it, "the actual voice of a dead man," or if he is just horrified by the artist's shoddy work in this Monty Pythonesque illustration.

What I find especially interesting about this image is the absence of a phonograph horn, which might be expected on a home device, and instead the presence of six headsets, or what were called at the time "hearing tubes." Jonathan Sterne has claimed that the modern headset originates with the invention of the binaural stethoscope by Arthur Leared in 1851 (see figure 2.2). The binaural stethoscope can be regarded as a quintessential Victorian invention: the first documented appearance of Leared's device is as an item on display at the Great Exhibition, whose catalog describes it as a "double stethoscope, made of gutta percha."[24] Several phonograph models in the 1880s and 1890s were intended to be used with binaural headsets, such as dictation phonographs and coin-in-the-slot machines in phonograph parlors.

A Voice from the Dead.

The above group represents a notable moment in the history of science and literature. The voice of the poet Browning, preserved by the phonograph, was being heard after death. It was the first occasion on which science had reproduced the actual voice of a dead man. "Every word," says Colonel Gouraud, "was perfectly distinct and of life-like fidelity."

MISS FERGUSON. COLONEL GOURAUD. REV. JOHN PHILLIPS. REV. H. R. HAWEIS.
DR. FURNIVAL. MRS. HAWEIS.

**Figure 2.1** "A Voice from the Dead," *Review of Reviews* 5 (1892), 468.

The evolution of the headset also represents the development of what Sterne calls "private acoustic space" in the fin de siècle. The Browning recording was made in a period when the skill that doctors applied in listening to the body through the stethoscope migrated into phonography and, in Sterne's words, into "a specific kind of bourgeois sensibility *about* hearing and acoustic space."[25] The phonograph headset in this illustration can be thought of as a disembodied stethoscope, in the sense that the participants are listening not to a live body, but to a speech machine playing the voice of an absent corpse. (The figure on the left, Dr. Furnivall, in particular seems to strike the pose of a listening doctor.)

**Figure 2.2** Arthur Leared's binaural stethoscope; William Aitken, *The Science and Practice of Medicine*, 6th ed., vol. 2 (London, 1872), 496.

The illustration captures the moment, and the crude rendering I think only draws attention to this, when the move was on to privatize and make clinical and respectable the middle-class activity of close listening to reproduced sound, even if, as in this early case, that meant the sound of a botched recital. The late Victorian phonograph rendered Browning the unconventional poet into Browning the awkward sound object.

## Tennyson and Pure Sound

The greatest cache of literary recordings from this early period is the better-known cylinders made by Alfred Tennyson, of which about two dozen survive. In May 1890, Tennyson was visited at Farringford on the Isle of Wight by Charles Steytler, an associate of Gouraud, for the purposes of obtaining some specimens of the poet laureate reading several poems, including "Charge of the Light Brigade"; Gouraud planned to use these in a fundraising event for survivors of the charge later that year.[26] Tennyson somehow ended up keeping the phonograph, and in the ensuing weeks and months he recorded all or part of about a dozen long and short poems.[27] He was proud of these records and had them played for visitors such as Bram Stoker (whose *Dracula*, as I have discussed elsewhere, uses the phonograph in ambiguous ways).[28] The cylinders, however, fell into obscurity until about 1920, when Charles Tennyson found them, in his words, "standing in a brown paper parcel, with the old phonograph, against the fortunately not very effective hot-water pipes, in the room at Farringford which had been the poet's library."[29] On one of the Steytler records *not* stored at Farringford, and thus in much better condition, Tennyson recited the first verse of "The Bugle Song" from *The Princess*:

> [*Tennyson*:] I thank you, Mr. Steytler, for making me acquainted with Edison's miraculous invention.
>
> [*aside*] Is that it at the top, or is that it?
>
> The splendour falls on castle walls
> And snowy summits old in story:
> The long light shakes across the lakes,
> And the wild cataract leaps in glory.
> Blow, bugle, blow, set the wild echoes flying,
> Blow, bugle; answer, echoes, dying, dying, dying.
>
> Tennyson

In Browning's case, the phonograph had, ironically if also pathetically, left speechless that master of the dramatic monologue, the poet whom A. S. Byatt has called the "great ventriloquist." Even the poor quality of the recording seems on a certain level to demonstrate a kind of technological respect for Browning's desire to remain hidden behind his speakers' voices, and imperceptible to his audience. But for Tennyson, who was equally shy of public reading—he never gave public recitals, and "would not even, as an undergraduate, give the customary public declamation of his Prize poem *Timbuctoo*"—it was something quite different, yet still consistent with his poetic tendencies: the new machine so intrigued him that he willingly committed many of his famous works to wax and had them replayed for himself and his guests.[30] As if to protest Kittler's claim that the "record grooves dig the grave of the author," the eighty-year-old Tennyson enthusiastically used audio technology to show that he would not go quietly.[31] The phonograph gave the great poet of divided mind the opportunity to perform a kind of audible self-fragmentation, literally to etch in ostensibly permanent fashion different voices of the self. Even on the short recording of "The Bugle Song," a listener can detect four different idiolects, beginning with Humorous Thanks (spoken with something like a mock American accent), then the Confused Aside, followed by the Declamatory Reading, and ending with the Signature. Tennyson's move to record himself may seem strikingly modern in its act of mechanical reproduction, yet it was in keeping with the aims of his poetic project: to express the plurality of voices that constitutes the self. As he neared the end of his life, Tennyson began to hear what his son referred to as "perpetual ghostly voices," the "Silent Voices of the dead" that whispered to him in his last completed poems.[32] For the aging laureate, the faithful sounds of the phonograph articulated with enduring presence a message that, like the song of the bugle, not only echoed but also could resist the ethereal, enigmatic voices he heard murmuring to him of his own mortality.

Along these lines, it is striking that Tennyson's recitation, in this recording as well as some of his others, resembles chanting or even singing. It is as if Tennyson, in choosing to record "The Bugle Song" and read it in this way, is implicitly acknowledging the musicality of the verses in a lyric that other Victorian and later readers and critics characterized (not entirely approvingly) as "pure sound."[33] If Browning's reluctant, partial recitation constitutes, as I have suggested, a counterintuitively significant interpretation of "'How They Brought the Good News from Ghent to Aix,'" Tennyson's songlike recitation of "The Bugle Song" effectively conveys the essential aurality of the poem. In so reading his lyric, Tennyson anticipates the treatment it would receive in the hands of later composers. The most famous setting of "The Bugle Song" is that of Benjamin Britten, from 1943, as the "Nocturne" in his "Serenade for Tenor, Horn, and Strings," which, though Britten altered the lyrics, actually employed a real horn. But earlier, in 1923, about three decades after Tennyson's recording, Frederick Delius had composed a version that not only set the text, at least the first two verses of it, as Tennyson wrote it, but also featured no instrumentation beyond the voices of the chorus. Delius's version is effectively realized in a performance from the 1990s by the Cambridge Singers, and conducted by John Rutter.[34] Apart from the flowing chromatic harmonies of this setting, what is most valuable about it is that it is composed for unaccompanied voices—that is, a cappella. This is important because this arrangement is entirely in keeping, not with the page-text, exactly, but rather with the cylinder-text, Tennyson's songlike rendition of it on Edison's machine. Delius uses voiced language as "pure sound" much as Tennyson did on the cylinder, and Delius's setting in its purely vocal musicality picks up where Tennyson's reading leaves off. I should add that I have no knowledge of whether Delius ever heard this or any of the other Tennyson recordings; but rather than a strict line of influence, what I am suggesting is that there exists here a kind of interpretive consistency or coherence.

## Voice of a Salesman: George Gouraud

Replaying the voices of Browning and Tennyson, I have somewhat morbidly fixated on the ways the phonograph came to signify or even serve as a kind of summing-up for those eminent Victorians near death, but I want to end on a more upbeat note by suggesting the kind of liveliness the machine captured as well. George Gouraud's voice is typically off at the margins of these recordings, even if his controlling influence is not, but in his phonographic correspondence his own voice takes center stage. The final extract I want to cite is one of his audio letters, or "phonograms" as he called to them, sent to Edison in 1888. I provide the transcript for what is a surprisingly intelligible recording (likely due to the fact that it was not played very often, if even more than once):

> Gouraud to Edison, [September 1888,] midnight, the rooms of the Inventors Institute, Chancery Lane, London, England
>
> Dear Edison
> The phonograph tonight is in its element. In the rooms of the Inventors Institute is where it should be. It has been the guest of honor and has distinguished itself as usual. A large and appreciative audience has greeted its presence here. The company was presided over by his serene highness the Prince of Mantua and Montserrat. I am pronouncing his name in the English fashion: *Mantua et Montserrat* it would be rendered in the true vernacular. He is the lineal representative of the ancient dukes of Gonzaga—*Gonzaga*. His family has been distinguished, not the least among its many distinguished gifts, by giving a gold medal to those disciples of science who have most distinguished themselves as benefits mankind. I am not in the present moment prepared to state that you will be the recipient of one of those medals, but I will give long odds that you will be. Many eminent men of science have supported his serene highness by their presence, amongst whom I must not fail to mention the name of Mr. Mackay, to whom you are already indebted for many very appreciative and intelligent descriptions of your latest and greatest. I was myself to have had the honor of addressing this meeting, but unfortunately a previous engagement prevented my being here until a very late hour. My chief duty in another place, at the end of a most sumptuous repast, due to the hospitality which is traditional of the great companies, the city guilds of London, involved upon me the present duty of speaking in response to most complimentary and appreciative allusions to your good self. Nothing else could excuse my absence, and as my paper is exhausted, I will conclude by saying, yours ever, Gouraud.[35]

Although this record is not of a celebrated writer, and it is not "literary" in any conventional sense, this is compelling because it captures Gouraud's sense of linguistic playfulness, particularly regarding accent and pronunciation—that is, a self-consciousness about the sound of language that the phonograph newly enabled and would not have been expressible in print. An American living in England, he would naturally have become quite self-conscious about his own accent, which to me at least sounds as if it wavers happily between that of a New Yorker and that of a Londoner, a bit like P. T. Barnum crossed with W. S. Gilbert. Browning has his James Mason, and Tennyson his Delius, but Gouraud has remained relatively invisible, or unheard, in the history of voice recording. In conclusion, then, to listen to Gouraud now, as well as to the recordings he made—not only of celebrities, but also some of his other firsts: the first recorded public concert (the Handel Festival at the Crystal Palace) and the first record of a Shakespearean actor (Henry Irving)—is to recapture a sense of late nineteenth-century American globalism, with its eagerness to engage with the world around it through the latest communications technologies, and to engage creatively with that other, more fundamental technology of communication, language itself. Gouraud was an important, if unsung, figure in the popularization of voice libraries, archival audio, and home recording more generally, working as he did to preserve vanishing Victorians on cylinder. He recognized the potential for the phonograph to transform the conventions of communications; he played an instrumental role in the securing of Browning's and Tennyson's voices for posterity; and he helped to bring about at home and abroad a kind of cultural stethoscopy—a form of modern close listening that Poe and Eliot could only imagine, and that we in the twenty-first century distantly echo every time we strap on our earbuds.

## Notes

\* This chapter revises and expands on material from my chapter "Aural Anxieties and the Advent of Modernity" in *The Victorian World*, ed. Martin Hewitt (London and New York, Routledge, 2012), 603–18, as well as selections from my book *Victorian Soundscapes* (Oxford and New York, Oxford University Press, 2003).
1. In the time that has passed since I originally wrote this paragraph, several more scholarly and trade books on noise have appeared. The most notable of these are Hillel Schwartz's sonic history of near-biblical proportions *Making Noise: From Babel to the Big Bang and Beyond* (New York, 2011) and, from a more journalistic angle, David Hendy's *Noise: A Human History of Sound and Listening* (London, 2013), which is based on a 30-part BBC radio series.
2. Stanley Joel Reiser, *Medicine and the Reign of Technology* (Cambridge, 1978), 38.
3. John Forbes, "Translator's Preface," in R.T.H. Laennec, *A Treatise on the Diseases of the Chest* (London, 1821), xix.
4. See James Lastra, *Sound Technology and the American Cinema* (New York, 2000), 1–3.

5. Quoted in Edgar Allan Poe, *Collected Works of Edgar Allan Poe*, ed. Thomas Ollive Mabbott (Cambridge, 1978), 791.

6. Edgar Allan Poe, "The Tell-Tale Heart," in *Collected Works of Edgar Allan Poe*, 792; hereafter cited in text.

7. George Eliot, *Scenes of Clerical Life*, ed. Thomas A. Noble (Oxford, 1985); hereafter cited in text. The argument about Eliot in the following paragraphs is dramatically condensed from my *Victorian Soundscapes* (Oxford and New York, 2003), 82–109, where it is made with special emphasis on *Daniel Deronda*.

8. George Eliot, *Middlemarch*, ed. David Carroll (Oxford, 1986), 189.

9. George Eliot, *The George Eliot Letters*, ed. Gordon Haight (New Haven, 1954–1978), 7: 28; William Baker, "A New George Eliot Manuscript," in *George Eliot: Centenary Essays and an Unpublished Fragment*, ed. Anne Smith (Totowa, NJ, 1980), 10.

10. [George Augustus Sala,] "A Little More Harmony," *Household Words* 10 (1854): 1.

11. Thomas Carlyle, *Sartor Resartus* (London, 1838), 251. A fuller discussion of Carlyle's soundproof study can be found in *Victorian Soundscapes*, 43–44 and 55–56.

12. All citations to Carlyle's letters are taken from *The Carlyle Letters Online* [CLO], 2007. http://carlyleletters.org; accessed 26 March 2014.

13. Rudolf Lehmann, quoted in Michael Hancher and Jerrold Moore, "'The Sound of a Voice That Is Still': Browning's Edison Cylinder," *The Browning Newsletter*, no. 4 (1970): 22. For more details of the Browning recording and its replaying, see *Victorian Soundscapes*, 122–24.

14. This is my transcription, based on my own listening and adapted from that of Hancher and Moore. Extracts of the recording are widely available on YouTube and commercial compact discs.

15. Robert Browning, "'How They Brought the Good News from Ghent to Aix,'" *The Poems, Volume 1*, ed. John Pettigrew (London, 1993), 395, ll. 1–6.

16. *The Poetry of Browning*, HarperCollins Audio Books audiocassette, HCA 169 (originally released on Caedmon Records in 1965).

17. Available at http://www.nationalgallery.org.uk/paintings/joseph-mallord-william-turner-rain-steam-and-speed-the-great-western-railway; accessed 26 March 2014.

18. W.M. Thackeray, "May Gambols; or, Titmarsh in the Picture-Galleries," *Fraser's Magazine*, no. 29 (1844): 712–13.

19. Michel Laffut, "Belgium," in *Railways and the Economic Development of Western Europe, 1830–1914*, ed. Patrick O'Brien (New York, 1983), 205–6.

20. *A Handbook for Travellers on the Continent*, 8th edn. (London, 1851), 92–93.

21. I am partly responding here to Yopie Prins's response to my *Victorian Soundscapes* and a subsequent essay of mine in her essay "Voice Inverse," *Victorian Poetry*, no. 42 (2004): 43–60. Prins's penetrating points about the metrical force of the poem have influenced but not entirely converted me. For more on the connections between Browning's poetry and railways, see Prins's "Robert Browning, Transported by Meter," in *The Traffic in Poems: Nineteenth-Century Poems and Transatlantic Exchange*, ed. Meredith McGill

(New Brunswick, 2008), 205–30; and Richard Altick, "Robert Browning Rides the Chicago and Alton," *The New Colophon: A Book Collector's Miscellany*, no. 3 (1950): 78–81.

22. Letter to Katherine Bradley, [December?] 1890, quoted in William S. Peterson, *Interrogating the Oracle: A History of the London Browning Society* (Athens, OH, 1969), 29–30.

23. Hugh Reginald Haweis, "Robert Browning's Voice," *The Times*, 13 December 1890, 10. A summary of various accounts of the event can be found in Hancher and Moore, "'The Sound of a Voice That Is Still,'" 21–33. The illustration was published in *The Review of Reviews*, no. 5 (1892): 468.

24. *Great Exhibition of the Works of Industry of All Nations, 1851. Official Descriptive and Illustrated Catalogue* (London, 1851), vol. 1, 477.

25. Jonathan Sterne, *The Audible Past: Cultural Origins of Sound Reproduction* (Durham, NC, 2003), 159–61.

26. Bennett Maxwell, "The Steytler Recordings of Alfred, Lord Tennyson: A History," *Tennyson Research Bulletin*, no. 3 (1980): 153. The two Tennyson recordings Steytler obtained (an abbreviated "Charge of the Light Brigade" and "The Bugle Song" from *The Princess*) are available with the Browning record in edited versions on the CDs accompanying *Poetry Speaks: Hear Great Poets Read Their Work from Tennyson to Plath*, ed. Elise Paschen and Rebekah Presson Mosby (Naperville, 2001). This discussion of the Tennyson recordings recapitulates and further develops some of the points made in my *Victorian Soundscapes*, 123–26.

27. A nearly complete listing of the Tennyson cylinders is given in Sir Charles Tennyson's "The Tennyson Phonograph Records," *British Institute of Recorded Sound Bulletin*, no. 3 (1956): 2–8.

28. See Picker, *Victorian Soundscapes*, 134–37.

29. Charles Tennyson, "The Tennyson Phonograph Records," 3. *Alfred, Lord Tennyson Reads from His Own Poems*, introduced by Sir Charles Tennyson, Craighill LP, TC 1; CRS audiocassette, CR 9000.

30. Philip Collins, *Reading Aloud: A Victorian Métier* (Lincoln, 1972), 26.

31. Friedrich Kittler, *Gramophone Film Typewriter* (Stanford, 1999), 83.

32. See *The Poems of Tennyson*, ed. Christopher Ricks, 2nd edn. (Berkeley, 1987), 3: 251.

33. Among the more influential critics of what he called "the cult of Pure Sound" was William Empson, in *Seven Types of Ambiguity* (London, 1930), 16.

34. Available at http://www.youtube.com/watch?v=vvAGaksLBJs; accessed 26 March 2014.

35. My transcription, derived from a recording housed at the Edison National Historic Site.

# Bibliography

*Alfred, Lord Tennyson Reads from His Own Poems*. Introduced by Sir Charles Tennyson. Craighill LP, TC 1; CRS audiocassette, CR 9000.

Altick, Richard. "Robert Browning Rides the Chicago and Alton." *The New Colophon: A Book Collector's Miscellany*, no. 3 (1950): 78–81.

Baker, William. "A New George Eliot Manuscript." In *George Eliot: Centenary Essays and an Unpublished Fragment*. Ed. Anne Smith. Totowa, NJ, 1980, 9–20.

Browning, Robert. *The Poems, Volume 1*. Ed. John Pettigrew. London, 1993.

Carlyle, Thomas. *Sartor Resartus*. London, 1838.

Collins, Philip. *Reading Aloud: A Victorian Métier*. Lincoln, 1972.

Eliot, George. *The George Eliot Letters*. Ed. Gordon Haight. New Haven, CT, 1954–1978.

———. *Scenes of Clerical Life*. Ed. Thomas A. Noble. Oxford, 1985.

———. *Middlemarch*. Ed. David Carroll. Oxford, 1986.

Empson, William. *Seven Types of Ambiguity*. London, 1930.

Forbes, John. "Translator's Preface." In R. T. H. Laennec, *A Treatise on the Diseases of the Chest*. London, 1821, vii–xxviii.

*Great Exhibition of the Works of Industry of All Nations, 1851. Official Descriptive and Illustrated Catalogue*. London, 1851.

Hancher, Michael, and Jerrold Moore. "'The Sound of a Voice That Is Still': Browning's Edison Cylinder." *The Browning Newsletter*, no. 4 (1970): 21–33.

*Handbook for Travellers on the Continent*. 8th edition. London, 1851.

Haweis, Hugh Reginald. "Robert Browning's Voice." *The Times*, 13 December 1890, 10.

Hendy, David. *Noise: A Human History of Sound and Listening*. London, 2013.

Kittler, Friedrich. *Gramophone Film Typewriter*. Stanford, 1999.

Laffut, Michel. "Belgium." In *Railways and the Economic Development of Western Europe, 1830–1914*. Ed. Patrick O'Brien. New York, 1983, 203–26.

Lastra, James. *Sound Technology and the American Cinema*. New York, 2000.

Maxwell, Bennett. "The Steytler Recordings of Alfred, Lord Tennyson: A History." *Tennyson Research Bulletin*, no. 3 (1980): 150–57.

Paschen, Elise, and Rebekah Presson Mosby, eds. *Poetry Speaks: Hear Great Poets Read Their Work from Tennyson to Plath*. Naperville, 2001.

Peterson, William S. *Interrogating the Oracle: A History of the London Browning Society*. Athens, OH, 1969.

Picker, John M. *Victorian Soundscapes*. Oxford and New York, 2003.

———. "Aural Anxieties and the Advent of Modernity." In *The Victorian World*. Ed. Martin Hewitt. London and New York, 2012, 603–18.

Poe, Edgar Allan. *Collected Works of Edgar Allan Poe*. Ed. Thomas Ollive Mabbott. Cambridge, 1978.

*Poetry of Browning*. HarperCollins Audio Books audiocassette, HCA 169.

Prins, Yopie. "Voice Inverse." *Victorian Poetry*, no. 42 (2004): 43–60.

———. "Robert Browning, Transported by Meter." In *The Traffic in Poems: Nineteenth-Century Poems and Transatlantic Exchange*. Ed. Meredith McGill. New Brunswick, 2008, 205–30.

Reiser, Stanley Joel. *Medicine and the Reign of Technology*. Cambridge, 1978.

[Sala, George Augustus.] "A Little More Harmony." *Household Words* 10 (1854): 1–5.

Schwartz, Hillel. *Making Noise: From Babel to the Big Bang and Beyond*. New York, 2011.

Sterne, Jonathan. *The Audible Past: Cultural Origins of Sound Reproduction.* Durham, NC, 2003.

Tennyson, Alfred. *The Poems of Tennyson.* Ed. Christopher Ricks. 2nd ed. Berkeley, 1987.

Tennyson, Charles. "The Tennyson Phonograph Records." *British Institute of Recorded Sound Bulletin*, no. 3 (1956): 2–8.

Thackeray, William Makepeace. "May Gambols; or, Titmarsh in the Picture-Galleries." *Fraser's Magazine*, no. 29 (1844): 700–16.

3

# THE HUMAN TELEPHONE
## Physiology, Neurology, and Sound Technologies
*Anthony Enns*

Some historians describe the telephone as a prosthetic device designed to simulate, enhance, and extend the sensory functions of the ear, thus overcoming the limitations of the body and enabling the perception of sound across vast distances. Other historians describe the development of the telephone as part of the history of acoustic automata, which were designed to simulate the organs of sound production, such as the lungs, the larynx, and the lips. However, few historians explain how the development of the telephone was connected to a broader crisis in perception that occurred in the nineteenth century. This crisis is more often associated with the rise of new optical media technologies, such as panoramas and motion pictures, which reflected a new understanding of visual perception as dependent on the material properties of the eye. This chapter will demonstrate that this crisis in perception also informed the development of new sound technologies, such as the phonautograph, the telephone, and the audiometer, which were similarly based on a new mechanistic understanding of auditory perception.

According to Jonathan Crary, this crisis in perception was inspired by scientific advances in the field of physiological perception. Crary explains that Immanuel Kant's notion of the "transcendental synthetic unity of apperception ... gave an apodictic or absolute character to perceptual experience,"[1] yet nineteenth-century physiological studies revealed that human perception was "dependent on the complex and contingent physiological makeup" of the individual subject.[2] Sensory perception could "no longer claim an essential objectivity or certainty," and it was gradually understood as "faulty, unreliable, and ... arbitrary."[3] This new understanding of perception as subjective and unreliable led to the scientific calculation of perceptual thresholds, which revealed the precise limitations of the perceptual apparatus. The calculation of perceptual thresholds also enabled the development of new media technologies, which were specifically designed to take advantage of these newfound limitations. The development of the panorama, for example, was made possible by the discovery of the limitations of depth perception. Optical media technologies were thus able to overcome the newfound limitations of visual perception by effectively deceiving the eye. By standardizing and optimizing the performance of sensory organs, in other words, nineteenth-century media technologies identified the inherent flaws in human perception and compensated for these flaws by manipulating the perceptual apparatus: "Once the empirical truth of vision was determined to lie in the body, vision (and similarly the other senses) could be annexed and controlled by external techniques of manipulation and stimulation."[4] Crary thus concludes that the development of new media technologies in the nineteenth century was part of "a broader process of normalization and subjection" that transformed "the individual ... into something calculable and regularizable."[5]

Friedrich Kittler agrees with Crary that "the turn away from physically natural optics ... towards physiologically embodied optics was a veritable scientific paradigm shift," yet he questions Crary's overemphasis on the body: "Crary's thesis would ... be more precise if he had not spoken about physiology but rather material effects in general, which can impact human bodies equally as well as technical storage media."[6] Instead of describing nineteenth-century media technologies as devices that standardized and optimized human sensory functions, therefore, Kittler points out that these media technologies were also capable of registering the material effects of sensory stimuli in the absence of a perceiving subject. The logical consequence of this shift is that media technologies no longer represented prosthetic extensions of the central nervous system, as Marshall McLuhan famously argued;[7] rather, they functioned as technological reconstructions of the perceptual apparatus that rendered the central nervous system superfluous: "In order to implement technologically (and thus render superfluous) the functions of the central nervous system, it first had to be reconstructed."[8] Instead of arguing that these media technologies simply manipulated and deceived the sensory organs, therefore, Kittler argues that these technologies were independent and autonomous reconstructions of the perceptual apparatus capable of registering the material effects of sensory stimuli in the absence of a perceiving subject, which rendered the body superfluous.

While Crary and Kittler primarily focus on optical media, this chapter will explore Crary's suggestion that the same claim can be made for "the other senses," including hearing. Just as the development of nineteenth-century optical media technologies was based on the study of physiological optics, so too was the development of nineteenth-century sound technologies based on the study of physiological acoustics, which similarly introduced a mechanistic understanding of auditory perception. Some historians, like James Lastra and Jonathan Sterne, have already examined the impact of physiological studies on the development of new sound technologies in the nineteenth century, yet these scholars do not explore how the development of these new technologies was related to a broader crisis in perception. Lastra may come closest by suggesting that the telephone was not only understood as a device that simulated the functions of the ear, but it was also the result of a sustained effort to translate sonic vibrations into visual inscriptions. Lastra also argues that these acoustic inscriptions extended the "inhuman" qualities of writing to the experience of auditory perception. By recording and preserving sounds over time, for example, sound-recording technologies like the phonograph and the gramophone were capable of separating voices from bodies and introducing them into new contexts, thereby transforming their meaning. Like Kittler, therefore, Lastra concludes that the "automatization" of auditory perception resulted in a "lack of subjectivity."[9] However, Lastra primarily associates this lack of subjectivity with the "inhuman" qualities of writing rather than the ability of sound technologies to register the material effects of sensory stimuli. This chapter will show, however, that physiological studies of auditory perception introduced a new understanding of the ear as a technical apparatus or transducer capable of converting sonic vibrations into electrical impulses. This new understanding of the ear represented an epistemological shift in the scientific understanding of auditory perception, as it conceived of the body itself as a machine rather than conceiving of the machine as a prosthetic extension of the body. This new mechanistic understanding of auditory perception thus revealed that the ear not only functioned as a technological apparatus, but it was also capable of registering material effects in the absence of a perceiving subject.

In order to trace this epistemological shift, the chapter will examine the connections between the development of new sound technologies in the nineteenth century, such as the phonautograph, the telephone, and the audiometer, and scientific studies of physiology, otology, and neurology, which introduced a new mechanistic understanding of auditory perception. It will also examine how these new sound technologies displaced the body through the technological conversion of sonic vibrations into electrical impulses, which reflected a new understanding of auditory perception as not only mechanistic, but also electronic. The standardization, automatization, and electricization of auditory perception enabled the technological reconstruction of the perceptual apparatus, which made bodies and machines indistinguishable and interchangeable. Nineteenth-century sound technologies can thus be considered inhuman not only because they introduced the qualities of writing into speech, but also because the conversion of sonic vibrations into electrical impulses resulted in an epistemological shift from the notion of technology as a prosthetic device to the notion of the body as a technological device.

## Perception

As Crary points out, the most significant nineteenth-century experiments on physiological perception were conducted by German physician-scientist Hermann Ludwig Ferdinand von Helmholtz. Crary primarily focuses on Helmholtz's work in the field of physiological optics, yet Helmholtz was even more famous for his groundbreaking work on physiological acoustics. In his 1857 lecture "Über die physiologischen Ursachen der musikalischen Harmonie" (On the Physiological Causes of Musical Harmony), Helmholtz introduced a distinction between vibrations and sounds that became the basis of all subsequent work on auditory perception. In order to explain this distinction, Helmholtz described an experiment using a siren, which revealed that some vibrations have such a low frequency that they are not perceived by the ear as sounds:

> When the siren is turned slowly, and hence the puffs of air succeed each other slowly, you hear no musical sound. By the continually increasing rapidity of its revolution, no essential change is produced in the kind of vibration in the air. Nothing new happens externally to the ear. The only new result is the sensation experienced by the ear, which then for the first time begins to be affected by the agitation of the air. Hence the more rapid vibrations receive a new name, and are called Sound. If you admire paradoxes, you may say that aerial vibrations do not become sound until they fall upon a hearing ear.[10]

In other words, Helmholtz's siren experiment revealed that some frequencies were perceived by the ear as sounds, while others were not. In the process of identifying and calculating the thresholds of auditory perception, therefore, Helmholtz introduced a new understanding of sound as a subjective experience that depended on the physiological properties of the ear.

Helmholtz's lecture also provided a detailed description of how the ear translates atmospheric vibrations into sounds. Helmholtz explained that the cochlea contains "about three thousand arches ... lying orderly beside each other, like the keys of a piano,"[11] and a series of "elastic appendages," each "tuned to a certain tone like the strings of a piano."[12] When a vibration of a certain frequency strikes the cochlea, "the corresponding hairlike appendage may vibrate, and the corresponding nerve-fibre experience a sensation,"[13] just as the strings on a piano produce sympathetic vibrations when a tuning fork of a certain pitch is placed in close proximity (see figure 3.1). In other words, the sounds perceived by the ear do not originate in the external world, but rather they are generated from within the ear itself. Helmholtz thus argued that the ear not only receives but also reproduces and transmits sounds. Helmholtz's use of the piano metaphor to describe the function of the ear also shows that auditory perception was increasingly understood in mechanistic terms.

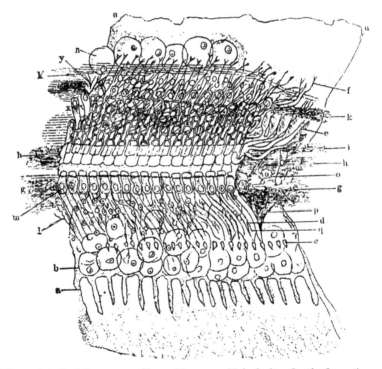

**Figure 3.1** Cochlean nerve fibres; Hermann Helmholtz, *On the Sensations of Tone* (New York, 1954), 141.

Helmholtz added, however, that auditory perception is based not only on the physiological properties of the ear, but also on the subject's methods of listening, which shape and determine the sounds that are perceived. Helmholtz thus distinguished between what he called a "material" and a "spiritual" ear: "We must distinguish two different points—the audible *sensation*, as it is developed without any intellectual interference, and the *conception*, which we form in consequence of that sensation. We have, as it were, to distinguish between the material ear of the body and the spiritual ear of the mind."[14] This distinction between the "material" and the "spiritual" ear was most clearly evident in Helmholtz's experiments on upper partial tones:

> No perceptions obtained by the senses are merely sensations impressed on our nervous systems. A peculiar intellectual activity is required to pass from a nervous sensation to the conception of an external object, which the sensation has aroused. The sensations of our nerves of sense are mere symbols indicating certain external objects, and it is usually only after considerable practice that we acquire the power of drawing correct conclusions from our sensations respecting the corresponding objects … All sensations which have no direct reference to external objects, we are accustomed, as a matter of course, entirely to ignore, and we do not become aware of them till we make a scientific investigation of the action of the senses … It is not enough for the auditory nerve to have a sensation. The intellect must reflect upon it.[15]

According to Helmholtz, therefore, auditory perception is not only conditioned by the physiological properties of the ear, but it is also a conscious act of interpretation that takes place within the intellect or "spiritual ear" of the listening subject. Helmholtz's concept of the "spiritual" ear thus represented an attempt to reconcile his new mechanistic understanding of auditory perception with Kant's notion of the "unity of apperception," and he reconciled these two contradictory theories by separating the physical operations of the perceptual apparatus from the psychological process of interpreting sensory perceptions. In short, Helmholtz's theories reflect a certain degree of anxiety concerning the implications of his own physiological experiments, and they testify to his unwillingness to surrender traditional notions of subjectivity.

## Automata

In 1846, Melville Bell, a student of acoustics and elocution, witnessed a demonstration of Joseph Faber's "Wonderful Talking Machine" at the Egyptian Hall in London. Faber's machine consisted of a talking head that could allegedly speak in complete sentences, as Alfred Mayer explains:

> Faber worked at the source of articulate sounds, and built up an artificial organ of speech, whose parts, as nearly as possible, perform the same functions as corresponding organs in our vocal apparatus. A vibrating ivory reed, of variable pitch, forms its vocal chords. There is an oral cavity, whose size and shape can be rapidly changed by depressing the keys on a keyboard. A rubber tongue and lips make the consonants; a little windmill, turning in its throat, rolls the letter *R*, and a tube is attached to its nose when it speaks French.[16]

Melville Bell was particularly impressed by the machine's ability to simulate the physiology of the human voice, and in 1863 he took his sons, including sixteen-year-old Alexander Graham Bell, to see another "speaking machine" developed by British scientist Charles Wheatstone. He then offered them a prize if they could build an automaton of their own:

> Following their father's advice, the boys attempted to copy the vocal organs by making a cast from a human skull and molding the vocal parts in guttapercha. The lips, tongue, palate, teeth, pharynx, and velum were represented. The lips were a framework of wire, covered with rubber which had been stuffed with cotton batting. Rubber cheeks enclosed the mouth cavity, and the tongue was simulated by wooden sections—likewise covered by a rubber skin and stuffed with batting. The parts were actuated by levers controlled from a keyboard. A larynx "box" was constructed of tin and had a flexible tube for a windpipe. A vocal-cord orifice was made by stretching a slotted rubber sheet over tin supports.[17]

According to Alexander Graham Bell, this automaton could be made to say vowels and nasals, and could be manipulated to produce a few simple utterances, like the word "mamma."[18] Long before he conceived of the telephone, therefore, Bell was already familiar with the history of talking automata, and he was actively engaged in the technological reconstruction of the organs of human sound production.

In 1865, Alexander Graham Bell also became interested in simulating the functions of the human ear, and he began to employ bottles as artificial cavities to determine the precise pitch of vowel sounds. Alexander Ellis, one of his father's colleagues, pointed out that Bell was actually replicating Helmholtz's experiments in physiological acoustics, and Bell subsequently attempted to learn more about Helmholtz's work. In the summer of 1866, Bell tried to recreate Helmholtz's "tuning fork sounder" or "resonator," a device designed to duplicate the

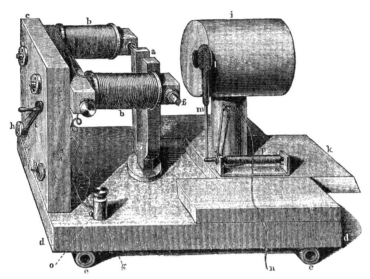

**Figure 3.2** Tuning fork sounder; Hermann Helmholtz, *On the Sensations of Tone* (New York, 1954), 121.

physiological structure of the ear by combining and resonating multiple tones using tuning forks kept in motion by electricity (see figure 3.2).[19] Like Helmholtz, therefore, Bell's early experiments were based on an understanding of auditory perception as a mechanistic process that could be systematically measured and regularized, which enabled the reconstruction of the ear as a technological apparatus.

## Phonautograph

At the same time that Alexander Graham Bell was fascinated with the problem of simulating human physiology by mechanical means, he also inherited an interest in the inscription of sound from his father, who had devoted his life to developing a universal phonetic alphabet. This alphabet consisted of visual icons that denoted "the organs of speech and of the way in which they were put together in uttering sounds."[20] Bell's father published this system in his 1867 book *Visible Speech*, and Bell was the first to master it. Its primary use was in teaching the deaf to speak, and in 1871, at the age of twenty-four, Bell began working as a teacher at the Boston School of the Deaf. He not only employed his father's universal alphabet, but he also drew diagrams of the mouth and the positions of the tongue to help his students visualize the formation of sounds. Bell's interest in phonetics gradually led him to search for other ways of visually representing acoustic information:

> [I]t was thought that my father's system of pictorial symbols, popularly known as visible speech, might produce a means whereby we could teach the deaf and dumb to use their vocal organs and to speak. The great success of these experiments urged upon me the advisability of devising methods of exhibiting the vibrations of sound optically, for use in teaching the deaf and dumb.[21]

In 1874, Bell began using Karl Rudolph Koenig's "manometric flame" to provide his students with images of various sounds. Koenig's device consisted of a membrane diaphragm stretched over a hole in a gas pipe. A speaking tube carried the sound to the diaphragm, causing the membrane to vibrate. The vibrating diaphragm made the gas pressure fluctuate, which made the flame vary in shape and height. The flame resembled a broad band of light, and each vowel sound had its own characteristic pattern. In order to see the shapes of the flame more clearly, it was also reflected from four mirrors mounted on the circumference of a revolving wheel. Bell intended to use this apparatus to show his students what a sound looked like and then help them to reproduce it themselves: "[P]ictures of the vibrations due to each sound could be given, and thus the sounds be identified through all eternity."[22] The experiment failed, however, as Bell was unable to photograph the shapes of the flame.

Bell then turned to Édouard-Léon Scott's phonautograph, the earliest known sound recording device, with which he hoped to make permanent inscriptions of sounds (see figure 3.3). Originally patented in 1857, Scott's phonautograph recorded the movements of a membrane set in motion by sonic vibrations:

> If one spoke or sang into the large end of a wooden cone, the sound vibrated a membrane diaphragm stretched over the small end. A thin wooden rod, hinged at one end of the diaphragm, ran across the center of it and projected beyond the opposite edge. A bit of cork and glue joined the center of the diaphragm to the wooden rod, so that the vibrations were magnified at the rod's projecting free end. A bristle fastened to that end traced a curve on a piece of smoked glass being drawn past it. Each sound left a characteristic trace.[23]

Melville Bell's phonetic system and Édouard-Léon Scott's phonauto-graph thus represent two contemporaneous methods of converting sounds into images. Like Helmholtz's "tuning fork sounder," Scott's phonautograph was also designed to simulate the physiological

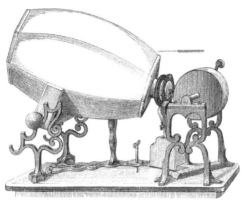

**Figure 3.3** Phonautograph; Franz Josef Pisko, *Die neueren Apparate der Akustik* (Vienna, 1865), 73.

properties of the ear, and it was directly inspired by research on human anatomy: the large cone was designed to simulate the external ear, the diaphragm was designed to simulate the tympanic membrane, and the stylus with the attached bristle was designed to imitate the middle ear ossicula.

Koenig constructed an improved version of Scott's phonautograph in 1859, and in 1861 an improved version of Koenig's phonautograph was constructed by Adam Politzer, a lecturer in Otology at the University of Vienna. In order to study the vibrations of the tympanic membrane and the ossicles, Politzer attached an actual human ear to the phonautograph, and he thus became the first person to obtain a record of the actual movements of the tympanic membrane. An American otologist named Clarence Blake served as Politzer's assistant during these experiments, and their initial work was first published in 1864. When Blake returned to Boston in 1869, he established an Aural Clinic at the Massachusetts Charitable Eye and Ear Infirmary, where he continued Politzer's research.

Blake first met Bell after attending one of Bell's demonstrations of visible speech in 1871. In 1873, Bell became a professor of Vocal Physiology and Elocution in the School of Oratory at the newly established Boston University. In 1874, Bell witnessed a demonstration of an improved phonautograph developed by Charles Morey, one of Koenig's students.[24] Bell was also given the opportunity to experiment with this apparatus at the Massachusetts Institute of Technology.[25] Bell noted that there was "a remarkable likeness between the manner in which this piece of wood was vibrated by the membrane of the phonautograph and the manner in which the ossiculae of the human ear were moved by the tympanic membrane," and he decided "to construct a phonautograph modeled still more closely on the mechanism of the human ear."[26] Bell subsequently built a series of phonautographs using membranes made with different materials, but he was not satisfied with the results as none of the devices were sensitive enough. He then turned to Blake for help, and the two men began to collaborate on another series of experiments.

Blake had seen Politzer use human ears for similar purposes, so with Bell's assistance he constructed two phonautographs using actual human ears (see figure 3.4). In a paper delivered to the British Society of Telegraphic Engineers in 1878, Blake provided the following guidelines for constructing what he called a "human ear phonautograph":

> In preparing the ear for use as a phonautograph, the roof of the cavity of the middle ear is first cut away; through this opening a narrow-bladed knife may be introduced to divide the tendon of the tensor tympani muscle and the articulation of the incus with the stapes. By means of a hair-saw a section of the middle ear is then made from before, backward through the divided articulation. This section removes the inner wall of the middle ear cavity with the portion of the bone containing the internal ear and exposes the inner surface of the drum membrane, with the malleus and incus attached … [A] stylus made of a single fibre of wheat-straw is glued to the descending part of one of the small bones, parallel to the long axis of the bone. With this, tracing may be made upon a plate of smoked glass, sliding upon a glass bed at a right angle to the line of excursion of the drum membrane, and moved by clock-work or a falling weight.[27]

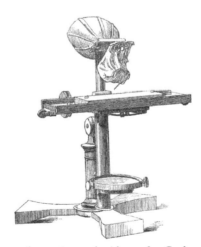

**Figure 3.4** Human ear phonautograph; Alexander Graham Bell, *The Telephone* (London, 1878), 21.

In other words, sonic vibrations caused the membrane to vibrate and these vibrations were then carried to the straw stylus, which left a tracing of its path on the smoked glass that was drawn along at a predetermined speed. The result was a wavy line that corresponded to the pitch of the original sound. Blake's "human ear phonautograph" thus provides a perfect illustration of this new mechanistic understanding of auditory perception: as soon as the middle ear was understood as a transducer that was capable of registering acoustic signals, then the next step was to transform the middle ear into a technological apparatus that was capable of inscribing sounds. As Jonathan Sterne points out, "the use of human ears in experiments was thus intimately tied to the development of a mechanical understanding of the ear—an ear that had to be physically extracted and abstracted from a human body. The ear could become part of the phonautograph in part because it was already being treated as a mechanism to be understood through mechanical means."[28] Blake claimed that he chose a real human ear because it possessed "the greatest delicacy of structure," yet he also emphasized the importance of using "a specimen as nearly normal as possible."[29] While he provides no precise guidelines for determining the normalcy of an ear, it is clear that the "human ear phonautograph" was part of a general trend toward the standardization and regularization of auditory perception.

It should be emphasized that the original purpose of this phonautograph was to teach deaf children to speak. As Bell explains, his efforts to find a method of visually transcribing sounds had led him to "devise an apparatus that might help children …, a machine to hear for them, a machine that would render visible to the eyes of the deaf the vibrations of the air that affect our ears as sound … It was a failure, but that apparatus, in the process of time, became the telephone."[30] This passage reveals that Bell's device was based not only on a mechanistic understanding of auditory perception, but also on the assumption that auditory perception could be technologically reconstructed. As Sterne notes, the phrase "a machine to hear for them" refers not to the amplification of sound but rather to the delegation of hearing to the machine, and therefore "Bell's planned practical application of the phonautograph … implies a programme for the use [of] the phonautograph's mechanical descendents by people who were not deaf."[31] In other words, Bell was not simply attempting to create a machine that would extend or enhance the sensory functions of the ear; rather, he was attempting to create a machine that would replace the ear, thereby rendering human sensory organs superfluous.

## Telephone

During his experiments with the "human ear phonautograph," Bell was particularly struck by the fact that sound waves acting on a thin membrane were capable of moving relatively heavy bones:

> While engaged in these experiments I was struck with the remarkable disproportion in weight between the membrane and the bones that were vibrated by it. It occurred to me that if a membrane as thin as tissue paper could control the vibration of bones that were, compared to it, of immense size and weight, why should not a larger and thicker membrane be able to vibrate a piece of iron in front of an electromagnet, in which case the complication of steel rods shown in my first form of telephone … could be done away with, and a simple piece of iron attached to a membrane be placed at either end of the telegraphic circuit.[32]

This inspiration led to the construction of Bell's first membrane diaphragm telephone in 1875. In a letter to his parents, Bell described this telephone as "an instrument modeled after the human ear."[33] According to his assistant, Thomas Watson, Bell constructed several different versions of this membrane diaphragm telephone using different materials, including one that incorporated the internal bones and drum of an actual human ear that had been supplied to him by Blake, and "[t]hey all worked, even the real ear telephone."[34] According to Watson, however, the "real ear telephone" was "the poorest of the lot,"[35] so Bell eventually decided to focus his efforts on developing an all-metal diaphragm magneto telephone, which he completed in 1876.

Blake also provided a description of Bell's "real ear telephone" in a paper delivered to the British Society of Telegraphic Engineers in 1878:

> With an ear so prepared, having a disk of ferrotype plate, seven millimeters in diameter, glued to the descending portions of both the malleus and incus, and with a proportionately small magnet and coil (resistance 44 ohms), I have been able to carry on conversation without difficulty over a line something more than six hundred feet in length, the ear telephone being used only as a receiving instrument.[36]

Blake thus described the "ear telephone" as a technological enhancement that enabled the ear to surpass the perceptual thresholds of human sensory organs. Blake also argued that the design of the all-metal diaphragm magneto telephone was based on the structure of the human ear: "The mouth-piece of the hand telephone may be compared to the external ear, the metal disc to the drum membrane, the air-chamber to the middle-ear cavity, the damping effect of the magnet to the traction of the tensor tympani muscle, and the induced current in the coil to the sentient apparatus."[37] Like the phonautograph, therefore, the telephone also represented a technological reconstruction of the human ear, so it similarly reflected a mechanistic understanding of auditory perception. Watson's claim that the "real ear telephone" was "the poorest of the lot" further illustrates how this technological reconstruction surpassed the limitations of the perceptual apparatus. The telephone was not simply a prosthetic device that simulated, enhanced, and extended the sensory functions of the ear; rather, it was a technological reconstruction that rendered the ear superfluous.

The notion that the telephone could potentially replace the ear was most clearly illustrated by Bell's proposal to construct a direct link between the telephone and the tympanic membrane. Bell described his initial inspiration for such a device in a letter written to Blake on 15 December 1874:

> When we take hold of the handles of an ordinary electro-magnetic machine, the muscles of our arms are made to *vibrate* at a rate corresponding to the making and breaking of the primary circuit. Now the thought struck me that if we could make the direct and reversed induced impulses succeed one another as regularly as the crests and depressions of waves, then an electrode applied to the ear so as to induce a vibration in the membrana tymp. *should create the sensation of sound without the aid of any intermediate apparatus.*[38]

If the telephone circuit could be attached directly to the tympanic membrane, in other words, then there would be no need for a telephone receiver to translate the electrical impulses back into sonic vibrations. Bell also claimed that he had already constructed a working model of such a device:

> A number of permanent magnets were arranged upon a cylinder, which was revolved in front of electro-magnets [see figure 3.5]. On filling my ears with water and applying the wires … as in the diagram, a soft musical note was heard. The sound stopped the moment the electrical circuit was broken … Two ladies who were present submitted to the experiment and heard the note as clearly as I did. A gentleman, however … heard nothing more than the *noise*.[39]

Although the legitimacy of this experiment is doubtful, Bell's proposal clearly reflects a popular belief at the time that the telephone could be connected directly to the nervous system. The most striking example of this idea was J.C. Chester, who was popularly known as the "living telephone." Chester was a deaf mute who learned to speak using Bell's methods: "Chester learned to articulate and can make the awful

**Figure 3.5** Electrical stimulation of the tympanic membrane; Alexander Graham Bell, *The Bell Telephone: The Deposition of Alexander Graham Bell in the Suit Brought by the United States to Annul the Bell Patents* (Boston, 1908), 45.

guttural sounds peculiar to the deaf and dumb speakers."[40] After experimenting with a telephone apparatus, however, Chester discovered that "the dulled nerves of the ear are quickened by these powerful electric appliances and that he does hear."[41] Chester then decided to attach a telephone permanently to his ear:

> A gentleman meeting this walking telephone upon the road is offered the transmitter and receiver that hang upon the hook. The gentleman places one to the ear and talks through the other, sound being much assisted by the receiver in his ear. When he replies, he speaks through a tin horn connecting with the wires and trusts to the carrying effect of the telephone.[42]

According to Chester, the goal of this experiment was "to hear and speak as well as anyone," and with the help of this apparatus he was reportedly able to "converse over a space of several feet as easily as any other man."[43] Chester's device thus represents one of the earliest attempts to construct an electrical hearing aid,[44] and Chester's claim that "the dulled nerves of the ear are quickened by these powerful electric appliances" reflects a widespread belief at the time that auditory perception was inherently flawed and that electrical sound technologies could compensate for the newfound limitations of the perceptual apparatus. By converting sonic vibrations into electrical impulses, the telephone appeared to be capable of bypassing the sensory organs altogether. The telephone was thus conceived as a cure for deafness because it supplemented, imitated, and ultimately replaced the human ear.

# Audiometer

Like the telephone, the audiometer was also a technological apparatus that supplemented, imitated, and replaced the human ear. Although the audiometer was originally designed to provide an accurate measurement of hearing loss, it was commonly believed that this device could also compensate for the limitations of impaired hearing. The first function illustrates how the audiometer promoted the normalization and standardization of auditory perception, as it allowed hearing to be empirically measured, tested, and verified. The second function illustrates how the audiometer was conceived as a technological means of overcoming the inherent flaws and deficiencies of the ear.

Following the development of the telephone in 1876, a variety of audiometers were invented in Germany, Hungary, Russia, Scotland, USA, and England. These early audiometers were known as "induction coil audiometers." They were based on the same principle as the telephone, and they employed actual telephone receivers as transducers to convert sounds into electrical impulses. These audiometers typically consisted of two circuits linked to each other by an induction coil. The primary circuit consisted of a battery, an interrupter, and a primary induction coil. Interrupting the current in this circuit induced a transient current in the secondary coil. A variety of systems in the secondary circuit enabled the operator to control the intensity of the induced current passing to one or more telephones. In most induction coil audiometers the stimulus was a ticking or clicking sound, or the interruption of the circuit by an electrically driven tuning fork.

The first induction coil audiometer was developed by Arthur Hartmann in 1878. Hartmann devised this instrument to conduct hearing tests using a telephone receiver. He described the apparatus as follows:

> After the invention of the telephone, the author endeavored to obtain an exact graduation of sound by means of electric currents. In the circuit is placed 1. a tuning fork, by which the current is interrupted at regular intervals; 2. a rheocord, or a sliding induction apparatus, by means of which the intensity of the current can be varied and exactly regulated at will; and 3. a telephone, at which is heard a tone corresponding with that of the vibrating tuning fork, of more or less intensity according to the strength of the current.[45]

In Hartmann's audiometer, therefore, the primary circuit was interrupted by an electrically driven tuning fork that induced a stimulus of a certain frequency in the secondary circuit.

The first commercial audiometer was developed by David Edward Hughes in 1879. This device employed a carbon microphone, and the stimulus was generated by the ticking of a clock. The current from a battery passed through two identical primary coils mounted on a rigid bar. A third coil, connected to the telephone receiver, would slide on the rigid bar toward either primary. The induced alternating current in the secondary circuit was zero whenever it was midway between the primary coils. As it approached either primary, the induced current would increase proportionately. Hughes referred to this device as an "electric sonometer," but later that year B.W. Richardson wrote, "the world of science in general, and the world of medicine in particular, is under a debt of gratitude to Prof. Hughes for his simple and beautiful instrument which I have christened the audimeter, or less accurately but more euphoniously, the audiometer."[46] The word "audiometer" proved to be more popular than "sonometer" or "audimeter," and it quickly became the standard term for such devices.

Bell designed his own audiometer in December of that same year. Like Hartmann and Hughes, Bell's primary goal was to repurpose the telephone into an instrument for measuring hearing loss. Like these other audiometers, Bell's device also consisted of two induction coils. One coil carried an intermittent electrical current of a precise frequency, which was produced by the rotation of an armature between the poles of a magnet. The other coil was attached to a telephone receiver. As the coils were brought closer to one another on a graduated scale, the sound of the induced current would grow louder in the telephone receiver. Bell described the design of the electrical circuit as follows:

> Interrupt the current passed through a flat coil. Observe sound induced in a secondary or telephone circuit … Rotate secondary or flat spiral until sound becomes inaudible. Continue to rotate until sound is again audible … Coils … might be fixed upon a base [see figure 3.6]. At point *a* a "dead spot" can be found—complete silence. Now let a sound be brought by a separate circuit to telephone B and let C be the telephone.[47]

Using this device, Bell was able to generate sounds of varying frequencies that could then be used to measure a listener's hearing ability. Bell's own name even came to represent the standard measure of relative differences in sound intensity (each "bel" corresponds to a tenfold increase in sound intensity).

Bell's audiometer was first reported in October 1884 in the *Deaf-Mute Journal*, and it was first exhibited before the National Academy of Sciences the following year. Bell noted that the device had already been used to measure hearing loss among schoolchildren in Washington:

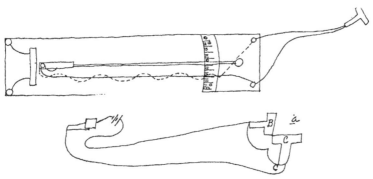

**Figure 3.6** Audiometer; George Fellendorf, "Bell's Audiometer"; *Asha* 18, no. 9 (1976), 564.

> The use of this instrument proved that ten per cent of the more than seven hundred pupils examined ... were hard of hearing (in their best ear), and seven per cent had very acute powers; the general range of audition being measured on the scale by the separation of the disks to a distance of from fifty to eighty centimeters, while the total range was from twenty to ninety centimeters.[48]

Some students, who had previously been classified as "distracted" or "stupid," actually turned out to be suffering from hearing impairments. The audiometer also revealed that many people who had previously been classified as deaf were actually only semi-deaf: "[I]n some institutions for the deaf as many as fifteen per cent are merely hard of hearing."[49] Bell's audiometer thus provided a more accurate method of calculating hearing loss, and it introduced a more precise set of standard sound frequencies for identifying and classifying hearing levels.

Some people were also convinced that Bell's audiometer could enhance auditory perception. In the editorial published in the *Deaf-Mute Journal*, for example, the anonymous commentator reported:

> We had an opportunity to test our hearing capacity a few days since. Hitherto we believed it to be at zero, but much to our astonishment it was registered at 11 in one ear and 9 in the other. But the most curious part of it all was that immediately after, a very strong ear-trumpet was tried, and with the result that we could distinguish several of the vowel sounds, although six months previous we could hear no sound at all. Two days after, the trumpet was again tried, but we could not hear any of the sounds except the letter O. Can it be that the testing apparatus had a stimulating effect upon the auditory nerves? Perhaps, in time, the question of teaching deaf-mutes may be solved through some kind of an instrument that will give them a certain power to hear and distinguish magnified vocal sounds.[50]

Like J.C. Chester, the "living telephone," this commentator was convinced that telephone technology could be employed not only to measure hearing loss but also to compensate for hearing impairments. He even predicted that scientists and engineers would eventually cure deafness by developing an instrument capable of electrically stimulating the auditory nerves, thus bypassing the ear altogether.

## Conclusion

In his discussion of the history of the telephone, Marshall McLuhan noted that "the receiver of the phone was directly modeled on the bone and diaphragm structure of the human ear," and "it is very much in the nature of the electric telephone, therefore, that it has such natural congruity with the organic."[51] McLuhan's claim that the telephone "was directly modeled on the bone and diaphragm structure of the human ear" clearly echoes the claims made by Bell and Blake; however, his claim that the telephone has a "natural congruity with the organic" fails to acknowledge the ways in which the organic was increasingly understood in technological terms. Helmholtz's studies on physiological acoustics, for example, introduced a mechanistic understanding of auditory perception that revealed the limitations of human hearing and simultaneously provided a means of compensating for these limitations through the technological reconstruction of the ear. Like Helmholtz's "tuning fork sounder," Édouard-Léon Scott's phonautograph was also designed to simulate the physiological properties of the ear, and it was directly inspired by research on human anatomy, as the large cone was designed to simulate the external ear, the diaphragm was designed to simulate the tympanic membrane, and the stylus with the attached bristle was designed to imitate the middle ear ossicula. Bell and Blake's "human ear phonautograph" went one step further by literally severing the ear from the body and transforming it into an autonomous machine. The technological reconstruction of the ear thus revealed that the perceptual apparatus was capable of registering the material effects of sensory stimuli in the absence of a perceiving subject, which effectively replaced Helmholtz's notion of the "spiritual ear" with the notion of the ear as a purely technological apparatus. The "human ear phonautograph" then led to the invention of the "real ear telephone," which incorporated a membrane taken from an actual human ear, yet this device was quickly surpassed by the diaphragm magneto telephone, which proved to be more sensitive than even the tympanic membrane. The superiority of the diaphragm magneto telephone encouraged a widespread belief that the telephone could potentially compensate for the inherent deficiencies of the perceptual apparatus. The telephone was thus based on the physiological structure of the ear, and it was designed to simulate auditory perception, yet it also threatened to replace the ear by rendering the sensory organs superfluous. The telephone also inspired the development of induction coil audiometers, which employed the same technology to measure the hearing capacity of the ear. Auditory perception could then be measured according to the same technical standards used to measure the strength of electrical circuits. The development of new sound technologies like the phonautograph, the telephone, and the audiometer was thus driven by a mechanistic understanding of auditory perception, and the ultimate goal of these experiments was the establishment of a direct link between the electrical circuit and the nervous system. In other words, the phonautograph, the telephone, and the audiometer did not simply represent prosthetic extensions of the human sensorium, but rather they promised to replace the sensory organs with a technological apparatus that would make hearing itself obsolete. The "inhuman" quality of these new sound technologies, therefore, is that they not only extended the qualities of writing to the experience of auditory perception, but they also promised to transform the body into a machine.

## Notes

1. Jonathan Crary, *Suspensions of Perception: Attention, Spectacle, and Modern Culture* (Cambridge, 1999), 56–57.
2. Ibid., 12.
3. Ibid.
4. Ibid.
5. Jonathan Crary, *Techniques of the Observer: On Vision and Modernity in the Nineteenth Century* (Cambridge, 1991), 17.
6. Friedrich Kittler, *Optical Media*, trans. Anthony Enns (Cambridge, 2009), 148.
7. Marshall McLuhan, *Understanding Media: The Extensions of Man* (New York, 1964).
8. Friedrich Kittler, *Gramophone, Film, Typewriter*, trans. Geoffrey Winthrop-Young and Michael Wutz (Stanford, 1999), 74.
9. James Lastra, *Sound Technology and the American Cinema: Perception, Representation, Modernity* (New York, 2000), 58.
10. Hermann Helmholtz, "On the Physiological Causes of Harmony in Music," trans. Alexander J. Ellis, in *Helmholtz on Perception: Its Physiology and Development*, eds. Richard M. Warren and Roslyn P. Warren (New York, 1968), 34.

11. Ibid., 43.
12. Ibid., 44.
13. Ibid.
14. Ibid., 46.
15. Ibid., 49–50.
16. Alfred M. Mayer, "On Edison's Talking Machine," *Popular Science Monthly* 12 (April 1878): 719.
17. J.L. Flanagan, "Voices of Men and Machines," *Journal of the Acoustical Society of America* 51 (March 1972): 1381.
18. Alexander Graham Bell, "Prehistoric Telephone Days," *National Geographic Magazine* 41 (March 1922): 236.
19. Lastra, *Sound Technology and the American Cinema*, 40.
20. Bell, "Prehistoric Telephone Days," 228.
21. Alexander Graham Bell, *The Telephone: A Lecture Entitled Researches in Electric Telephony* (London, 1878), 20.
22. Quoted in Robert V. Bruce, *Bell: Alexander Graham Bell and the Conquest of Solitude* (Boston, 1973), 111.
23. Ibid., 110–11.
24. Bell, *The Telephone*, 20.
25. Ibid.
26. Ibid., 21.
27. Clarence Blake, "Sound in Relation to the Telephone," *Journal of the Society of Telegraph Engineers* 7 (1878): 250–51.
28. Jonathan Sterne, "A Machine to Hear for Them: On the Very Possibility of Sound's Reproduction," *Cultural Studies* 15, no. 2 (2001): 273.
29. Clarence Blake, "The Use of the Membrana Tympani as a Phonautograph and Logograph," *Archives of Ophthalmology and Otology* 5 (1878): 110.
30. Quoted in Charles Snyder, "Clarence John Blake and Alexander Graham Bell: Otology and the Telephone," *Annals of Otology, Rhinology and Laryngology* 83, no. 4 (July–August 1974): 30.
31. Sterne, "A Machine to Hear for Them," 267.
32. Bell, *The Telephone*, 22.
33. Quoted in Snyder, "Clarence John Blake and Alexander Graham Bell," 19.
34. Thomas Watson, *Exploring Life: The Autobiography of Thomas A. Watson* (New York, 1926), 90.
35. Watson, *Exploring Life*, 90.
36. Blake, "Sound in Relation to the Telephone," 251.
37. Ibid., 252.
38. Alexander Graham Bell, *The Bell Telephone: The Deposition of Alexander Graham Bell in the Suit Brought by the United States to Annul the Bell Patents* (Boston, 1908), 44–45.
39. Ibid., 45.
40. Grant Eldredge, "A New Telephone That Is Alive," *Buffalo Times*, 24 January 1897, from the Audiology Folder, Medical Sciences Division, National Museum of American History, Smithsonian Institution.
41. Ibid.

42. Ibid.
43. Ibid.
44. The first U.S. patent for a "magneto telephone for personal wear" was actually issued to Alonzo E. Miltimore in 1892, but the device was never produced.
45. Quoted in C.C. Bunch, "The Development of the Audiometer," *The Laryngoscope* 51, no. 12 (December 1941): 1101.
46. Ibid., 1102.
47. Quoted in George W. Fellendorf, "Bell's Audiometer," *Asha* 18, no. 9 (September 1976): 564.
48. "The April Meeting of the National Academy of Sciences," *Science* 5, no. 117 (1 May 1885): 354.
49. Ibid.
50. "Dr. Bell's Audiometer," *Deaf-Mute Journal*, 9 October 1884, from Library of Congress, Alexander Graham Bell Family Papers 1862–1939, http://memory.loc.gov/ammem/bellhtml; accessed 16 May 2012.
51. McLuhan, *Understanding Media*, 238.

# Bibliography

Anon. "The April Meeting of the National Academy of Sciences." *Science* 5, no. 117 (1 May 1885): 353–55.

———. "Dr. Bell's Audiometer." *Deaf-Mute Journal*, 9 October 1884. From Library of Congress, Alexander Graham Bell Family Papers 1862–1939; http://memory.loc.gov/ammem/bellhtml; accessed 16 May 2012.

Bell, Alexander Graham. *The Telephone: A Lecture Entitled Researches in Electric Telephony*. London, 1878.

———. *The Bell Telephone: The Deposition of Alexander Graham Bell in the Suit Brought by the United States to Annul the Bell Patents*. Boston, 1908.

———. "Prehistoric Telephone Days." *National Geographic Magazine* 41 (March 1922): 223–41.

Bell, Alexander Melville. *Visible Speech: The Science of Universal Alphabetics*. New York, 1867.

Blake, Clarence. "Sound in Relation to the Telephone." *Journal of the Society of Telegraph Engineers* 7 (1878): 247–59.

———. "The Use of the Membrana Tympani as a Phonautograph and Logograph." *Archives of Ophthalmology and Otology* 5 (1878): 1–6.

Bruce, Robert V. *Bell: Alexander Graham Bell and the Conquest of Solitude*. Boston, 1973.

Bunch, C.C. "The Development of the Audiometer." *The Laryngoscope* 51, no. 12 (December 1941): 1100–18.

Crary, Jonathan. *Techniques of the Observer: On Vision and Modernity in the Nineteenth Century*. Cambridge, 1991.

———. *Suspensions of Perception: Attention, Spectacle, and Modern Culture*. Cambridge, 1999.

Eldredge, Grant. "A New Telephone That Is Alive." *Buffalo Times*, 24 January 1897. From the Audiology Folder, Medical Sciences Division, National Museum of American History, Smithsonian Institution.

Fellendorf, George W. "Bell's Audiometer." *Asha* 18, no. 9 (September 1976): 563–65.

Flanagan, J.L. "Voices of Men and Machines." *Journal of the Acoustical Society of America* 51 (March 1972): 1375–87.

Helmholtz, Hermann. "On the Physiological Causes of Harmony in Music." Trans. Alexander J. Ellis. In *Helmholtz on Perception: Its Physiology and Development*. Eds. Richard M. Warren and Roslyn P. Warren. New York, 1968, 27–58.

Kittler, Friedrich. *Gramophone, Film, Typewriter*. Trans. Geoffrey Winthrop-Young and Michael Wutz. Stanford, 1999.

———. *Optical Media*. Trans. Anthony Enns. Cambridge, 2009.

Lastra, James. *Sound Technology and the American Cinema: Perception, Representation, Modernity*. New York, 2000.

Mayer, Alfred M. "On Edison's Talking Machine." *Popular Science Monthly* 12 (April 1878): 719–24.

McLuhan, Marshall. *Understanding Media: The Extensions of Man*. New York, 1964.

Snyder, Charles. "Clarence John Blake and Alexander Graham Bell: Otology and the Telephone." *Annals of Otology, Rhinology and Laryngology* 83, no. 4 (July–August 1974): 3–31.

Sterne, Jonathan. "A Machine to Hear for Them: On the Very Possibility of Sound's Reproduction." *Cultural Studies* 15, no. 2 (2001): 259–94.

Watson, Thomas. *Exploring Life: The Autobiography of Thomas A. Watson*. New York, 1926.

PART III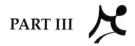

# SOUND OBJECTS AS ARTIFACTS OF ATTRACTION

4

# Listening to the Horn
## On the Cultural History of the Phonograph and the Gramophone
*Stefan Gauß*

The act of listening (and seeing), the construction of sense, occurs as a historically determined process. The modality and models of this process vary according to place, time, and community. The multifaceted and changeable implications of an acoustic event depend upon the means by which the listener receives it. The listener is never confronted with an abstract, ideal sound detached from all materiality. Thus the question of the history of auditory perception leads to a further question of material conditionality and its effect on this history.

Listening is an activity that is always connected with gestures, spaces, and habits. Those who listen to technically reproduced sounds are dealing with something, the properties and characteristics of which are determined by their means of hearing, as is their appropriation and their understanding of the perceived sound. The act of listening in the presence of devices, such as MP3 players, is part of our mental disposition. It belongs to our personal store of senses and emotions, in the same way that we are educated in forms of cultural identity and social differentiation.

An acoustic event, while remaining identical in tone, takes on new meaning as soon as the conditions of its technical reproduction or the manner of delivering sound to the perceptive organs change. Sense is produced from the various forms in which sound is created, processed, and made audible. It therefore seems appropriate to inquire into the historicity of practices based on listening to technically reproduced sounds and on the way we handle these practical objects; that is, to inquire into the effective conditions that have resulted from more than 130 years of the phonograph and the gramophone. The detachment of sound from the place and time of its production, which defines its technical reproducibility, has continually been carried over into new generations of objects, the long and widespread acceptance of which can only be explained by the beneficial experiences that people have had with them.[1]

As my primary interest is neither the "technical medium" nor listening as such, some remarks on my research approach seem appropriate in order to sketch out the epistemic interest of some methodological assumptions and key terms. In connection to this, I will focus on the characteristics of the object and its transition from small-scale manufacture into industrial product, followed by an inquiry into the sound from the acoustic horn, its nature as an artifact, and its complement, the listener. Finally, I will consider the central place of the use of sound objects, particularly in the context of the city's acoustic culture, and their importance in the conflict between "culture" and "civilization."

## Listening in Industrial Mass Culture

The following remarks are based on my study of the cultural history of the phonograph and the gramophone in Germany between 1900 and 1940.[2] That work was composed as a monograph based on the "Industrial Mass Culture"[3] field of research developed by Wolfgang Ruppert, building upon its theories and methodological implications. It inquires into the mutually dependent processes of production, the use of these objects, and their position in long-term historical trends of modern civilization. The epistemic interest lies in the connection between material and immaterial culture. In the present case, this means objectifying the relationships between the properties and characteristics of the objects, on the one hand, and the ideas, mental images, emotions, attributions, perceptions, and practices on the other.

It is necessary to clarify the meaning of certain terms. We are starting out from a concept of culture that explicitly deals with things as an integral part of culture.[4] Artifacts are to be understood as objectifications of "a socially structured and culturally formed human behavior"[5] of historical actors, who can thus be read as part of this behavior. The determination of what the object is or can be underlies historicity itself. Following the definition of the psychologist, Wolfram Heubach, we speak of an object as "the concept of concreteness through which the grown person realizes things by way of behavior and perception."[6] It is clear from this perspective that—for example, in media studies, where the dominant opinion is that "phonographs" have to do with a technical medium—all that is presented is a concept of concreteness that touches on the intended usage of the object, prioritizing the technical development of the apparatus over its other properties and characteristics, and leaving the impression that the objects were only created for the investigation of this single aspect. By regarding the concept of concreteness historically, it becomes clear what contemporaries saw, in the course of history, in the objects for the technical reproduction of sound. Integrated into research are symbolic examples of the "phonograph" and "gramophone" as signs of progress, of modernity, and of epochal change; whereas, in the wake of obsolescence, its meaning has changed into, for example, a coveted "antique," or garbage, or even imbued with magical qualities, as in Werner Herzog's film, *Fitzcarraldo*.

Devices for the technical reproduction of sound have been invented and produced in multiple ways. They differ from each other in their wide range of technical constructions and features, their practical value, and their aesthetic appearance (design). The terms "phonograph" and "gramophone" capture this range of devices only in a vague and incomplete way; moreover, both terms have historical connotations and are attached to company brandings and product lines. In the absence of a suitable preexisting term, the term "phono-object" will be introduced here. This will allow us to speak comprehensively of those objects that reproduce sound by means of a recording medium, and will, at the same time, create the distance necessary for intellectual investigation into those terms connected to objectivity.

## The "Eternal Return" of Sound

In 1889, Thomas Alvar Edison, the American "inventor" of the phonograph, and Emile Berliner, the "inventor" of the gramophone who had emigrated from Hannover in Germany to the United States, found themselves on business trips in Europe at the same time. Edison arrived in Paris at the beginning of August and then went on to Berlin in September, where he showed his phonograph to scientists at the Siemens & Halske company, run by his friend and business partner, Werner Siemens. Berliner arrived in his hometown in September and presented his gramophone in Berlin in November.

In the United States, Edison had started getting famous contemporaries to speak into the phonograph. He planned to continue this PR strategy in Germany, which led him to establish contact with Kaiser Wilhelm II, Chancellor Otto von Bismarck, and Count Helmuth von Moltke. As Edison did not have the opportunity for personal meetings with these luminaries during his stay in Germany, he commissioned his assistant, Theo Wangemann, to meet these men and complete the recordings.

In October 1889, after meeting with Wilhelm II and Bismarck, Wangemann was received by Moltke, who, in the course of recording multiple cylinders, remarked: "This new invention by Mr. Edison is in fact quite remarkable. The phonograph makes it possible for a man who has already laid long in the grave to raise his voice again and speak his greetings to the present."[7] Moltke thus described a fundamental usage of the phono-object. The phonograph has the ability to transform a fleeting sound into a material, lasting, and reproducible record, thus releasing the sound from its original context. It separates the spoken word from the body of the speaker, just as it does the sound of a trumpet from the instrument itself, or street noises from the city.

With the possibility of making the past audible in the present, the phono-objects created an access point to the past and expanded historical knowledge:

> Currently, in order to find out about the attitude and presence of this or that actor or singer, we have to content ourselves with consulting the writings that have been handed down to us. We can only instruct ourselves about the development of language through written works. In the future, however, this will be handed down via the gramophone, and in addition to the instructive written works, we will also have the opportunity to immerse ourselves via our ears, with the help of the gramophone, in the past.[8]

In 1909, in the *Phonographische Zeitschrift* (Phonographic Journal), Wilhelm Kronfuss composed a multipart study on the "Style of Phonographs and Phonograms."[9] With the goal of defining the specific essence of the phono-object, he compared it with objects that possess properties and characteristics that are as similar as possible—for example, the optic lens, the telephone, or the flat mirror. The telephone, with its transmission of sound over long distances, had already overcome the spatial connection to its point of origin. Kronfuss acknowledged this and went further, saying that the phono-object, in contrast to the telephone, also overcame the temporal connection to the sound's origin. This, however, was true in only one direction on the axis of time—that is, endlessly in the direction of the future—since of course recordings from past acoustic events are impossible, even if certain contemporaries expressed a wish for this usage and were enthusiastic about having unique experiences hearing, for example, the voices of "great" poets, such as Johann Wolfgang von Goethe.

For Kronfuss, the phono-object effectively cancelled time, or even destroyed time, and allowed a time-free space to emerge: "In the phonograph, we possess a sort of time machine, for which time in fact does not exist at all, fixing and inscribing in its phonograms an eternal present."[10]

Among the objects of cultural modernity, phono-objects have the ability to reorder the space–time coordinates of acoustic events, sharing a close connection with the railroad and the automobile, which likewise influenced the dimensions and perceptibility of space and time, as, for example, the "panoramic" view from a train.[11]

Contemporaries who were attempting to define the aesthetic of the acoustic horn's sound employed many spatial metaphors. Thomas Mann spoke of an aesthetic analog to looking through the wrong end of opera glasses,[12] and others—possibly borrowing from the novelist—through the wrong end of a telescope.[13] Individual sounds were emphasized at the expense of the overall impression, according to Thomas Mann, and, like a painting viewed in this way, the sound seemed transported away and reduced in size, without losing any of its definition. Then again, Mann may have known of the music critic Max Chop's 1909 description of a sound characteristic, in connection with the *Starktonplatte* (amplifying plate), which pointed out an "anatomical tendency," like looking through a magnifying glass, which diverts from the *Totaleindruck* (total sound impression) and instead stresses the individual components of the sound image.[14]

The anthropologist, Helmut Plessner, with respect to the audibility of the spaciousness of sound, spoke of "volume," which suggests expansion, intensity, and duration.[15] In this sense, the phono-object would produce or support the perception of compression in the auditory elements within a given volume of sound. This would give the phono-object a twofold dimensionality: in the technical reproduction, the volume of sound would expand itself in time. At the same time, in the manner of a "time machine," the phono-object permanently secures the ephemeral sound in a timeless space, an archive of "eternal return"[16]—the original purpose of the phonograph, according to Kronfuss. This "eternal" space gives Moltke's "voice from the grave" its ability to remain current. The recordings of Moltke, Bismarck, and all the other contemporaries are a historical remnant that has stretched into the present, and, by listening to them in their original volume, they can be made present for us again, as they will also be for future generations—saved and accessible on the Internet and as technically modern MP3 files.

## Phono-objects as Industrial Mass-Market Product

On 26 November 1889—Edison had left Germany two months earlier, and Wangemann was already in Budapest for the second time to make a recording of Kaiser Franz Joseph—the presentation of the phonograph and gramophone appeared on the program for the monthly meeting of the Electro-Technical Society.[17] In the main auditorium of the Imperial Post Office in Berlin's Artilleriestrasse (now Tucholskystrasse), various entrepreneurs, engineers, officers, and scientists from the city had gathered, including the regional secretary of the imperial postal service, Heinrich von Stephan, special advisor to the government, Werner von Siemens, and head telegraph engineer, Grahwinkel. Müller, the telegraph engineer of the imperial postal service, presented the phonograph to those assembled. He explained the technical details of the machine, spoke a few sentences that were recorded onto a cylinder, and played the cylinder back for the auditorium. A man named Költzow, a foreman from an electro-technical factory, described the experience: "The voice was pure and clear, with a bit of background noise, yet so faint that only those standing directly in front of it could hear anything."[18] At the end of the presentation, a coachman blew a signal into the phonograph, which was played back into the room as a weak but clear recording, according to Költzow.

Emile Berliner, a member of the society, then followed up with a presentation and demonstration of a gramophone that he had built himself. Költzow stressed the simplicity of the construction in comparison to the phonograph, and wrote about the sound it gave: "As Berliner put his machine into operation, an awful noise arose, which was almost unendurable, but which soon became a complete orchestra sound, out of which one could make out almost every individual instrument, despite the noise."[19]

Emile Berliner explained to those present that Edison's phonograph had already reached a technical cul-de-sac. He came to this conclusion on the basis of his experiences, as well as considerations he had made on the basis of physics. His gramophone, on the other hand, was still at the beginning of its development. Berliner's criticism of the phonograph concerned the dependence between amplification and sound quality. Edison's machine would not permit a reproduction of sound that was simultaneously loud and true to nature. Berliner explained that the reason for this was the high level of energy needed to bring plate lines vertically into the record. By contrast, the plate lines in the gramophone were inscribed horizontally—and therefore with greater energy efficiency. The difference between the phonograph and the gramophone corresponded to the impression given on hearing them, as was reported by Költzow: a soft and clear tone from the phonograph; and loud with a lot of background noise from the gramophone.

The difference in the way that the two phono-objects functioned in the form of the record had far-reaching consequences for the use and the marketability of the two devices. Edison saw in the phonograph first and foremost a new tool for the office, which would be used along with the telephone and typewriter as a means of streamlining communication. In the United States, his machine was being successfully marketed as a coin-operated entertainment device, against which Edison protested. By contrast, Berliner was of the opinion that the future of sound recording lay precisely in the entertainment industry. For this reason, he saw the laborious and expensive reproduction of cylinders as the decisive weakness of the phonograph, neglecting the possibility for self-recording on the gramophone.

With the benefit of hindsight, we can see Berliner's position as clear sighted. The industrialization of the phono-object has been driven by record consumption. This has established a sensible, long-term, and traditional relationship for the phono-object, which secured the existence of the recording industry over a long period. However, from the viewpoint of Berliner's contemporaries, who were participating in the commercialization of the machine, it remained unclear which utilization concept would prove most marketable in the future. The question was, which general consumer need would reach the critical mass required to push this new device from a limited-run article into an industrial, mass-market product.

In contrast to our more or less self-evident relationship with the phono-object today, at that time it still played no role in people's economic mindset, and its trade possibilities would appear negligible for some time. In 1878, the *Leipziger Illustrierte* newspaper wrote that the phonograph was "scarcely more than an interesting experiment" and "for the present [is capable] of no practical uses."[20] This verdict remained virtually unchanged for another ten years. After the monthly meeting of the Electro-Technical Society, which almost all the Berlin newspapers had reported on, Emile Berliner wished to make his gramophone accessible to a wider public and installed it for that purpose in a small room of the Belle Alliance theater in Berlin; admission was priced at fifty Pfennig per hour for each visitor. The response to this, however, was well below expectations. Only a few visitors took up the offer, and the installation had to be dismantled after only four days.

The example of Költzow, the factory foreman, can help explain the problem of commercialization in an open field of disparate business concepts. Költzow, who became an enthusiastic proponent of sound recordings following the meeting of the Electro-Technical Society, first experimented with improving the sound of the gramophone, and then focused his energies on the phonograph, which he saw as having greater commercial potential. The possibility of recording sound, and then playing it back again immediately, indicated to Költzow that it had better chances in the marketplace than a device that simply played back sound. He then built his own phonograph, showed it to his superiors at the factory, and suggested that they produce the device commercially. However, they viewed this new "invention" as merely a curious toy, as did so many other skeptics at that time, and they declined the proposal. In response, Költzow handed in his resignation, and in 1890 he opened the "first German phonograph factory in Berlin." The business, which Költzow ran together with the pianist Bahre, entailed taking a "baby" device that they had purchased from the Columbia Phonograph Company, providing it with a glass casing, then reselling this to visitors at a considerable markup. A gallery, with up to a dozen hearing tubes connected to the phonograph, was used to draw in visitors. Working closely with Költzow and Bahre was the locksmith, Paul Pfeiffer. In the 1890s, with his brother-in-law, the mechanic Carl Lindström, Pfeiffer founded the company "Pfeiffer & Lindström, technical workshop for innovations and mass produced articles of all kinds."[21] Shortly after the turn of the century, Lindström Inc. was formed out of that workshop, and it became a global player in the recording industry in the period of the Kaiser, second only to the German Gramophone Company. The enormous growth in the recording industry was attributed to the context of the second industrial revolution, with its major electro-technical and chemical sectors. From the 1880s onwards, Germany experienced a period of general prosperity, and the increased prevalence of modern means of communication and transportation led to a boost in globalization. The increase in the recording industry was an international phenomenon. It took hold in many countries at the same time, especially in the United States, France, England, and also, to a certain extent, in Germany. The German recording industry grew as part of the "new economy" of the period before 1914, becoming a world market leader and dominant exporter. Companies such as Lindström Inc. and the German Gramophone Company

**Figure 4.1** Shipping department of Lindström Inc.; *Die Sprechmaschine* 4, no. 20 (1909), 568; Bildarchiv Preußischer Kulturbesitz, Berlin.

ran numerous international production centers and operated a worldwide trade network (see figure 4.1).

Berlin was the "capital" of the recording industry. In the export quarter around Berlin's Ritterstrasse, a large number of businesses had established themselves or opened branches. In addition, the rich music culture of Berlin offered many opportunities for making recordings— for example, the German Gramophone Company recorded the star tenor, Enrico Caruso, during his visit to the city—and the citizens of Berlin functioned as a test market for new products.

The phonograph had virtually no part in the growth of the recording sector. It was true that improved technical innovations created the possibility of industrially reproducing recording cylinders, slightly diminishing the advantage of the flat gramophone record. But there were also technical improvements in the gramophone record. The substantial background noise and poor sound quality of the record, listening to which required "iron nerves" according to Költzow, had been considerably improved since October 1896 through the use of shellac. The potential of the phonograph for creating one's own recordings remained its particular domain for some time. However, consumers scarcely took advantage of this function, so that eventually the self-recording feature of the phonograph was only provided to customers upon demand.

The recording industry had trouble explaining the reluctance of its customers to use the self-recording function and believed that they could increase acceptance of this use with the help of advertising. They compared the creation of "records" with photographs, and they promoted a cylinder album (with recordings of children) as the ideal addition to the family archive, next to the photo album. But these rescue attempts for the phonograph were futile. The decline of the phonograph continued steadily in the years following 1900. Lindström Inc. discontinued the product in 1907, and Edison ceased producing phonographs entirely in 1913.

## The Sound from the Horn: Musical Adaptations

The sound that emerges from the acoustic horn is an artifact, with a variety of factors having contributed to its formation. The recording possibilities were first determined by the recording equipment. The duration of the recording was only a few minutes, and the frequency spectrum and power were very limited. Furthermore, the machine reproduced its own operating noise. Recordings had to proceed without pause from beginning to end, and making any corrections afterwards was impossible.

In the commercially equipped studio recording, the producers attempted to retain as complete control over the sound as possible. In a time of purely mechanical recording technology, which was replaced in the 1920s by electrical recording technology, experimental recording methods were dominant, driven by the expertise gained by sound engineers (see figure 4.2).

Musical material was brought into an appropriately new form to match the machine, unless compositions were directly cut in order to fit the limits of what could be recorded. Longer musical pieces were shortened, split over multiple recordings, or simply played faster, so that they fitted the time limits of the recording device. Improvements were planned for sound sources that could only be partially or poorly reproduced. Examples of these improvements are the omission of certain instruments; or substitution, for example, wind instruments for strings; or playing short notes one after the other instead of holding one note.

**Figure 4.2** Choral recording at the Brussels World Exposition; *Die Sprechmaschine* 5, no. 6 (1910), 124; Bildarchiv Preußischer Kulturbesitz, Berlin.

Not only were adjustments made to the musical material, but they were also made to the musicians and singers themselves. While in the recording studio, they had to submit to the acoustic, technical, and organizational conditions of the recording procedures, as well as to the sound engineer, who would be directing the operation, and the record producer's agents.

## Processing the Artists before the Horn

For the artists, sound recording meant, first of all, acquiring and practicing discipline and control of their emotions. Since a recording could neither be "edited" nor reworked, the participants could not let any mistakes slip through during the entire recording period. The various levels of sound intensity, the power of the instruments and singing disallowed any "correction," so the actors each had to be arranged according to the intensity of their instruments while still as close as possible to the recording horn, which led to some very tightly packed arrangements. At the same time, these arrangements, once decided on, were still subject to change and were of necessity altered in the course of the recording, according to the varying sound dynamic of the composition.

The singer, Frieda Hempel, who was engaged at the Berlin Court Opera from 1907 to 1912, describes in her 1955 autobiography her experiences during the first recordings for the Odeon in 1907. Hempel writes that she was "prodded" in the back when it was time to start singing, and when the score required her to sing powerfully, a recording technician pulled on her skirt, so that she stepped away from the recording horn. During softer sections, she was given another energetic push back toward the horn: "With all of this pushing and pulling, it was not easy to maintain musical continuity. The recording often had to be repeated, as the voice was not at the appropriate level. And when the recording really worked, then the record itself would take every opportunity to go and break."[22]

Moreover, sound recording meant that the artists could not play for a distinct and present audience, as they would at a concert. The sound that had been inscribed "forever" onto the record now implied, in the act of performing, an impalpable, imaginary audience, which seemed to the artist as spatially and temporally unlimited, socially indifferent, and quantitatively undefined. One sang, played music, and recited words before a world public that stretched into all future generations. The majority of artists did not seem affected by this; others responded with a "fear of the horn," a fear that overcame even celebrated performing artists who were well accustomed to the stage, and which led them to falter in their recordings. Sound engineers reported cases similar to a "black out"; a complete memory block caused by stress.

And there was something else, too, that sound recording demanded of the artists: playing for "eternity," together with the potentially endless repetition of a flawed recording, led to increased urgency for artistic perfection. Especially notable is the description of pianist Artur Schnabel, writing to his wife on 26 March 1932, of his distress during the recording of Beethoven's sonatas in London.[23] It was the first time that he had played for a recording. The pianist considered the "plating process," as he called it, to be a kind of "destruction through preservation." What cannot die has never lived, according to Schnabel. These machines created by man have an imperfection that does violence against man, in that the "miserable technology" forces humans to be flawless, which can never be the case. Schnabel wrote that he found himself on the brink of a nervous breakdown while recording: "I almost began to weep when I was alone on the street. ... The delivery unto evil, the betrayal of life, the objectification of blood, the marriage to death. It is complete madness and absolute perversion. ... It is only happening because it is possible."[24] In view of this mechanical requirement of unconditional perfection, a feeling of shame overcame Schnabel for a human performance that was perceptible only in its inadequacies.

## Listening in Front of the Horn

Just as recording conditions underlay the formation of sounds from the horn, so it was with its counterpart, the listener in front of the horn: this time the process was reversed, with sound playback determined by the conditions of the machine and the formation of his subjective perception. The ear, just like the eye, is a historical product. Sound is perceptible to the ear as sensory "input" from which the listener deduces a mental representation. Sound that permeates the ear is continuously identified and evaluated: as speech, noise, music, as known or unknown, as pleasant or unpleasant, or even as a pathogenic experience of the body—as with tinnitus, for example. Listening is therefore not only a physiological stimulus, but also and above all a cultural process of the views and orders of sensory impression, which then leads to different impressions based on the individual's own social modes of experience.

The production of sound and its perception correlate with one another: they are drawn to each other in ways that are both arbitrary and determined. Just as with the record producer—who has to take into account different patterns of consumer taste, as well as change in music and sound styles—so the listener's perception will undergo a process of adaptation to the specific quality of technically reproduced sound. Along with the pressure to reach perfection that was imposed on the artists while recording, there was also the listener's own expectation of perfection. In a letter to his wife, Schnabel mentions a conversation with a "record enthusiast" who judged the artistic achievements of a live concert differently to those of a recorded concert: he tolerated mistakes made by the artist on stage but not mistakes on the record.

From the listener's point of view, the phono-object pluralized the possibilities of listening, in that it opened up entirely new interconnections in which listening could now take place—interconnections that were essentially closed off by conventional forms of listening, for example, the concert performances of music, and listening to the spoken word. Listening became more individually structured and more intensely perceptible, in particular in the way music from the acoustic horn was more "closely" experienced. For example, in his novel *The Magic Mountain*, Thomas Mann vividly depicts how the consumption of gramophone music became an intimate act of introspection for the novel's protagonist, Hans Castorp.[25] Castorp develops a love affair with a gramophone with the trade name "Polyhymnia" and listens to music in tranquil isolation. He longs for togetherness and falls into an intimate dialogue with himself, whose deeper layers he is able to fathom by way of music. Through Schubert's Lied, "Der Lindenbaum," Castorp makes the shocking discovery that the object of his love is death. With "Der Lindenbaum" still on his lips, he heads into World War I.

Thomas Mann demonstrates, as had Artur Schnabel and others, the cultural importance of the phonograph and gramophone in the semantics of the dual relationship between life and death, art and machine. In the case of Hans Castorp, a fatal love of music amounted to a death wish, which Thomas Mann viewed as a central cultural phenomenon of pre-World War I society. Of course, the listener in front of the machine is in possession of all his five senses. The person listening to sound from the horn is affected by the entire materiality of the machine, meaning also the visual appearance, always a crucial component and reference point for its functionality, which corresponds to the modality and forms of hearing and seeing.

In 1908, a writer attempting to obtain criteria for the design of phono-objects described the use of senses as an indicator for the musicality of the listener:

> In larger groups, where almost everyone was musically educated (or at least behaved as if they were!), or had studied music to some extent, I often had the opportunity to make psychological observations of my acquaintances during presentations of the speaking machine. Those who were truly musical did not look at the machine, while those less appreciative, in contrast, tended to look on the enormous copper horn as though it were something fascinating to behold.[26]

Instead of through his ear, the listener reveals himself through his gaze, the most visible, tangible signal that a body puts out to a third party. A gaze is interpretable. The musically uneducated listeners prefer machines with a large amplifying horn, due to the wider visual effect, which gives him the common man's pride of ownership as he looks at it; the artistic and knowledgeable music lover can be identified precisely because he does not bother to look at the machine, even closes his eyes at

**Figure 4.3** The "Weber" phono-object; *Phonographische Zeitschrift* 11, no. 36 (1910); Bildarchiv Preußischer Kulturbesitz, Berlin.

the intensity of the experience as if in a concert, and prefers machines that take on the shape of furniture, blending into the style of the household without giving any indication of its use. Countless models took on this ideal of making the intended purpose invisible, including the so-called "hornless machine," which had a sound amplifier integrated into its housing (see figure 4.3), as well as cabinet and chest models, and also sculpturally overdesigned machines such as the "Belophon" (see figure 4.4).

**Figure 4.4** The "Belophon" of the Karl Below Company, Leipzig, 1905; *Phonographische Zeitschrift* 6, no. 49 (1905), 1096; Bildarchiv Preußischer Kulturbesitz, Berlin.

## Between Original Sound and "Phonograph Sound"

The phono-object provoked the question of how technically reproduced sound, and its associated listening experience, should be evaluated. There are two contrary positions on the best approach to the production of sound and its appropriation. First, the reproduction could be judged according to the degree of its consistency with the original. From this perspective, the phonograph and gramophone promised faithful reproducibility in the sense of authenticity and detailed precision: after a 1906 debate, the phonograph, in comparison with written descriptions, retained "the subjectivity, the individuality of each of the singers or his regional variation, the color in tone and word."[27] The phonogram recording—analog to photography—would take on the responsibility of straightforward recording of reality: "If the phonograph is to provide perfectly faithful reproduction of people's speech and people's songs, still it would need to be much improved; its goal must be to capture a song like a Kodak captures a picture."[28]

But this ideal, which was so closely bound to technical advancement, is fundamentally not achievable. The phono-object does not simply capture sound and then play it back again; rather, it replaces the captured acoustic reality with something new, with its own specific qualities. The original is represented by its reproduction merely on the basis of the similarity between them. The original disappears not with its technical reproduction; rather it survives as a symbolic representation. The similarity between the original and its reproduction allows the listener to create a relationship between the two. The listener manages to perceive the intention or the desire to reproduce the original, provided he or she views and arranges the sensory input out of the horn, and this confirms, supports, enriches, or recalls the idea of what is heard.

Given the impossibility of being able to hear the original, as well as the impression that the sound quality had not made any notable improvement in some time, a contrary position to "true to the original" was put forward in 1910. The apologists of this new point of view claimed that the "phonograph sound," as the sound out of the horn was described, should be viewed as something independent in itself. An aesthetic quality, independent of the original, was ascribed to the "phonograph sound." It should not be measured against the original, for it possessed a potential for its own beauty, which in certain cases could even surpass the original. Following this proposition, the listener should integrate all details of the sound into his listening experience, and perceive and enjoy the music from the horn with particular awareness of its technical reproduction.

## The "Beautiful" Sound

The question of what constituted the "beauty" of the sound from the horn was directed toward the objective sound itself as well as toward the listener. In this, there were different intentions: the debate about tonal properties of a "beautiful" sound concerned the determination of fundamental criteria for the development and judgment of recording principles. This looked to improve the technical properties of the phono-object, foregrounding the listener's experience and the way in which he or she arrives at the most enjoyable and intense listening experience possible.

Georg Rothgiesser, publisher of the *Phonographische Zeitschrift*, endeavored to create a "theory of beautiful sound" in an article in 1901.[29] His intention was to determine a criterion that would transcend the vicissitudes of taste and could find recognition as a universal principle. Rothgiesser came to the conclusion that the reverberation of sound was decisive in the perception of beauty, and thus recommended that a "sound shadow" should take place during recording as well as playback. Sound is "beautiful," if we follow the conclusion of Helmut Plessner, through its intensity over a stretch of time, or, in the words of Thomas Mann, when sound carries in it the "fullness of melody."[30]

In 1924, Rudolf Lothar examined the subjective side of the listener in a paper about the "speech machine"; in this paper, he puts forward a theory for the pleasurable appropriation of recorded music.[31] At the center of his discussion he addresses the capacity of the individual for imagination, which he calls the "power of illusion." According to Lothar, this "power of illusion" served the listener in two ways: by suppressing the undesirable background noise of the machine on the one hand, and providing the perceived sounds with the listening pleasure of increased imagination, internal visions, and fantasy on the other. This manner of perception provided one of the conditions for the technical reproduction of a decent listening experience. With the concept of the "power of illusion," Lothar laid out—theoretically at least—a path toward recorded music for the educated classes, whose attitude had been one of reluctance mixed with total refusal. Lothar's view was that listening to technically reproduced sound would be more difficult to dismiss as a culturally limited practice if people were really challenged to understand the entire subject, and put it to the test. If the phono-object with all its inadequacies could be said to present an obstacle to musical pleasure, the passive recipient, not understanding the challenges of the experience, will likewise have trouble adjusting his or her ears accordingly.

## Dealing with the Phono-object, the City, and Noise

There are numerous different ways in which phono-objects are used, and these can be divided into three major context areas. The first area is that of leisure: practices including making use of the objects as a pastime, which can be thought of as a hobby; forms of intensive listening, for instance solitary and introverted listening to music, which I touched upon lightly in an example from Thomas Mann's *The Magic Mountain*; the consumption of music by World War I veterans as a kind of mental support; and in early cinemas, where very loud amplifiers were installed to play during intermissions, and to provide sound or acoustic accompaniment to the film program. A second context area is the use of the phono-object in professional life: for example, the phonograph would be used for recording and later for making transcriptions of parliamentary debates, and for streamlining and increasing the flexibility of written work.

In factories, gramophone music helped relieve the tedium of rather monotonous tasks and diverted the workers and employees, and in Berlin's municipal transport system a proposal to replace train conductor announcements with phonographs was considered. The third context field encompasses education and science. In science, researchers used the phonograph as a new medium for identifying acoustic phenomena, using new methods of detailed analysis with the help of the machine. The research of comparative musicology was based on the phonograph, which opened up the possibility of innovative ethnological studies. The cylinder provided new source material, which enabled the collection and archiving of acoustic materials, for example of representatives of folk culture, who were motivated by the impending disappearance of their original cultural modes of expression. There were cultural and political motivations for saving "what is still left to save" before the inevitable technical advances spread further across the world by Western civilization, and all regional characteristics had been swept away. Through using the phonograph, linguists hoped to hit upon the generative principle of language, and doctors recorded bodily noises for educational purposes. Dentists began to offer their patients recorded music to help diminish the sense of pain during procedures.

In the field of education, speech recordings helped students with correct pronunciation while learning foreign languages, and music and singing teachers used the machine to make their students more attentive to mistakes, and to play model performances for them. In secretarial training, gramophone music was used to clock typing speeds.

## The Shot at the Gramophone

When we inquire into the different practices that played a role in the leisure time of urban auditory culture, almost all involved filling public space with sound. Shopkeepers, for instance, played records at high volume as a kind of advertisement or to give their customers a taste of the music. Among these shopkeepers was Anton Witte, who installed three different brands of "amplification machines" for one of his "concerts" in the park at Lastrup (Oldenburg) (see figure 4.5). An "Auxetophon," a "Trompophon," and several "Mammutapparate" (Mammoth Machines) played music, and it was reported that they were still "fairly audible" even up to three kilometers away.[32] Moreover, restaurant and pub owners used automated machines for the entertainment of their guests, including in outdoor establishments, and owners of garden allotments would play their gramophones in the open air (see figure 4.6). Travelers and day-trippers would listen to music while on the road, and apartment dwellers would fill their neighborhoods with sound from their open windows. This practice of playing music from open widows was particularly contentious, and many of the conflicts that arose had to be handled by the court. In Vienna, for example, a composer was suspected of shooting at a

**Figure 4.5** Anton Witte concert; private collection of Gisbert Witte.

**Figure 4.6** Idyll with speech machine; *Phonographische Zeitschrift* 12, no. 23 (1911), 506; Bildarchiv Preußischer Kulturbesitz, Berlin.

bookbinder's gramophone with a 16-millimeter hunting rifle. The composer admitted to having fired six shots into the air, which he argued had not been done in anger at the gramophone playing, but rather as a result of the "precise consideration" that he had the same right to create noise as his neighbor.[33]

The filling of public spaces with sound from phono-objects happened as part of an increasingly dense, pluralized, and intense "acoustic environment," especially in large cities. It was part of a new sensory experience, which contemporaries processed in different ways. Urban sounds counted as a significant part of the city structure, which were perceived as an elemental identifier of the city in the same manner as large buildings, the construction of modern infrastructure, or factories: "We can endorse it as correct, that in large cities, and in particular in Berlin, a great deal of noise will be made on the streets. Noise, however, is the expression of pluralized life, which is exactly what the imposing and dynamic aspects of a large city present."[34] "Noise"—the word was a call to arms for those who viewed the noise of the large city as a malady of excessive aggression.

## The Phono-object and the Anti-noise Movement

An organized form of combating noise took place first in the United States, then also in Germany, in 1908, with the establishment of the Antilärmverein (Anti-noise Society) by the journalist and philosopher, Theodor Lessing. According to the mission statement of the society, members would seek to exert an influence on the "entire national way of life," not just battle against "noise," but in general combat "culture offenses" and even "hygiene offenses"[35] of all kinds such as fell in the no man's land between the law and ethics. The society used the term "abuse of music" in their battle against harassment from phono-objects ("the gramophone plague").[36]

With a view toward better cultural education, the society's supporters sought a turn to aesthetic training in music: workers were to develop, through members of the society, more culturally valuable forms of auditory culture than the "dirt and filth" of popular songs. In place of these popular songs, there would be a music that was to be valued for its representation of genuine "nature," as well as its spontaneous expression of the "soul of the people."[37] Alongside legislative change and special permissions from the police, further recommendations from the society for effectively combating noise included establishing quiet zones around hospitals, implementing the quietest possible type of street paving (for example, asphalt with the use of rubber tires), discontinuing the use of metal components on carts, banning noisy use of whips, and breaking up the city into areas of habitation, which would be separated from traffic centers. The suggestions were discussed with clear awareness of how limited their possible effects would be, as is evident in the case of using noise-reducing building materials and building methods for apartments: "If a tenant places a parrot or a gramophone on the balcony, then the best ceilings and walls in the world will not prevent it from being bothersome!"[38]

Lessing received broad support for his society, including from a number of well-known contemporaries, among them the writer Hugo von Hofmannsthal, the sculptor Hermann Obrist, the patron and collector of the arts Karl Ernst Osthaus, and the historian Karl Lamprecht.[39] Also among the active supporters was the sociologist and economist, Werner Sombart, who delivered a polemical lecture against phono-objects in 1908 and said that a "tasteful century" would give the inventor of the phonograph a life sentence in prison.[40] As for the ability to implement the Antilärmverein's demands in Berlin, it could not have been without significance that Traugott Achatz von Jagow, who had been the police commissioner since 1909, was an outspoken enemy of noise with a particularly important position. His disgust for any type of noise whatsoever—most of all he hated the "melodic clangs of coin-operated music machines" used in taverns[41]—had already been established during his time as mayor of Potsdam. He posted security guards in front of both his apartment and his office, who were charged with keeping things quiet.

## The Phono-object between "Culture" and "Civilization"

What were the reasons for this aversion to sounds that had been branded as "noise"? What arguments were used to legitimize this "battle"? In 1908, Theodor Lessing published his *Pamphlet for the Battle against Noise*, in which he laid out his position.[42] His attack against noise revealed itself through his differentiation between the cultivated individual and the masses of modern civilization. Those who "work with the brain" were being refused the outward conditions necessary for their thoughts to come to maturity, as they required quiet and solitude. All noise, whether a machine, a baker's cart, a gramophone, or a piano, was inimical to creative thought. Using the contemporary semantics of "nerves," Lessing referred to the energy required to overcome the noise caused by the telephone, the horns of automobiles, a train, or an electric trolley, in order to enable more spiritual and creative work. This effort required all of the individual's spiritual energies, and their nerves could be seriously affected.

Lessing dedicated himself to his criticism of capitalistic business methods and their manifestations, in the area of production as well as related forms of modern leisure activity, namely tourism and various forms of regenerating the energy to work. The masses, arising from the processes of civilization, are described by him as inconsiderate, vain, and obsessed with power and success. Lessing reveals his deep contempt for the masses in a polemic in which he holds them responsible for the omnipresence of music. They have desecrated the "innocence of the most beautiful landscape"[43] and are as superfluous as they are innumerable, just like sturgeon, rabbits, or tapeworms.

It is here that he develops the contrast between the coarse, cheap, and superfluous human masses and the sensitive and cultivated intellectual. Thus Lessing puts forward the concept that the "natural" world, untouched by technical civilization and cultural modernity, exists simply to provide ideal working conditions for intellectuals. This adoption of nature and its mythical primitive qualities follows two modes: the masses of modern civilization transgress nature and fill it with noise, while the cerebral man of culture keeps nature's best interests at heart by leaving it just as it is.

It is precisely the central quality of the phono-object, to bring sound into a completely new relationship with listening—the point of departure for the cultural pluralization of listening—that pushes Lessing into making a false connection between the source of the sound and its perception. As an example, he refers to the technical reproduction of a recording of "Hymn to Solitude," sung and performed by Caruso in New York, being heard on the Jungfrau mountain in Switzerland. Every sound, of course, only occurs at the site of its creation: "And wherever 'advancement' and 'cultivated Europeans' go, there you will find 'noise.'"[44]

For Lessing, noise is the central anthropological moment by which to classify people. He sees noise as the "deepest characteristic of the human being,"[45] and there is nothing more challenging to man as to "die in silence." The basis of his anthropological impression of man's urge to cry out derives from nature, which he understands as silent, and thus at the same time he manages to raise himself above his noise-making contemporaries. "Culture is an evolution into silence!"[46] The cultivation of man into an intellectual and his social distinction from the human masses with their animalistic nature are closely connected in Lessing's way of thinking. The relationship between man and sound is, in this model, the axis of culture, which can be located as the point where ontogenetic cultivation successfully overcomes phylogenetic preconditioning.

Sound, noise, amplification—these are not just interpretable phenomena for Lessing, they are real instruments for exercising power that have been put into action by uncultivated people for exclusively base purposes, motivated by a sadistic desire to inflict pain. According to Lessing, noise is ultimately an act of moral murder against an innocent victim, that is, against the cultivated man: "When people are assembled, lungs are the deciding factor."[47]

The argument for resistance, such as that proposed by Lessing, was based on the contrasts between culture and civilization,[48] and the secret meanings that these words carry but which are rarely expressed:

> Culture is ennobling, civilization is vulgarizing. Culture belongs to the few, civilization is for those who say: "We may be idiots, but we're the majority, too!" … To be cultured means to be considerate of one's fellow man, while civilization meanwhile tramples on the individual's rights and desires only to turn us into a race of uniform anthropoids; this civilization belongs to the well-behaved, mechanically functioning middle-class citizen, who is repulsed equally by powerful revolutionaries as by energetic reactionaries.[49]

From this perspective, the phono-object doubtlessly belongs in the category of "civilization"; however, it also belongs in a sense to "culture," since it reproduces not only the music of the lower classes, denigrated as "popular songs" and presented as contemptible, but also canonical music known as "classical," with recordings of heroes such as Ludwig van Beethoven and Richard Wagner, who both played a critical role in forming German identity. The conclusion that the phono-object is identical with "dirt and filth" simply does not stand up.

The restriction of culture to intellectuals and ideas, which has become more qualified in German cultural studies over the last few decades, still more or less adheres to the hierarchy of subjects deemed legitimate for intellectual thought, as can be seen, for example, in the high regard in which art objects are held in comparison to objects of everyday life. This needs to be reconsidered in the light of the case of listening to technically reproduced sound, which cannot be separated from the materiality of the phono-object and which is deeply interwoven into social and cultural contexts. From the first functional phonograph of 1877 through the succeeding objects for technically reproducing sound—in view of their industrial production as well as their adaptation to mass culture and its uses—there have been deep changes affecting daily life. The history of these "industrial mass culture" objects makes clear how production methods establish their use and interpretation, and ultimately lead to new environments and ways of living.

## Notes

1. On a thesis for general everyday objects of the nineteenth and twentieth centuries, cf. Wolfgang Ruppert, ed., *Fahrrad, Auto, Fernsehschrank* (Frankfurt am Main, 1993).
2. Stefan Gauß, *Nadel, Rille, Trichter: Kulturgeschichte des Phonographen und des Grammophons in Deutschland (1900–1940)* (Cologne, 2009).
3. Cf. Wolfgang Ruppert, "Plädoyer für den Begriff der industriellen Massenkultur," in *Europäische Kulturgeschichte: Zur Gesellschafts- und Kulturgeschichte des Konsums (18. bis 20. Jahrhundert)*, ed. Hartmut Kaelble, Jürgen Kocka, and Hannes Siegrist (Frankfurt am Main, 1997), 563–82; and Ruppert, "Zur Kulturgeschichte der Alltagsdinge," in Ruppert, *Fahrrad, Auto*, 14–36.
4. For detailed cultural terminology, see Wolfgang Ruppert, *Der moderne Künstler: Zur Sozial- und Kulturgeschichte der kreativen Individualität in der kulturellen Moderne im 19. und frühen 20. Jahrhundert* (Frankfurt am Main, 1998), 46ff.
5. Ruppert, "Plädoyer," 563–82, here 565–66.

6. Friedrich Wolfram Heubach, *Das bedingte Leben: Entwurf zu einer Theorie der psychologischen Gegenständlichkeit der Dinge. Ein Beitrag zur Psychologie des Alltags* (Munich, 1987), 14.

7. "Diese neue Erfindung des Herrn Edison ist in der Tat staunenswert. Der Phonograph ermöglicht, dass ein Mann, der schon lange im Grabe ruht, noch einmal seine Stimme erhebt und die Gegenwart begrüßt." Recording of Helmuth von Moltke on 21 October 1889 http://www.nps.gov/av/ner/avElement/edis-05-tenhp_edison_c_E-5777_edis-93951_20110415.mp3, accessed 14 April 2014.

8. "Wir müssen uns heute damit begnügen, aus überlieferten Schriften über Gestaltungsart und Wesen von diesem oder jenem Schauspieler oder Sänger etwas zu erfahren. Über die Entwicklung der Sprache können wir uns selbst ebenfalls nur durch Schriftwerke unterrichten. In künftigen Zeiten aber wird dieses durch das Grammophon überliefert werden, und neben den belehrenden Schriftwerken wird man auch Gelegenheit haben, sich durch das Ohr mit Hilfe des Grammophons in die Vergangenheit einleben zu können." Carl Stahl, "Die Grundlagen falscher Urteile über Sprechmaschinen," *Phonographische Zeitschrift* 4 (September 1908): 114–15, here 115.

9. Wilhelm Kronfuss, "Studien über den Stil von Phonographen und Phonogrammen," *Phonographische Zeitschrift* 10, no. 13 (1909): 367–69; and here no. 14 (1909): 388–90.

10. "Wir besitzen also im Phonographen eine Art Zeitmaschine, für welche die Zeit eigentlich gar nicht existiert, und in deren Phonogrammen eine ewige Gegenwart fixiert und niedergelegt ist." Kronfuss, "Studien über den Stil," 388–90, here 389.

11. Cf. Wolfgang Schivelbusch, *The Railway Journey: The Industrialization and Perception of Time and Space* (Berkeley, 1987).

12. Thomas Mann, *Der Zauberberg* (Frankfurt am Main, 1991), cf. 874.

13. Anon., "Beethovens IX. Symphonie auf der Platte," *Phonographische Zeitschrift* 25, no. 1 (1924): 24; also, Wilhelm Hoffmann, "Das Mikrophon als akustisches Fernglas," *Rufer und Hörer* 2, no. 10 (January 1933): 453–57.

14. Cf. Max Chop, "Ein Rückblick auf die Sprechmaschinen-Literatur an der Jahrhundertwende," *Phonographische Zeitschrift* 10, no. 2 (1909): 29–32.

15. Cf. Helmut Plessner, *Anthropologie der Sinne* (Frankfurt am Main, 2003), 231ff.

16. Kronfuss, "Studien über den Stil," 367–69, here 367.

17. *Elektrotechnische Zeitschrift* (Elektrotechnischer Verein, October 1889), no. 23, Vereins-Angelegenheiten, 552–54.

18. "Die Sprache war rein und klar mit etwas Nebengeräusch, jedoch sehr leise, so, daß nur die Umstehenden, die sich in nächster Nähe befanden, etwas hören konnten." Albert Költzow, "Aus der Entstehungsgeschichte der Sprechmaschinen," *Die Sprechmaschine* 9, no. 26 (1913): 409–10, here 409.

19. "Als Berliner seinen Apparat in Tätigkeit setzte, entstand ein fürchterliches Geräusch, welches fast unerträglich war, bald aber ertönte eine

vollständige Orchestermusik, aus welcher man trotz des Geräusches fast jedes einzelne Instrument heraushören konnte." Költzow, "Aus der Entstehungsgeschichte," 409.

20. Horst Wahl, *Die Chronik der Sprechmaschine*, vol. 1, ed. Hansfried Sieben (Düsseldorf, 1986), 94.

21. Anon., "Glückwünsche," *Phonographische Zeitschrift* 26, no. 16 (1925): 638–62; see report by Herrmann Eisner, 660–62.

22. "Bei diesem handgreiflichen Verfahren die musikalische Kontinuität zu wahren, fiel nicht leicht. Die Aufnahmen mußten sehr oft wiederholt werden, weil die Stimme nicht gleichmäßig war. Und wenn eine Aufnahme wirklich glückte, dann zerbrach womöglich die Platte." Frieda Hempel, *Mein Leben dem Gesang. Erinnerungen* (Berlin, 1955).

23. The letter is transcribed in *Artur Schnabel. Musiker, Musician, 1882–1951*, ed. Werner Grünzweig on commission from the Stiftung Archiv der Akademie der Künste (Kat. der Ausstellung der Akademie der Künste Berlin, 2.9.–14.10.2001) (Hofheim, 2001), 124–25.

24. "Ich begann fast zu weinen, wenn ich allein auf der Straße war. ... Die Auslieferung an das Böse, der Verrat am Leben, die Verdinglichung des Blutes, die Ehe mit dem Tod. Es ist der vollkommene Unsinn, die vollkommene Unnatur. ... Es geschieht nur, weil es möglich ist." *Artur Schnabel. Musiker*, 124.

25. Mann, *Der Zauberberg*. Cf. the chapter "Fülle des Wohllauts," 871ff.

26. "In grösseren Gesellschaften, deren Mitglieder fast durchgängig musikalisch gebildet waren (oder so taten!), z. T. Musik studiert hatten, hatte ich häufig Gelegenheit, meine Bekannten beim Vorführen der Sprechmaschine psychologisch zu beobachten. Die wirklich Musikalischen sahen den Apparat nicht an, die weniger Empfänglichen dagegen pflegten nach dem riesigen Messingtrichter wie nach etwas Faszinierendem zu blicken." Roering-Helsingborg, "Musikalische Illusionen und Architektur der Sprechmaschine," *Phonographische Zeitschrift* 9, no. 8 (1908): 216–17, here 216.

27. Franz Scheirl, "Der Phonograph im Dienste des Volksliedes," *Das Deutsche Volkslied, Zeitschrift für seine Kenntnisse und Pflege*, published by the Deutsche Volksgesang-Vereine in Vienna, official paper of the choral society "Deutsches Volkslied," H. 6, August 1906, 85–89, here 86.

28. "Soll der Phonograph für die naturgetreue Wiedergabe der Volkssprache und des Volksgesanges Tadelloses leisten, so wird er sich allerdings noch sehr vervollkommnen müssen; sein Ziel muß sein, gleichsam das Lied so abzuknipsen wie der Kodak das Bild." Scheirl, "Der Phonograph," 85–89, here 87.

29. Georg Rothgiesser, "Zur Theorie des schönen Tons," *Phonographische Zeitschrift* 2, no. 4 (1901): 22.

30. Mann, *Der Zauberberg*, 871.

31. Rudolf Lothar, *Die Sprechmaschine* (Leipzig, 1924).

32. Anon., "Garten-Sprechmaschinen-Konzert," *Die Sprechmaschine* 3, no. 40 (1907): 998. The sound was reported to be "full and ample," the lectures "faultless and understandable."

33. Anon., "Der Wiener Grammophon-Prozeß," *Recht auf Stille: Der Antirüpel: Antirowdy* 1, no. 11 (1909): 220–21.
34. Joco.: "Viel Lärm um den Lärm," *Phonographische Zeitschrift* 9, no. 6 (1908): 150–52.
35. Anon., "Hygienische Delikte," in *Recht auf Stille: Der Antirüpel: Antirowdy* 1, no. 3 (1909): 38–40.
36. For example, the Berlin member, Gretel Meier-Heß, complained of domestic servants singing from open windows just as she complained of the "gramophone plague," from which she also suffered. Gretel Meier-Heß et al., "Lärm-Enquete," *Recht auf Stille: Der Antirüpel: Antirowdy* 1, no. 3 (1909): 34–38, here 37.
37. Cf. Hans Brandenburg and Theodor Lessing, "Briefwechsel coram publico. Offener Brief an Dr. Theodor Lessing," *Recht auf Stille: Der Antirüpel: Antirowdy* 1, no. 5 (1909): 86–88.
38. "Stellt ein Mieter einen Papagei oder ein Grammophon auf den Balkon, dann werden freilich alle guten Decken und Mauern vor Belästigung nicht schützen!" Oskar Gellért, "Ruhestörungen im Berliner Mietshause," *Recht auf Stille: Der Antirüpel: Antirowdy* 1, no. 12 (1909): 225–28, here 227. The author is an architect in Berlin. The article concerns the possibility of protecting buildings against noise.
39. Anon., "Antilärmiten," *Recht auf Stille: Der Antirüpel: Antirowdy* 1, no. 4 (1909): 53–57.
40. Following the representation by Baron von Hagen, "Wie kann ein grösseres Interesse für die Sprechmaschine erreicht werden?," *Phonographische Zeitschrift* 9, no. 20 (1908): 597–98; here 597.
41. Anon., "Der neue Polizeipräsident als 'Antilärmit,'" *Recht auf Stille: Der Antirüpel: Antirowdy* 1, no. 12 (1909): 231–32.
42. Theodor Lessing, *Der Lärm: Eine Kampfschrift gegen die Geräusche unseres Lebens* (Wiesbaden, 1908).
43. Ibid., 16.
44. Ibid.
45. Ibid.
46. Ibid.
47. Ibid., 21.
48. Cf. the varying meanings of the terms "civilization" and "culture" in French and German: Norbert Elias, *Über den Prozeß der Zivilisation*, vol. 1 (Frankfurt am Main, 1989), 1–64.
49. "Kultur ist Adel, Zivilisation eine Verpöbelung. Kultur ist eine Sache der wenigen, Zivilisation eine Sache derjenigen, die da sagen: 'Die Dümmern san mer schon, aber die Mehrern san mer aa!' ... Kultur haben, heißt Rücksicht nehmen auf den Nebenmenschen, die Zivilisation tritt jegliches Recht der Individualität mit Füßen und möchte aus uns am liebsten ein Geschlecht uniformierter Anthropoiden machen; sie ist eine Sache der brav maschinell funktionierenden Staatsbürger, denen die starken Revolutionäre geradeso zuwider sind wie die energischen Reaktionäre." Julius Bittner, "Über Kultur," *Der Antirüpel: Recht auf Stille* 3, no. 1 (1911): 5.

# Bibliography

Anon. "Antilärmiten." *Recht auf Stille: Der Antirüpel: Antirowdy* 1 (1909): 53–57.
———. "Beethovens IX. Symphonie auf der Platte." *Phonographische Zeitschrift* 25 (1924): 24.
———. "Der neue Polizeipräsident als 'Antilärmit.'" *Recht auf Stille: Der Antirüpel: Antirowdy* 1 (1909): 231–32.
———. "Der Wiener Grammophon-Prozeß." *Recht auf Stille: Der Antirüpel: Antirowdy* 1 (1909): 220–21.
———. "Garten-Sprechmaschinen-Konzert." *Die Sprechmaschine* 3 (1907): 998.
———. "Glückwünsche." *Phonographische Zeitschrift* 26 (1925): 638–62.
———. "Hygienische Delikte." *Recht auf Stille: Der Antirüpel: Antirowdy* 3 (1909): 38–40.
Bittner, Julius. "Ueber Kultur." *Der Antirüpel. Recht auf Stille* 3 (1911): 5.
Brandenburg, Hans and Theodor Lessing. "Briefwechsel coram publico. Offener Brief an Dr. Theodor Lessing." *Recht auf Stille: Der Antirüpel: Antirowdy* 1, no. 5 (1909): 86–88.
Chop, Max. "Ein Rückblick auf die Sprechmaschinen-Literatur an der Jahrhundertwende." *Phonographische Zeitschrift* 10 (1909): 29–32.
Elias, Norbert. *Über den Prozeß der Zivilisation*, vol. 1. Frankfurt am Main, 1989.
Gauß, Stefan. *Nadel, Rille, Trichter: Kulturgeschichte des Phonographen und des Grammophons in Deutschland (1900–1940)*. Cologne, 2009.
Gellért, Oskar. "Ruhestörungen im Berliner Mietshause." *Recht auf Stille: Der Antirüpel: Antirowdy* 1 (1909): 225–28.
Grünzweig, Werner, ed. *Artur Schnabel: Musiker, Musician, 1882–1951* (on commission from the Stiftung Archiv der Akademie der Künste). Hofheim, 2001.
Hagen, Baron von. "Wie kann ein grösseres Interesse für die Sprechmaschine erreicht werden?" *Phonographische Zeitschrift* 9 (1908): 597–98.
Hempel, Frieda. *Mein Leben dem Gesang: Erinnerungen*. Berlin, 1955.
Heubach, Friedrich Wolfram. *Das bedingte Leben: Entwurf zu einer Theorie der psychologischen Gegenständlichkeit der Dinge: Ein Beitrag zur Psychologie des Alltags*. Munich, 1987.
Hoffmann, Wilhelm. "Das Mikrophon als akustisches Fernglas." *Rufer und Hörer* 2 (1933): 453–57.
Joco. "Viel Lärm um den Lärm." *Phonographische Zeitschrift* 9 (1908): 150–52.
Költzow, Albert. "Aus der Entstehungsgeschichte der Sprechmaschinen." *Die Sprechmaschine* 9 (1913): 409–10.
Kronfuss, Wilhelm. "Studien über den Stil von Phonographen und Phonogrammen." *Phonographische Zeitschrift* 13 (1909): 367–69.
Lessing, Theodor. *Der Lärm: Eine Kampfschrift gegen die Geräusche unseres Lebens*. Wiesbaden, 1908.
Lothar, Rudolf. *Die Sprechmaschine*. Leipzig, 1924.
Mann, Thomas. *Der Zauberberg*. Frankfurt am Main, 1991.
Meier-Heß, Gretel. "Lärm-Enquete." *Recht auf Stille: Der Antirüpel: Antirowdy* 1 (1909): 34–38.
Plessner, Helmut. *Anthropologie der Sinne*. Frankfurt am Main, 2003.

Roering-Helsingborg. "Musikalische Illusionen und Architektur der Sprechmaschine." *Phonographische Zeitschrift* 9 (1908): 216–17.

Rothgiesser, Georg. "Zur Theorie des schönen Tons." *Phonographische Zeitschrift* 2 (1901): 22.

Ruppert, Wolfgang. *Fahrrad, Auto, Fernsehschrank.* Frankfurt am Main, 1993.

———. "Plädoyer für den Begriff der industriellen Massenkultur." In *Europäische Kulturgeschichte: Zur Gesellschafts- und Kulturgeschichte des Konsums (18. bis 20. Jahrhundert).* Ed. Hartmut Kaelble, Jürgen Kocka, and Hannes Siegrist. Frankfurt am Main, 1997, 563–82.

———. *Der moderne Künstler: Zur Sozial- und Kulturgeschichte der kreativen Individualität in der kulturellen Moderne im 19. und frühen 20. Jahrhundert.* Frankfurt am Main, 1998.

Scheirl, Franz. "Der Phonograph im Dienste des Volksliedes." *Das Deutsche Volkslied, Zeitschrift für seine Kenntnisse und Pflege* 7 (1906): 85–89.

Schivelbusch, Wolfgang. *The Railway Journey: The Industrialization and Perception of Time and Space.* Berkeley, 1987.

Stahl, Carl. "Die Grundlagen falscher Urteile über Sprechmaschinen." *Phonographische Zeitschrift* 4 (1908): 114–15.

Wahl, Horst. *Die Chronik der Sprechmaschine*, vol. 1. Ed. Hansfried Sieben. Düsseldorf, 1986.

5

# Phones, Horns, and "Audio Hoods" as Media of Attraction
## Early Sound Histories in Vienna between 1883 and 1933
*Christine Ehardt*

In her "Lectures from the Future," the peace activist and Nobel Prize winner Bertha von Suttner wrote in 1889:

> The prospects of the immediate future already offer a lot of pleasure: the phonograph, which records and reproduces both our words and our voices; the telephone, which broadcasts those same voices across vast distances; … the opera performances and political speeches brought into our homes in this way …, indeed, all those marvelous valves and channels that carry everything imaginable into our homes.[1]

The idea of listening to voices that are far away, or that are even already in the past, was an important impulse in the invention of sound transmission and conversion methods at the end of the nineteenth century. Two aspects dominated the horizon of expectations about audio media: "liveness," the possibility of being part of an event; and "attraction," the staging of the experience of listening itself.

These two dimensions correspond to particular notions of modernity: the overcoming of space and time, and the period's interest in new forms of distraction.[2] International exhibitions around 1900 displayed technical achievements, the value of which for everyday life had not yet been determined. New acoustic media attracted their audience, not in spite of this, but because their contingent use offered many varied uses. As well as telephone, phonograph, and gramophone, the radio in its early years was part of such media of attraction. As I shall argue here, it is not isolated discoveries and ostensibly linear developments that can be considered the forerunners of contemporary new media, but rather it is technical, social, and cultural processes of change that form the foundation of new communication techniques.[3] Objects of sound, and headphones and horns in particular, became the iconographic symbols for new acoustic media conceptions. In this chapter I will draw upon images, articles, and official documents of sound technologies between 1883 and 1933 in order to trace a cultural history of listening in the age of mechanical reproduction.[4]

## The First International Electrical Exhibition of 1883 in Vienna

"So much that was new had entered our lives, so much that had never been there before was now there,"[5] continues Bertha von Suttner in her "Lectures from the Future" about the technical discoveries, political changes, and social upheavals that intensified at the end of the nineteenth century. The development of the electrical industry and economic changes associated with it, such as the formation of stock companies and national businesses, accompanied the "beginning of the machine age."[6] In the international exhibitions promoted in Europe and America from the middle of the nineteenth century, the technical achievements of the industrial world were put on show. In 1883, ten years after the Vienna World Exhibition, a special exhibition of electro-technical apparatus was opened. It was the first of such industrial exhibitions in Austro-Hungary: two years earlier, the first worldwide electrical exhibition had opened in Paris; another in Munich followed in 1882;[7] and in 1883, Crown Prince Rudolf opened the exhibition in the Rotunda in the Vienna Prater Park—built in 1873 on the occasion of the World Exhibition—with the words:

> We stand today with pride before a work that owes its origin solely to the patriotic self-sacrifice of a number of men. The exploitation of a powerful force of nature through scientific work, and the application of the same in daily life, breaks new ground.[8]

With over 33,000 square meters of exhibition space, the Vienna Exhibition was the largest of its kind to date.[9] National and international companies displayed new inventions and already familiar machines and apparatus for industrial, as well as private, use. In the forward to the "Illustrirten Führer" for the *Internationale Elektrische Ausstellung*, the public was guided through a bewildering number of exhibits.

> "Without understanding there can be no pleasure!" is the Electrical Exhibition's motto. Whoever hopes, in visiting the same, merely to be amused for a few hours while viewing all kinds of strange new things will be strangely disappointed. For he will see so much that is new and strange that his head will soon be spinning if no one is there to kindly explain the chaos to him and to show him the meaning and purpose of the new objects on show in such abundance.[10]

To avoid this mental chaos, the exhibition brochure offers a prescribed path which is supposed to meaningfully connect the great number of technical inventions. Following the signposts, and after traversing the entire exhibition area, the visitor comes via the east gate to a specially erected exhibition theater. There, theater and musical performances conveyed over electrical connections are presented and transmitted throughout the city by sixty international and national telephone companies into "telephone auditoria."[11]

A great number of new and ingenious devices appeared at the end of the nineteenth century, and they had a vast array of possible uses. What is common to all these inventions is their contingent use. They were media of attraction and served predominantly the pleasure of the public. They were, as stated in the exhibition catalogue, "interesting demonstrations," but nevertheless "without practical value."[12] They had first to be given their proper place in a discourse of leisure and consumption. Nevertheless, they are already manifestations of typical wishes and expectations at the turn of the century, such as the aforementioned desire to overcome time and space by means of technical devices. In the following decades a reciprocal process of technical possibilities, economic and political interests, as well as social changes, made products suitable for the mass market out of the "interesting demonstrations"[13] that were displayed at the fairs and exhibitions.

## The Beginning of the Telephone and Electrical Industry in Austro-Hungary

> In summoning up this mood and disseminating it, the greatest contribution to this was made by the well-known little miracle ... the telephone. The railway line to Lichtenfels ..., the huge expansion of submarine cables, the heroic deeds of telegraphy, none of this would have electrified the masses as much as that little instrument, which brought the personal element, that independence from time and space, which is in electricity, to the astonished senses.[14]

The Electrical Exhibition of 1883 offered the numerous, newly founded telephone and telegraph companies the chance to seize on these wishes and expectations by presenting the visitors with products for sale.

> The telephone booths in the Rotunda still have the appearance of a never-ending spectacle—excuse me, an ear-fest. It is as if these chambers are condemned to a condition of a ten-week siege; on and on come the people, occupy the booths, continue on their way, and troops of

reinforcements continuously jostle forward (among whom there is no shortage of officers)—in short, the booths are always filled.[15]

At the International Exhibition in Vienna, along with firms still well known today, such as Ericsson, Siemens, and Berliner, it was the Wiener Privat-Telegraphen-Gesellschaft above all, which, with its music broadcasts, attempted to convince the public of the new possibilities of voice and sound transmission. A report on the exhibition reads:

> The "micro-telephone" transmission of the opera and concert music of the Wiener Privat-Telegraphen-Gesellschaft to the Rotunda was only possible by means of two double-core cables. For the purposes of the telephone transmission of the operas to the Rotunda, twelve microphones patented by the Wiener Privat-Telegraphen-Gesellschaft were placed on the stage of the Court Opera alongside the footlights.[16]

So-called "audio hoods"[17] were connected to the cables in the Rotunda and it was by means of these that these stereophonic transmissions could be heard (see figure 5.1).

During the exhibition, theater stars from the Viennese Opera and the Burgtheater performed songs and scenes that could also be received in coffeehouses around the exhibition hall. The performances were transmitted by microphones that were placed at various points on

**Figure 5.1** An "audio hood"; Anon.: *Bericht über die Internationale Elektrische Ausstellung in Wien 1883* (Vienna, 1885), 303.

stage. The audience in the telephone cabins could not only hear the performance, but also the movements off and on stage, the reactions of the audience, and the whole atmosphere during the live performance; the newspaper reports of such demonstrations focused mainly on the live character of the transmissions. Although the technology of stereophonic recording would not be successfully invented until the late 1940s, the character and descriptions of radiophonic transmission via telephone had already raised the issue of the stereophonic phenomenon.

The reports explicitly relate to the stereophonic effect created by the experimental setup. These kinds of descriptions were also to be found at the Electrical Exhibition of 1881 in Paris: there, too, "on the stage at each side of the prompter's box 12 Ader type transmitters"[18] were symmetrically positioned. The listening pleasure of the public lay not only in the actual transmission of the music, song, or speech of the Opera House and the *Comédie française*,[19] but the live transmission of the spatial listening experience was also emphasized:

> To protect these from shocks and extraneous sounds which could emanate from the wooden stages, the microphone cases had a base of a thick sheet of lead, which rested on rubber feet. Each listener was given two … telephone receivers to equip his ears. One of these electrically connected listening instruments stood to the right of the transmitter at the prompter's box, the other to the left, so that the listener could thereby acoustically determine whether the actor had stood still or had moved to the right or left.[20]

In Paris the "Théâtrophone" described by Marcel Proust had already been successfully introduced shortly after the first Electrical Exhibition in 1881, and had received international acclaim.[21] The pleasure lay not simply in the participation of the performances themselves, but in being able to hear the reactions of the audience.

The "telephone newspaper" became a much discussed topic of the modern age in Europe, a discourse that anticipated the early ideas about the radio and its potential. In large cities like Paris and Budapest there were already regular news and entertainment services transmitted by telephone connections. In Hungary, the telephone subscription service even existed into the 1930s. The *Telefon Hírmondó* (Telephone Herald) was conceived by a colleague of Edison's, Theodor Puskás. In 1878, he appointed his brother, Ferenc Puskás, as chief representative of the European Edison Telephone Company in Austro-Hungary. The "talking newspaper," as it was also called in the international press, began its permanent operation and delivered a regular program of commercial news, musical entertainment, and weather forecasts to its customers.

To gain access to this facility, the public had only to connect "via the normal telephone to the 'telephone newspaper' for an extra fee."[22]

From 1893, in Vienna as well, daily stock market news could be received by the telephone via the Imperial and Royal Central Telephone Exchange. No concert, opera, or theater performances could be received regularly in Vienna. Such performances were only organized occasionally for demonstration or promotion purposes. For example, on the occasion of the opening of the Vienna–Prague telephone line in 1890, a concert was transmitted between the Prague telephone exchange and the hall of the Austrian Trade and Industry Association.[23] The necessary apparatus was assembled by the Czeija & Nissl Company. Franz Nissl, a Viennese engineer and long-time technical director of the Budapest Central Telephone Exchange, and Karl August Czeija, an industrialist from the high Viennese bourgeoisie, had founded the company of Czeija & Nissl, which had an important share in the development of the telephone system in the Austro-Hungarian monarchy. In 1893, Czeija & Nissl took over the "telegraph and telephone production company C. Schäffler, in existence since 1871,"[24] and from then on, they called their company the Vereinigte Telephon- und Telegraphenfabrik Czeija, Nissl & Co. The Western Electric Company, "the biggest American telephone company at that time,"[25] also took a share in this transaction. In 1896, Czeija & Nissl acquired the first Vienna telephone exchange and also obtained the overall contract for the construction of two new telephone exchanges in Vienna.[26]

The use of the telephone as an entertainment and news medium was not pursued further in the following years, apart from a few exceptions such as the aforementioned journal *Telefon Hírmondó* in Budapest. The telephone was soon limited to a one-to-one communication medium. The experiments of the earlier developmental phase were forgotten. Many ideas and concepts, however, were taken up again in the development of radio transmission, and influenced the first years of radio.[27]

By 1876 the telephone was in use across the world as a means of communication. In 1883, the year of the Electrical Exhibition, there were three towns in Austria with their own telephone network, and 870 subscribers were registered at this time. In contrast, Great Britain already had seventy-five towns with networks and over seven thousand telephone users; Germany, too, already had more than twenty telephone providers. "Judging by the low numbers of telephones in Austria as a whole, we can conclude that the telephone systems here have still achieved no great distribution. This year's exhibition will certainly be a stimulus."[28]

In actual fact, the Austrian telephone network recorded an increase in subscribers from the middle of the 1880s, and the number of telephones produced by industry also grew. As in many European countries, private telephone networks were also nationalized in Austro-Hungary at the end of the nineteenth century. In 1893, ten out of the total of eleven private networks passed into state ownership; the urban telephone network of the Wiener Privat-Telegraphen-Gesellschaft was taken over by the Trade Ministry in 1895 after lengthy negotiations and public debates about the company's business methods.[29]

The development of the telephone network was still a costly investment for the postal and telegraph service. While 3.1 million gulden (guilder) had been earned since its inception, by 1890, a total of 4.13 million gulden had already been expended on the inter-urban expansion of the network.[30] These numbers show the potential ascribed to the telephone, in contrast to the telegraph, which, despite its many years on trial, did not become a mass market communication instrument. In view of international development, industry and the national government looked forward to a rapid increase in private telephone use.

> The telegraph, although part of our social fabric, has not become an instrument of the people. Shall the telephone also succumb to this fate? This is not in line with the democratic nature of our day. The telephone must not become a privilege of the rich, but must be for the good of all.[31]

Thus an important foundation stone in the development of new (mass) media was laid. Technical inventions were no longer to only be directed at "a restricted circle of socially elite user groups," but were to offer the possibility "of reaching social, regional, and national, non-specific publics."[32] Boundless communication and entertainment beyond spatial and temporal frontiers were "inscribed in the contract"[33] for the new media.

## Talking Machines and the Aura of Reproduction

Boundless communication and entertainment without spatial or temporal frontiers were important promises in this process of addressing a general public. The requirements of "liveness" and "attraction" were the central topics in the new electronic media discourse. And this was not only the concern of transmissions by telephone—gramophone and phonograph companies also solicited the simultaneity of live performances.

Telephones were classified as inventions of "speech telegraphy" (*Sprachtelegraphie*) at the end of the nineteenth century: they are "telegraphs with transient characters."[34] In contrast to telegraph machines, which allowed only a "copy of the *meaning* of the original," telephones and microphones made possible the production of a "copy of the *form* of the original".[35] Furthermore, talking machines like the gramophone and the phonograph offered the possibility of hearing the disembodied voice over great distances for the first time, and also of making this voice temporally independent, since it could be recorded, thus circumventing its impermanence and transience.[36]

> By the Telephone, Sound is converted into Electricity, and then by completing the circuit, back into sound again. Jones converts all the pretty Music he hears during the Season into Electricity, bottles it and pops it away in Bins for his Winter Parties. All he has to do, when his guests arrive, is to select, uncork, and then complete the Circuit. And there you are.[37]

The phonograph made it possible to record and preserve music, sounds, and the voice. Collecting and indexing phonograms became a favorite leisure activity for the affluent social classes. "The band of phonograph friends has already reached an impressive number today, and everywhere where there are modern people the talking machines are to be found."[38] In addition to the classic phonograph, numerous other variations on talking machines were introduced to the market at the end of the nineteenth century. Thus the Viennese company, A. Bückl, produced "specialties in talking machines from 6 Kronen upwards." Among them were "fantasy and luxury machines, singing flower pots, automatic gramophones, talking alarm clocks, machines for recording on records and cylinders," as well as "the most famous, giant concert graphophones for theater and concert halls."[39]

Actors and musicians who were hired for the recordings by the record companies put a greater price on their loss of prestige as artists than on the commercial success of a recording. Thus in 1900 the Austrian actor, Joseph Kainz, demanded a large part of his remuneration, not as payment for his performance, but as compensation for "the damage which he will suffer in posterity because of this recording."[40]

Whether these statements are down to coquetry or the promotion of their own market value is open to debate. They make clear, however, that the cultural and economic discourse centered on the new mass media inventions. Their value for art, culture, and the economy had first to be negotiated. This is also revealed by the numerous handbooks and instruction manuals, as well as the debates in newspapers, on the methods and ways of utilizing mass media forms of entertainment meaningfully, and, simultaneously, of exploiting them commercially. The discussion fluctuated between the requirements of a didactic appropriation of new procedures, and fascination and skepticism with regard to their use as entertainment and diversion.

> Unfortunately, the sales success [of recordings] is at the cost of placing it in the service of the lower instincts and willingly reproducing every kind of musical rubbish and drivel. The most empty and worthless that could be obtained in the musical field, pop tunes of the day and doubtful couplets of the least and lowest kind.[41]

In actual fact, the new storage media were used for recordings of all kinds, from scenic representations of important political events to recordings "of dubious jokes for so-called gentlemen's clubs."[42] Sound cylinder recordings of artistic and cultural importance were made and distributed. With artists like Caruso, Moissi, and Kainz, some of the best-known speech and music recordings were produced for a mass audience, and their performances were played in cinemas, theaters, and tavern halls.

In Vienna, the internationally famous Deutsche Grammophon-Gesellschaft had set up its own limited company.[43] The Deutsche Grammophon-Aktiengesellschaft Wien advertised over fifteen thousand recordings by famous national and international artists. Every month saw the addition of new recordings, from the "k.k. Infanterie-Regiments Hoch- und Deutschmeister" polka to humorous talks and folk songs; all were recorded and distributed.

> All of the more popular German records are now produced in Austria itself. Recently … the DACAPO Record Company arranged for a new factory to be built in Austria … In their own mass production factory, the DACAPO Record Company already presses ten thousand records per day.[44]

The production of the recordings took place quickly after premiers and successful performances. Thus, the much celebrated performance of *The Merry Widow* in London was on sale as a record within the shortest possible time, and in the first week of sales "10,000 records were demanded and supplied."[45]

The aura of the original gave way to the aura of its reproduction, as Walter Benjamin wrote in his essay, "The Work of Art in the Age of Mechanical Reproduction." The producers of talking machines promoted the possibility of perfect sound reproduction and the impossibility of hearing a difference between the original and the copy. To hear a record or a transmission via telephone suggested a special way of being part of the live event. "Period use made no real distinction between the 'liveness' of simultaneity and the 'liveness' of storage medium,"[46] writes William Uricchio in his article, "Technologies of Time." Both offered the possibility of being part of an event.

## The Idea of Broadcasting

"Everything by Radio" (*Alles per Radio*) was the title of an extravaganza held in the Viennese Ronacher Theater in 1924 that was directed by the cabaret artists Karl Farkas and Gustav Beer, and in which favorites of the public like Hans Moser, Fritz Heller, and Lilian Harvey took part. The revue, whose title promised a small sensation—after all, the new medium was still more a fashion trend than an everyday practicality— in no way involved radio in any scene. It was more the fact that Karl Farkas had used a simple but effective trick: "The title must comprise three words and be relevant."[47] In 1924, it was scarcely possible to imagine something more current or a greater attraction than the theme represented by radio and radio transmission in its infancy.[48]

Despite overcoming time and space, the attraction value of new inventions was foremost. Like film, phonograph and gramophone were predominantly used for pleasure and amusement. The radio had also been advertised as a media of attraction, whose multifarious facilities had not yet been recognized, as pictures of listeners in magazines and newspapers illustrate. The public authorities, however, revealed a concern about the unlimited and apparently uncontrollable possibilities of wireless communication. The allocation of a transmission license for the Austrian national radio service was correspondingly difficult and laborious.

It was the radio industry above all that competed for a broadcasting license at the beginning of the concession process. Many of these firms were established at the turn of the century, and some of them, like Ericsson, Berliner, and Siemens & Halske, had already taken part in the Electrical Exhibition of 1883. In the course of the negotiations over the license allocation, these firms had successively to withdraw their offers and share capital involvement. In contrast, the influence of politics and state control strengthened, and the allocation of a license and allotment of share capital reflects the political power balance of the First Republic. The Czeija & Nissl Company also applied for a broadcasting license to establish an Austrian broadcasting company after World War I. The applications for transmission licenses reveal very different expectations for possible use. In addition to the

Kremenetzky electric light bulb factory, the Vereinigte Telephon- und Telegraphenfabriks-Aktiengesellschaft of Czeija & Nissl had already set up their transmitters in the technological industry museum for experimental purposes. By 1923, Radio Hekaphon was transmitting regularly, and enjoyed a certain degree of popularity, with one of their announcers, Oskar Koton, celebrated in the Austrian newspapers as a radio star.[49]

The two companies that had cooperated with the Western Electric Company since 1893 proposed in their application to use the transmitter "for the transmission of concerts, music, song, etc. by means of wireless telephone to the public" and, furthermore, to offer "theater and entertainment shows, lectures, and reports of general interest."[50] The necessary apparatus for the transmissions was to be "sold or leased to the public for a subscription or license fee,"[51] and, furthermore, for "the recording of the performance, the proprietors of the receiving stations are to be charged subscription or license fees."[52] The scheduled daily program was to be presented to the national government for approval, which also reserved its right to broadcast news without charge.

Broadcasting proposals by the Schrack-Czeija Group were also put forward by Oskar Czeija, the son of Karl August Czeija, and the telephone company of Kapsch and Eduard Schrack, together with the Austrian Creditinsitut. In their financial plan of March 1923, the operating company estimated a sale of five hundred radio sets in the first year. These sets were to be produced by the Schrack Company and distributed as "single sale items" (*Alleinverkauf*), and in addition, over two million kronen were to be raised annually in fees from "telephone subscribers" (*Telephon-Abonnenten*).[53] The idea of the new stock company was to divide broadcasting into two parts: a general program called *Broadcastingteil*, and a special commercial broadcast called *Wirtschaftsrundfunk*. The general program was to include "musical and declamatory"[54] elements, news, and weather reports, as well as to transmit fairy tales for children. The commercial broadcast was to be transmitted "not as speech, but by Morse code,"[55] and was only to be made available to banks and big businesses. This split corresponded to the experiences and ideas about the use of the new communications pathways up to that time. No great commercial success was ascribed to an entertainment broadcasting station, despite the euphoric announcements from Germany, America, and England, which had already established regular broadcasting enterprises prior to 1924; financial gain was anticipated only from commercial radio.

As discussed already, Radio-telephony, with so-called "broadcasting" as its most lucrative branch on the one hand and the possibility of total or partial instant speech between people in different places on the other, is, despite the expansion of the broadcasting service in particular, more a luxury activity than a compelling need. At this moment in time, wireless telegraphy must be given precedence, for it is above all the abundant experience so far on this topic that speaks for profitability—insofar as the commercial point of view is given priority.[56]

The idea of a commercial broadcasting station—in other words, a possible combination of radio and telegraph—was soon rejected in this form, however, even before its introduction. Instead, shortly after the beginning of the program, the station was developed as an entertainment radio station based on the German and Anglo-American model.

These two proposals were now joined by that of the Radiovox Company, backed by the Marconi Company, along with Austrian firms in the light electrical industry. In their proposal of 29 July 1922, they put forward their program plan of "broadcasting opera performances, theatrical productions, every kind of musical performance and broadcasts of entertainment shows, lectures and talks, reports on parliamentary and other bodies, as well as weather reports, political, financial, sport, and general news ... of every kind."[57] Another applicant was the Österreichische Drahtlose Verkehrsgesellschaft, which entered the race on behalf of A.E.G. Telefunken, and, in the course of the licensing procedure, also the Viennese Literarische Anstalt A.G. In the end, after tough and prolonged negotiations, as well as numerous exertions of political influence, the RAVAG—Radioverkehrsaktiengesellschaft,[58] from which Austrian radio would arise in 1955—represented an amalgam of banks, the post office, and big industry. At the time of the celebrations of the birth of Austrian radio there were already eleven thousand listeners, mostly long-time registered radio amateurs. In the same year, licenses increased to ninety-four thousand, and the exponential increase continued in the succeeding years.[59]

## Dancing Headphones: The Development of Radio from Medium of Attraction to Mass Medium

In 1925, Hermann Leopoldi composed the song "Lovely Adrienne has a radio antenna," sung by Max Kuttner. The foxtrot, with its catchy melody, became a hit in the German-speaking world. In the lyrics, the progress of radio from an object of attraction to an everyday object is made clear. It becomes part, not only of a new medium, but also of the new culture of everyday life: "Momentan sucht ein junger Mann / schnell ein Zimmer, schwer kommt's ihm an. / Bad, Telefon und wie's heut Brauch, / Radioanschluß auch" (Now a young man is looking / for a room to rent quick, though he's finding it tough. / Bathroom, telephone, and, as is customary today, / radio connectivity, too). The wishes and hopes of the electronic age appear to be fulfilled. Bertha von Suttner's ideas for the machine age were a reality: by the beginning of the twentieth century, piped water supply, heating, electric light, and telecommunications were taken for granted as part of everyday life.

Yet the overcoming of space and time, one of the essential promises of the technical achievements of the modern age, lost none of its fascination with the coming of the medium of radio. An enthusiastic radio amateur wrote about his experience:

> Every innovation, particularly the innovation of broadcasting, enhances our power. With just a few hand grips, I command the airwaves. Tremendous distances disappear into the ether, and I can get the better of space and time.[60]

No wonder Alfred Kuh, an Austrian writer, wrote about the new medium: "I am frightened of the radio."[61]

Sound reproduction by headphones and horns staged the audible in a certain way. To accomplish this new technology, the whole discourse of sound production, distribution, and reception had been embedded into a culture of leisure and entertainment. Film, revue, operetta, dance halls, and amusement parks became successful forms of entertainment for the masses, and they all focused on pleasure and spectacle. The early years of broadcasting were also influenced by this development. The audience used the radio as a superior medium of attraction. Listening to the radio was synonymous for being part of an event, and listening to technically reproduced sound meant a certain lifestyle and was considered a fashionable artifact of modernity. "Being part of an event": this phrase does not just describe the audible world inside the headphones and horns; in fact, the modes of listening itself were considered an event.

Along with the invention of the radio, headphones soon become a specific iconographic symbol for this new media. In particular, the radio was part of a set of electronic products, the promises of which still reflected the period's interest in technologies of time, space, and event. The year 1926, two years after the establishment of the Austrian RAVAG broadcast station, brought a major burst of innovation, and the newspapers and journals were reporting the new medium's successes.

Cars with a radio, radio in the train, at the hairdressers, in the park, on the rowboat, and so on—the radio was omnipresent, and the papers suggested that everyone wanted to be part of this evolution. For instance, the conservative newspaper *Neuigkeitsweltblatt* published a cover story about the successful rail trip of a new "Radio Rail Car" (*Radio-Zug*) from Vienna to Graz. During the trip the passengers had the option of listening to the radio. By looking at those pictures, it is possible to gain the impression that listening to the radio can always be combined with other possibilities of spending time—together or alone.[62] Every listening experience mentioned here could be under-taken alongside other forms of amusement or daily activities. For example, the cover story, "Radiohörer im Grünen" (Radio listeners outdoors), announced the reception of radio in the city park of Vienna.

> An innovation for cities has recently been created in the Viennese City Park. A limited number of "radio friends" can now avail themselves of this pleasure while enjoying a view of the blossoming shrubs and flowerbeds. As our picture shows, thirty pairs of headphones have been installed for the audience for a fee of 20 cents per hour. The novelty is well received by the public.[63]

During this period, when radio was establishing itself, pictures of listening always show groups with at least one pair of headphones. Although radio producers already offered horns for collective listening, it seemed to be considered rather chic to have headphones instead.

While the use of stethoscopes, as used in medicine, was normal for use with talking machines in the nineteenth century, with the expansion of the telephone, so-called earpieces were normal, and in the Electrical Exhibition of 1883 these earpieces were combined to form a pair of headphones, for which the term *Telephonhaube*[64] (audio hood) was used. For communication by means of telephone, however, only one earpiece was used; it was only with the coming of radio that headphones with two earpieces became popular. Produced in their thousands in the radio factories of the land, they represent a mass product, but they became scarce items soon after the establishment of the first radio stations. The periodical, *Radiowelt*, writes, "[The] great interest led to a big demand for headphones which, as a result of that present demand, cannot be met."[65] In numerous articles, radio listeners discussed the headphone misery.[66] Up to 20,000 were produced monthly in Austria; in addition, an import consignment of 3,000 to 6,500 was permitted to be imported from neighboring countries—primarily from Germany.[67]

Cartoons, sketches, and photographs that had radio as their subject used the headphone as a symbol of the new technology. While the radio sets themselves were still frequently perceived as cumbersome and complicated, the fascination for the new medium appeared to be better expressed in the form of a pair of headphones. They were an iconographic symbol of a contemporary urban lifestyle, a chic accessory and a fashion trend in which everyone wished to participate, even before the use and employment of the new medium had been fully determined:

> Put a set of radio headphones on your head just once. Allow what you hear to wash over you. Give in to your impressions. And then consider. This is not an invention like any other. It is not like the gramophone and the telephone. It is more, it is different. It is a message from an unknown world.[68]

The radio and, with it, the headphones were present everywhere; the press spoke of a "radio fever" that had gripped the whole of Europe. This development was commented upon by some with interest, some with amusement, but, by some, also with irritation. A Swiss daily newspaper, for example, captions one of its cartoons in which they make fun of the new mass phenomenon "Dancing Headphones" (*Tanzende Kopfhörer*),[69] and the *Radiowelt* endorses a new invention for the irritated radio refuseniks: the "completely silent headphone" (*Kopfabsolutnichthörer*; see figure 5.2).[70] Portable receivers and headphones also offered the possibility of listening to the radio undisturbed in all sorts of places, and the installation of receivers in public baths, hospitals, and vehicles was discussed and, in part, actually realized.

The illustrations demonstrate a diverse spectrum of possibilities for the use of radio. While the content and formation of the radio service and radio programs at the beginning of regular transmission traffic in Austria oriented themselves above all to known educational and entertainment media, following the bourgeois-conservative concept of culture, and had first to develop a proper program for radio, the radio itself had advanced to become a symbol of an innovative, modern, and urbane lifestyle. What counted above all was the "how" and not the "what" of radio listening. The possibilities for use and exploitation did not exclude any combination with other media systems. Like the spectacular demonstrations in the exhibitions at the turn of the century, the media technologies at the beginning of the twentieth century were still open to a variety of potential uses, and many inventions participated in the development of the new entertainment and communications media.[71]

At this point, the radio was integrated in a discourse of spectacle and distraction, or, as Walter Benjamin stated for the medium of film,

Zeichnung von Trier.

## IM RADIO-KAFFEEHAUS.

„*Ja, da staunste, Herr Müller, was ? Das ist nämlich meine
Erfindung : Kopfabsolutnichthörer !*" *(Lustige Blätter)*

**Figure 5.2** The "completely silent headphone"; *Radiowelt*, no. 15 (1925), 3.

the collective modes of listening "require no attention."[72] To hear the radio did not mean being a concentrated listener of the radio program, it meant being part of a set of leisure activities—"being part of mass culture," but not "being part of a mass medium."

Although there had been trials in which the radio set had been combined with horns to amplify the volume, headphones continued to be the main form of listening to the radio. It was not until the late 1920s that the loudspeaker became a primary part of the talking machines. Along with this simplification and improvement of the radio set, it was established as a normal and integrated artifact of daily life. Together with the development of cheap and compact radio receivers, the range of operating distances that could be received had to be reduced. Overcoming time and space—as had previously been promised—was no longer interesting. This development went along with the idea of a national listening community that overcomes the limits of individuality and gets together as a collective *Volkskörper* (national body). Even during Austrofascism, the period of authoritarian rule between 1934 and 1938 in Austria, the discussion of collective modes of listening was dominated by national and political interests. It seems to be a historical anachronism that the integration of the loudspeaker into the radio receiver went alongside a focus on propaganda and nationalism; an anachronism because listening with headphones requires much more concentration and interest for the program, instead of being free to move (and less prone to concentrate), as you are with loudspeakers.

The competition among generally accepted modes of listening influenced the apparatus itself. Objects of sound—their shape and mode—are the result of different discourses. As Trevor Pinch and Wiebe Bijker have commented, the path of development does not always follow technical feasibilities. Different social groups, such as engineers, consumers, and producers, as well as organizations and institutions, "influence the meaning given to an artifact,"[73] and the outcomes of those discussions have to satisfy different expectations. The construction of an artifact is always accompanied by several discussions, which configure the meaning ascribed to it. In my examples, the meaning and use of acoustic media around 1900 was an expression of the period's notion of time, space, and event, which were still important for the successful establishment of the radio. At the end of the 1920s, other requirements and notions from several social groups came to the fore and changed not only the object itself—in a technical and aesthetical sense—but also changed the modes of listening, so that the medium of attraction could turn into a mass medium.

## Notes

1. Bertha von Suttner, *Das Maschinenzeitalter: Zukunftsvorlesungen über unsere Zeit* (Düsseldorf, 1983), 295. All German quotations translated by the author. "Die zunächst liegenden Erwartungen boten schon des angenehmen genug: Der Phonograph, welcher das Wort samt der Stimme fixieren und vervielfältigen sollte; das Telephon, welches diese selbe Stimme über weite Entfernungen hinüberträgt; … die auf diese Weise ins Haus gebrachten Opernvorstellungen und Parlamentsreden … überhaupt alle diese Wunderröhren, die alles erdenkliche in die Wohnung leiten."
2. See Wiliam Uricchio, "Technologies of Time," in *Allegories of Communication: Intermedial Concerns from Cinema to the Digital*, eds. Jan Olsson and John Fullerton (Eastleigh, 2004), 123–38.
3. On these methodological prerequisites, see: Raymond Williams, *Television: Technology and Cultural Form* (London, 1990); Siegfried Zielinski, *Audiovisionen: Kino und Fernsehen als Zwischenspiele in der Geschichte* (Reinbek, 1989); Trevor J. Pinch and Wiebe E. Bijker, "The Social Construction of

Facts and Artifacts: Or How the Sociology of Science and the Sociology of Technology Might Benefit Each Other," in *The Social Construction of Technological Systems: New Directions in the Sociology and History of Technology*, eds. Trevor J. Pinch and Wiebe E. Bijker (Cambridge, 1987), 17–50.

4. Some of the examples and ideas presented here can also be found in: Christine Ehardt, "Audioprojektionen: Radio im Spannungsfeld soziotechnischer Mediensysteme," in *Ungeplante Strukturen: Tausch und Zirkulation*, eds. Maik Bierwirth, Oliver Leistert and Renate Wieser (Munich, 2010), 47–58.

5. von Suttner, *Das Maschinenzeitalter*, 335. "Es war ja so viel Neues ins Leben getreten, so viel nie noch Dagewesenes war nun da."

6. Werner Faulstich, *Medienwandel im Industrie- und Massenzeitalter (1830–1900)* (Göttingen, 2004), 21.

7. See Roman Sandgruber, *Strom der Zeit: Das Jahrhundert der Elektrizität* (Linz, 1992), 15.

8. Kronprinz Rudolf, "Preface," *Internationale Zeitschrift für die elektrische Ausstellung in Wien 1883* (19 August 1883): 83. "Mit stolzen Gefühlen stehen wir heute vor einem Werke das seine Entstehung allein dem opferfreudigen Patriotismus einer Anzahl von Männern verdankt. Der Verwerthung einer mächtigen Naturkraft durch wissenschaftliche Arbeit und der Ausnützung derselben für das tägliche Leben neue Bahnen zu brechen."

9. Josef Kareis, *Über die culturelle Bedeutung der Elektrischen Ausstellung in Wien* (Vienna, 1884), 2.

10. Anon., *Illustrirter Führer durch die Internationale elektrische Ausstellung in Wien 1883* (Vienna, 1883), 5. "Ohne Verständnis kein Genuss! heißt es bei der elektrischen Ausstellung. Wer etwa hofft, dass er beim Besuch derselben sich nur einige Stunden amüsiren und dabei allerhand Neues und Sonderbares schauen könnte, der dürfte doch in einer ganz seltsamen Weise enttäuscht werden. Denn er wird dort soviel Neues und Sonderbares sehen, dass es ihm bald wie ein Mühlrad im Kopf herumgehen wird, wenn niemand da ist, der ihm freundlichst das Chaos klärt und ihm Zweck und Wesen der dort in Fülle vorhandenen neuen Erscheinungen deutet."

11. Ibid., 41. ("Telephon-Auditorien")

12. Ibid., 91.

13. Ibid.

14. Anon., *Internationale Zeitschrift für die elektrische Ausstellung in Wien 1883* (19 August 1883): 5. "Diese Stimmung zu erregen und zu verbreiten, dazu trug am meisten bei das kleine wohlbekannte Wunderding, ... das Telephon. Die Eisenbahn zu Lichtenfels ..., die ungeheure Ausbreitung der unterseeischen Kabel, die Siegesthaten der Telegraphie, all dies hätte nicht so sehr die Massen elektrisirt, als das kleine Instrument, welches das persönliche Moment, die Unabhängigkeit von Zeit und Raum, die in der Electricität steckt, vor die erstaunten Sinne rückte."

15. Anon., "Notizen," *Internationale Zeitschrift für die elektrische Ausstellung in Wien 1883* (16 September 1883): 159. "Die Telephonkammern in der Rotunde bieten äusserlich noch immer den Anblick einer nie abnehmenden Schau—, pardon Hörlust. Es ist als wären dieselben zu einem dritthalbmonatlichen

Belagerungszustande verdammt; fort und fort kommen die Leute, occupiren die Zellen, ziehen wieder ab, und stets zucken neue Entsatztruppen (bei denen es auch nicht an Officieren fehlt) heran.—Kurz—die Kammern sind immer gefüllt."

16. Anon., *Bericht über die Internationale Elektrische Ausstellung in Wien 1883* (Vienna, 1885), 300. "Die mikrotelephonische Übertragung der Opern- und Concertmusik der Wiener Privat-Telegraphen-Gesellschaft nach der Rotunde geschah nur mittelst zweier Doppelleitungen. Zum Behuf der tele- phonischen Opernübertagung in die Rotunde wurden auf der Bühne der k. k. Hofoper und zwar längs der Beleuchtungsrampe derselben 12 Mikrophone, Patent der Wiener Privat-Telegraphen-Gesellschaft aufgestellt."

17. Ibid., 303. ("Telephonhauben")

18. Anon., *Bericht über die Internationale Elektrische*, 299. "auf der Bühne auf jeder Seite des Souffleurkastens symmetrisch je 12 Ader'sche Transmitter."

19. Ibid., 299.

20. Ibid. "Um dieselben vor Erschütterungen und fremden Geräuschen, welche von den Bretterbühnen ausgehen könnten, zu schützen, erhielten die Kästchen der Mikrophone als Boden dicke Bleiplatten, welche auf Kautschukfüssen ruhten. Jeder Hörer bekam zwei … Empfangs-Telephone zur Bewaffnung seiner Ohren. Von diesen Hör-Instrumenten stand das eine mit einem rechts, das andere mit einem links vom Souffleurkasten angebrachten Transmitter in leitender Verbindung, so dass der Lauscher dadurch akustisch wahrnehmen konnte, ob der Acteur stehen geblieben oder ob er nach rechts oder links geschritten war."

21. See Asa Briggs, "The Pleasure Telephone: A Chapter in the Prehistory of the Media," in *The Social Impact of the Telephone*, ed. Ithiel the Sola Pool (Cambridge, 1977), 40–65.

22. Adalbert Kukan, "Der Vorläufer des Rundfunks: der Telephon-Bote," *Blätter für Technikgeschichte*, ed. Rolf Niederhuemer, no. 46 (Vienna, 1986): 179–86, here 184. "über den normalen Telefonapparat mit der 'Telefonzeitung' gegen Extragebühr."

23. See Regine Rohrböck, *Die Entwicklung der Nachrichtentechnik bis zum Beginn des 20. Jahrhunderts unter besonderer Berücksichtigung der Telegraphie und der Telephonie in Österreich-Ungarn* (Vienna, 1989), 77.

24. Andreas Resch and Reinhold Hofer, *Österreichische Innovationsgeschichte seit dem späten 19. Jahrhundert: Indikatoren des Innovationssystems und Muster des Innovationsverhaltens* (Innsbruck, 2010), 240.

25. Ibid., 239.

26. See Rohrböck, *Die Entwicklung*, 82.

27. "Meanwhile, the telephone industry developed on the basis of a service to customers carrying out their own exchanges, and much of the early talk about theaterphones and electrophones was forgotten, buried in a rejected past. Fortunately, the idea of 'the pleasure telephone' never completely disappeared." Briggs, "The Pleasure Telephone," 59.

28. A. Oberbeck, "Telephon und Mikrophon auf der Elektrischen Ausstellung in Wien," *Internationale Zeitschrift für die elektrische Ausstellung in Wien 1883* (22 July 1883), 276. "Aus der im Ganzen nur geringen Zahl telephonischer

Apparate in der österreichischen Abtheilung kann man wohl schließen, dass die Fernsprech-Einrichtungen hier noch keine größere Verbreitung gefunden haben. Sicher wird auch nach dieser Richtung die diesjährige Ausstellung anregend wirken."

29. On the history of the Austrian telephone network, see: Josef Wanka, *Das Telegraphen- und Telephonwesen in Österreich* (Vienna, 1896); Hans von Hellrigl, "Die Entwicklung der Telephonie in Österreich," *Zeitschrift für Elektrotechnik*, vol. 16 (1898): 205–32; Rohrböck, *Die Entwicklung.*

30. See Anon., *Österreichische Verkehrs-Zeitung: Fachblatt für Post, Telegraph und Telephon, Wien* (3 February 1892), 36.

31. Ibid., 1. "Die Telegraphie, obwohl mit unseren gesellschaftlichen Zuständen innig verwachsen, ist doch keine volksthümliche Einrichtung geworden. Soll es die Telephonie auch nicht werden? Es steht des nicht im Einklange mit dem demokratischen Zuge, welcher der Gegenwart eigen ist. Die Telephonie darf nicht zu einem Privileg der Reichen, sondern sie muss Allgemeingut warden."

32. Siegfried Zielinski, *Archäologie der Medien: Zur Tiefenzeit des technischen Hörens und Sehens* (Reinbek, 2002), 322.

33. Ibid.

34. Karl Eduard Zetzsche, "Die elektrische Telegraphie und die Arten der elektrischen Telegraphen," *Internationale Zeitschrift für die elektrische Ausstellung in Wien 1883* (22 July 1883): 31. "Telegraphen mit vergänglichen Zeichen."

35. Ibid., 31, "*sinngetreue* Nachbildung des Originals," "Erzeugung einer *formgetreuen* Nachbildung des Originals."

36. On the history of phono-objects, see Stefan Gauß, *Nadel, Rille, Trichter: Kulturgeschichte des Phonographen und des Grammophons in Deutschland (1900–1940)*, (Cologne, 2009), and his chapter in this volume.

37. Punch's Almanack for 1878; http://www.terramedia.co.uk/Chronomedia/years/punch_telephone_predictions_4.htm; accessed 15 January 2012.

38. [Advertisement], *Kinematographische Rundschau*, no. 3 (1907): 7. "Die Schar der Phonographenfreunde hat heute schon eine stattliche Zahl erreicht und überall dort, wo es moderne Menschen gibt, auch die Sprechmaschine nicht fehlt."

39. Ibid., "Spezialitäten in Sprechmaschinen von 6 Kronen aufwärts," "Phantasie- und Luxusapparate, singende Blumenstöcke, Grammophonautomaten, sprechende Weckeruhren, Aufnahmeapparate für Platten und Walzen," "die rühmlichst bekannten Riesenkonzert-Graphophone für Theater- und Konzertsäle."

40. Quoted after Klaus Amann, *Vor dem Hörspiel war das Tongemälde: Rezitationen, Melodramen und Hörbilder der Schallplattenindustrie von 1890–1930*, Radiofeature SDR, 1982.

41. Ibid., "Leider wurde die Verbreitung [von Schallaufnahmen; C.E.] dadurch erkauft, daß sie sich in den Dienst der niederen Instinkte stellte und willig jeden musikalischen Quatsch und Tratsch vervielfältigte. Das Inhaltsloseste und Wertloseste, was es auf musikalischem Gebiet nur gab, Gassenhauer und Couplets der geringsten und niedrigsten Art."

42. Ibid., "zweifelhafter Witze für sogenannte Herrengesellschaften."

43. The establishment of a distribution company in Austria had also become necessary for many other companies because Austria continually increased the custom duty on recordings.

44. Anon., "DACAPO Rekord Company," *Kinematographische Rundschau*, no. 38 (1908): 5. "Alle beliebteren deutschen Schallplatten werden nunmehr in Österreich selbst fabriziert. Neuestens haben ... die DACAPO Rekord Company veranlasst in Österreich eine eigene Fabrik zu erbauen ... In der eigenen Massefabrik der DACAPO Rekord Company werden schon heute bis 10000 Stück Platten pro Tag gepresst."

45. Anon., "Notizen," *Kinematographische Rundschau*, no. 8 (1907): 4. "10000 Platten verlangt und geliefert."

46. Uricchio, "Technologies of Time," 123.

47. Karl Farkas, "Alles per Radio," *Illustriertes Wiener Extrablatt*, 3 March 1924, 15. Thanks for this quotation to Hilde Haider-Pregler, University of Vienna. "Der Titel muss aus drei Wörtern bestehen [und] Aktualität zeigen."

48. In 1926, Farkas and Grünbaum also wrote the lyrics of the operetta revue "Journal der Liebe" (Journal of Love) centered around a simultaneous transmission in Prague, Vienna and Budapest "sparkling of telephonic witticism," quoted after Hans Veigl, *Lachen im Keller* (Vienna, 1986), 103.

49. See Anon., "Dem lieben Radioonkel," *Radiowelt*, no. 23 (1923): 3.

50. Letter 20 April 1923, in rec. 7847/1923, Ministry of Transport [Austrian public record office], "zum Senden von Konzerten, Musik, Gesang etc. mittelst drahtloser Telephonie an das Publikum zu benützen," "Theater und Unterhaltungsvorstellungen, Vorträge und Berichte von allgemeinen Interesse."

51. Ibid., "an das Publikum gegen Abonnements- oder Lizenzgebühren verkauft oder vermietet."

52. Ibid., "die Aufnahme der von ihr verbreiteten Vorführung den Inhabern der Empfangsstationen Lizenz- oder Abonnementsgebühren."

53. Letter 15 May 1923, in rec. 9843/1923, Ministry of Transport [Austrian public record office].

54. Anon., "Was bringt der österreichische Radioverkehr?," *Reichspost*, 23 March 1924 (Vienna, 1924), 4; "musikalische und deklamatorische."

55. Ibid., "nicht gesprochen, sondern mittels Morsezeichen."

56. Oskar Czeija, "Radiotelegraphie," [transcript] undated, Oskar Czeija Gedächtnisfonds Vienna; "Die schon früher in Erörterung gezogene Radiotelephonie mit ihrem lukrativsten Zweige, dem sogenannten 'Broadcasting' einerseits und der gänzlichen oder teilweisen unmittelbaren Gesprächsmöglichkeit zwischen Personen an verschiedenen Orten andererseits bildet trotz der Verbreitung besonders des Broadcastingdienstes dennoch eher einen Luxusbetrieb als ein zwingendes Bedürfnis. Derzeit muss der drahtlosen Telegraphie noch der Vorrang eingeräumt werden, denn vor allem spricht auch die auf diesem Gebiete reichlichst gesammelte Erfahrung für die Rentabilität—soweit der kaufmännische Gesichtspunkt in den Vordergrund gerückt wird."

57. Quoted after Theodor Venus, "Das österreichische Beispiel. Rundfunkpolitische Weichenstellungen von den Anfängen des Funks

bis zur Gründung der RAVAG 1897–1924," in *Die Idee des Radios: Von den Anfängen in Europa und den USA bis 1933*, eds. Edgar Lersch and Helmut Schanze (Konstanz, 2004), 165–204, 191f, "Opernvorstellungen, Theatervorstellungen, allerlei andren musikalischen Vorstellungen und alle andren Übertragungen von Unterhaltungsvorstellungen, Vorträgen und Reden, Berichte von parlamentarischen und sonstigen Körperschaften, sowie Wetterberichte, politische, finanzielle, sportliche und allgemeine Nachrichten … jeder Art."

58. Ibid.
59. See *Radio-Wien*, no. 17 (1946): 4.
60. A. Mitzriegler, "Der Radioteufel," *Neues Wiener Journal* (23 March 1924): 8, "Jede Erfindung vor allem aber die Erfindung des Radios bedeutet einen Machtzuwachs. Mit einigen Handgriffen beherrsche ich das Äthermeer. Ungeheure Entfernungen versinken im nichts, Raum und Zeit werden überwunden."
61. Anton Kuh, "Angst vor dem Radio," in *Luftlinien: Feuilletons, Essays und Publizistik* (Berlin, 1981), 232; "Ich fürchte mich vor dem Radio."
62. On the individualized and collective modes of listening, see Jonathan Sterne, *The Audible Past: Cultural Origins of Sound Reproduction* (Durham, NC, 2003), 161ff.
63. Anon., "Radiohörer im Grünen," *Neuigkeitsweltblatt* (9 May 1926): 1, "Eine Neuheit für die Großstadt wurde jüngst im Wiener Rathauspark geschaffen, wo nunmehr bei schönem Wetter eine beschränkte Anzahl von Radiofreunden sich diesen Genuss angesichts der blühenden Sträucher und Blumenbeete verschaffen können. Wie unser Bild zeigt, wird ein Radioapparat mit Rahmenantenne aufgestellt und 30 Paare Kopfhörer stehen dem Publikum gegen eine Gebühr von 20 Groschen pro Stunde zur Verfügung. Die Neueinführung findet großen Zuspruch."
64. Anon., *Bericht über die Internationale Elektrische*, 303.
65. G. Walter, "Der Mangel an Kopfhörern," *Radiowelt*, no. 39 (1926): 5, "[Das] große Interesse führte zu einer großen Nachfrage an Kopfhörern, die durch den augenblicklichen Bedarf nicht gedeckt werden kann."
66. Anon., "Die Kopfhörermisere," *Radiowelt*, no. 38 (1926): 2.
67. See Walter, "Der Mangel an Kopfhörern," 5.
68. Anon., "Versuchen Sie's!," *Radiowelt*, no. 2 (1924): 1, "Legen Sie einmal den Kranz eines Radio-Kopfhörers um die Stirne. Lassen Sie das, was Sie hören, voll auf sich wirken. Geben Sie sich Ihrem Eindruck hin. Und dann überlegen Sie. Das ist nicht eine Erfindung wie andere. Es ist nicht wie Grammophon und Telephon. Es ist mehr, es ist andres. Es ist Botschaft aus einer unbekannten Welt."
69. "Dancing Headphones" was the title of a Swiss satirical magazine. "First we have a fancy dinner and afterwards a merry little dance with excellent orchestra music," read the ironic text beside the cartoon. See Kurt Stadelmann and Rolf Wolfensberger, eds., *Wunschwelten: Geschichten und Bilder zu Kommunikation und Technik* (Zurich, 2000).
70. This cartoon from 1925 shows a radio-café with horns and headphones on the tables and an irritated non-listener with pillows instead of

headphones, saying: "Amazed, Mr. Miller? That's my invention, the absolutely-nothing-to-hear headphone!," *Radiowelt*, no. 15 (1925): 3.
71. See Ehardt, "Audioprojektionen," 54f.
72. Walter Benjamin, *Das Kunstwerk im Zeitalter seiner technischen Reproduzierbarkeit* (Frankfurt a.m., 1977), 41, "Aufmerksamkeit nicht ein."
73. Pinch and Bijker, "The Social Construction of Facts and Artifacts," 46.

# Bibliography

Anon. *Bericht über die Internationale Elektrische Ausstellung in Wien 1883.* Ed. Niederösterreichischer Gewerbeverein. Vienna, 1885.

———. *Illustriertes Wiener Extrablatt* (3 March 1924).

———. *Illustrirter Führer durch die Internationale elektrische Ausstellung in Wien 1883.* Vienna, 1883.

———. *Internationale Zeitschrift für die elektrische Ausstellung in Wien 1883* (19 August 1883).

———. *Kinematographische Rundschau*, no. 3 (1907), no. 8. (1907), no. 38 (1908).

———. Letter 15 May 1923, in rec. 9843/1923, Ministry of Transport [Austrian public record office].

———. "Radiohörer im Grünen," *Neuigkeitsweltblatt* (9 May 1926): 1.

———. "Notizen," *Internationale Zeitschrift für die elektrische Ausstellung in Wien 1883* (16 September 1883): 159.

———. *Österreichische Verkehrs-Zeitung. Fachblatt für Post, Telegraph und Telephon*, Wien (3 February 1892).

———. "Die Kopfhörermisere," *Radiowelt*, no. 38 (1926): 2.

———. "Dem lieben Radioonkel," *Radiowelt*, no. 23 (1923): 3.

———. *Radiowelt*, no. 15 (1925), no. 39 (1926).

———. *Radio-Wien*, no. 17 (1946).

———. "Versuchen Sie's!" *Radiowelt*, no. 2 (1924): 1.

———. "Was bringt der österreichische Radioverkehr?," *Reichspost* (23 March 1924).

Amann, Klaus. *Vor dem Hörspiel war das Tongemälde: Rezitationen, Melodramen und Hörbilder der Schallplattenindustrie von 1890–1930.* Radiofeature SDR, 1982.

Benjamin, Walter. *Das Kunstwerk im Zeitalter seiner technischen Reproduzierbarkeit.* Frankfurt a.M., 1977.

Briggs, Asa. "The Pleasure Telephone: A Chapter in the Prehistory of the Media." In *The Social Impact of the Telephone.* Ed. Ithiel the Sola Pool. Cambridge, 1977, 40–65.

Czeija, Oskar, "Radiotelegraphie," [transcript] undated, Oskar Czeija Gedächtnisfonds Vienna.

Ehardt, Christine. "Audioprojektionen: Radio im Spannungsfeld soziotechnischer Mediensysteme." In *Ungeplante Strukturen: Tausch und Zirkulation.* Eds. Maik Bierwirth, Oliver Leistert, and Renate Wieser. Munich, 2010, 47–58.

Faulstich, Werner. *Medienwandel im Industrie- und Massenzeitalter (1830–1900)*. Göttingen, 2004.

Gauß, Stefan. *Nadel, Rille, Trichter: Kulturgeschichte des Phonographen und des Grammophons in Deutschland (1900–1940)*. Cologne, 2009.

Hellrigl, Hans von. "Die Entwicklung der Telephonie in Österreich," *Zeitschrift für Elektrotechnik*, vol. 16 (1898): 205–32.

Kareis, Josef. *Über die culturelle Bedeutung der Elektrischen Ausstellung in Wien*. Vienna, 1884.

Kronprinz Rudolf, "Preface," *Internationale Zeitschrift für die elektrische Ausstellung in Wien 1883* (19 August 1883): 83.

Kuh, Anton. "Angst vor dem Radio." In *Luftlinien: Feuilletons, Essays und Publizistik*. Berlin, 1981.

Kukan, Adalbert. "Der Vorläufer des Rundfunks: der Telephon-Bote." In *Blätter für Technikgeschichte*. Ed. Rolf Niederhuemer. Vienna, 1986, vol. 46, 179–86.

Mitzriegler, A. "Der Radioteufel," *Neues Wiener Journal* (23 March 1924): 8.

Oberbeck, A. "Telephon und Mikrophon auf der Elektrischen Ausstellung in Wien," *Internationale Zeitschrift für die elektrische Ausstellung in Wien 1883* (22 July 1883): 276.

Pinch, Trevor J., and Wiebe E. Bijker. "The Social Construction of Facts and Artifacts: Or How the Sociology of Science and the Sociology of Technology Might Benefit Each Other." In *The Social Construction of Technological Systems: New Directions in the Sociology and History of Technology*. Eds. Trevor J. Pinch and Wiebe E. Bijker. Cambridge, 1987, 17–50.

*Punch's Almanack for 1878*; http://www.terramedia.co.uk/Chronomedia/years/punch_telephone_predictions_4.htm; accessed 15 January 2012.

Resch, Andreas, and Reinhold Hofer. *Österreichische Innovationsgeschichte seit dem späten 19. Jahrhundert: Indikatoren des Innovationssystems und Muster des Innovationsverhaltens*. Innsbruck, 2010.

Rohrböck, Regine. *Die Entwicklung der Nachrichtentechnik bis zum Beginn des 20. Jahrhunderts unter besonderer Berücksichtigung der Telegraphie und der Telephonie in Österreich-Ungarn*. Vienna, 1989.

Sandgruber, Roman. *Strom der Zeit: Das Jahrhundert der Elektrizität*. Linz, 1992.

Stadelmann, Kurt, and Rolf Wolfensberger, eds. *Wunschwelten: Geschichten und Bilder zu Kommunikation und Technik*. Zurich, 2000.

Sterne, Jonathan. *The Audible Past. Cultural origins of sound reproduction*. Durham, NC, 2003.

Suttner, Bertha von. *Das Maschinenzeitalter: Zukunftsvorlesungen über unsere Zeit*. Düsseldorf, 1983.

Uriccio, Wiliam. "Technologies of Time." In *Allegories of Communication: Intermedial Concerns from Cinema to the Digital*. Eds. Jan Olsson and John Fullerton. Eastleigh, 2004, 123–38.

Veigl, Hans. *Lachen im Keller*. Vienna, 1986.

Venus, Theodor. "Das österreichische Beispiel. Rundfunkpolitische Weichenstellungen von den Anfängen des Funks bis zur Gründung der RAVAG 1897–1924." In *Die Idee des Radios: Von den Anfängen in Europa und den USA bis 1933*. Eds. Edgar Lersch and Helmut Schanze. Konstanz, 2004, 165–204.

Walter, G. "Der Mangel an Kopfhörern," *Radiowelt*, no. 39 (1926): 5.

Wanka, Josef. *Das Telegraphen- und Telephonwesen in Österreich*. Vienna, 1896.

Williams, Raymond. *Television: Technology and Cultural Form*. London, 1990.

Zetzsche, Karl Eduard. "Die elektrische Telegraphie und die Arten der elektrischen Telegraphen," *Internationale Zeitschrift für die elektrische Ausstellung in Wien 1883* (22 July 1883): 31.

Zielinski, Siegfried. *Audiovisionen: Kino und Fernsehen als Zwischenspiele in der Geschichte*. Reinbek, 1989.

———. *Archäologie der Medien: Zur Tiefenzeit des technischen Hörens und Sehens*. Reinbek, 2002.

# PART IV

# MUSIC LISTENING IN THE LABORATORY AND IN THE CONCERT HALL

6

# From the Piano Pestilence to the Phonograph Solo
## Four Case Studies of Musical Expertise in the Laboratory and on the City Street

*Alexandra E. Hui*

In 1884 the music critic Eduard Hanslick lamented how dangerous the streets of Vienna had become. The refined listener was defenseless against the cacophony of, not the noise of the city, but the bad music of its inhabitants. The assault on the ear was both physical and psychological. It had to be stopped. Hanslick, for his part, proposed reducing the number of piano students.

Thirty years later and a continent away, a brigade of demonstration experts were dispatched by the Edison Company to instruct the public in the proper operation of the new Edison Diamond Disk Phonographs. Through demonstration recitals, phonograph listeners were trained not only in the proper generation of sound but also the proper reception of sound; they were taught to only receive certain sounds. They would have been safe on the streets of Vienna.

This chapter presents four relatively small case studies toward an understanding of how the clatter of practicing piano students was rendered non-threatening in a single generation. The multiple and evolving forms of musical expertise changed in relation to the simultaneously shifting listening culture. I therefore presume that an examination of specific cases of changing definition and value of musical expertise can provide insight into listening culture generally. Both expertise and listening culture are defined broadly so as to capture and validate the skills of the New Jersey housewife alongside those of the director of the Berlin Psychological Institute. Musical expertise, listening practices, and sounds themselves were intertwined and evolving at the end of the long nineteenth century. Further, these shifts and upheavals were not limited to the music world. Both anxiety and enthusiasm about the value of practitioners' musical expertise plagued the academic world as well.

The first two of the case studies have been discussed at much greater length and with a different analytical thrust in previous publications.[1] Here Eduard Hanslick's writing on the piano-scourge and Carl Stumpf's debate with Wilhelm Wundt over the role of music-consciousness are examined only in relation to the larger argument of this chapter about the renegotiation of musical expertise's role in conceptions of listening, both scientific and non-scientific. At the end of the nineteenth century, conceptions of listening were bound up with specific understandings of musical skill. This was the case both within the walls of the laboratory as well as on the city streets. There was a right and wrong way of listening and it was rooted in the listener's musical training. This criterion for proper listening was, however, beginning to come under attack. In the psychological laboratory, the standards for scientific expertise shifted. On the city streets, the sounds themselves began to change. The first two case studies in this chapter are a testament to this period of negotiation.

The long-term decline of experimental studies of sound sensation that were both psychophysical and aesthetic projects is a testament to the fundamental shift away from the use of musical skill in the laboratory.[2] The way in which individuals began and continued to experience music through recording and replay technology rather than live performances (by themselves or with others) paralleled the attenuating importance of individual musical skill for the experience of listening to music. The third and fourth case studies in this chapter— the use of the phonograph in ethnomusicological field studies and the Edison Company's demonstration recital program—were chosen in order to bridge the introduction of recording-replaying technology. The phonograph buttressed, but also fundamentally changed, musical expertise. Because the phonograph liberated the listener from the need to experience a music performance "live," it separated the expertise of receiving sound from the expertise of generating it. It increased credibility (both scientific and social), but also reduced the need for musicality, both in performing and listening to music.

That said, the use of the phonograph at the beginning of the twentieth century complicated this steady decline in the value of musical expertise. The third and fourth case studies suggest that the phonograph was employed to preserve and even cultivate expertise, and in this sense maintained a place for expertise both in the worlds of field research and popular music. The definition of expertise was, however, markedly changed and dependent on the technology itself. The phonograph was the expert listener, and the human listener no longer needed to maintain a superior level of individual, musical skill.

In turn, the phonograph made a new kind of listening both possible and important. The phonograph encouraged the cultivation of an entirely new kind of listening, capable of distinguishing an entirely new kind of music. This new listener focused on the recorded sound's fidelity to a now separate (temporally and spatially) original performance and, as a consequence, no longer heard the noise of the device.

## Case One: The Aesthetic Listener Takes on the Piano Scourge

Eduard Hanslick's work as a music critic, historian, and aesthetician dominated the Viennese music scene in the second half of the nineteenth century. He reviewed performances for the Wiener Zeitung and Neue Freie Presse, adjudicated at competitions, and was one of the first individuals to hold an ordinarius professorship in the History and Aesthetics of Music (at the University of Vienna). The pieces Hanslick chose to review helped to shape the classical canon.[3] His writings also helped fuel growing criticism of the cult of the virtuoso. Hanslick was deeply suspicious of the flamboyant spectacle of such performers as Nicolò Paganini and Franz Liszt. This suspicion aligned with Hanslick's distaste for the compositions of the cadre of composers who termed themselves the New German School, and included Richard Wagner, Franz Liszt, Anton Bruckner, and Hector Berlioz. Hanslick instead celebrated the music of the predominantly Leipzig-based performers, Joseph Joachim and Clara Schumann, both known for their ascetic style of music interpretation, and the composers Robert Schumann, Felix Mendelssohn, and Johannes Brahms—Brahms being a close personal friend.

Hanslick's writings are generally considered to denote the beginning of a new musical aesthetic discourse in Europe. His 1854 treatise on aesthetic theory, *Vom Musikalisch-Schönen* (The Beautiful in Music), proposed that the beautiful in music was sonically moving forms (*tönend bewegte Formen*), both the structure and content of the structure.[4] Beauty in music was the specifically beautiful, with no object or goal beyond itself. Music therefore had no aim of giving the listener pleasure. It was instead the role of the listener to locate the beauty in the music (not the role of the composer or performer to present it to the listener). Attention and/or intellectual contemplation was therefore critically important to the listener's experience of music.

Form as musical idea framed Hanslick's analysis of musical works. His program of formalist analysis was, he claimed, more exacting than the imprecise aesthetics of emotion.[5] He would criticize music in which the formalist elements, both the structure of the piece and the musical idea within, were, by his analysis, incongruent with the historical moment in which the piece was composed. Hanslick derided such pieces as primitive, pre-verbal, and pathological.

The individuals listening to music were also subject to Hanslick's critique. Just as there was pathological music, there were pathological listeners. These pathological listeners experienced music in a state of continuous passive reception. They allowed the elemental forms so critical to understanding the beauty in music, according to Hanslick, to wash over them and affect them only in a "supersensible" manner—a twilight state of sounding nullity.[6] There was also the observant listener. The observant listener was misguided by the aesthetics of emotion (rather than form) and, because he or she was emotional, fancied him or herself to be musical. Because they sought only abstract feeling or emotion, and did so with a complete lack of reasoning, Hanslick derided the observant listeners as the lowest common denominators in the audience. They experienced music as if chloroformed.[7] Then there was the aesthetic listener, the practitioner of the true method of listening. Aesthetic listening was, according to Hanslick, an act of pure contemplation, diligent attention, and thoughtfulness. To listen in this way, with unflagging attention, was "a truly aesthetic art in itself."[8] Those who listened in this way, actively following and anticipating the composer's (formalist) intentions, would be rewarded with satisfaction and delight.[9]

Johannes Brahms—an additional example—similarly emphasized "proper" listening, though as a generational and cultural critique.[10] Brahms complained about the lack of rigor in musical education and training. The music historian and conductor, Leon Botstien, argues that Brahms's concerns reflect an anxiety about the intertwined development of increased piano-based music education and increased opportunity for individuals to listen to music without generating it. These trends intertwined, according to Brahms, to weaken musical literacy.[11] Brahms preferred an audience full of listeners who could experience his musical performances as if they were playing the music themselves (and could have). Certainly the performances of virtuosos, aiming only to audiovisually dazzle, demanded no such engagement from their audiences. Listening itself was conscripted into battle against the aesthetics of the New German School.

Hanslick's celebration of the aesthetic listener is indicative of the rising status of musical expertise in the act of listening. The ability to employ formalist analysis—dependent on extensive music theory knowledge and rigorous ear training—was now required for a satisfactory musical experience. In turn, the musical experience of the aesthetic listener was unquestioned. As long as the listening technique was correct (i.e. it employed formalism) the sounds the listener heard were legitimate.

In fact, the musical experience of the aesthetic listener determined which sounds were legitimate. Thirty years after Vom Musikalisch-Schönen, Hanslick published an article titled, "Ein Brief über die 'Clavierseuche'" (A Letter on the "Piano Pestilence").[12] He lamented the latest scourge of the modern cityscape: the mediocre piano playing of the neighbors. The errors and missteps of the "tinkling dilettantes" practicing their scales and mis-executing chords were a continuous assault on the ear of the refined listener. The torments of these aural assaults were both physical and psychological, and the aesthetic listener was defenseless.

Hanslick's solution—because the aesthetic listener must be protected—was to reduce the number of piano students. Certainly the entire piece was a bit tongue-in-cheek, but it is worth examining the larger cultural critique at work here. The 1791 introduction of the single-piece cast iron frame marked the beginning of a century-long flurry of innovation in piano design. All of the major European piano firms were established by the middle of the nineteenth century. The robust piano market mirrored economic growth and stability (and fueled further design innovation). By the end of the century, the piano was the emblem of the newly emergent middle classes; which is to say, the piano pestilence dovetailed with the growing middle class—likely observant listeners, all. These "tinkling dilettantes" would have been enraptured by the music of Wagner, or hoped to play the piano like Liszt themselves.

Hanslick's concern about the health effects of music is the tail end of a longer history of anxieties over the dangers of music to both listeners and performers.[13] Consider the contemporary writings of Max Nordau or Friedrich Nietzsche lamenting physical, psychological, social, spiritual, and/or cultural degeneration brought on by the creations of "mystics," "egomaniacs," and Richard Wagner.[14] For Hanslick, however, it was not simply poorly composed or poorly performed music that was at fault for assaulting the aesthetic listener. It was the rigorous musical training that made the aesthetic listener so vulnerable. If the musical aesthetics of the masses were the basis of a pestilence, then the musical expertise of the aesthetic listener was a preexisting condition. It was not, however, a vulnerability to be cured or avoided. Instead, the musical expertise of the aesthetic listener was to be prized and protected.

## Case Two: The Bias of Music-Infected Consciousness

Musical expertise was not just prized and protected in concert halls and on the city streets. For much of the nineteenth century, musical training was seen as a critically important skill for the scientific study of sound sensation. Experimenters such as Hermann von Helmholtz and Ernst Mach were so steeped in the music world that they thought of sound and music as interchangeable.[15] The ability to properly read, play, and above all hear music was necessary to properly do science. In the 1890s this assumption came under attack. The vicious debate between Carl Stumpf and Wilhelm Wundt illustrates the extent to which the value of musical expertise was being negotiated at the end of the nineteenth century.

In 1890, Carl Lorenz, a student in Wundt's Leipzig experimental psychology laboratory, published the results of his experiments on tone differentiation. He would sound two tones (*Grenztöne*) for the experimental subject, at either musical or non-musical intervals. He would then sound a lengthy series of tones, increasing in intervals of four cycles per second, between the previously sounded *Grenztöne*. The observers were asked to judge and indicate which tone was the middle one between the *Grenztöne*. This experiment was repeated for several different intervals, several ranges, from high to low, and low to high, and resulted in over 110,000 judgments. Lorenz claimed that his results revealed two significant features about sound sensation and its experimental study. First, his work showed that the psychophysical method of just noticeable difference measurements (in the form of the Tondistanzen judgments he collected) could be applied successfully to the study of tone sensation. Lorenz's work also showed that Tondistanzen judgments were the arithmetic mean of the *Grenztöne* and therefore likely to be unrelated to musical intervals.[16] Tone differentiation did not appear to be rooted in the Western tuning system.

Lorenz also claimed that his results demonstrated that earlier studies of tone fusion (the perception of two simultaneously sounded tones as one single tone) by Carl Stumpf had been performed incorrectly. Or, rather, that Stumpf's use of musically trained experimental subjects biased Stumpf's data. These individuals would have, according to Lorenz, been more inclined to identify certain tone intervals (musical ones) than follow instructions to be honest in their judgments.

Stumpf responded by publishing a scathing article in which he meticulously picked apart Lorenz's work.[17] His critiques ranged from the insultingly minute (the way Lorenz formatted his tables) to systematic error in Lorenz's analysis. Stumpf rearranged Lorenz's data from a "musical point of view" to reveal two major oversights. First, Stumpf found that when the *Grenztöne* were a musical interval, the various middle tone judgments were significantly more definite (that is, a small standard deviation in the distribution of judgments). Second, he showed that the tone around which these judgments clustered was actually the geometric mean, which corresponded to the "musical" middle; for example, when the *Grenztöne* were an octave apart, the judged middle tone was the tone a fifth above the lower pitched *Grenztöne*.[18]

These results indicated, Stumpf continued, that Lorenz's data showed that tone differentiation was related to Western tuning after all. Listeners were subject to what Stumpf termed "music consciousness" (*Musikbewusstsein*) and heard musical intervals out of musical habit.[19] This explained why Lorenz's rearranged data showed that for non-musical *Grenztöne* intervals, though there was far more variation in the distribution of judgments, the middle tone was judged to be the nearest musical middle. The ear sought musical intervals, even when they did not exist.

The roots of Stumpf's conception of music consciousness, or music-infected consciousness as he also called it, can be traced back to his earlier *Tonpsychologie* text, but he did not employ such terms in that work. While the language is suggestive of menace or disease, Stumpf, like Hanslick, believed that musical expertise provided better insight. In Stumpf's case, the music-infection of the listener's consciousness granted him or her access into the processes of sound sensation. The close adherence of the judgments by musically skilled experimental subjects to a geometric mean suggested that the applicability of a psychophysical law of tone differentiation sensitivity could vary according to the musical expertise of the listener. Stumpf did not address the issue directly; but if, say, the Fechner-Weber law only applied to musical experts, there were significant implications for contemporary theories (even Stumpf's) about the origins of music.

According to Stumpf, the rearranged results also indicated that musical interval consciousness was the most influential factor in tone differentiation. Of Lorenz's various experimental subjects, those who were musically skilled made the most definitive judgments. Some of the experimental subjects who lacked musical training could not even determine which of the *Grenztöne* was higher in pitch. Stumpf stated that, "a single judgment by one such [musically skilled] observer [was] worth more than a thousand by the unmusical and unskilled,"[20] and Lorenz and Wundt should have employed only experimental subjects that had musical training. Their work, Stumpf explained, was so arbitrary that they might as well have "put it to a vote of the people."[21]

Wundt responded, defending his student from Stumpf's attacks. He explained that Stumpf misunderstood both Lorenz's research and the proper application of psychophysics generally. In fact, Wundt continued, Stumpf was undermining psychophysics.[22]

If Wundt was going to accuse Stumpf of being incapable of understanding psychophysics, then Stumpf was going to accuse Wundt of being incapable of hearing correctly. He fired back another article, expressing his doubt in both Wundt's musical skills and his hearing generally.[23] Wundt had disputed whether an experimental subject could detect interference beats pulsing at a frequency greater than 60 beats per second and, according to Stumpf, set this as the upper limit of what Wundt's "expert" was capable of detecting.[24] Not only was this well below what Helmholtz had claimed to be able to detect (up to 132 beats per second), it was far inferior to his own ability (up to 264 beats per second!). Stumpf had devoted the previous two decades to studying the intersection of musical experience, psychology, and sound sensation.[25] Stumpf had collaborated with the instrument maker and acoustician, Georg August Ignatius Appunn. He had also worked closely in his studies with such performers as Georg Schünemann and Joseph Joachim, and was himself proficient on several musical instruments. It is of little surprise, then, that Stumpf insisted on employing musical expertise as a criterion for scientific credibility; in this clash with Wundt, he had more of it.

In his rebuttal, Wundt insisted that not only were experimental subjects who lacked musical training perfectly usable, they were actually preferable.[26] The experimental subject should reflect something approaching the universal experience of sound sensation, not the ideal or expert. Even Hanslick had noted that the majority of people were not aesthetic listeners. Because Wundt believed the experimental subject should approximate a general experience of sound sensation, he sought large volumes of data. By excluding experimental subjects who lacked musical training, Wundt continued, Stumpf was missing out on valuable data. So whereas for Stumpf the bias of music consciousness was beneficial, for Wundt the bias of music consciousness was a liability.

Experimental expertise for Wundt was the combination of the experimental subjects' introspection (a technique of careful self-observation that Wundt developed and promoted) and the experimenter's ability to properly analyze large volumes of data. Musicianship among the subjects or the experimenter threatened to bias both introspection and analysis. Not, Wundt insisted, that there was any indication of music-training-related bias. He reanalyzed the data and argued that consciousness could not be music-infected. One could only find an indication of such if they limited themselves to a superficial analysis. Taking one final, personal swing at Stumpf, Wundt concluded: "[I]f Stumpf has such an insurmountable dislike of arithmetic, [then] that is his problem; nobody is making him do psychophysical research."[27]

Stumpf was troubled by Wundt's insistence on moving away from the unique and superior skills of musically trained observers. He equated musical skill with scientific skill. Indeed, Wundt and Lorenz's masses of mediocre observers distorted results and threatened, in their flood of data, to overwhelm the contribution that Stumpf, with his musical training, could offer. Stumpf later described being deeply hurt by Wundt's attacks. Although the debate had fizzled out anticlimactically, Stumpf insisted that he was correct, not least because Lorenz's research was never again mentioned anywhere except in Wundt's textbook.[28]

In his recounting of the debate during his 1928 Presidential Address before the American Psychological Association, the psychologist Edward Boring explained that he could not determine who had won.[29] He noted that Edward Titchener, who had studied with Wundt, also admitted that he could not consistently agree with either Wundt or Stumpf. This suggests that, at least in the retelling, the tension at the core of the debate was the possibility that rigorous engagement could fail to produce a correct answer. Perhaps the young field of experimental psychology held only false potential. The question of the role of musical expertise in the laboratory threw into relief a deeper anxiety in experimental psychology, namely that the new experimental protocols, statistical analysis in particular, might not be the means of better understanding psychological phenomena after all.

### Context Pause: New Sounds and Re-Created Sounds

It is important to note that music was also changing dramatically at this time. Acceptance of the 440 cycles per second concert pitch and the steady implementation of equal-temperament had appeared to standardize the harmonies of musical ensembles and organs across Europe. Almost mocking this standardization effort were the composers who sought to generate completely new, previously unheard harmonies. Arnold Schoenberg, for example, deliberately rejected the Western tonal system and refused to organize any of his works around a tonal center.[30] Dissonance was emancipated, and tonality, he would claim, was dead.

This was not necessarily a surprising claim. Already in 1885, the mathematician and philologist, Alexander Ellis, had declared that there was no single, "natural" universal scale.[31] He based this claim on a comparison between the traditional musical scales of Greece, "Arabia," "India," "Java," China, and Japan. Like many in England and in Europe, Ellis gained much of his knowledge about non-Western music from performances by touring groups of native musicians. Exposure to these new sounds was inspiring for many—Claude Debussy credited his use of pentatonic scales (commonly found in traditional African and Indonesian music) to encounters with native music ensembles at the 1889 Paris Exhibition.[32] The sophisticated music performed by these groups prompted many to question the primacy of the Western tonal system and, as indicated by the subsequent development of atonal music, whether a tonal system was even a requirement of music at all.

Exposure to non-Western music also fueled an interest in local traditions and folk music. Composers such as Maurice Ravel, Béla Bartók, Leoš Janáček, Manuel de Falla, and Igor Stravinsky referenced their own folk heritage in their works, drawing on melodies and rhythms of the countryside, hills, and woods. These exercises of compositional nostalgia were, in part, aimed at combating the twin traditions of Beethoven and Wagner—that is, the perceived dominance of German and Austrian styles. Such efforts to develop new sounds dovetailed with growing nationalist movements. Bartók's efforts to develop a modernist Hungarian art music, for example, began as a project to collect and classify Hungarian folk tunes, which itself had been initially inspired by the 1896 millennial celebration of the Magyar presence in Hungary.[33]

In addition to the new sounds of the new century, consider also the increasing volume of the major cities of America and Europe. At the end of the nineteenth century, a series of anti-noise campaigns were launched in the major capital cities, in most cases a consequence of middle-class anxieties about rapid industrialization. For example, historian Peter Payer documents how the Viennese anti-noise movement, though framing their cause in language of hygiene and health, was most critical of the noise of the lower classes—the clanging of delivery vehicles, the shouts of the street vendors, the banging of construction, the barking of dogs, and the poor piano playing of Hanslick's wrath.[34] Very few complaints were made about the sound of factories, which were associated with modernity, and churches. Some noises were silent in the rising din of the cityscape, at least for those who claimed to be the most disturbed by other noises.[35]

So there were new harmonies, new tonalities, new sounds from far away places, and new sounds from very close, but deeply hidden, places. And then, with the introduction of Thomas Edison's 1877 device, sounds could be recorded and repeatedly replayed, new once again. If formalist listening or music consciousness was used to defend musical expertise against the unskilled masses within the narrow realms of the Viennese streets or psychological laboratory, the cascade of new sounds opened up a number of new soundscapes in which to negotiate new forms of musical expertise.

## Case Three: Melody under the Microscope

In 1900, Stumpf's extensive acoustic instrument and phonograph cylinder collection was given its own space and official status as the Berlin Phonogramm-Archiv. The Phonogramm-Archiv was devoted to the comparative musicological study of non-Western music. Stumpf's student, Erich von Hornbostel, managed and expanded the collection mostly through the implementation of a system in which he provided recording equipment and training to field ethnomusicologists in exchange for their original cylinders. The field researchers would then be provided with copies of the originals. The establishment of the Phonogramm-Archiv under Stumpf's direction can be seen as an indication of the growing legitimacy of ethnomusicology as a discipline.

The phonograph made the field study of music rigorous, mostly because the music could leave the field. Through the phonograph, music gained a new kind of materiality, one that liberated it from space and time. The wax roll was transportable and preservable. The system of exchange employed by the Phonogramm-Archiv, for example, meant that the expert analysis of a musical performance often occurred completely separate from the performance itself. But the walls of the laboratory did not expand or fall down. Instead, the experimental object, a unique musical moment, could exist in multiples. A folk song that was fleeting in the hills of Romania could reappear in material form in Berlin (or, presently, in digital form everywhere).

By employing the phonograph in the field, the ethnomusicologist was freed of the need to document a performed piece on paper. The latter practice required significant concentration in order to retain subtle details long enough to be transcribed. It also inevitably suffered from reduction in the case where musical effects and tone colors occurred for which there was no appropriate musical sign. The phonograph meant that performers were much less likely to tire or become bored from repeating pieces for transcription. The phonograph therefore increased both the accuracy and efficiency of documentation.[36]

Otto Abraham and Erich von Hornbostel noted in their 1904 article on the use of the phonograph in comparative musicology that eliminating the need for transcriptions eliminated an opportunity for the researcher to impose his own European aesthetic assumptions.[37] They described the great effort required for the researcher to overcome the harmonies of his heritage. Stumpf's term *Musikbewusstsein* was not used, but Abraham and von Hornbostel were clearly concerned about exactly such a bias, one in which musical training would make the researcher hear different sounds. The phonograph, by circumventing the researcher, saved the musical expert from his or her own expertise. It was the objectivity of the phonograph, both in recording and replaying the folk song for analysis that, Bartók similarly explained, made folk song collecting a scientific enterprise.[38]

Perhaps the greatest appeal of the phonograph for the researcher was the repeatability of replay. Unlike its human performers, the recording was exactly the same with every replay—that is until the researcher altered the rotational speed of the cylinder. Bartók explained that this allowed the researcher to observe the melody "like an object under the microscope."[39] The slowed cylinder revealed intricate and nearly imperceptible rhythmic shifts and musical ornaments with, Bartók claimed, "an accuracy unobtainable from hearing the natural song."[40] The phonograph, like a microscope, supplemented a sensory organ, improving its abilities. Or, put another way, the phonograph altered sounds to accommodate the limits of even the expert listener.

Stumpf defended musical expertise as scientific expertise. He insisted that musical skill was necessary for the scientific study of sound sensation. The ethnomusicologists (some his own students), however, employed the phonograph to replace musical skill. Bartók described his hope that the recording and classification of folk songs could eventually be entrusted entirely to a machine.[41] The phonograph did not simply give ethnomusicology the trappings of science; it gave ethnomusicology expertise.

The phonograph was transformative, and in multiple ways. For one, it materialized music. As a scientific object, materialized music could be approached in a new way. Not that this was the first time music was the subject of scientific scrutiny, but the type of scrutiny changed once music was materialized on a wax cylinder. It could be manipulated, repeated indefinitely, and slowed interminably. Bartók described the phonograph as being like a microscope. Just as the images seen through the microscope were presumed (admittedly after substantial debate) to reflect the actual and real, the inaudible sounds rendered audible by the phonograph were presumed to be important features. So the phonograph protected against the bias of musical expertise while simultaneously granting a new expertise of its own making. It created new, extra-human standards of musical expertise (and met them).

If we consider, then, the relationship between musical expertise and listening practice, we see a shift from the previous two cases. The techniques of aesthetic listening were still employed by the ethnomusicologist, albeit with hopefully little bias to Western music consciousness. The expertise, however, was not located in the musical training of the ethnomusicologist, or at least not entirely. Expertise came from the supplemental use of the phonograph.

### Case Four: First Re-creations (the Phonograph Solo)

Not only did the phonograph grant the ability to hear inaudible sounds, it also rendered other sounds inaudible. This selective deafness was also framed as a form of listening expertise. Extensive scholarship has shown that the phonograph changed listening practices among the public, from increasing accessibility to a diverse array of musical styles (especially fueling the growth of such American traditions as Blues, Rock and Roll, and Country) to shared popular behavior in choosing and replaying commercially mediated music. The phonograph was first and foremost a commercial device. To cultivate a consumer base, it was necessary for its purveyors to teach the public how to select from among the new sounds the phonograph generated—hearing some, not hearing others. In the long term, this ability contributed to the development of a new kind of listening.

In 1914, the Edison Company launched a program of what they termed demonstration recitals or tone tests.[42] This program was a product of Edison's anxiety about accusations of charlatanry rooted in his early years as an inventor in a late nineteenth-century American landscape replete with professional swindlers and carpetbaggers. Edison wanted consumers to embrace his phonograph and cylinders because of their superior sound quality, not because they had signed famous musicians for their recordings (as the Victor Talking Machine Company had). This practice was a distinctly Edison Company phe-nomenon. Victor Talking Machine Company and Berliner Gramophone relied almost entirely on print advertising to promote their brand.[43] Several distributors credited the demonstration recitals for their robust sales.[44] The demonstration recitals functioned as an opportunity for the public to experience the superiority of his machine over others. It was also an opportunity for consumers to learn how to operate the device properly to generate a unified product. Further, the demonstration recitals were a means of training listeners to receive the phonograph's sound in a very specific way.

The demonstration recitals were conducted by a team of demonstrators that answered to a Mr. Riley in the Edison Company. These demonstrators were dispatched to organize recitals in cooperation with local distributors. The recitals would take place in stores that sold Edison products, at churches, in schools, YMCAs, and private homes. The audiences would range in size from a dozen to 150 people. Some recitals—especially those at schools, who would be considering investing in a machine for the school district—were sought out and requested of the demonstrators. For the most part, however, the demonstrators initiated the demonstration recitals.[45]

Demonstrators were instructed not to explicitly advertise or promote the purchase of the Edison machine at the recitals.[46] The recitals were supposed to approximate a proper concert. Sometimes the recitals were complemented by lectures on music history by an academic or a music critic.[47] Public demonstration recitals were promoted as such. Programs were distributed. The audience applauded between pieces. The demonstrators would then report back to Riley on the location and size of the recital, the pieces performed, and a few sentences summarizing the audience reaction. These reports were initially just handwritten letters but were later standardized with an official form.[48]

After the Edison Company caved to consumer pressure and began signing well-known performers to make recordings, the recording artist was sometimes recruited to participate in the demonstration recitals. These "re-creation recitals", as they were called, juxtaposed the live performer against the recording of his or her voice (see figure 6.1). The recording artist would sing a duet with the phonograph, and then he or she would stop and allow the phonograph to perform solo. Sometimes, in an act of generosity, the phonograph would go silent, and the recording artist would be allowed to perform solo. Audiences seemed to appreciate the additional human element offered by the re-creation recitals. One respondent noted that she liked when the recording artist gestured to the phonograph, humanizing the machine.[49] Since the goal of these re-creation recitals was to showcase the fidelity of the sound recordings, the recording artists were encouraged to conform their voices to match the sounds generated by the phonograph.[50] Certainly they would be forbidden from "showing up" the phonograph recording of themselves with the bending of notes or additional musical flourishes.

**Figure 6.1** Promotional material for a 1921 Re-Creation Recital, Box 18, William Maxwell Files. Credit: U.S. Dept. of the Interior, National Park Service, Thomas Edison National Historical Park.

The demonstrators would instruct the audience before, during, and after (in follow-up letters) the concert on what to listen for, sometimes to the point of irritating audience members.[51] They would emphasize the fidelity and clarity of the phonograph's tone. They would, of course, deemphasize the scratching and buzzing sounds of the device. It is illustrative that these recitals were also called tone tests. The demonstrators did not, however, discuss the music itself. They did not discuss the formal structures of the pieces, nor the chord progressions, nor the interesting melodic elements. They were not training aesthetic listeners. Instead, the demonstration recitals functioned to highlight good sounds to the point that they sonically eclipsed bad ones. Listeners were taught to not hear.

This emphasis on tone would be reinforced in the record catalogs distributed to Edison customers. The description of Anna Case's "Somewhere a Voice is Calling" Re-Creation explained that the recording "displays remarkably her sympathetic personality and her glorious voice, supreme in its golden purity, exquisite in its tenderness, pure as the morning dew that graces the petals of the wild rose."[52] Or, Ms. Hempel's voice was "luscious, glowing, a veritable golden flood, ranging upward, ranging downward in undiminished body and beauty." The pure, beautiful tone of the artist and the pure, beautiful tone of the record were equivalent. Listeners were encouraged to understand them as the same.

This was not musical expertise. The phonograph did not make its listeners more musical. Nor did it communicate their preexisting musical sophistication, if they had any (if anything, it functioned to communicate their wealth and/or sophistication). This is not to say that the demonstration and re-creation recitals did not cultivate an expertise of sorts. The audiences were taught to be experts on sound quality. Further, they were trained to be experts at a new kind of listening. They could separate music from noise, and ignore, possibly not even hear, the latter. They could have walked down the streets of Hanslick's Vienna untroubled by the clatter of bad piano playing.

## Conclusion

The end of the long nineteenth century was a deeply unstable soundscape. With the introduction of new tonal systems and new compositional styles, it was a period in which sounds and harmonies proliferated, no longer tethered to a unifying aesthetic. Complementing the explosion of new sounds was a democratization of listening. Some individuals—Hanslick and Stumpf—perceived the increased access to music or science to be rooted in a reduced standard of musical expertise.[53] The new listening practices cultivated by phonograph manufacturers in a way realized Hanslick's fears. Musical expertise was not only left unprotected, it was rendered completely irrelevant by the listening demands of the phonograph. The only expertise necessary, the ability to not hear non-music, was a deafening of sorts.

Stumpf's belief that musical skill was necessary for the practice of science was becoming increasingly rare but had not disappeared completely. Echoes are apparent in the practices of field ethnomusicologists. Careful listening skills were necessary for the rigorous musical analysis that their work required. The researcher, however, did not need to posses them: he only needed a phonograph. The phonograph both increased and fulfilled standards of expertise.

This chapter's examination of the changing definition and value of musical expertise at the turn of the century illuminates the development of a new kind of listening, one in which the listener heard less. In his discussion of audification, Jonathan Sterne frames the introduction of recording and replay technology as an alienation of sound generation from the self.[54] This fits into a more general feature of modernity—the alienation of the individual from the self. I would add that we might think of the Edison demonstration recitals as an alienation of music from music. Again, the demonstrators emphasized fidelity of tone, not composition or recorded performance. They instructed listeners to notice how similar the phonograph sounded to real music, celebrated as re-creations. There was a separation of product from producer; in comparing recording to recorded artist, there was no charade that the recording was the recording artist. They were standing there next to each other, deliberately coordinated in their performances, and then uncoordinated. One was a wooden box.

The question remains whether this new form of listening was an ability not to hear but to ignore certain sounds, or to not hear said sounds at all. I would venture that listeners of the early twentieth century were increasingly unable to hear certain sounds. A quick survey of the letters to the Edison Company in 1915 and 1916 finds very few complaints about the noise of the new Diamond Disk phonograph.[55] Far more are overwhelmingly enthusiastic about the quality of the phonograph's sound. Certainly compared to earlier models of phonographs, victrolas, and gramophones, the Diamond Disk device and disks promoted through demonstration recitals had a much cleaner sound. It is possible that the noise generated went unnoticed.[56]

If this was the case, then it is an exception to other noise abatement narratives.[57] Now, the hiss of the phonograph needle was not necessarily a terribly intrusive sound, at least not when compared with the clanging of trains or the roar of a factory floor. But the separation of the listener from a direct experience of the generation of music— watching the violinist struggle to eliminate the scratching sounds of the bow or the vocalist serenely hit a high, clear note—made possible by the phonograph, eliminated many of the visual cues that might have reinforced the subtler sounds of a "live" performance. Scratches and hisses revealed something important about the skills of the performer. They had no meaning in the case of the phonograph whose quality, the demonstrator explained, was one of fidelity. The noise problem was eliminated in the case of the phonograph, not through the actual elimination of noise, but through the cultivation of a new kind of listening, which, physically separated from the original musical performance, could not hear noise.

## Notes

1. Portions of this chapter have previously appeared in print in the *Journal for the History of the Behavioral Sciences* 48, no. 3 (2012), published by Wiley-Blackwell; *Culture Unbound: Journal of Current Cultural Research* 4 (2012), published by the Linköping University Electronic Press; as well as my book, *The Psychophysical Ear: Musical Experiments, Experimental Sounds, 1840–1910* (Cambridge, MA, 2013), and I am grateful to the original publishers for kindly granting me permission to draw upon this earlier material of mine.
2. Psychophysics was a subdiscipline that developed as both a philosophical and experimental approach to the study of sensory perception. The basic assumption of psychophysics, developed from touch sensitivity studies in the 1840s by Gustav Fechner and Ernst Heinrich Weber, was that there was a direct (logarithmic, it turns out) relationship between physical stimulation and psychical sensation. This Fechner–Weber law allowed sense perception to then be quantified.
3. These were mostly new works and included virtually nothing composed prior to 1700. Such selectivity reflected Hanslick's belief in the historicity of musical compositions: "There is no art which, like music, uses up so quickly such a variety of forms. Modulations, cadences, intervals, and harmonious progressions become so hackneyed within fifty, nay, thirty years, that a truly original composer cannot well employ them any longer, and is thus compelled to think of a new musical phraseology. Of a great number of compositions which rose far above the trivialities of their day, it would be quite correct to say that there was a time when they were

beautiful." Eduard Hanslick, *The Beautiful in Music*, ed. Morris Weitz, trans. Gustav Cohen (New York, 1957), 58.

4. "To the question: What is to be expressed with all this material? the answer will be: Musical ideas. Now, a musical idea reproduced in its entirety is not only an object of intrinsic beauty but also an end in itself, and not a means for representing feelings and thoughts. The essence of music is sound and motion." Hanslick, *The Beautiful in Music*, 48.

5. There was also a parallel growing interest in the emotional experience of music during this period. See Hansjakob Ziemer's contribution to this volume.

6. "The number of those who thus listen to, or rather feel, music is very considerable. While in a state of passive receptivity, they suffer only what is elemental in music to affect them, and thus pass into a vague 'supersensible' excitement of the senses produced by the general drift of the composition. Their attitude toward music is not an observant but a pathological one. They are, as it were, in a state of waking dreaminess and lost in a sounding nullity; their minds are constant only the rack of suspense and expectancy." Hanslick, *The Beautiful in Music*, 89–90.

7. Ibid., 91.

8. Ibid., 99.

9. Musicologist Rose Subotnik argues that Hanslick's conception of aesthetic listening (the basis of what she calls "structural listening") assumed that the listener's mental framework was ideologically and culturally neutral, and required neither self-criticism nor awareness of individual or cultural biases. She sees the introduction of structural listening as central in the distancing of listeners—by condescendingly comparing other types of listening to drug intoxication, irrationality, etc.—from the sensuous experience of art music, an effect that is bound up with contemporary music today and contributing to its social irrelevance. Rose Subotnik, *Developing Variations: Style and Ideology in Western Music* (Minneapolis, 1991), 280–83.

10. Leon Botstein, "Time and Memory: Concert Life, Science, and Music in Brahms's Vienna," in *Brahms and his World*, ed. Walter Frisch (Princeton, 1990), 7.

11. Ibid.

12. Hanslick, "Ein Brief über die 'Clavierseuche,'" in *Suite. Aufsätze über Musik und Musiker* (Vienna, 1884).

13. Myles Jackson, "Physics, Machines, and Musical Pedagogy," in *Harmonious Triads: Physicists, Musicians, and Instrument Makers in Nineteenth-Century Germany* (Cambridge, 2006), 231–79; James Kennaway, "From Sensibility to Pathology: The Origins of the Idea of Nervous Music around 1800," *Journal of the History of Medicine and Allied Sciences* 65 (2012): 396–426.

14. See Friedrich Nietzsche, *Zur Genealogie der Moral: Eine Streitschrift* (Leipzig, 1887); *Der Fall Wagner* (Leipzig, 1888); *Nietzsche Contra Wagner: Aktenstücke eines Psychologen* (Leipzig, 1889); Max Nordau, *Dégénérescence* (Paris, 1894).

15. Alexandra Hui, "Instruments of Music, Instruments of Science: Hermann von Helmholtz's Sound Sensation Studies, his Classicism, and his

Beethoven Sonata," *Annals of Science* 68, no. 2 (2011): 149–77; Hui, *The Psychophysical Ear*.

16. Lorenz's data analysis suggested that observers usually selected the tone that corresponded with the arithmetic mean between the *Grenztöne* to be the middle tone. In the Western tuning system, the arithmetic mean only corresponded with a music interval in relation to the *Grenztöne* when the *Grenztöne* were two octaves apart. So, in tending to choose arithmetic intervals, the experimental subjects were not choosing musical intervals. Carl Lorenz, "Untersuchungen über die Auffassung von Tondistanzen," *Philosophische Studien* 6 (1890): 26–103.

17. Carl Stumpf, "Über Vergleichungen von Tondistanzen," *Zeitschrift für Psychologie und Physiologie der Sinnesorgane*, no. 1 (1890): 419–62.

18. Take A and B as the *Grenztöne* and C as the middle tone. Lorenz claimed that his data showed that C was the arithmetic mean, that is, C = (A+B)/2. Stumpf claimed that Lorenz's data showed that, in the case that the *Grenztöne* were a musical interval, C was the geometric mean, that is, C = $(AB)^{1/2}$.

19. Stumpf, "Über Vergleichungen von Tondistanzen," 433.

20. Ibid., 457.

21. Ibid., 456.

22. Wilhelm Wundt, "Ueber Vergleichungen von Tondistanzen," *Philosophische Studien* 6 (1891): 609, 632.

23. Carl Stumpf, "W. Wundt, Grundzüge der physiologischen Psychologie; E. Luft, Über die Unterschiedsempfindlichkeit für Tonhöhen," *Vierteljahrsschrift für Musikwissenschaft* 4 (1888): 540–50.

24. Carl Stumpf, "Wundts Antikritik," *Zeitschrift für Psychologie und Physiologie der Sinnesorgane*, no. 2 (1891): 276.

25. Carl Stumpf, "Autobiography of Carl Stumpf," in *History of Psychology in Autobiography*, vol. 1, ed. C. Murchison (Worcester, 1930), 396.

26. Wundt, "Ueber Vergleichungen von Tondistanzen," 616–17.

27. Ibid., 617.

28. Stumpf, *History of Psychology in Autobiography*, 401.

29. Edward Boring, "The Psychology of Controversy," *Psychological Review*, no. 36 (1929): 116–17.

30. Arnold Schoenberg, "Composition with Twelve Tones (I) (c.1941)," in *Style and Idea: Selected Writings of Arnold Schoenberg*, ed. Leonard Stein, trans. Leo Black (Berkeley, 1985).

31. "The Musical Scale is not one, not 'natural,' nor even founded necessarily on the laws of the constitution of musical sound, so beautifully worked out by Helmholtz, but very diverse, very artificial, and very capricious." Alexander Ellis, "On the Musical Scales of Various Nations," *Journal of the Society of Arts*, no. 33 (1885): 527.

32. Annegret Fauser, *Musical Encounters at the 1889 Paris World's Fair* (Rochester, 2005), 165–214.

33. Julie Brown, "Bartók, the Gypsies, and Hybridity in Music," in *Western Music and Its Others: Difference, Prepresentation, and Appropriation in Music*, eds. Georgina Born and David Hesmondhalgh (Berkeley, 2000).

34. Peter Payer, "The Age of Noise: Early Reactions in Vienna, 1870–1914," *Journal of Urban History*, no. 5 (2007): 773–93. See also Karin Bijsterveld, *Mechanical Sound: Technology, Culture, and Public Problems of Noise in the Twentieth Century* (Cambridge, 2008).
35. This phenomenon might be juxtaposed against the phenomenon of hearing loss among factory workers. See Karin Bijsterveld, "Listening to Machines: Industrial Noise, Hearing Loss and the Cultural Meaning of Sound," *Interdisciplinary Science Reviews* 31, no. 4 (2006): 323–37.
36. See Béla Bartók's discussion of the advantages of the phonograph and gramophone in ethnomusicological studies in the preface to Romanian Folk Songs from Bihor County, originally published in 1913, in Benjamin Suchoff, ed., *Béla Bartók: Studies in Ethnomusicology* (Lincoln, 1997); as well as "Why and How Do We Collect Folk Music?" and "Some Problems of Folk Music Research in East Europe," reprinted in Benjamin Suchoff, ed., *Béla Bartók Essays* (Lincoln, 1992).
37. Otto Abraham and Erich Moritz von Hornbostel, "Über die Bedeutung des Phonographen für vergleichende Musikwissenschaft," *Zeitschrift für Ethnologie* 36 (1904): 226–27.
38. Bartók, "Why and How Do We Collect Folk Music?," 14.
39. Bartók, "Some Problems of Folk Music Research in East Europe," 175.
40. Bartók, "Why and How Do We Collect Folk Music?," 14.
41. Ibid. He admitted that this might never be achieved.
42. I have discussed these demonstration recitals more extensively in my article, "Sound Objects and Sound Products: Creating a New Culture of Listening in the First Half of the Twentieth Century," *Culture Unbound: Journal of Current Cultural Research* 4 (2012): 599–616. See also Emily Thompson, "Machines, Music, and the Quest for Fidelity: Marketing the Edison Phonograph in America, 1877–1925," *The Musical Quarterly* 79, no. 1 (1995): 131–71.
43. Conversation with Leonard DeGraaf, Archivist, Thomas Edison National Historic Park, West Orange, New Jersey, 11 Aug. 2011.
44. Letters dated 4/10/1915, 4/16/1915, 4/22/1915, 5/4/1915, and 5/14/1915 from distributors to William Maxwell detailing their respective techniques of promoting the Edison instrument, Box 1, William Maxwell Files, Edison Historic Site Archives, Thomas Edison National Historic Park.
45. This sometimes led to friction between the demonstrators and the local distributors. Distributors would complain that the demonstrators would sweep into town and, unaware of local mores, would plan recitals in the wrong part of town or among the wrong kind of people, and in the process alienate actual prospective buyers. Letter dated 4/24/1915 to William Maxwell, Box 1, William Maxwell Files, Edison Historic Site Archives, Thomas Edison National Historic Park.
46. Bulletin (no. 43) to distributors, dated 4/1/1914, and letters dated 4/17/1915, 4/24/1915, and 4/30/1915, Box 1, William Maxwell Files, Edison Historic Site Archives, Thomas Edison National Historic Park.
47. A Frank Hildebrand, for example, gave a series of Lecture-Recitals in 1915 with such titles as "The Growth of Music", "Music and Life," and

"The Opera". Programs included in Box 1, William Maxwell Files, Edison Historic Site Archives, Thomas Edison National Historic Park.

48. Reports and letters, dated 4/21/1915, 4/22/1915, 4/26/1915, 5/4/1915, 5/6/1915, 5/16/1915, 6/6/1915, 6/21/1915, and 6/23/1915, Box 1, William Maxwell Files, Edison Historic Site Archives.

49. Comment on Recital At Woman's Club, dated 6/21/1915, Box 1, William Maxwell Files, Edison Historic Site Archives, Thomas Edison National Historic Park.

50. Greg Milner presents a nice discussion of several of these demonstration recitals in his book, *Perfecting Sound Forever: An Aural History of Recorded Music*. He finds the vocalists' manipulation of their voices' tone and volume to match the sounds of the phonograph as early evidence of a larger trend in which recording technology led the representation of and the real in music to collapse into one. Greg Milner, *Perfecting Sound Forever: An Aural History of Recorded Music* (New York, 2007). See also Thompson, "Machines."

51. "Mrs. Rouland also said that she didn't like very much the idea of Mr. Fuller [the demonstrator] acting as though the audience knew nothing whatsoever about music, and had to be told every point to look for in the records ... Mrs. Edison's [likely no relation to Thomas Edison] chief objection was that the whole thing seemed to be more mechanical than artistic. The machine was too much in evidence and the artistic part too much in the background. She thought Mr. Fuller's efforts to be funny did not get over very successfully." Comment on Recital At Woman's Club, dated 6/21/1915, Box 1, William Maxwell Files, Edison Historic Site Archives, Thomas Edison National Historic Park.

52. Re-Creations for the New Edison: "The Phonograph with a Soul" pamphlet, November 1919, Edison Companies, Primary Printed Material, Edison Historic Site Archives, Thomas Edison National Historic Park.

53. Their language of the pestilence of the rising middle class or arbitrariness of liberal democracy suggests a deep anxiety about the masses generally. It is worth noting, in light of the knowledge that this was a period of brittle socio-political stability, that both Hanslick and von Hornbostel were ethnically Jewish.

54. Jonathan Sterne, *The Audible Past: Cultural Origins of Sound Reproduction* (Durham, 2003).

55. I refer here to both the William Maxwell Files (box 1) and the Thomas Edison Files (boxes 22–25, 63 and 64 especially), held at the Edison National Historic Site Archives, Thomas Edison National Historic Park. Two letters to Maxwell (dated 4/26/1915 and 4/29/1915) included complaints about instrument noise. Several letters were written to Edison through the early 1920s complaining about instrument noise. Some included possible causes of the noise, and suggested solutions.

56. The noise did become noticeable toward the end of World War I, when disc quality worsened. War shortages required a change in the chemical process used to make the discs. Correspondence in both the William Maxwell Files and the Thomas Edison Files indicate that the Edison Laboratories knew of

the problem and scrambled both to find alternatives during the war and to return the discs to their pre-war quality once the chemicals became available again after the end of the war. Conversation with Leonard DeGraaf, Archivist, Thomas Edison National Historic Park, West Orange, New Jersey, 16 July 2013.

57. See Bijsterveld, *Mechanical Sound*; Emily Thompson, *The Soundscape of Modernity: Architectural Acoustics and the Culture of Listening in America, 1900–1933* (Cambridge, 2002).

# Bibliography

Abraham, Otto, and Erich Moritz von Hornbostel. "Über die Bedeutung des Phonographen für vergleichende Musikwissenschaft." *Zeitschrift für Ethnologie* 36 (1904): 222–36.

Bijsterveld, Karin. "Listening to Machines: Industrial Noise, Hearing Loss and the Cultural Meaning of Sound," *Interdisciplinary Science Reviews* 31, no. 4 (2006): 323–37.

———. *Mechanical Sound: Technology, Culture, and Public Problems of Noise in the Twentieth Century*. Cambridge, 2008.

Boring, Edward. "The Psychology of Controversy." *Psychological Review*, no. 36 (1929): 97–121.

Botstein, Leon. "Time and Memory: Concert Life, Science, and Music in Brahms's Vienna." In *Brahms and his World*, ed. Walter Frisch. Princeton, 1990, 3–25.

Brown, Julie. "Bartók, the Gypsies, and Hybridity in Music." In *Western Music and Its Others: Difference, Prepresentation, and Appropriation in Music*, eds. Georgina Born and David Hesmondhalgh. Berkeley, 2000, 119–42.

Ellis, Alexander. "On the Musical Scales of Various Nations." *Journal of the Society of Arts*, no. 33 (1885): 485–527.

Fauser, Annegret. *Musical Encounters at the 1889 Paris World's Fair*. Rochester, 2005.

Hanslick, Eduard. *Suite: Aufsätze über Musik und Musiker*. Vienna, 1884.

———. *The Beautiful in Music*, ed. Morris Weitz, trans. Gustav Cohen. New York, 1957.

Hui, Alexandra. "Instruments of Music, Instruments of Science: Hermann von Helmholtz's Sound Sensation Studies, his Classicism, and his Beethoven Sonata." *Annals of Science* 68, no. 2 (2011): 149–77.

———. "Sound Objects and Sound Products: Creating a New Culture of Listening in the First Half of the Twentieth Century." *Culture Unbound: Journal of Current Cultural Research* 4 (2012): 599–616.

———. *The Psychophysical Ear: Musical Experiments, Experimental Sounds, 1840–1910*. Cambridge, MA, 2013.

Jackson, Myles. "Physics, Machines, and Musical Pedagogy." In *Harmonious Triads: Physicists, Musicians, and Instrument Makers in Nineteenth-Century Germany*. Cambridge, 2006, 231–79.

Kennaway, James. "From Sensibility to Pathology: The Origins of the Idea of Nervous Music around 1800." *Journal of the History of Medicine and Allied Sciences* 65 (2012): 396–426.

Lorenz, Carl. "Untersuchungen über die Auffassung von Tondistanzen," *Philosophische Studien* 6 (1890): 26–103.

Milner, Greg. *Perfecting Sound Forever: An Aural History of Recorded Music*. New York, 2007.

Nietzsche, Friedrich. *Zur Genealogie der Moral: Eine Streitschrift*. Leipzig, 1887.

———. *Der Fall Wagner*. Leipzig, 1888.

———. *Nietzsche Contra Wagner: Aktenstücke eines Psychologen*. Leipzig, 1889.

Nordau, Max. *Dégénérescence*. Paris, 1894.

Payer, Peter. "The Age of Noise: Early Reactions in Vienna, 1870–1914." *Journal of Urban History* 33 (2007): 773–93.

Schoenberg, Arnold. "Composition with Twelve Tones (I) (c.1941)." In *Style and Idea: Selected Writings of Arnold Schoenberg*, ed. Leonard Stein, trans. Leo Black. Berkeley, 1985, 245–49.

Sterne, Jonathan. *The Audible Past: Cultural Origins of Sound Reproduction*. Durham, 2003.

Stumpf, Carl. "W. Wundt, Grundzüge der physiologischen Psychologie; E. Luft, Über die Unterschiedsempfindlichkeit für Tonhöhen." *Vierteljahrsschrift für Musikwissenschaft* 4 (1888): 540–50.

———. "Über Vergleichungen von Tondistanzen." *Zeitschrift für Psychologie und Physiologie der Sinnesorgane*, no. 1 (1890): 419–62.

———. "Wundts Antikritik." *Zeitschrift für Psychologie und Physiologie der Sinnesorgane*, no. 2 (1891): 266–93.

———. "Autobiography of Carl Stumpf." In *History of Psychology in Autobiography*, vol. 1. Ed. C. Murchison. Worcester, 1930, 389–441.

Subotnik, Rose. *Developing Variations: Style and Ideology in Western Music*. Minneapolis, 1991.

Suchoff, Benjamin, ed. *Béla Bartók Essays*. Lincoln, 1992.

———, ed. *Béla Bartók: Studies in Ethnomusicology*. Lincoln, 1997.

Thompson, Emily. "Machines, Music, and the Quest for Fidelity: Marketing the Edison Phonograph in America, 1877–1925." *The Musical Quarterly* 79 (1995): 131–71.

———. *The Soundscape of Modernity: Architectural Acoustics and the Culture of Listening in America, 1900–1933*. Cambridge, 2002.

Wundt, Wilhelm. *Grundzüge der physiologischen Psychologie*. Leipzig, 1887.

———. "Ueber Vergleichungen von Tondistanzen." *Philosophische Studien* 6 (1891): 605–40.

7

# THE INVENTION OF SILENCE
## Audience Behavior in Berlin and London in the Nineteenth Century
*Sven Oliver Müller*

In this chapter I will argue that the analysis of audience behavior calls for a historical approach. The reasons why talking, eating, and even fighting in the aisles ceased to be acceptable forms of behavior is a question that is significant not only for musicologists, but for historians as well. I suggest that we need a change of perspective, moving away from the study of musical works or the aesthetic debates on music to an investigation of the actual experiences and practices of participants.

To draw out the historical importance of music, I suggest substituting a works-based approach with an events-based one.[1] We know much more about scores, styles, aesthetic shifts, and the music of great, male—and, generally, dead—German composers than we know about the impact of musical practices upon the formation of the sociocultural sphere. Musical meaning is constituted less through the reproduction of a score than by the reception of performances and by the space provided for, and constituted through, the consumption of music. The primary problem to be investigated is whether it is the music or its entire performative context and the network of social relations that shapes audience behavior.

I will argue that the impact of opera and concert performance in the nineteenth century hinged less on its musical content and more on the power of the social relations of musical reception. This does not mean that the music itself does not count—quite the opposite. The reception of music by audiences provides a link between musical production and society. Only the interaction between musical and social factors can explain audience behavior and illuminate the production of historical meaning. One does not have to follow the radical constructivist approach of Ola Stockfelt and declare that "the listener, and only the listener, is the composer of the music,"[2] in order to acknowledge that musical meaning is not fixed. From the historian's point of view, it is crucial to acknowledge that especially audiences make music meaningful and relevant.[3]

Musical performances in Europe have changed since 1830 in particular. The development of common practices and a common market allows not only the investigation of patterns of musical production, but the analysis of genres, practices, and styles from the perspective of the consumers whose cultural demands conducted the transfer of music. The change of these demands and the transformation of tastes and fashions can only be investigated by focusing on the various local adaptations of musical works across modern Europe. Mid-nineteenth-century Europe witnessed an extraordinary rise in cultural exchange between various metropolises and cultural centers, and the development of new repertoires and audiences—a so-called "modern musical culture." This time frame is chosen on the basis of perceptions of Europe within musical history, since important developments show this to be a period within which cultural modernity was formulated and common practices and tastes were appropriated.

This opens up a new perspective for examining spatial dimensions, social dynamics, and inner conflicts. This chapter will draw attention to the sites in which to investigate the social functions of "serious music": opera houses and concert halls. Musical performances were an integral part of the leisure time of the aristocracy and the bourgeoisie. Therefore opera houses and concert halls are the ideal places to analyze the social order and cultural manners of an audience. Here, I take Berlin and London as my focus, but I suggest that the findings of these two case studies would apply equally to the audience cultures of other European cities as well.

The first section deals with changes in cultural practices and the new evaluation of musical taste in nineteenth-century Berlin. It will demonstrate how a more or less inattentive audience became "listeners" during this period. Public acts of listening strategies and self-discipline during performances were used for the identification and the demarcation of social groups. Some of the questions of the first part are: Who were the people attending the performances? Why did the behavior of audiences in Germany change so dramatically in the nineteenth century? Why did people stop talking, drinking, and eating during performances and become silent? The second part of this article focuses on the transfer of manners, and analyzes how the continental habit of silent listening eventually spread to Britain as well. Although music can be regarded as the ideal vehicle for successful and harmonious transfer, I will emphasize that getting to know each other and learning about each other's music and manners can sometimes also involve conflict and hatred.

## Social Distinctions: Disciplining Audiences in Berlin

Opera houses and concert halls constituted one of the most important social spheres of the nineteenth century. The auditoriums became meeting places where high- and lowbrow audiences, men and women, different classes, confessions, and political groups interacted. Although opera houses and concert halls were in fact highly segregated places of social inequality, they were in theory accessible to anyone willing (or able) to purchase a ticket. It will be shown that the audience was regulated by certain social, cultural, and financial restrictions. Seating arrangements, clothes, codes of behavior, and often even the ability and the permission to buy tickets, divided music lovers. Because of that, musical performance facilitates detailed study of the development of classes, social inequality, and the formation of tastes. Here, the aristocracy and the middle classes, men and women, do not appear as abstract constructions or isolated objects, but as groups and individuals acting in a defined social space. The public musical event temporarily illuminated the invisible power structure of the European societies of the 1800s.[4]

The characteristic features of opera and concert-going revolved around a matter of "seeing and being seen." This is not just a modern, but also a contemporary, phrase. True, the music itself was important, but it was only part of a package that also included social contacts, sophisticated conversation, a good meal, and contact with the opposite sex. The dress worn by opera audiences was highly formalized, and participation took place within the habitual boundaries of established conventions. Appropriately, up to the second half of the century, the lights were not dimmed in the auditorium during performances. That would have diminished the social function of mutual observation. Although petty bourgeois audiences had, to some extent, access to state opera and high-class concerts, both of these places remained strongholds of elite culture. It could even be argued that audiences attended certain musical performances because they wanted to emphasize and publicly display their social position. Opera houses and concert halls offered the attraction of social exclusivity, hand in hand with the possibility of interacting with other elites. In spite of their fierce political and economical struggles, members of the aristocracy and the bourgeoisie found themselves united in the public consumption of high-class music. In 1901 the *Illustrirte Zeitung* regarded the contacts between the two classes in the Royal Opera in Berlin as a form of successful social adjustment: "Nothing unites more swiftly than common practices and common interests."[5]

According to Pierre Bourdieu, no social practice has a stronger classifying effect, or expresses and shapes the patterns of behavior of a social group more strongly, than the public consumption of music. With the increase in opera and concert attendance and the rise of musical activity by amateurs, music gradually became an important public affair. The appreciation of high-class music was not only the expression of a certain lifestyle; it was also a mark of social distinction. The splendid self-display of the audiences and above all the knowledge about music, singers, composers, and styles—these were important power resources.[6] For the aristocracy and the middle classes, both men and women alike, attending musical performances served to identify them as people of good taste and social importance. This allowed the initiated to differentiate between those who belonged to the elites and those who did not.[7] The social impact of these patterns of distinction was quite remarkable. Noble elites, for instance, sought to legitimize their privileges with reference to their cultural, and thereby moral, superiority. Simultaneously, the rising middle class tried to imitate and to adopt cultural conventions and certain modes of behavior, because they were crucial for the acquisition of social privileges and the enforcement of social distinction.[8] Thus, in the framework of social conventions, the public appropriation and evaluation of music had a dual function in metropolitan societies during the nineteenth century. On one hand, it confirmed social identity through habitualized social practice; on the other hand, it reflected a taste for art displayed in public, which served as a means of distinction. All this aimed to maintain boundaries and distances within society, and allowed one to label oneself as an individual or as part of a social group.

Architecture and audiences had reciprocal effects on each other. The grand ceremonial design of opera houses and concert halls imposed certain social codes on visitors and increased theatrical behavior and self-representation.[9] The audiences divided musical spaces into different social spheres: they entered the auditorium by separate entrances, remained in separate areas during the performances, and even spent the intervals in separate foyers. In the way in which the social classes celebrated the art event, both the bourgeois and the aristocratic audiences paid meticulous attention to closing themselves off from each other, but also from the petty bourgeoisie and the working class. Although the London King's Theatre and Berlin Royal

Opera did not physically segregate aristocracy and middle classes, as the Vienna Opera did, opera-going remained, especially in London, a matter of class distinction. The management of the opera houses emphasized the social function of this establishment by publishing a list of every subscriber and the box or seats taken by them. Because of this, everybody knew who was "a part of the club," and who was not. It was easy to spot people at the center and on the peripheries, and those who liked or disliked each other. The plan of the theater helped to make sense of the social maze of opera-going.[10]

Emphasizing the social function of opera-going does not necessarily mean that the audience behaved according to the common rules, or that everything always went well for the elites. Contemporary reports and articles tend to present a different picture. When, for instance, the management of an opera business ran out of funds—and this happened quite frequently—the social status of the audiences tended to decline as well. Members of the elite did not want to associate with badly dressed individuals, as a report on a performance of Rossini's *La Donna del Lago* in 1829 revealed:

> The Performance of *La Donna del Lago* was quite ... disgraceful to the Establishment. ... Whether the manager fills the pit of the Opera with orders, or not, we cannot say: but we never saw such a collection of odd looking and ill dressed people assembled together ... Vulgar looking men in old black stocks, dirty neck cloths, muddy boots, drab trousers, yellow waistcoats, and greasy *casquettes*, and a mob of ill-dressed and dowdy women, fill the pit nightly, after they have squeezed themselves into it by means of shoving, elbowing, oaths and blows. This should really be reformed. If the Opera-house once loses its aristocratic character, its occupation is gone. Fashionable people will not sit in an atmosphere of orange-peel and city-dust, or be squeezed between a fat citizen and his apprentice or shop man, or a female dealer in tallow candles from the Borough, who has engaged to *chaperon* a tribe of milliners.[11]

The behavior of concert and opera audiences changed fundamentally during the nineteenth century. The most noticeable shift took place in the public assessment and consumption of music. Above all else, people began to listen more closely during performances. They concentrated quietly on the music. Although the process of learning to listen marked a decisive cultural shift, and although it took place all over Europe, we still know very little about the nature of this development. Why did people start to concentrate on the music? Why did the practices of listening develop more or less in the same direction (although with certain delays) in different European countries? Whereas, from the 1830s onwards, concert and opera audiences on the Continent in general, and in Germany and France in particular, learned to listen quietly to music and tried to avoid unnecessary talk and movement, matters were quite different in Britain until the last third of the same century.[12] Analyzing the evolution in musical practices and musical tastes helps to reveal the emergence of new cultural values and mentalities of the audience in a transnational context.

Contradictory public assessments about the relation of opera and concert performances in the musical culture of the time can be observed. On the one hand, both institutions were crucial for the development of musical life in nineteenth-century Europe; on the other hand, the differences are important as well. We have to distinguish the traditional social representation in opera houses—remains of the fashionable aristocratic culture—from the new taste politics of middle-class elites in concert halls. In the view of German members of the educated classes, it was the distinction between the audience behavior in opera houses and concert halls that was lamentable. The German educated elites did not attach an imminent or functional quality to music, but rather a transcendental one. Music contained the promise of new horizons, a new orientation, and individual experience that could give life meaning. At this point the influence of the new bourgeois "religion of art,"[13] which increasingly regarded a piece of music as a valuable "opus" as opposed to an entertaining ornament, made itself felt. Music was not simply to be enjoyed—it was to be comprehended and to provide edification. Therefore, concert halls and the "absolute music" performed in them were regarded as semi-sacral spaces—spaces to be protected from conventional desecration.[14]

Today's patron of a typical classical musical event would probably feel ill at ease with the audience behavior at an early nineteenth-century performance. Until well into the second half of the century, behavior in European concert halls and opera houses was more like that at a soccer match. While the music was being played, people would talk to one another (both quietly and loudly), eat and drink, call upon the boxes of other patrons, and promenade in the hall. The visitors were not totally inattentive; they simply concentrated—rather selectively—on certain brilliant achievements of the artists and the "beautiful" passages of a musical score. At such moments, however, the audience participated extremely noisily in the event, applauding or booing in the middle of a piece or an aria. Often the performances dragged on considerably, because single movements or arias had to be repeated, sometimes even several times, in response to the demands of the audience. Moreover, it was quite common that noble patrons who were unable to find a place in the auditorium were allocated seats on the stage itself. Indeed, these were highly sought after places. Therefore, from a certain point of view, there was little distinction between the artists and the observers. Both parties shaped the character of an evening so that it was often unclear whether the more interesting performance took place on the stage or in the auditorium.

This interaction between artists and audiences can be illustrated by examining the behavior of the audience of the Royal Berlin Opera. In 1818, after the bass singer, Josef Fischer, had complained about the audience's lack of enthusiasm during previous performances, a number of patrons apparently decided to teach him a rather public lesson. As the *Haude- und Spenersche Zeitung* reported:

> 1st Scene: ... (Fischer, playing the cobbler "Geloso") is sitting next to his table and working on a shoe. ... Suddenly a tremendous noise from all parts of the crowded house was heard. ... A clapping like from one hundred giants and a hiss like from a thousand rattlesnakes arose toward the sky. ... Finally Geloso moved and he and the orchestra started to make music, but—not a single tone was audible. ... One, two, three times Herr Fischer and the orchestra tried to recommence—in vain. ... Only for a brief moment the clapping and the shouting of "bravo" seemed to prevail and Herr Fischer bowed to the audience, but eventually the noisy flood only became louder. Curtain. "Apologize!" "On your knees!" "Off you go!" People shouted from all parts of the auditorium and those patrons clapping, shouting "bravo" and asking for silence were finally beaten. ... 2nd Scene: The audience alone and amusing itself with swearwords of all kinds, many crying "da capo." 3rd Scene: (Herr Maurer and the audience). Herr Maurer (barely audible): "Nevertheless, Herr Fischer is anxious now to sing—if the audience wishes him to continue. A hundred voices—"No! No No!" A few voices—"Yes! Yes! Yes!" ... 4th Scene: (Herr Devrient and the audience). The audience continued clapping and shouting "bravo." Herr Devrient (with a shrug of his shoulders and a smile): "Because Herr Fischer is unable to sing, the performance is finished!" Then he left the stage. The audience applauded, shouted "bravo"—and went home.[15]

Modes of behavior began to change simultaneously in the German states and in Vienna and Paris after 1830. A new silence emerged in the auditorium as audiences gradually ceased to express themselves. The listeners silently paid attention to the music, restricting unruly expressions of satisfaction or dissatisfaction, and ceasing communication with the artists. This newly developed practice originated in concerts of serious music and gradually found its way into the operatic world as well—not least as a result of the international success of Richard Wagner's musical dramas, as we will see. Noteworthy among the reasons for this development is the massive expansion of opera and concert performances during this period, as well as the enhanced seating capacity provided by nineteenth-century musical theaters. Because of this, and alongside the growing commercialization of musical performances, audiences became increasingly heterogeneous, and patrons became less likely to be acquainted with one other. This new anonymity hindered public communication and discouraged moving about the auditorium. Of equal importance was the growing influence of a new aesthetic ideal promoted by music critics and musical periodicals. The educated middle classes (*Bildungsbürgertum*) began to attach a transcendental quality to music; it was to lend meaning to life. Instrumental "absolute" music, which had been considered the lowest form of art, was elevated, thanks to its "ephemeral" quality, to the highest form of art.

This new evaluation of taste and of public self-restriction can usefully be described, following Norbert Elias, as a "process of civilization."[16] With regard to early modern Europe, Elias has rightly emphasized the growing impact of individual self-control and the decline of spontaneous expressions of affects and emotions in public as a form of mutual coercion. This development was by no means the achievement of a single class or group but resulted from the interaction between them in the social sphere. Opera houses and concert halls fulfilled the function of social spheres, where elites and lower ranks increasingly became dependent on observing, and being much more self-aware of, their social habits. Mutual perception in the auditorium triggered feelings of shame, and gradually stimulated a new, disciplined appreciation of music. While the contrast in individual behavior became more muted, the sensibility for refinements in tastes, gestures, and behaviors deepened. Learning to listen quietly meant, therefore, observing the bourgeois ideal of self-discipline.

Toward the middle of the nineteenth century, musical journals were full of articles addressing the question of when and how to applaud and when to remain silent. The repeated complaints about "misbehavior" revealed not only the gradual change in habitual manners and cultural morals, but also the persistence of traditional forms of behavior. When the Berlin critic, Ludwig Rellstab, who had evidently been able to acquire a notoriously scarce ticket, complained in 1844 about the unbound enthusiasm of the audiences during Jenny Lind's performance of "Norma," his verdict did not remain unchallenged. Although Rellstab emphatically praised Lind's interpretation of "Casta Diva," he added: "The singer accomplished something outstanding here. Her aria was demanded *da capo*, and the artist was loudly acclaimed and shouted at in the midst of the act. We trust that this barbarity of applause, which destroys the dramatic context of a musical work, will soon be terminated for good."[17] But this notion of disciplined self-restriction was by no means a matter of common consensus. A few days later an angry reader of this article replied to the same newspaper, emphasizing the importance of spontaneous musical ardor: "The critic of this newspaper called the public acclamation during the performance an act of barbarity of applause, instead of regarding it as the purest outpouring of enthusiasm and well-earned gratitude—particularly because the performance was not at all disturbed by the applause."[18]

European concert halls and opera houses witnessed this competition between different tastes and modes of behavior—not a one-sided process of imposition and imitation of a "modern" listening practice—into the 1870s. There was a bilateral negotiation process among different "taste publics."[19] In fact, as William Weber has demonstrated, different social groups formed around currents of tastes and practices of certain preferences and dislikes. Middle class and aristocratic, high- and lowbrow values and tastes interacted contentiously in the social arena of the auditorium and gradually began to shape the new behavior of audiences.[20] The history of listening can be read as an excellent case study of an interaction between "elite" and "popular" manners, because the barrier between popular and elevated forms of entertainment and taste were originally very low, and the two were often difficult to distinguish.[21]

The importance of listening in silence as an aesthetic expression of the middle classes remained, therefore, an object of bitter cultural controversy for the best part of the nineteenth century. When, for instance, the famous conductor and pianist, Hans von Bülow, admonished a vociferous audience in 1859 during a concert at the Berlin Singakademie, he caused quite a scandal. After he had conducted Franz Liszt's symphonic poem, "The Ideal," he received a hostile reception: "Only some applause was heard accompanied by some marks of disapprobation, though not in the mode of an explicit demonstration. In spite of that the conductor reprimanded the patrons, requested that the dissatisfied should leave the hall and shouted … 'I beg the noisy gentlemen to leave the auditorium, that behavior is inappropriate here.'"[22] Bülow's words caused much talk and outrage in Berlin society in the days that followed. The press commentary on the incident was mixed in tone. While some journals underlined the legitimacy of Bülow's admonition, others, like a writer in the *Haude-Spenersche Zeitung*, stated that "in a concert, restrained marks of disapproval have the same right as applause." And one critic openly asked "whether a common piano player may provoke the audience in such a way."[23]

## The Transfer of Manners: Learning to Listen in London

The development of public codes of behavior simultaneously reflected and created changes in cultural values. An analysis of changes in musical practices and tastes reveals the social norms and mentalities of the audience. The question arises as to why people started to concentrate on the music, and why listening practices in different European countries developed in more or less the same direction. Why did the German states and Austria lead the way, while Britain only followed later? Was there a relationship between certain types of music and certain effects?

As previously mentioned, while concert and opera audiences on the Continent in general, and in France and Germany in particular, learned to listen to music quietly from the 1830s on, avoiding unnecessary talk and movement, matters were quite different in Britain until the last third of the nineteenth century.[24] When in London, German musicians, critics, and journalists were often disagreeably struck by the primarily social function of "serious music," which was just seen as an entertainment. The Italian opera in particular, as Eduard Hanslick observed sternly, was the favorite of "the vogue, the fashion of the day, this most powerful tyrant of London society."[25] Hanslick went on to complain:

> There is a strange restriction of personal freedom in the theater and concert life here: the explicit regulation of evening dress. For the Italian opera, this fashion rendezvous of the wealthy and elegant, the childish rule, "evening dress indispensable," may still be tolerable. Yet who gives anybody the right to dictate—and without any exception, mind you—a tuxedo and white cravat to a music lover who wants to attend a Philharmonic concert at his own cost? This idea forces the impertinent question from our lips of whether, in truth, it can be a musical nation that complicates and spoils delight in one of Beethoven's symphonies by a ridiculous dress code?[26]

Another lamentable example of British "superficiality" and "lack of appreciation" of art was observed in 1914 by Oscar Schmitz who noted the Londoners' admiration for the performances of top-notch musicians. Unlike in Germany, he thought, it was not sincerity of feeling, but admiration for circus-like accomplishments that made people flock to the concert halls in London: "Englishmen find an access to music not via the heart, but by sport and the church. They appreciate that it takes a lot to play a difficult concerto and they turn up when those who are currently regarded as the 'champions' of this sport appear on stage."[27]

Time and again, German journalists and musicians contrasted appropriate listening behavior (that is, their own silent and concentrated listening) with the garrulous and hedonistic behavior of British audiences during a concert. They had the impression that the art of music was but a triviality for the London elites; the audience did not follow the music in a focused way, they pointed out, and were even asleep at times. However, things could be even worse in London. In March 1886 the *Vossische Zeitung* commented in a somewhat irritable tone that a strike had disrupted the performance in one of London's most famous theaters; the temple of music had been profaned by a labor dispute:

> Gounod's *Faust* could not be continued in Her Majesty's Theater because the members of the choir and the stagehands had not received their wages and went on strike. When the performance was about to be drowned in a wild commotion, they lined up in front of the apron and begged the audience for alms to satisfy their hunger. Many people think that this outrageous scandal has buried the Italian opera in London for good.[28]

These German assessments were more or less correct. Businessmen discussed their commercial concerns, women presented the latest fashions, and courtesans tried to attract the attention of potential lovers. However, the audience usually took an extremely lively part in the event, applauding or booing each piece of music or aria, and might be repeated once or even several times in response to audience demand. It could, therefore, be argued that both artists and observers shaped the character of a performance.

However, there were also a number of British critics of this behavior. Toward the end of the nineteenth century music journals were full of articles discussing how and when to applaud, and when to remain silent:

> Some severe penalty—say fourteen days' imprisonment without the option of a fine—should be inflicted on those gentlemen who insist on bursting out in the middle of a song or an instrumental solo with the strident shout of 'Bra! Bra!' the second syllable being quite inaudible. This peculiar noise, though ostensibly intended to express delight, is much more suggestive of the wrath or indignation of an infuriated gorilla.[29]

Repeated complaints revealed not only a gradual change in habitual manners and cultural morals, but also the persistence of traditional forms of behavior. According to Lawrence Levine's *Highbrow/Lowbrow*, the history of the behavior of English audiences can be read as an excellent case study of interaction between "elite" and "popular" manners. With regard to the United States, Levine argues, the barrier between popular and elevated forms of entertainment and taste was extremely low for much of the nineteenth century, and the two were often difficult to distinguish.[30] A somewhat irritated reader of *Musical World* noticed this simultaneity, and reported on a Wagner night at Covent Garden Opera:

> It is a frequent source of annoyance to hear individuals applauding with more enthusiasm than discretion at inopportune times, generally immediately after the last note of anything sung that pleases them, thus drowning the finishing bars to be played by the orchestra. ... Last night, at the *finale* of the first act of *Tannhäuser*, the "gods", as usual, began to applaud before the singing had ceased, and a little sensation was created by a gentleman resenting their bad taste (though in somewhat noisy manner) by shouting "Order!!!" in stentorian tones, and afterwards (when the band had finished) calling out "Now!!!" setting the example by then clapping vigorously. Cannot Mr Gye set up a signal post of some kind to teach people when to be quiet and when to give vent to their enthusiasm?[31]

The German example led the way in Britain. In Germany, music was held to be a higher "counter-world" or, according to Schopenhauer, a matrix of the real world, a key to the soul and to happiness. The very concept of music held by the German middle classes, the social assessment of serious music as a quasi-holy achievement of mankind, created new cultural images that spread all over Europe. Learning from Germany, therefore, for many educated Britons meant an improvement in taste and manners, though occasionally this could be uncomfortable, as the *Morning Post* observed: "The British, unlike the Germans, have never become accustomed to long sittings, to continual concentration of [the] mind on the drama or opera."[32] But in Edwardian England the silent and concentrated reception of music eventually became widely accepted. Only occasionally, when superstars such as Enrico Caruso performed, did audiences give way to uncontrolled enthusiasm: "once the audience broke through the custom borrowed from Germany of observing silence until the end of the act, and greeted Signor Caruso when he made his appearance with drum and cart."[33]

It took a long time for people to become accustomed to silence during performances. Until the turn of the century a part of the English elite still lamented the lack of principles in the listening behavior of the bourgeoisie in contemporary musical life. From this new educated perspective, English audiences seemed to lack a true understanding of music and had to be taught better manners. Enjoyment was to be replaced by understanding. The new habit that was required fully to appreciate the deeper values of music was silent listening. In an ideal-typical view, the medium of art music closely corresponded to the cosmos of values held by the aspiring middle classes, and the harmony of music reflected the ideal of societal concord. The middle classes could recognize their principles of order in the repetitious structures of music. "Correct" behavior in public during performances was therefore more than the expression of good taste; it was a form of social promotion. The rising middle classes made themselves visible in their public demonstration of allegedly superior manners.[34]

The British reception of Richard Wagner's musical dramas apparently played a central part in the development of this new behavior. For decades, English critics and audiences had been haunted by the specter of Wagner, and it was not until the 1890s that his works became broadly accepted. But then the change was almost complete. What was more, English critics not only urged native composers to look to Wagner's music for inspiration, but his operas themselves seemed to have a lasting impact on the behavior of English audiences. As early as 1882, when the first *Ring des Nibelungen* was performed in London, audiences were obviously not only impressed, but spellbound by the music, as a somewhat puzzled report in the *Morning Post* demonstrated:

> The Prince of Wales and the Duke of Edinburgh were present at the beginning and remained to the end. … All applause was checked during the progress, to be allowed full expression at the end of the scenes. Everything seemed new and fascinating. When, after the prelude, the curtain rose and discovered the beautiful scene of the bottom of the river, with the Nixies or Rhine maidens floating in the flood, a murmur of approval was heard from the audience, but nothing more, for all seemed intent upon observing the course of the story.[35]

Ten years later the *Illustrated London News* noted the familiar concentrated attention, reinforced by a darkened auditorium, during a performance of *Siegfried* at Covent Garden:

> The house was crowded, and the representation was followed throughout with the same intense earnestness and absorbing interest that have invariably characterised the attitude of previous audiences at similar Wagnerian performances. All lights in the house were extinguished whilst the music was in progress, and such perfect silence was kept that at the rare moments when a pause occurred, the proverbial pin might have been heard to drop.[36]

There were various reasons for transfer of the new silence amongst European audiences in the second half of the nineteenth century: although one cannot overlook the importance of the self-discipline among the middle classes, one should also take into account the influence of certain musical works and styles. The argument seems self-evident and even somewhat trivial: the musical dramas of Richard Wagner apparently had a similar effect in the opera houses as the symphonies of Ludwig van Beethoven had in the concert halls.[37] Wagner himself did all he could to promote the silent habits of concert audiences in the operatic realm. It goes without saying that the semi-sacral cult of the "Meister" of Bayreuth also stimulated a reverent reception of Richard Wagner's works.[38] But the cultural importance of his highly original music can hardly be overestimated. Apart from the outstanding dramatic quality of Wagner's operas and the absorbing storyline, the constant flow of music does not leave any space for the inappropriate expression of noisy enthusiasm, as is often the case in the much shorter arias of earlier operas. Wagner's audiences were thus hardly able to escape his music, for his music never ended. The darkening of the auditorium lights during performances also signifi-cantly aided the general concentration of audiences and increased the self-restraint of those who attended.

Therefore, the performance of Wagner helped to transform behavior and educate the public in middle-class values. In 1902 the *Musical Times* was firmly convinced of the impact of Wagner's dramas:

> The necessity of educating audiences—of making good listeners—has often been the subject of comment. … If only the people who go to concerts went to hear the music, I make little doubt but that the methods of Bayreuth would, by common consent, be largely imitated in our concert-rooms, for they are all devised with a view to concentrating attention upon the performance. Perfect quiet so long as a composition is in progress, and an auditorium sufficiently darkened to prevent one's being distracted by the appearance and movements of one's neighbours; these are attained at Bayreuth, and in many other theatres where Bayreuth is being more or less sincerely flattered by imitation.[39]

The successful transfer of cultural norms and practices between the major European capitals epitomizes the emergence of a common European culture of music. It was by no means a natural phenomenon, which meant that by the latter part of the century, a German bourgeois and an English aristocrat exhibited similar behavior during a concert, and that they cultivated similar aesthetic preferences. The new habit required a full appreciation of the "deeper values" of music by listening in silence. In an ideal-typical manner, the medium of art music closely corresponded to the cosmos of values of the aspiring middle classes, and the harmony of music concurred with the ideal of societal concord. In the structure of musical rituals and in the repetitious structure of the music itself, the middle classes could recognize their notions of order.

A "correct" and self-restrained behavior in public during performances was therefore more than the expression of good taste; it was a form of social self-promotion. The rising middle classes made themselves visible by their public demonstration of allegedly superior manners.[40]

## Concluding Remarks

Opera- and concert-going can be understood as a public self-production of political and cultural relations. It is absolutely misleading to regard the public representation of culture as merely a superficial staging, or a delusion. What counts is that there are no fixed social relations or political issues before the collective actors construct them by means of communication. People have to create differences in order to be influenced by them. Any cultural phenomenon, and especially something as highly valued as serious music, can become an important social issue if the collective actors deliberately decide to make it one. That is why the categories in which British and German critics, musicians, and journalists perceived the musical scene of their time were highly selective. These perceptions and ascriptions, which did not necessarily always correspond to "facts," reveal the values and images of the world shared by members of the educated classes in both countries. Therefore these patterns of interpretation cannot be considered as doing any noticeable service to the reconstruction of musical life or cultural transfer. Rather, they are revealing with regard to the aesthetic and nationalist ideals of their creators.

If we weigh up the mutual evaluation and influence of the German and British music cultures, we can observe the emergence of an international style of musical values and musical practices. In both countries, the productions of opera houses and the repertoires of concert halls became increasingly similar. Even the decor and staging followed common aesthetic values and customs. At the turn of the twentieth century, singers, directors, conductors, and composers traveled frequently between the two countries and exchanged concepts and tastes. The importance of traditional centers of musical culture in France and Italy were gradually challenged by the rising metropolises of London and Berlin. The mutual appreciation of absolute music in particular reflects the impact of the German–British cultural transfers. Even if German and British musicians stubbornly insisted on their national differences, the nationalist elevation of art music in Britain can be comprehended as a successful transfer. Around 1900, serious music was no longer considered a foreign commodity imported into London. Moreover, with the help of their contacts in Berlin and Leipzig, many London musicians had transferred particular musical values and forms of behavior developed in Germany to their own art scene. It was by no means a natural phenomenon that at the beginning of the twentieth century a German bourgeois and an English aristocrat behaved in the same way during a concert and cultivated similar aesthetic preferences. The transfer of cultural norms between Germany and Britain—above all the habit of silent listening and the elevation of absolute music—epitomizes the emergence of a common European culture of music. German–English communication about music, therefore, can be understood as an integral part of an emerging European elite culture that referred to common cultural institutions, ideals, and practices.[41]

## Notes

1. This is regularly called for, but is seldom accomplished. Cf. Richard Taruskin, *Text and Act: Essays on Music and Performance* (New York, 1995); Nicholas Cook, "Music as Performance," in *The Cultural Study of Music: A Critical Introduction*, eds. Martin Clayton, Trevor Herbert, and Richard Middleton (New York, 2003), 204–14; William Weber, *Music and the Middle Class: Social Structure of Concert Life in London, Paris and Vienna* (London, 1975), 144–45; David Gramit, *Cultivating Music: The Aspirations, Interests, and Limits of German Musical Culture, 1770–1848* (Berkeley, 2002), 164–65.

2. Ola Stockfelt, quoted in: Ruth Finnegan, "Music, Experience, and the Anthropology of Emotion," in *The Cultural Study of Music*, eds. Martin Clayton, Trevor Herbert, and Richard Middleton (New York, 2003), 181–92, here 184.

3. Cf. Susan Bennett, *Theatre Audiences: A Theory of Production and Reception* (London, 1990); Christopher Small, *Musicking: The Meanings of Performing and Listening* (Middleton, CT, 1998). Among the various scholars highlighting the importance of the analysis of receptions are Hermann Danuser and Friedrich Krummacher, eds., *Rezeptionsästhetik und Rezeptionsgeschichte in der Musikwissenschaft* (Laaber, 1991); Hans-Joachim Hinrichsen, "Musikwissenschaft: Musik—Interpretation—Wissenschaft," *Archiv für Muskwissenschaft* 57 (2000): 78–101; Martyn Thompson, "Reception Theory and the Interpretation of Historical Meaning," *History and Theory* 32 (1993): 248–72; Wolfgang Kemp, ed., *Der Betrachter ist im Bild: Kunstwissenschaft und Rezeptionsästhetik* (Berlin, 1992).

4. Cf. James H. Johnson, *Listening in Paris: A Cultural Study* (Berkeley, 1995), 9–34. The debate about the methodological and empirical impact of Johnson's book is continuing. Quite a few scholars complain that Johnson's focus is directed solely on Paris and demand an international comparison.

Cf. John M. Picker, *Victorian Soundscapes* (Oxford, 2003); William Weber, *The Great Transformation of Musical Taste: Concert Programming from Haydn to Brahms* (Cambridge, 2008). The book by Colin Lawson and Robin Stowell, *The Historical Performance of Music* (Cambridge, 1999), offers an overview of historical performance, surveying the various current issues (including the influence of recording) and examining the impact of the period performer's myriad primary source materials.

5. "Nichts eint bekanntlich Menschen schneller und nachhaltiger als gemeinsame Interessen." *Illustrirte Zeitung*, 28 March 1901, 471–74.
6. Pierre Bourdieu, *Distinction: A Social Critique of the Judgment of the Taste* (London, 1986); Cf. Ivo Supicic, *Music in Society: A Guide to the Sociology of Music* (New York, 1987), esp. 141–68.
7. Cf. Richard Sennet, *The Fall of the Public Man* (London, 1977); idem., *The Conscience of the Eye: The Design and Social Life of Cities* (London, 1993).
8. Cf. Rudolf Braun and David Gugerli, *Macht des Tanzes–Tanz der Mächtigen: Hoffeste und Herrschaftszeremoniell 1550–1914* (Munich, 1993), 166–202.
9. Cf. Bennett, *Theatre Audiences*, 133–47; Small, *Musicking*,19–29.
10. Cf. *The Morning Post*, 8 June 1844.
11. The British Library, Haymarket Theatre (HM) Cuttings from Newspapers, 1807–29, Bl. Th.Cts. 43, 8. June 1829.
12. Cf. Picker, *Victorian Soundscapes*; Johnson, *Listening in Paris*; Jennifer Hall-Witt, "Representing the Audiences in the Age of Reform: Critics and the Elite at the Italian Opera in London," in Christina Bashford and Leanne Langley, eds., *Music and British Culture, 1785–1914: Essays in Honour of Cyril Ehrlich* (Oxford, 2000), 121–44; Steven Huebner, "Opera Audiences in Paris 1830–1870," *Music and Letters* 70 (1989): 206–25; William Weber, "Did People Listen in the 18th Century?" *Early Music* 25 (1997): 678–91; Christina Bashford, "Learning to Listen: Audiences for Chamber Music in Early-Victorian London," *Journal of Victorian Culture* 4 (1999): 25–51; Sven Oliver Müller, *Das Publikum macht die Musik: Musikleben in Berlin, London und Wien im 19. Jahrhundert* (Göttingen, 2014).
13. Thomas Nipperdey, "'Bürgerlich' als Kultur," in Jürgen Kocka, ed., *Bürger und Bürgerlichkeit im 19. Jahrhundert* (Göttingen, 1987), 143–48.
14. Cf. Bernd Sponheuer, *Musik als Kunst und Nicht-Kunst: Untersuchungen zur Dichotomie von "hoher" und "niederer" Kunst im musikästhetischen Denken zwischen Kant und Hanslick* (Kassel, 1987); Celia Applegate, *Bach in Berlin: Nation and Culture in Mendelssohn's Revival of the St. Matthew Passion* (Ithaca, NY, 2005), 45–79; Leon Botstein, "Listening through Reading: Musical Literacy and the Concert Audiences," *19th Century Music* 16 (1992): 129–45; ibid., *Music and its Public: Habits of Listening and the Crisis of Musical Modernism in Vienna 1870–1914* (Ph.D. diss., Harvard University, 1985).
15. *Haude- und Spenersche Zeitung*, 21 March 1818.
16. Norbert Elias, *The Civilising Process* (Cambridge, 1994). Cf. Sennet, *Fall of the Public Man*.
17. "Die Sängerin erreichte hier was noch keiner unsers Wissen bei uns begegnet ist, daß die Arie Dacapo verlangt, und die Künstlerin danach mitten im Akt gerufen wurde. Möchte diese Barbarei des Beifalls, der allen

dramatischen Zusammenhang des Kunstwerks zerstört, indeß bei uns nicht heimisch werden." *Vossische Zeitung*, 17 December 1844.

18. "Der Referent dieser Blätter nennt den Hervorruf während des Aktes Barbarei des Beifalls, anstatt ihn als den reinsten Erguß der Begeisterung und des wohlverdienten Dankes zu betrachten, zumal die Handlung der Oper dadurch gar nicht gestört ward." *Vossische Zeitung*, 20 December 1844.

19. Cf. Weber, *The Great Transformation*; Sven Oliver Müller et al., eds., *Die Oper im Wandel der Gesellschaft: Kulturtransfers und Netzwerke des Musiktheaters in Europa* (Vienna, 2010); idem., "A Musical Clash of Civilisations? Musical Transfers and Rivalries in the 20th Century," in Dominik Geppert and Robert Gerwarth, eds., *Wilhelmine Germany and Edwardian Britain: Essays on Cultural Affinity* (Oxford, 2009), 305–29; Jeffrey S. Sposato, "Saint Elsewhere: German and English Reactions to Mendelssohn's Paulus," *19th-Century Music* 32 (2008): 26–51.

20. Cf. Heinz-Dieter Meyer, "Taste Formation in Pluralistic Societies: The Role of Rhetorics and Institutions," *International Sociology* 15 (2000): 33–56; Andreas Gebesmair, *Grundzüge einer Soziologie des Musikgeschmacks* (Opladen, 2001).

21. That is the argument of Lawrence Levine, *Highbrow/Lowbrow: The Emergence of Cultural Hierarchy in America* (Cambridge, 1988).

22. "Nach ihrer Ausführung gab sich unter den Zuhörern ein sehr mäßiger Beifall kund, der von ebenfalls mäßigen Zeichen des Mißfallens begleitet wurde, die jedoch in keiner Weise als Demonstration aufzufassen waren. Dessenungeachtet hielt es der Conzertgeber für gut, den Anwesenden sofort einen Verweis zu ertheilen, indem er die Unzfriedenen aufforderte den Saal zu verlassen. …, Ich bitte die Herren Zischer den Saal zu verlassen, das ist hier nicht üblich!'" *Vossische Zeitung*, 16 January 1859.

23. "… in einem Privat-Concert haben indeß maaßvolle, nicht in das Rohe übergehende Zeichen des Mißfallens dasselbe Recht, wie die des Beifalls." "Ob ein Clavierspieler in höherem Grade das Recht hat, das Publikum in solcher Weise herauszufordern, als ein Schauspieler, wissen wir nicht; wohl wissen wir aber, daß man Aenliches einem Schauspieler nicht verzeihen würde." *Haude und Spenersche Zeitung*, 16 and 18 January 1859.

24. See Johnson, *Listening in Paris*; Jennifer Hall-Witt, "Representing the Audiences"; Huebner, "Opera Audiences," 206–25; and Weber, "Did People Listen," 678–91.

25. Eduard Hanslick, *Musikalisches Skizzenbuch: Der "Modernen Oper," IV. Theil: Neue Kritiken und Schilderungen* (Berlin, 1888), 260.

26. "Im Theater- und Concertleben existirt hier … eine seltsame Beschränkung der persönlichen Freiheit: die ausdrückliche Vorschrift der Abend-Toilette. Sei nach der Italienischen Oper, diesem Mode-Rendezvous der Reichen und Vornehmen, das kindische Gebot: ‚Evening dress indispensable!' vergönnt. Aber mit welchem Rechte kann man einem Musikfreunde, der für sein Geld ein philharmonisches Concert besuchen will, vorschreiben, er müsse unbedingt in Frack und weißer Cravatte erscheinen? … Kann das in Wahrheit eine musikalische Nation sein, welche uns den Genuß einer

Beethovenschen Symphonie durch lächerliche Kleider-Ordnung erschwert und verleidet?" Hanslick, *Musikalisches Skizzenbuch*, 303.

27. Oskar A.H. Schmitz, *Das Land ohne Musik: Englische Gesellschaftsprobleme* (Munich, 1914), 98.

28. "In Her Majestys Theater konnte Gounods ‚Faust' nicht weitergespielt werden, weil die Choristen und Bühnenarbeiter, die ihre Löhnung nicht erhalten konnten, Strike machten. Sie traten, als die Vorstellung im wilden Tumult unterging, bettelnd vor die Rampe und baten das Publikum um Almosen, um ihren Hunger zu stillen. Mit diesem unerhörten Skandal wähnten Viele die italienische Oper in London für immer begraben." *Vossische Zeitung*, 9 Mar. 1886.

29. "The Art of Applause," *Musical Times*, 1897, 448–49.

30. Levine, *Highbrow/Lowbrow*.

31. "When to Applaud," *Musical World*, 23 June 1877, 431 (original emphasis).

32. *Morning Post*, 21 Feb. 1910.

33. Ibid., 21 May 1913.

34. See Richard Leppert, "The Social Discipline of Listening," in Hans Erich Bödeker, Patrice Veit, and Michael Werner, eds., *Le Concert et son public: Mutations de la vie musicale en Europe de 1780 à 1914 (France, Allemagne, Angleterre)* (Paris, 2002), 459–79; Johnson, *Listening in Paris*, 228–38; Leo Balet and E. Gerhard, *Die Verbürgerlichung der deutschen Kunst, Literatur und Musik im 18. Jahrhundert*, ed. Gert Mattenklott (Frankfurt am Main, 1972), 334–94, 468–81; Ute Daniel, *Hoftheater: Zur Geschichte des Theaters und der Höfe im 18. und 19. Jahrhundert* (Stuttgart, 1995), 126–57.

35. *Morning Post*, 6 May 1882.

36. *Illustrated London News*, 18 June 1892, 747.

37. Cf. Ullrich Schmitt, *Revolution im Konzertsaal: Zur Beethovenrezeption im 19. Jahrhundert* (Mainz, 1990); Elisabeth Eleonore Bauer, *Wie Beethoven auf den Sockel kam: Die Entstehung eines musikalischen Mythos* (Stuttgart, 1992); Johnson, *Listening in Paris*, esp. 257–69.

38. Cf. David C. Large and William Weber, eds, *Wagnerism in European Culture and Politics* (Ithaca, NY, 1985); Veit Veltzke, *Der Mythos des Erlösers: Richard Wagners Traumwelten und die deutsche Gesellschaft* (Stuttgart, 2002).

39. *Musical Times*, August 1902, 523. Cf. *Musical Times*, July 1892, 406.

40. Cf. Leppert, "The Social Discipline of Listening," 459–79; Johnson, *Listening in Paris*, 228–38; Balet and Gerhard, *Die Verbürgerlichung*, 334–94, 468–81; Daniel, *Hoftheater*, 126–57.

41. See Helga de la Motte-Haber, ed., *Nationaler Stil und Europäische Dimension in der Musik der Jahrhundertwende* (Darmstadt, 1991); Philipp Ther, *In der Mitte der Gesellschaft: Opertheater in Zentraleuropa 1815–1914* (Munich, 2006), 395–421.

# Bibliography

Applegate, Celia. *Bach in Berlin: Nation and Culture in Mendelssohn's Revival of the St. Matthew Passion.* Ithaca, NY, 2005.

Balet, Leo, and Eberhard Gerhard. *Die Verbürgerlichung der deutschen Kunst, Literatur und Musik im 18. Jahrhundert*, ed. Gert Mattenklott. Frankfurt am Main, 1972.

Bashford, Christina. "Learning to Listen: Audiences for Chamber Music in Early-Victorian London." *Journal of Victorian Culture* 4 (1999): 25–51.

Bauer, Elisabeth Eleonore. *Wie Beethoven auf den Sockel kam: Die Entstehung eines musikalischen Mythos*. Stuttgart, 1992.

Bennett, Susan. *Theatre Audiences: A Theory of Production and Reception*. London, 1990.

Botstein, Leon. "Listening through Reading: Musical Literacy and the Concert Audiences." *19th Century Music* 16 (1992): 129–45.

———. *Music and its Public: Habits of Listening and the Crisis of Musical Modernism in Vienna 1870–1914*. Ph.D. diss., Harvard University, 1985.

Bourdieu, Pierre. *Distinction: A Social Critique of the Judgment of the Taste*. London, 1986.

Braun, Rudolf, and David Gugerli. *Macht des Tanzes—Tanz der Mächtigen: Hoffeste und Herrschaftszeremoniell 1550–1914*. Munich, 1993.

Cook, Nicholas. "Music as Performance." In *The Cultural Study of Music: A Critical Introduction*. Eds. Martin Clayton, Trevor Herbert, and Richard Middleton. New York, 2003, 204–14.

Daniel, Ute. *Hoftheater: Zur Geschichte des Theaters und der Höfe im 18. und 19. Jahrhundert*. Stuttgart, 1995.

Danuser, Hermann, and Friedrich Krummacher, eds. *Rezeptionsästhetik und Rezeptionsgeschichte in der Musikwissenschaft*. Laaber, 1991.

Elias, Norbert. *The Civilising Process*. Cambridge, 1994.

Finnegan, Ruth. "Music, Experience, and the Anthropology of Emotion." In *The Cultural Study of Music: A Critical Introduction*. Eds. Martin Clayton, Trevor Herbert, and Richard Middleton. New York, 2003, 181–92.

Gebesmair, Andreas. *Grundzüge einer Soziologie des Musikgeschmacks*. Opladen, 2001.

Gramit, David. *Cultivating Music: The Aspirations, Interests, and Limits of German Musical Culture, 1770–1848*. Berkeley, 2002.

Hall-Witt, Jennifer. "Representing the Audiences in the Age of Reform: Critics and the Elite at the Italian Opera in London." In *Music and British Culture, 1785–1914: Essays in Honour of Cyril Ehrlich*. Eds. Christina Bashford and Leanne Langley. Oxford, 2000, 121–44.

Hanslick, Eduard. *Musikalisches Skizzenbuch: Der "Modernen Oper" IV. Theil: Neue Kritiken und Schilderungen*. Berlin, 1888.

Hinrichsen, Hans-Joachim. "Musikwissenschaft: Musik—Interpretation—Wissenschaft." *Archiv für Muskwissenschaft* 57 (2000): 78–101.

Huebner, Steven. "Opera Audiences in Paris 1830–1870." *Music and Letters* 70 (1989): 206–25.

Johnson, James H. *Listening in Paris: A Cultural Study*. Berkeley, 1995.

Kemp, Wolfgang, ed. *Der Betrachter ist im Bild. Kunstwissenschaft und Rezeptionsästhetik*. Berlin, 1992.

Large, David C., and William Weber, eds. *Wagnerism in European Culture and Politics*. Ithaca, NY, 1985.

Lawson, Colin, and Robin Stowell. *The Historical Performance of Music*. Cambridge, 1999.

Leppert, Richard. "The Social Discipline of Listening." In *Le Concert et son public: Mutations de la vie musicale en Europe de 1780 à 1914 (France, Allemagne, Angleterre)*. Eds. Hans Erich Bödeker, Patrice Veit, and Michael Werner. Paris, 2002, 459–79.

Levine, Lawrence. *Highbrow/Lowbrow: The Emergence of Cultural Hierarchy in America*. Cambridge, 1988.

Meyer, Heinz-Dieter. "Taste Formation in Pluralistic Societies: The Role of Rhetorics and Institutions." *International Sociology* 15 (2000): 33–56.

Motte-Haber, Helga de la, ed. *Nationaler Stil und Europäische Dimension in der Musik der Jahrhundertwende*. Darmstadt, 1991.

Müller, Sven Oliver. "A Musical Clash of Civilisations? Musical Transfers and Rivalries in the 20th Century." In *Wilhelmine Germany and Edwardian Britain: Essays on Cultural Affinity*. Eds. Dominik Geppert and Robert Gerwarth. Oxford, 2009, 305–29.

———. *Das Publikum macht die Musik: Musikleben in Berlin, London und Wien im 19. Jahrhundert*. Göttingen, 2014.

———, et al., eds. *Die Oper im Wandel der Gesellschaft: Kulturtransfers und Netzwerke des Musiktheaters in Europa*. Vienna, 2010.

Nipperdey, Thomas. "'Bürgerlich' als Kultur." In *Bürger und Bürgerlichkeit im 19. Jahrhundert*. Ed. Jürgen Kocka. Göttingen, 1987, 143–48.

Picker, John M. *Victorian Soundscapes*. Oxford, 2003.

Schmitt, Ullrich. *Revolution im Konzertsaal: Zur Beethovenrezeption im 19. Jahrhundert*. Mainz, 1990.

Schmitz, Oskar A.H. *Das Land ohne Musik: Englische Gesellschaftsprobleme*. Munich, 1914.

Sennet, Richard. *The Fall of the Public Man*. London, 1977.

———. *The Conscience of the Eye: The Design and Social Life of Cities*. London, 1993.

Small, Christopher. *Musicking: The Meanings of Performing and Listening*. Middleton, CT, 1998.

Sponheuer, Bernd. *Musik als Kunst und Nicht-Kunst: Untersuchungen zur Dichotomie von "hoher" und "niederer" Kunst im musikästhetischen Denken zwischen Kant und Hanslick*. Kassel, 1987.

Sposato, Jeffrey S. "Saint Elsewhere: German and English Reactions to Mendelssohn's Paulus." *19th-Century Music* 32 (2008): 26–51.

Supicic, Ivo. *Music in Society: A Guide to the Sociology of Music*. New York, 1987.

Taruskin, Richard. *Text and Act: Essays on Music and Performance*. New York, 1995.

Ther, Philipp. *In der Mitte der Gesellschaft: Opentheater in Zentraleuropa 1815–1914*. Munich, 2006, 395–421.

Thompson, Martyn. "Reception Theory and the Interpretation of Historical Meaning." *History and Theory* 32 (1993): 248–72.

Veltzke, Veit. *Der Mythos des Erlösers: Richard Wagners Traumwelten und die deutsche Gesellschaft*. Stuttgart, 2002.

Weber, William. "Did People Listen in the 18th Century?" *Early Music* 25 (1997): 678–91.

———. *Music and the Middle Class: Social Structure of Concert Life in London, Paris and Vienna*. London, 1975.

———. *The Great Transformation of Musical Taste: Concert Programming from Haydn to Brahms*. Cambridge, 2008.

# PART V

# THE SOUNDS OF WORLD WAR I

# CHEERS, SONGS, AND MARCHING SOUNDS
## Acoustic Mobilization and Collective Affects at the Beginning of World War I
*Daniel Morat*

The so-called *Augusterlebnis* ("August experience") is no longer a source of contention in historical research. The term refers to the idea that the outbreak of World War I in August 1914 led to a wave of nationalistic enthusiasm for the war throughout the German Empire that leveled internal political divisions and gave rise to national unity in the face of an external threat. This contemporary perception was long characteristic of the general image of the beginning of World War I in Germany and was in many cases still being restated in the historiographical literature in the 1980s.[1] The 1990s then witnessed the emergence of critical research on the *Augusterlebnis*, which has shown that enthusiasm for the war was by no means as unanimous or ubiquitous as had long been assumed. It was concentrated above all in the centers of the cities and was rooted in the bourgeoisie and a nationalistic student body. In rural areas and among the working classes, on the other hand, the war was by no means unanimously welcomed, let alone seen with enthusiasm.[2] The idea of national unity at the outbreak of war and a special "spirit of 1914" is thus more the result of military and bourgeois-nationalist propaganda than a true reflection of a widespread enthusiasm for the war.

This interpretation is the current consensus in historical studies, and in this sense the deconstruction of the "myth" of the *Augusterlebnis* can be considered complete. Even this deconstruction, though, does not deny that scenes of exuberant, nationalistic fervor were indeed to be observed in parts of the German population, and in the centers of the cities in particular, at the outbreak of war. In this sense, there most certainly was such a thing as the *Augusterlebnis*, even if it was less widely spread across space and society than was long thought to be the case.[3] In what follows, I want to examine these scenes of nationalistic enthusiasm for war in the summer of 1914 once again. But this time, the emphasis lies neither on the question of how widespread it was in society or how it was politically exploited, nor on the question of the extent to which an already existing mood for war found expression in the celebrations that took place when it came.[4] Instead, I want to focus on the mechanisms of collective self-mobilization and self-intoxication that came into play in the specific contexts of the mass demonstrations and mass meetings that took place in July and August 1914. The analysis is guided by the assumption that collective singing and shouting took on a central role in this self-mobilization.

Although such singing and shouting is omnipresent in contemporary reports, and although "hurrah patriotism" and the noise of the war rallies are referred to again and again in the scholarly literature, the acoustic dimension of the *Augusterlebnis* has hitherto hardly ever been thematized in its own right. This is due, among other things, to the fact that it is only in recent years that historians have, as a whole, begun to engage with acoustic communication and the history of hearing. The aim of what follows is to apply, for the first time, the questions and approaches developed in this context to the mass meetings and demonstrations of summer 1914; in the process, particular attention is given to the significance of sound and acoustic communication for the stimulation and reinforcement of collective emotions. The history of emotions has been an established field of research in its own right within historical studies for some time now,[5] but even here, acoustic and auditory issues have to date had only a secondary role to play. For this reason, as a first step, the relationship between sound and emotions is considered more closely in a methodological section; here, the case is made for a theoretical shift from the concept of emotions to the concept of affects. Then, in a second section, the methodological remarks on the acoustic transmission of affects are applied to the analysis of acoustic mobilization in the summer of 1914. It will become clear in the process that the *Augusterlebnis* of 1914 cannot only be considered the climax of the mood for war in the urban bourgeoisie of Wilhelmine Germany, but also that in it there appeared new forms of acoustic mass mobilization that pointed ahead to the subsequent history of the twentieth century.[6]

## Sound, Emotions, and Affects

The idea of a close connection between hearing and emotion is to a certain extent a commonplace. In the words of Gerald Fleischer, who works on auditory medicine, "the soul clings to the ear," from which the social scientist Stephan Marks concludes that hearing is the sensory faculty "that is most directly connected to the emotions."[7] This applies in a distinctive sense to listening to music, with respect to which, according to the neuroscientists Michael Grossbach and Eckart Altenmüller, it has been "undisputed throughout history" that music "has a particularly strong effect on the emotions."[8] It is not possible here to consider in detail the debates about the relationship between music and emotions that have taken place not only between neuroscientists and musicologists but also in other contexts.[9] Even so, it is striking that relatively little thought has been given to this relationship, or more generally to the significance of hearing for the emotions, in the context of the history of emotions. This may change as a result of the current popularity of sound studies and auditory history. The uncritical assumption that hearing is closer to the emotions than seeing, though, belongs to a tradition of sound studies that can already be considered somewhat antiquated. One of the most important pioneers of this earlier tradition is the Canadian composer and sound researcher, R. Murray Schafer, who brought the World Soundscape Project into being at Simon Fraser University in British Columbia in 1971. This project, which is still being pursued today, is devoted to the comparative study of soundscapes— of sonic environments and how they change as a result of processes of urbanization and industrialization. An extended edition of *The Tuning of the World* (1977), Schafer's most influential book in this area, was published as *The Soundscape: Our Sonic Environment and the Tuning of the World* in 1994.[10]

One of Schafer's assumptions is that the sense of sound, in contrast to that of sight in particular, has very specific qualities—that the different sensory organs produce fundamentally different forms of emotional and cognitive perception. He also believes that a historical development in which seeing has become increasingly important and gained supremacy over hearing has taken place in Western societies. Where this latter point is concerned, the influence of the media theory of Marshall McLuhan and Walter Ong becomes apparent. McLuhan, philosopher and literary scholar, was himself a Canadian; in the media theory whose principles he developed in the 1960s, he divided history into four epochs: oral tribal culture, literate manuscript culture, the Gutenberg galaxy, and the electronic age. Each of these epochs, he believed, was marked by a particular media setting that in turn privileged individual senses. While McLuhan described oral culture as a "world of the ear," he felt that manuscript culture required the involvement of all the senses because dealing with manuscripts was a tactile activity, and they were often read aloud.[11] The subsequent age of printing, the Gutenberg galaxy, he proposed, was, however, clearly a visual age in which the sense of sight dominated the others. Following McLuhan, other historians of media and culture have also referred to a hegemony of the visual in modernity. According to the established narrative of modernity, this hegemony of the visual was also accompanied by a suppression of, in particular, the senses of touch, taste, and smell, associated as they are with proximity, and by an increase in inhibition, as described by Norbert Elias in his *Civilizing Process*.[12]

Criticisms of this grand narrative of a visual modernity defined by rationality and inhibition have been put forward numerous times from the perspective of a history of the senses in recent years.[13] In this context, Jonathan Sterne's study *The Audible Past: Cultural Origins of Sound Reproduction* (2003) was particularly influential on what could, to set it apart from Schafer, be called the new history of hearing.[14] In his book, Sterne takes issue with accepted narratives of effective history (*Wirkungsgeschichte*) that adopt as a starting point the discovery of acoustic media such as the telephone or the phonograph in order to then describe their effects on habits and practices of listening. Sterne inverts this argumentation and assumes that it was possible to discover the acoustic media only because changes had already taken place beforehand in the status and nature of hearing. This is what Sterne means with the cultural origins of sound reproduction that he traces back as far as the early nineteenth century in the process of a search that takes in the history of science, technology, and culture. In doing so, he describes the "objectification and abstraction of hearing and sound," their construction as objects to be studied and researched, as prerequisites for, not effects of, sound reproduction.[15] This objectification of hearing included the development of particular auditory techniques, which Sterne describes with reference to the history of the stethoscope, for example. In this way he hopes to show that hearing, too, played a crucial role in the development of modern knowledge cultures. "To take seriously the role of sound and hearing in modern life," Sterne writes, is therefore "to trouble the visualist definition of *modernity*."[16]

With this argument, though, Sterne not only takes issue with the idea of an unrivalled hegemony of the visual in modernity. He also, more fundamentally, calls for a new consideration of hearing itself. Even in the current scholarly discourse, Sterne suggests, a series of a priori assumptions crop up again and again, in which "hearing" is usually characterized by means of a contrast with "seeing." Thus, he continues, it is felt that "hearing is spherical, vision … directional"; that hearing generates nearness, vision distance; that "hearing immerses its subject, vision offers a perspective"; that "hearing tends toward subjectivity, vision … toward objectivity"; and so on. The above-mentioned idea that hearing privileges the emotions but vision the intellect is also included in this "audiovisual litany."[17] Taking issue with these assumptions, Sterne emphasizes that listening is a "directed, learned" cultural strategy, one that is just as historically variable as the use of the other sensory faculties.[18] Hearing and seeing are, for Sterne, not more emotional or more rational in themselves; instead, they are only so as a result of the historically variable cultural strategies and cultural meanings that make use of them and are ascribed to them.

Does this mean that the assumption of a particularly direct link between hearing and emotion is just a cultural convention, no more than a preconception? Sterne's intervention against a naive and frequently romanticizing engagement with hearing was most welcome, and the resultant historicization of human sense perceptions is perfectly sensible; yet, for all that, I believe that we should be careful not to throw the baby out with the bathwater. Human sensory activity is always bound to particular anatomical and physical foundations, and these foundations constrain the historical variability of the ways in which it is used and the meanings that are ascribed to it. How, then, against this background, can the relationship between sounds and emotions be described in a way that is not naive and that takes account of their historical construction?

To answer this question, we can turn to another book from the recent context of sound culture studies. In his study *Sonic Warfare: Sound, Affect, and the Ecology of Fear*, published in 2010, the English musicologist and scholar of cultural studies, Steve Goodman, reminds us, among other things, of the physical dimension of sound perception.[19] If we speak in a metaphorical manner about being gripped or touched by something we hear, this is also to be taken perfectly literally—for sound, with its vibrations, makes us move in a very real way. From the tympanic membrane to the cochlea, our hearing apparatus is set up in a special way to perceive these vibrations and translate them into an auditory impression. If the sound pressure is high enough, though, we can perceive it with the rest of our bodies as well.

What follows from this? Sound is a medium that brings bodies in relation to one another and sets them in collective motion.[20] It is thus also particularly suited to manipulating and influencing bodies. Steve Goodman's book is concerned with a particular form of such influence. In it, Goodman takes "sonic warfare" to mean any deployment of sound with the aim of having a violent effect on others. This is not limited to the deployment of acoustic weapons in war, which Goodman describes with reference to, for example, German Stukas in World War II. For Goodman, it also includes acoustic instruments of "crowd control" employed by the police, or the use of high-frequency tones to drive gangs of youths away from supermarkets, and ultimately certain forms of electronic music in the context of post-colonial "culture wars."

In studying "sonic warfare," Goodman turns not to the concept of emotions but to that of affects. In the process, he makes particular use of the transitive nature of the term: the associated verb "to affect" means to have an effect on others. The term "sonic effect" is therefore equally significant for Goodman. This has two consequences. One is a depsychologization of the problem. If with emotions we are always pursuing individual perceptions and mental states inside a person, then pursuing affects and "sonic effects" means that the focus shifts to the two-way connections and vibrating relationships between bodies and subjects in which the boundaries of those subjects become porous.[21] The second consequence is that focusing on acoustic effects means leaving the pursuit of essentialities behind. In Goodman's words, "the focus shifts from what a body is … to its powers—what it can do."[22] With this modified line of enquiry, there is no longer the temptation to try to make generalizing statements about "hearing" in relation to "the emotions." Instead, we can observe the use of acoustic means to stimulate and regulate collective emotions in specific historical situations, and try to describe the effects that this acoustic action had. In the next section, this approach is applied to the analysis of the *Augusterlebnis* in the German Empire in the summer of 1914.

## The Sound of the *Augusterlebnis*

Strictly speaking, the *Augusterlebnis* actually began in July. The course of events is familiar: the assassination of Archduke Franz Ferdinand, heir to the Austrian throne, in Sarajevo on 28 June 1914 initiated what is known as the July Crisis, which finally led to the outbreak of war in August.[23] After the German Empire declared its unconditional commitment to support Austria on 6 July, it was clear that an Austrian declaration of war on Serbia would also lead to Germany entering the war on the Austrian side. The expiry of the ultimatum that Austria issued to Serbia on 23 July was therefore awaited with much interest in the German Empire as well:

> In the late afternoon on 25 July vast crowds of curious and excited people gathered in the larger German cities at the sites where they expected the news of the Serbian response first to be distributed: at the city squares downtown, in front of the newspaper office buildings, in the downtown cafés. After learning that Serbia had rejected the ultimatum, in Berlin

and a few other large cities "parades" of enthusiastic youths marched through the streets, singing patriotic songs.[24]

It was these patriotic parades that provided the model for many other patriotic demonstrations and mass meetings in the last days of July and the first days of the war. In the bourgeois and conservative press, and later among many historians as well, these patriotic parades were treated as signs of national unity and enthusiasm for the war. These images of a sacred enthusiasm for war, and of the "unity of 1914" of which Gustav Stresemann spoke when looking back in 1921, supplied the core of the myth of the *Augusterlebnis.*[25] The extent of its mythical status has already been described above. For one thing, enthusiasm for the war was by no means ubiquitous. It was concentrated above all in the centers of the cities, but even here it was not universally evident. Instead, there are also many reports of a gloomy atmosphere on city squares after the announcement of mobilization and the declarations of war in the first days of August. The other thing is that recent research has shown that the bourgeoisie, and the students and bourgeois youth in particular, were the primary channels for the patriotic mood of exultation (see figure 8.1). The majority of the working classes were opposed to the war, despite the establishment of the *Burgfrieden,* or political truce between the parties, and despite the approval of war

**Figure 8.1** A group of enthusiastic students on Unter den Linden on 1 August 1914. Copyright: Bundesarchiv.

credits by the Social Democratic members of parliament on 4 August. This found expression before 4 August in large antiwar demonstrations organized by the Social Democrats. In quantitative terms, partici- pation in these antiwar protests was much greater than that in the patriotic demonstrations. In the greater Berlin area alone, thirty-two antiwar gatherings took place with a total of over a hundred thousand participants.[26] The numbers cited by historians as having been involved in the patriotic demonstrations vary, but never reach this level.

Nonetheless, Thomas Lindenberger speaks of a "hegemony of those in favor of war" on the streets of Berlin.[27] This was due not least to the political and ideological harmony between the patriotic pro-war demonstrators, the authorities, and those in power. It was not just that Traugott von Jagow, chief of the Berlin police, generally allowed war demonstrations to continue, despite approval not having been sought—those in favor of the war were also able to gain control of the symbolic central space of the authoritarian Wilhelmine state: the imposing route linking the palace and the Reichstag. Already in the years before World War I, the area around the palace and Unter den Linden had become the empire's central "hurrah quarter" and "district for ceremonial carry-ons," as the newspaper *Vorwärts* jested.[28] In the days of July and August, those in favor of the war were able to draw on a wide and well-rehearsed repertoire of patriotic events and symbolic demonstrations of power in order to play to the gallery in this "hurrah quarter." The extent to which these patriotic events shaped the political culture and education of the empire has been illustrated by Eric Hobsbawm with reference to the

> chronicles of one Gymnasium [that] record no less than ten ceremonies between August 1895 and March 1896 recalling the twenty-fifth anni- versary of the Franco-Prussian war, including ample commemorations of battles in the war, celebrations of the emperor's birthday, the official handing-over of the portrait of an imperial prince, illuminations and public addresses on the war of 1870–1, on the development of the imperial idea (*Kaiseridee*) during the war, on the character of the Hohenzollern dynasty, and so on.[29]

The various elements in the militaristic education and expressions of national identity found in the empire of which use could be made in the summer of 1914 have already been examined in numerous historical studies.[30] Thomas Lindenberger, though, has pointed out that something new, precedents for which had previously only appeared in isolated instances, came into play as well in the days of summer 1914: a higher level of self-mobilization among the bourgeois masses, who, with their nationalistic sentiment, now played more than just a supporting role at patriotic events. Lindenberger refers here to "new dimensions of mass mobilization" that surpassed the older forms of monarchic self-presentation.[31] One sign of this was the fact that bourgeois demonstrators for the first time vied with the workers in using the streets as an arena for making political statements, and refused to confine their rallies to clearly demarcated roads and squares. This led to extraordinary situations in which, in part, the previous boundaries between the population and the power of the state were crossed—for example, when the masses pushed their way closer to the Kaiser's car than they were really allowed to get. Verhey refers for this very reason to "carnivalesque crowds" in which the existing social order was turned on its head.[32] Paradoxically, the authorities therefore found themselves forced to take action against individual out-of-control groups of patriotic demonstrators whose unruly patriotism had, in some cases, also met with criticism in the bourgeois press.

But what does all this have to do with sounds and affects, and with acoustic mobilization? If we read contemporary accounts of events in the summer of 1914 in the press and other reports, it really is impossible to overlook the ubiquity of singing and cries of hurrah. Visual symbols such as flags and portraits of the Kaiser did, of course, play an important role too, but the central means of expressing patriotic sentiment seems to have been singing and shouting. In the periodical *Daheim*, Eduard Heyd summarized this when he wrote of the "roaring, singing exaltation of the fatherland."[33] In this respect, something resembling a standard course of events emerged: (usually improvised) patriotic speeches were followed by cheering and shouts of "hurrah," and then finally by the singing of patriotic songs. In the cafés and bars, which were often home to bands, the usual program of waltzes and light music was suspended. In its place, patriotic pieces and marches were played. Anyone who did not wish to join in the singing, or happened to ask the band for a waltz, had to reckon with the opprobrium of the impassioned masses. The Berlin correspondent of the Essen *General-Anzeiger* described such a scene as follows:

> Finally the doors opened. For a dozen walking out, two dozen pushed their way in. Once again music is played. A march, a war song. Pity those who did not want to accommodate their program to the mood of the day. Once the band attempted to sneak in a fashionable waltz. Scarcely had the first notes been played when the public answered with whistling protest. The conductor had to stop, and a dozen voices intoned *a capella* what he must play: "Deutschland, Deutschland über alles." The choir grew powerfully, and then the orchestra joined in. The music rose sublimely to the heavens. All rose. Two, three guests believed that

they could remain indifferent to the general enthusiasm, that they could remain seated. After two or three seconds a storm of indignation forced them to stand up. One still remained seated. He was thrown into fresh air, without being allowed to pay his bill or fetch his hat or coat. A new troop pushed in from outside. Over their heads a flag, black and gold [the Austrian colors]. That was the signal for a last raging increase in enthusiasm. Roaring yells of hurrah, glowing eyes, an exuberance which causes hearts to overflow. And once again music. And once again the song: Gott erhalte Franz den Kaiser.[34]

The Habsburg imperial hymn, composed by Joseph Haydn, was sung here out of solidarity with Austria, which came quite naturally to the German patriots not least because the "Lied der Deutschen," written after it, had the same melody. Collective singing was, indeed, a long-familiar practice when it came to expressing the national will. In the nineteenth century, the song movement became an important part of the German national movement. As Dietmar Klenke writes, the German choral societies with their national song festivals were "trailblazers on the road to modern mass mobilization."[35] In the empire, military music played an equally important role alongside the singing of patriotic songs at school, and at patriotic events and commemorations.[36] Granted, there was not an official German national anthem, but instead there were three unofficial ones: the "Lied der Deutschen," the Prussian song of homage "Heil dir im Siegerkranz" from as long ago as the late eighteenth century (which was sung to the tune of the English national anthem, "God Save the Queen"), and the anti-French "Wacht am Rhein" from the mid nineteenth century.[37] These were the three songs that were sung everywhere in the summer of 1914.

How, then, can we capture more precisely the significance of this ubiquitous singing and shouting in the specific historical situation of the weeks of July and August 1914? Following Christian Jansen, the reeling off of patriotic songs can be described—by analogy with speech acts—as a "music act," that is, as an action carried out with music.[38] From this perspective, the songs are not considered as acoustic messages whose senders and recipients can be studied (as is usually the case in classic studies in communication theory). Instead, the singing patriots are seen here as, in equal measure, both senders and recipients of their own message. In Steve Goodman's terms, we can say that the singing and shouting presents itself as an instrument for affecting oneself and others. It was a way to set oneself and others in motion acoustically. If we argue with Goodman's concept of affects in this way, it also seems less helpful to interpret the singing and shouting merely as an expression of patriotic feelings. Instead, it mattered because it was a way of bringing forth those patriotic feelings in the first place, or at least of intensifying and channeling them in oneself and others. A line of historical enquiry accentuated in this way is thus concerned not with singing and shouting as an aid to gauging a patriotic sentiment that existed separately from them, but instead with the function of the singing and shouting in the organization and management of collective moods and actions.

In order to follow this line of enquiry further, we must recall once again the specific communication situation that pertained in the last weeks of July and the first weeks of August: in the time before radio and television, not to mention the Internet, the extra editions that the daily newspapers published several times a day were the most up-to-date form of news media.[39] The extra editions were sold and read on the streets, and it was here, on the streets and squares, that news spread from mouth to mouth—which also meant that rumors and false reports were able to thrive unchecked. Thus, anyone who wanted to learn about the most recent developments had to go onto the streets. In Berlin, furthermore, he could even go straight to the places where decisions were made and, in many cases, directly announced—such as the palace, where the Kaiser's announcement of the imminent risk of war (*Zustand drohender Kriegsgefahr*) was read out on 31 July. Before anything else, then, it was curiosity and uncertainty that brought masses of people onto the streets. In this state of uncertainty, the tension was bound to be channeled in one direction or another sooner or later. This, too, was effected by collective singing and shouting. A journalist in Gelsenkirchen interpreted the situation there on 31 July in this very manner, writing that "until late in the evening people waited for news. Although at first the mood was very depressed, it soon improved through the singing of patriotic songs."[40]

As is also apparent from this description, we should not think that the air was constantly filled with shouts and songs. Instead, noise and silence alternated with each other. Tense stillness was broken by the "shrill screams of the newspaper sellers," as the Berlin *Tägliche Rundschau* wrote;[41] new escalations in the political crisis were greeted with demonstrations and songs. A change can also be seen to have taken place between July and August. If vocal demonstrations were predominant in the last weeks of July, the public gatherings fell silent more and more frequently after mobilization and the outbreak of war in the first week of August. The *Nürnberger Stadtzeitung*, for example, wrote on 2 August: "the feverish noise which echoed through the streets in the days before the mobilization has gradually become silent.

Most of the people walk by each other serious and depressed."[42] After the first victories were reported, though, the patriotic demonstrations and songs came back to life. On 22 August, for example, the *Tägliche Rundschau* contained the following report of a victory celebration in Berlin:

> The Berliner Liedertafel put on a fine victory celebration last night by giving an improvised concert on the Potsdamer Platz under the baton of its choirmaster, Max Wiedemann. The well-known society interrupted its evening rehearsal in order to provide some kind of outlet for the unstoppable tide of celebration triggered by the major victory of which news had just arrived, moved on to the Potsdamer Platz, and surprised and delighted the substantial crowd with its artistry. The "Niederländlisches Dankgebet" and a number of fiery war songs, among them "Lützows wilde, verwegene Jagd," were performed and received with thunderous applause by the ever-growing audience. For the last songs, "Deutschland, Deutschland über alles," "Die Wacht am Rhein," [and] "Heil dir im Siegerkranz," the crowd, which by then filled almost the entire square, joined in, so that the improvised concert ultimately became a patriotic demonstration of overwhelming beauty.[43]

The Berliner Liedertafel was one of the largest choral societies in the German Empire.[44] This report of a spontaneous concert shows how, in the summer of 1914, the organized singing of the choral societies could combine with the spontaneous singing of the masses on the streets. Just as the singing, the shouting also went on well into the first weeks of the war. On 2 September 1914, the *Rheinisch-Westfälische Zeitung* reported from the capital:

> This is a brand new pastime in Berlin: "cheering on" [*Abschreien*]. "Do you have any plans for tonight?" "We go cheering on." A crowd is gathering on busy squares and crossroads, and as soon as the people spot a field grey uniform in a car or a suitcase they sound a many-voiced "Hurrah!" That's how they bid farewell to the leaving soldiers. And the officers stand up and wave their hats. The crowd is waiting deep into the night. They would not go to bed unless they have "cheered on" at least 25 lieutenants.[45]

If the public singing and shouting can hence be understood as a means of affecting oneself and others, and as an instrument for defusing tension and manipulating moods, it could also, ultimately, be used very directly as a "sonic weapon" in Goodman's sense. This can be seen, for example, in an event at the end of July that Philipp Scheidemann later recalled as a "battle of singers" (*Sängerkrieg*): during the antiwar demonstrations of the Social Democrats on 28 July, bands of workers also marched into the city center and managed, circumventing police blockades, to reach Unter den Linden. At about 10 P.M., around one to two thousand Social Democrats passed up and down Unter den Linden while the bourgeoisie gave voice to patriotic songs on both sides. The correspondent of the *Frankfurter Zeitung* reported as follows:

> In front of the cafés and restaurants there were masses of people. The "Wacht am Rhein" and "Heil dir im Siegerkranz" sounded out of thousands of throats, but one could also hear the "Arbeitermarseillaise" sung powerfully by closely organized parades in the night. The cheers for the Kaiser and his Austrian ally were interspersed with cheers for international social democracy and cries of "down with the war!" It was an incredible confusion of heated calls, of demonstrations for and against, which rose to a raging noise, and which increased ever more the general excitement. The police were completely powerless at 10.00 against this mass of people.[46]

Here, therefore, singing was, in a very immediate way, a means of political confrontation between those in favor of and those opposed to the war.

Finally, the special affective quality of acoustic mobilization was also exploited for propaganda and commercial purposes. In 1915, for example, the Deutsche Grammophongesellschaft produced a number of *Hörbilder* (sound scenes), as they are called, which it marketed as "patriotic zonophone recordings" (*vaterländische Zonophonaufnahmen*— the zonophone was a device that competed with the gramophone). These *Hörbilder* involved scenes that were reenacted acoustically in the studio and can be considered the predecessors of the later radio plays. Alongside scenes such as "The Storming of Liège" ("Die Erstürmung von Lüttich") and "Welcoming U 21" ("Begrüßung der U 21"—the submarine U 21 sank the British cruiser HMS *Pathfinder* on 5 September 1914), these patriotic recordings also included one with the title "The Mobilization of 1 August 1914" ("Die Mobilmachung am 1. August 1914"). In it, we hear first the address of a mayor to a departing regiment at the railway station. His address gives way to shouts of "hurrah" and the collective singing of the "Wacht am Rhein," accompanied by a military band. Further shouts of "hurrah" and the response of the regimental commander follow, then cheers to the Kaiser and "Heil dir im Siegerkranz," and finally a tangle of voices, the sounds of the train as it leaves, fanfares, and a final song, "Muss i denn, muss i denn zum Städtele hinaus."[47]

As it is a reenactment after the event, the value of this recording as a source is problematic. It does not, of course, provide an authentic reproduction of the mood of August 1914. But we can see in it something resembling a retrospectively constructed prototype for the patriotic demonstrations and ceremonies for departing troops in August 1914, one that contains all the elements with which we are familiar from the newspaper reports: speeches, shouts and cheers, and patriotic songs. The interpretation proposed here is not necessarily concerned with how real the patriotic emotions of the singing and cheering actors in this recording were, or with how "authentic" the scene they portrayed can claim to be; what it does provide, though, is a document of the significance of acoustic mobilization in August 1914, which, it was assumed, would still be able to arouse patriotic feelings in later listeners to the zonophone.

This *Hörbild* stands in contrast to other sound recordings that have been preserved from World War I. In January 1918, at Bellevue Palace, for example, Kaiser Wilhelm II repeated his famous address to the German people of 6 August 1914 and had it recorded. Unlike in the *Hörbilder*, there is no attempt to recreate a particular scene. Although the voice really is that of Wilhelm II, this address recorded at a later date does not provide an authentic aural impression of the excitement in the days of the summer of 1914. The latter can be better reconstructed on the basis of contemporary reports. The *Vossische Zeitung* of 1 August, for example, contained a report about the Kaiser's address that followed the announcement of the imminent risk of war on 31 July (see figure 8.2). This report provides a better impression of how we should imagine Wilhelm II's speeches in front of large crowds in the summer of 1914:

> The moment the purple royal standard was raised above the Royal Palace yesterday afternoon, countless thousands thronged towards the Schloßplatz square and the Lustgarten park, which were soon packed from the Cathedral to the Spree and from the terraces of the Palace to the National Gallery. Nationalistic songs thundered forth mightily: the "Wacht am Rhein," "Heil dir im Siegerkranz," "Deutschland, Deutschland über alles." Suddenly—it was just after six o'clock—the doors on the balcony opposite the Cathedral opened. The Kaiser, the Kaiserin, and Princes Adalbert and Oskar stepped out, enveloped in a thunder of extraordinary jubilation. It was quite some time before the thundering cheers faded away and the Kaiser was able to speak. His words rang out, clipped and filled with the most profound solemnity, with a force befitting this decisive moment. There are some sentences, spoken with trembling anger and standing out clearly from the rest of his speech, that left such a mark that they will never be forgotten by anyone who was among those who heard the indictment that the Kaiser hurled at our war-mongering neighbor. The crowd stood there staggered, with doffed hats, as the Kaiser concluded by calling on all to beseech Heaven

for the victory of German arms! … "Heil, Kaiser" was their response to him.[48]

This newspaper report is not in itself more authentic than the 1918 recording. The terseness and force of the Kaiser's voice, for example, might have been somewhat exaggerated on account of the situation. The report does, though, illustrate better than the studio recording the

**Figure 8.2** Wilhelm II speaks to the masses from the balcony of his palace on 31 July 1914. Copyright: Bundesarchiv.

dynamic situation of acoustic communication into which the Kaiser and the people entered at the moment of collective self-mobilization. This also marks the beginning of a new form of mass politics that, in the subsequent course of the twentieth century, continued to employ a wide variety of ways of acoustically affecting the self and others (which have in many cases become more powerful since being used with media such as radio and the loudspeaker).

## Conclusion

Even before the address that has just been described, the Kaiser was greeted with vocal enthusiasm on 31 July when he entered Berlin with his wife in an open-top car. Theodor Wolff, liberal journalist and editor-in-chief of the *Berliner Tageblatt*, observed the scene and described it in the following words in the memoirs of World War I that he later wrote: "the hurrah-yelling crowd heated itself up to a stormy enthusiasm."[49] With these words, he had already recognized the cheers as a means of collective self-stimulation. To an extent, this observation is perhaps banal. Collective singing, shouting, and noise-making were (and still are) among the means with which groups and crowds of people took shape, expressed themselves, and began feeling and moving together in other historical situations too. A number of historically specific features are apparent in the days of summer 1914, though. First, this was when, for the first time in the German Empire, the bourgeoisie and classes on which the state depended vied with the workers in using the streets as a medium for expressing opinion in public.[50] In the process, they were able to make use of rituals from the culture of patriotic ceremonies fostered in the empire, which, however, took on a life of their own that extended well beyond the context of demonstrations of agreement organized from above. This led to the monarch, too, being drawn into a new form of political interaction with the masses on the streets of Berlin, one that already anticipates the forms of political communication in the twentieth century after the monarchy. The significance of direct acoustic communication at this particular point in time—the dawning age of the mass media—also became apparent in the process. In addition, the crowds of loudly celebrating and singing people really did shout down the critics of the war, thus producing, in the act of affecting and convincing themselves, the perception of a unanimous enthusiasm for the war. In this way, they made possible the mythologization of the *Augusterlebnis* that, even at the end of the twentieth century, continued to shape the memory of, and historical research on, World War I.

# Notes

\* Translation from German by Alastair Matthews.

1. This was still the case in, for example, Thomas Nipperdey, *Deutsche Geschichte 1866–1918*, vol. 2: Machtstaat vor der Demokratie (Munich, 1992), 778–82.

2. See, above all, Jeffrey Verhey, *The Spirit of 1914: Militarism, Myth, and Mobilization in Germany* (Cambridge, 2000); further Thomas Raithel, *Das "Wunder" der inneren Einheit: Studien zur deutschen und französischen Öffentlichkeit bei Beginn des Ersten Weltkrieges* (Bonn, 1996); on the working classes, Wolfgang Kruse, *Krieg und nationale Integration: Eine Neuinterpretation des sozialdemokratischen Burgfriedensschlusses 1914/15* (Essen, 1993); on the rural *Augusterlebnis*, Benjamin Ziemann, *War Experiences in Rural Germany, 1914–1923* (Oxford, 2007).

3. See Gunther Mai, "1. August 1914: Gab es ein Augusterlebnis?," in *Tage deutscher Geschichte: Von der Reformation bis zur Wiedervereinigung*, eds. Eckart Conze and Thomas Nicklas (Munich, 2004), 177–94.

4. On this question, see Thomas Rohkrämer, "August 1914—Kriegsmentalität und ihre Voraussetzungen," in *Der Erste Weltkrieg: Wirkung, Wahrnehmung, Analyse*, ed. Wolfgang Michalka (Munich, 1994), 759–77.

5. For recent introductions, see Susan J. Matt, "Current Emotion Research in History: Or, Doing History from the Inside Out," *Emotion Review* 3, no. 1 (2011): 117–24; Barbara Rosenwein, "Problems and Methods in the History of Emotions," *Passions in Context: Journal of the History and Philosophy of the Emotions* 1 (2010): 1–32 <http://www.passionsincontext.de/index.php?id=557>; Anna Wierzbicka, "The 'History of Emotions' and the Future of Emotion Research," *Emotion Review* 2, no. 3 (2010): 269–73.

6. Peter Fritzsche, *Germans into Nazis* (Cambridge, 1998), 3–36, also argues that the patriotic crowds of July and August 1914 marked the beginning of a new form of nationalistic mass politics that prefigured the Nazi politics of the *Volksgemeinschaft*. He does not pay special attention to the acoustic dimension of these mass politics though. For the transformation of mass politics through World War I, see also Bernd Weisbrod, "Die Politik der Repräsentation: Das Erbe des Ersten Weltkrieges und der Formwandel der Politik in Europa," in *Der Erste Weltkrieg und die europäische Nachkriegsordnung: Sozialer Wandel und Formveränderung der Politik*, ed. Hans Mommsen (Cologne, 2000), 13–41; Benjamin Ziemann, "Germany 1914–1918: Total War as a Catalyst of Change," in *The Oxford Handbook of Modern German History*, ed. Helmut Walser Smith (Oxford, 2011), 378–99.

7. Gerald Fleischer, *Lärm—der tägliche Terror* (Stuttgart, 1990), 9; Stephan Marks, "Zur Bedeutung des akustischen Mediums für die sozialwissenschaftliche Forschung und Lehre," in *Akustisches Gedächtnis und Zweiter Weltkrieg*, ed. Robert Maier (Göttingen, 2010), 23. "Die Seele hängt am Ohr"; "das am unmittelbarsten mit den Gefühlen verbunden ist". Translator's note: translations of material quoted in German are either original or drawn from Verhey, *The Spirit of 1914*.

8. Michael Grossbach and Eckart Altenmüller, "Musik und Emotion—zur Wirkung und Wirkort von Musik," in *Die Macht der Töne: Musik als Mittel politischer Identitätsfindung im 20. Jahrhundert*, eds. Tillmann Bendikowski et al. (Münster, 2003), 13. "zu allen Zeiten unbestritten"; "besonders stark auf die Emotionen wirkt".

9. For a contemporary overview, see Patrik N. Juslin and John Sloboda, eds., *Handbook of Music and Emotion: Theory, Research, Applications* (Oxford, 2010).

10. R. Murray Schafer, *The Soundscape: Our Sonic Environment and the Tuning of the World* (Rochester, VT, 1994).

11. Marshall McLuhan, *The Gutenberg Galaxy: The Making of Typographic Man* (London, 1962), 18.

12. See Norbert Elias, *The Civilizing Process: Sociogenetic and Psychogenetic Investigations*, trans. Edmund Jephcott with some notes and corrections by the author, rev. edn, eds. Eric Dunning, Johan Goudsblom, and Stephen Mennell (Oxford, 2000).

13. See Mark M. Smith, *Sensing the Past: Seeing, Hearing, Smelling, Tasting, and Touching in History* (Berkeley, 2007).

14. Jonathan Sterne, *The Audible Past: Cultural Origins of Sound Reproduction* (Durham, NC, 2003).

15. Ibid., 23.

16. Ibid., 3.

17. Ibid., 15.

18. Ibid., 19.

19. See Steve Goodman, *Sonic Warfare: Sound, Affect, and the Ecology of Fear* (Cambridge, 2010).

20. For this argument, see also Steven Connor, "Feel the Noise: Excess, Affect and the Acoustic," in *Emotion in Postmodernism*, eds. Gerhard Hoffmann and Alfred Hornung (Heidelberg, 1997), 147–62.

21. Teresa Brennan, too, argues in her book *The Transmission of Affect* (Ithaca, NY, 2004) that affects are fundamentally social and that "there is no secure distinction between the 'individual' and the 'environment'" (ibid., 6).

22. Goodman, *Sonic Warfare*, 36.

23. For a brief overview of the events that led to the outbreak of World War I, see Roger Chickering, *Imperial Germany and the Great War, 1914–1918*, 2nd edn. (Cambridge, 2004), 10–17. For a recent revaluation of the July Crisis, see Christopher Clark, *The Sleepwalkers: How Europe Went to War in 1914* (London, 2012).

24. Verhey, *The Spirit of 1914*, 1. See also Gunther Mai, *Das Ende des Kaiserreichs: Politik und Kriegführung im Ersten Weltkrieg*, 2nd edn. (Munich, 1993), 9–30.

25. Verhey, *The Spirit of 1914*, 2–3.

26. Kruse, *Krieg und nationale Integration*, 31.

27. Thomas Lindenberger, *Straßenpolitik: Zur Sozialgeschichte der öffentlichen Ordnung in Berlin 1900 bis 1914* (Bonn, 1995), 360. "Hegemonie der Kriegsbefürworter".

28. Quoted following ibid., 60. "Hurrahviertel"; "Festklimbimrevier".

29. Eric J. Hobsbawm, "Mass-Producing Traditions: Europe, 1870–1914," in *The Invention of Tradition*, eds. Eric J. Hobsbawm and Terence Ranger (Cambridge, 1984), 277.
30. See Heinz Lemmermann, *Kriegserziehung im Kaiserreich. Studien zur politischen Funktion von Schule und Schulmusik 1890–1918* (Lilienthal, 1984); Thomas Rohkrämer, *Der Militarismus der "kleinen Leute."* Die *Kriegervereine im Deutschen Kaiserreich 1871–1914* (Munich, 1990); Jakob Vogel, "Militärfeiern in Deutschland und Frankreich als Rituale der Nation (1871–1914)," in *Nation und Emotion. Deutschland und Frankreich im Vergleich. 19. und 20. Jahrhundert*, eds. Etienne Francois, Hannes Siegrist, and Jakob Vogel (Göttingen, 1995), 199–214; Jakob Vogel, *Nationen im Gleichschritt. Der Kult der "Nation in Waffen" in Deutschland und Frankreich, 1871–1914* (Göttingen, 1995).
31. Lindenberger, *Straßenpolitik*, 376. "neue Dimensionen der Massenmobilisierung". See also Fritzsche, *Germans into Nazis*, 13–36.
32. Verhey, *The Spirit of 1914*, 82–89.
33. Eduard Heyd, "Quer durch die Mobilmachung," *Daheim* 50 (1914): 138. "brausende, singende Vaterlandserhebung".
34. Verhey, *The Spirit of 1914*, 28–29. "Endlich öffnen sich die Pforten. Für ein Dutzend Herausschreitende drängten sich zwei Dutzend hinein. Wieder spielt die Musik. Ein Marsch, ein Kriegslied. Wehe ihr, wenn sie das Programm nicht der Stimmung des Tages anpassen wollte! Gestern versuchte sie noch einmal, einen modischen Walzer einzuschieben. Kaum erklangen die ersten Takte, so antwortete das Publikum mit pfeifendem Protest. Der Kapellmeister mußte abklopfen und ein Dutzend Stimmen intonierte a capella, was er spielen soll: 'Deutschland, Deutschland über alles.' Der Chor schwillt gewaltig an, jetzt fällt die Musik ein. Erhaben rauscht die Hymne empor. Das ganze Publikum hat sich von den Sitzen erhoben. Zwei, drei Gäste glauben, ihre Gleichgültigkeit gegenüber der allgemeinen Begeisterung durch Sitzenbleiben bekunden zu dürfen. Aber nur zwei, drei Sekunden lang. Ein Sturm der Entrüstung fegt sie empor. Sie müssen aufstehen. Und als dennoch einer weiter sitzen bleiben will, wird er ohne Säumen gepackt, ohne daß er Zeit gehabt hätte, die Zeche zu zahlen, ohne daß ihm Frist geblieben, nach Hut und Stock zu greifen, findet er sich an der frischen Luft wieder. Ein neuer Trupp dringt von draußen herein. Über ihren Häuptern schwebt eine Fahne, schwarzgelb. Das ist das Signal zur letzten, tobenden Steigerung des Enthusiasmus. Brausende Hochrufe, leuchtende Augen, ein Überschwang, von dem die Herzen überfließen. Und wieder Musik. Und wieder Chorgesang: Gott erhalte Franz den Kaiser."
35. Dietmar Klenke, *Der singende "deutsche Mann": Gesangsvereine und deutsches Nationalbewusstsein von Napoleon bis Hitler* (Münster, 1998), 104. "Vorreiter auf dem Weg zur modernen Massenmobilisierung."
36. See Sabine Giesbrecht, "'Lieb' Vaterland, magst ruhig sein': Musik und Nationalismus im deutschen Kaiserreich," in *Vom hörbaren Frieden*, eds. Hartmut Lück and Dieter Senghaas (Frankfurt am Main, 2005), 413–42; Barbara James, "'Der Kaiser ist ein lieber Mann': Schullieder auf Kaiser

Wilhelm," in *Ich will aber gerade vom Leben singen …: Über populäre Musik vom ausgehenden 19. Jahrhundert bis zum Ende der Weimarer Republik*, ed. Sabine Schutte (Reinbek bei Hamburg, 1987), 169–86.

37. See Waltraud Linder-Beroud, "Von 'Heil dir im Siegerkranz …' zum 'Hymnenmix': Vom Kreuz mit den deutschen National- und Landeshymnen," in *Geschichte als Musik*, ed. Otto Borst (Tübingen, 1999), 32–67.

38. Christian Jansen, "Einleitung: Musik als Mittel politischer Identitätsstiftung," in *Die Macht der Töne: Musik als Mittel politischer Identitätsfindung im 20. Jahrhundert*, eds. Tillmann Bendikowski et al. (Münster, 2003), 9. "Musikhandlung."

39. For the importance of newspapers in Berlin before World War I, see Peter Fritzsche, *Reading Berlin 1900* (Cambridge, MA, 1996).

40. Verhey, *The Spirit of 1914*, 59. "Bis in die spätesten Nachtstunden hinein warteten die Leute auf endgültige Nachricht über den Stand der Dinge. Während vorerst eine bedrückte Stimmung vorherrschte, löste sich allmählich die Spannung und machte sich Luft durch Absingen patriotischer Lieder."

41. Ibid., 73. "gellenden Rufe der Zeitungsverkäufer."

42. Ibid., 70. "Der fieberhafte Lärm, der in den Tagen vor der Mobilmachung die Straßen durchhallte, verstummt allmählich. Die meisten Menschen gehen ernst und bedrückt aneinander vorüber."

43. *Tägliche Rundschau*, 22 August 1914, quoted following Dieter Glatzer and Ruth Glatzer, *Berliner Leben 1914–1918: Eine historische Reportage aus Erinnerungen und Berichten* (Berlin, 1986), 91. "Eine schöne Siegesfeier veranstaltete gestern Nacht die Berliner Liedertafel, indem sie unter der Leitung ihres Chormeisters Max Wiedemann ein improvisiertes Konzert auf dem Potsdamer Platz gab. Der bekannte Verein hatte seinen Übungsabend abgebrochen, um dem überquellenden Jubel über den eben bekanntgewordenen großen Sieg in irgendeiner Weise Luft zu machen, zog zum Potsdamer Platz und überraschte und erfreute die zahlreiche Menge durch seine Kunst. Das 'Niederländische Dankgebet' und einige feurige Kriegslieder, darunter 'Lützows wilde, verwegene Jagd', wurden vorgetragen und von dem immer mehr anwachsenden Publikum mit tosendem Beifall aufgenommen. Bei den letzten Liedern 'Deutschland, Deutschland über alles', 'Die Wacht am Rhein', 'Heil dir im Siegerkranz' fiel die schließlich fast den ganzen Platz füllende Menge ein, und so gestaltete sich schließlich das improvisierte Konzert zu einer patriotischen Kundgebung von überwältigender Schönheit."

44. See Klenke, *Der singende "deutsche Mann*," 13.

45. Bernd Ulrich and Benjamin Ziemann, eds., *German Soldiers in the Great War: Letters and Eyewitness Accounts* (Barnsley, 2010), 24. "Ein ganz neuer Berliner Sport 'Abschreien'. 'Was machen Sie denn heute abend?' 'Wir gehen abschreien.' Auf den belebteren Plätzen und Straßenkreuzungen sammelt sich die Menge und sowie eine feldgraue Uniform im Auto vorbeisaust, sowie ein Koffer irgendwo sichtbar ist, ertönt ein vielstimmiges Hurra! So nimmt man Abschied von den scheidenden Kriegern.

Und die Offiziere stehen auf und schwenken die Mütze—das Volk wartet
bis tief in die Nacht—ohne 25 'abgeschrieene' Leutnants geht niemand ins
Bett." For the German original: Bernd Ulrich and Benjamin Ziemann, eds.,
*Frontalltag im Ersten Weltkrieg: Wahn und Wirklichkeit* (Frankfurt am Main,
1994), 30.
46. Verhey, *The Spirit of 1914*, 54. "Vor den Cafés und Restaurants gab
es große Anhäufungen der Massen. Die 'Wacht am Rhein' und 'Heil
dir im Siegerkranz' erschollen aus Tausenden von Kehlen, aber
auch die Arbeitermarseillaise klang von geschlossenen Trupps her
machtvoll durch die Nacht. In die Hochs auf den Kaiser und seinen
österreichischen Verbündeten mischten sich die Hochrufe auf die internationale Sozialdemokratie und die Rufe 'Nieder mit dem Krieg!' Es war ein
Durcheinander von erhitzten Rufen, von Kundgebungen für und wider, die
zu einem brausenden Lärm anschwollen und wie die allgemeine Erregung
sich immer mehr steigerten. Die Polizei war um die zehnte Stunde gegen
diesen Massenandrang von Menschen vollkommen machtlos."
47. On the *Hörbilder*, see Heinz Hiebler, "Weltbild 'Hörbild': Zur Formengeschichte des phonographischen Gedächtnisses zwischen 1877 und 1929,"
in *Die Medien und ihre Technik: Theorien – Modelle – Geschichte*, ed. Harro
Segeberg (Marburg, 2004), 206–28; Sandra Rühr, *Tondokumente von der
Walze zum Hörbuch: Geschichte – Medienspezifik - Rezeption* (Göttingen,
2008), 50. The *Hörbild* can be listened to on, for example, the CD *Der
Kaiser kommt, der Kaiser geht: Tondokumente von 1900 bis 1918 (Stimmen
des 20. Jahrhunderts)*, eds. Deutsches Historisches Museum/Deutsches
Rundfunkarchiv, track 10.
48. *Vossische Zeitung*, 1 August 1914, 1. "Sobald gestern nachmittag auf dem
Königlichen Schlosse die purpurne Königsstandarte hochging, drängten
ungezählte Tausende nach dem Schloßplatz und dem Lustgarten, die
bald vom Dom bis zur Spree und von den Terrassen des Schlosses bis zur
Nationalgalerie dicht besetzt waren. Machtvoll brausten nationale Lieder
empor, die 'Wacht am Rhein', 'Heil dir im Siegerkranz', 'Deutschland,
Deutschland über alles'. Plötzlich—es war kurz nach sechs Uhr—öffneten
sich die Türen des Balkons, der dem Dom gegenüber liegt. Der Kaiser, die
Kaiserin und die Prinzen Adalbert und Oskar traten, von ungeheurem
Jubel umbraust, heraus. Es dauerte geraume Zeit, ehe die brausenden
Hochs verstummten und der Kaiser sprechen konnte. Markig und von
tiefstem Ernst erfüllt klangen die Worte, mit einer Wucht, die der entschei-
denden Stunde entspricht. Einige Sätze, zornbebend gesprochen und aus
dem Fluß der Rede markant hervorgehoben, müssen sich unvergeßlich
jedem einprägen, der die Anklage mitangehört, die der Kaiser vor versam-
meltem Volk gegen den friedenstörenden Nachbar schleuderte. Erschüttert
stand die Menge entblößten Hauptes da, als der Kaiser zum Schluß alle
aufforderte, den Himmel anzuflehen um den Sieg der deutschen Waffen! …
'Heil Kaiser dir!' war die Antwort."
49. Theodor Wolff, *Der Krieg des Pontius Pilatus* (Zurich, 1934), 357. "Die
hochrufende Menge erhitzte sich zu stürmischer Begeisterung" (trans.
from Verhey, *The Spirit of 1914*, 59).

50. This argument can already be found in Lindenberger, *Straßenpolitik*, 377–81, but not in Leif Jerram's new study, *Streetlife: The Untold History of Europe's Twentieth Century* (Oxford, 2011), which examines the street as a political place primarily with reference to revolutionary unrest, but not to demonstrations supporting the state.

## Bibliography

Brennan, Teresa. *The Transmission of Affect*. Ithaca, NY, 2004.

Chickering, Roger. *Imperial Germany and the Great War, 1914–1918*. 2nd edn. Cambridge, 2004.

Clark, Christopher. *The Sleepwalkers: How Europe Went to War in 1914*. London, 2012.

Connor, Steven. "Feel the Noise: Excess, Affect and the Acoustic." In *Emotion in Postmodernism*. Eds. Gerhard Hoffmann and Alfred Hornung. Heidelberg, 1997, 147–62.

Elias, Norbert. *The Civilizing Process: Sociogenetic and Psychogenetic Investigations*. Trans. Edmund Jephcott with some notes and corrections by the author. Rev. edn. Eds. Eric Dunning, Johan Goudsblom, and Stephen Mennell. Oxford, 2000.

Fleischer, Gerald. *Lärm—der tägliche Terror*. Stuttgart, 1990.

Fritzsche, Peter. *Reading Berlin 1900*. Cambridge, MA, 1996.

———. *Germans into Nazis*. Cambridge, 1998.

Giesbrecht, Sabine. "'Lieb' Vaterland, magst ruhig sein': Musik und Nationalismus im deutschen Kaiserreich." In *Vom hörbaren Frieden*. Eds. Hartmut Lück and Dieter Senghaas. Frankfurt am Main, 2005, 413–42.

Glatzer, Dieter, and Ruth Glatzer. *Berliner Leben 1914–1918: Eine historische Reportage aus Erinnerungen und Berichten*. Berlin, 1986.

Goodman, Steve. *Sonic Warfare: Sound, Affect, and the Ecology of Fear*. Cambridge, 2010.

Grossbach, Michael, and Eckart Altenmüller. "Musik und Emotion—zur Wirkung und Wirkort von Musik." In *Die Macht der Töne: Musik als Mittel politischer Identitätsfindung im 20. Jahrhundert*. Eds. Tillmann Bendikowski et al. Münster, 2003, 13–22.

Heyd, Eduard. "Quer durch die Mobilmachung." *Daheim* 50 (1914): 138–40.

Hiebler, Heinz. "Weltbild 'Hörbild': Zur Formengeschichte des phonographischen Gedächtnisses zwischen 1877 und 1929." In *Die Medien und ihre Technik: Theorien – Modelle – Geschichte*. Ed. Harro Segeberg. Marburg, 206–28.

Hobsbawm, Eric J. "Mass-Producing Traditions: Europe, 1870–1914." In *The Invention of Tradition*. Eds. Eric J. Hobsbawm and Terence Ranger. Cambridge, 1984, 263–307.

James, Barbara. "'Der Kaiser ist ein lieber Mann': Schullieder auf Kaiser Wilhelm." In *Ich will aber gerade vom Leben singen …: Über populäre Musik vom ausgehenden 19. Jahrhundert bis zum Ende der Weimarer Republik*. Ed. Sabine Schutte. Reinbek bei Hamburg, 1987, 169–86.

Jansen, Christian. "Einleitung: Musik als Mittel politischer Identitätsstiftung." In *Die Macht der Töne: Musik als Mittel politischer Identitätsfindung im 20. Jahrhundert*. Eds. Tillmann Bendikowski et al. Münster, 2003, 7–12.

Jerram, Leif. *Streetlife: The Untold History of Europe's Twentieth Century*. Oxford, 2011.

Juslin, Patrik N., and John Sloboda, eds. *Handbook of Music and Emotion: Theory, Research, Applications*. Oxford, 2010.

Klenke, Dietmar. *Der singende "deutsche Mann": Gesangsvereine und deutsches Nationalbewusstsein von Napoleon bis Hitler*. Münster, 1998.

Kruse, Wolfgang. *Krieg und nationale Integration: Eine Neuinterpretation des sozialdemokratischen Burgfriedensschlusses 1914/15*. Essen, 1993.

Lemmermann, Heinz. *Kriegserziehung im Kaiserreich: Studien zur politischen Funktion von Schule und Schulmusik 1890–1918*. Lilienthal, 1984.

Lindenberger, Thomas. *Straßenpolitik: Zur Sozialgeschichte der öffentlichen Ordnung in Berlin 1900 bis 1914*. Bonn, 1995.

Linder-Beroud, Waltraud. "Von 'Heil dir im Siegerkranz …' zum 'Hymnenmix': Vom Kreuz mit den deutschen National- und Landeshymnen." In *Geschichte als Musik*. Ed. Otto Borst. Tübingen, 1999, 32–67.

Mai, Gunther. *Das Ende des Kaiserreichs: Politik und Kriegführung im Ersten Weltkrieg*. 2nd edn. Munich, 1993.

———. "1. August 1914: Gab es ein Augusterlebnis?" In *Tage deutscher Geschichte: Von der Reformation bis zur Wiedervereinigung*. Eds. Eckart Conze and Thomas Nicklas. Munich, 2004, 177–94.

Marks, Stephan. "Zur Bedeutung des akustischen Mediums für die sozialwissenschaftliche Forschung und Lehre." In *Akustisches Gedächtnis und Zweiter Weltkrieg*. Ed. Robert Maier. Göttingen, 2010, 21–30.

Matt, Susan J. "Current Emotion Research in History: Or, Doing History from the Inside Out." *Emotion Review* 3, no. 1 (2011): 117–24.

McLuhan, Marshall. *The Gutenberg Galaxy: The Making of Typographic Man*. London, 1962.

Nipperdey, Thomas. *Deutsche Geschichte 1866–1918*. Vol. 2: Machtstaat vor der Demokratie. Munich, 1992.

Raithel, Thomas. *Das "Wunder" der inneren Einheit: Studien zur deutschen und französischen Öffentlichkeit bei Beginn des Ersten Weltkrieges*. Bonn, 1996.

Rohkrämer, Thomas. *Der Militarismus der "kleinen Leute." Die Kriegervereine im Deutschen Kaiserreich 1871–1914*. Munich, 1990.

———. "August 1914—Kriegsmentalität und ihre Voraussetzungen." In *Der Erste Weltkrieg: Wirkung, Wahrnehmung, Analyse*. Ed. Wolfgang Michalka. Munich, 1994, 759–77.

Rosenwein, Barbara. "Problems and Methods in the History of Emotions." *Passions in Context: Journal of the History and Philosophy of the Emotions* 1 (2010): 1–32. See http://www.passionsincontext.de/index.php?id=557; accessed 6 September 2013.

Rühr, Sandra. *Tondokumente von der Walze zum Hörbuch: Geschichte— Medienspezifik—Rezeption*. Göttingen, 2008.

Schafer, R. Murray. *The Soundscape: Our Sonic Environment and the Tuning of the World*. Rochester, VT, 1994.

Smith, Mark M. *Sensing the Past: Seeing, Hearing, Smelling, Tasting, and Touching in History*. Berkeley, 2007.

Sterne, Jonathan. *The Audible Past: Cultural Origins of Sound Reproduction*. Durham, NC, 2003.

Ulrich, Bernd, and Benjamin Ziemann, eds. *German Soldiers in the Great War: Letters and Eyewitness Accounts*. Barnsley, 2010.

Verhey, Jeffrey. *The Spirit of 1914: Militarism, Myth, and Mobilization in Germany*. Cambridge, 2000.

Vogel, Jakob. "Militärfeiern in Deutschland und Frankreich als Rituale der Nation (1871–1914)." In *Nation und Emotion: Deutschland und Frankreich im Vergleich. 19. und 20. Jahrhundert*. Eds. Etienne Francois, Hannes Siegrist, and Jakob Vogel. Göttingen, 1995, 199–214.

———. *Nationen im Gleichschritt: Der Kult der "Nation in Waffen" in Deutschland und Frankreich, 1871–1914*. Göttingen, 1995.

*Vossische Zeitung*, 1 August 1914.

Weisbrod, Bernd. "Die Politik der Repräsentation: Das Erbe des Ersten Weltkrieges und der Formwandel der Politik in Europa." In *Der Erste Weltkrieg und die europäische Nachkriegsordnung: Sozialer Wandel und Formveränderung der Politik*. Ed. Hans Mommsen. Cologne, 2000, 13–41.

Wierzbicka, Anna. "The 'History of Emotions' and the Future of Emotion Research." *Emotion Review* 2, no. 3 (2010): 269–73.

Wolff, Theodor. *Der Krieg des Pontius Pilatus*. Zurich, 1934.

Ziemann, Benjamin. *War Experiences in Rural Germany, 1914–1923*. Oxford, 2007.

———. "Germany 1914–1918: Total War as a Catalyst of Change." In *The Oxford Handbook of Modern German History*. Ed. Helmut Walser Smith. Oxford, 2011, 378–99.

9

# LISTENING ON THE HOME FRONT
## Music and the Production of Social Meaning in German Concert Halls during World War I

*Hansjakob Ziemer*

In 1915, while in the trenches of Verdun, the music journalist, Paul Bekker, wrote a review of the premiere of the *Alpensinfonie* by Richard Strauss without having actually attended the performance in Berlin's Philharmonic Hall. With only the score of the symphony at his disposal, he imagined his listening experience "as if" he had visited the concert hall. He wrote how, in his imagination, he arrived at the concert hall and noticed its faulty architecture, and made observations about other fellow listeners. He went on to describe the sounds, the development of the musical themes and structures, and he recorded his emotional experience of the music. He wrote, for example, about how the music had "stirring" moments or how it expressed a "tender glowing."[1] Finally, reflecting on the composition of the work, he acknowledged the musical craftsmanship of Strauss, but otherwise wrote a scathing review; in his view the piece was of minor quality and lacked a deeper understanding of nature. Defenders of Strauss, such as the noted Viennese journalist Richard Specht, dismissed Bekker's verdict, arguing that Bekker could not possibly be a legitimate judge of the music since he did not actually hear the work. He denied Bekker's claim that "inner listening" could take place without physically hearing the music, and he fumed over Bekker's sharp critique. Specht's rejection of Bekker's review culminated in a hyperbolic threat ("one should kill this critic"), illustrating just how much was felt to be at stake in this debate.[2]

The controversy between Bekker and Specht revolves ostensibly around differing judgments of Strauss' music. The underlying issue, however, was how "listening" on the front challenged notions of "listening" on the home front. In particular, Bekker called into question accepted ideas about the cultural methods and social meanings of listening, especially those that bound listening to time and space. Bekker severed the listening experience from its material, temporal, and spatial context—one that relied on a concert hall, musicians, instruments, and other listeners—and he replaced it with a listening experience that was exclusively governed by his knowledge of music and inner fantasy. Indeed, he claimed that the physical distance from the premiere was a precondition for "purer listening" that elevated the quality of the listening experience.[3] Bekker's ability to have a listening experience outside of the "normal" listening context brings to the fore the importance of the listening context for the listening experience, and opens the possibility that different listening contexts lead to different listening experiences. Indeed, Bekker shows us that the same is true for Specht's listening experience: his own listening context, although not in the trenches, was not static, but the changing social and political environment of the home front. Just as for Bekker, for listeners on the home front the changing social, political, and cultural context influenced the social meaning of the listening experience. At issue in Bekker's and Specht's dispute was the definition of listening, to what extent the social context and institutional background mattered, and—at root—the variable social meaning of the listening experience. For Bekker, listening in Verdun, the music meant a break from the war, a momentary escape, so that he did not attach any political or national significance to Strauss. For Specht, listening on the home front, the national significance of Strauss was crucial because, he argued, Strauss represented the superiority of the German musical tradition and offered a way for listeners to experience a "German feeling." Specht's social context was just as changed by World War I as Bekker's. The war altered social life on the home front by erasing boundaries between the military and civilian realms and by intruding on all aspects of social, political, cultural, and emotional life.[4] Listening experiences such as those of Bekker and Specht, I propose, were highly contested not so much for musical reasons, but because they were embedded in different social contexts of listening.

Recent historiography has done little to illuminate the effects of changing contexts on the practices of and discourses about listening in the concert hall. As an ephemeral subject that is hard to grasp with conventional methods of social history, assumptions about the history of music listening are often based on static models that rely on aesthetic treatises outlining ideals, rather than practices, of listening. Cultural historians of the second half of the nineteenth century, such as Peter Gay, have argued that "the nineteenth century campaign" attempted to achieve a "lonely, sacred eminence" of listening, and that its goal had been the "undivided silent attention to a musical performance" that culminated in the "triumph of inwardness."[5] But Gay's perspective on listening as focused attention to music, implies a self-disciplined and passive behavior that ignores the richness of opportunities for individual listeners to make active and public use of their emotional experiences, and, as a result, it misses the different social meanings that listening experiences could acquire under different circumstances. The notion of change has been notably absent from the history of listening, which has, instead, been emblematic for a history that sees culture as largely limited to a "civilizing effort." Such a perspective also suggests a certain inevitability and immutability of the passively listening audience, even up to today. Such questions as if and how social and cultural turning points, such as World War I, can influence changes in sensory perceptions, and how we can study them, have remained largely desiderata.

The model of the silent, passive listener has been challenged on methodological grounds by ethnomusicologists and music sociologists who study listening contexts other than the Western symphony concert hall. For these scholars, the underlying assumptions of the silent listener were simply not applicable to the musical experiences they encountered outside the concert halls. As a result, in attempting to explain the relationship between emotional responses to music and the listening contexts, they developed concepts that emphasized the cultural construction of listening habits.[6] Judith Becker, for example, has argued that the listener is defined "through continuous, interactive, ever-evolving musical structures and listener responses," and that the meaning of the event was created in this "mutual relationship established at any given moment."[7] Listening, then, is not exclusively characterized by the aesthetic ideals of a certain group of listeners but by a specific surrounding culture, by behavioral styles in the concert hall, by the imagination of social relationships, and by the definitions of music that all situate the listening activity at different levels. Listening emerges hereby as a product of the constant interaction of time, place, personal biography, and the shared context of culture. We study this interaction to gain insights into what sounds, and the emotional responses they elicit, meant to contemporaries in a specific historical moment.

Using these insights from sociological and ethnomusicological studies, this chapter attempts to reconstruct the historical contexts of emotional experiences of music. If we define culture not merely as an educational process with a capacity for cognitive conditioning, but, following Ann Swidler, as a "'tool-kit' of symbols, stories, rituals, and world-views, which people may use in varying configurations to solve different kinds of problems," then the emotional experiences of music were a useful way for listeners to actively construct social meaning.[8] Listeners could engage in the interpretive flexibility offered by symphonic music in order to find answers and meanings in the challenges that the total war posed for them. In this situation, listening was activated to help listeners manage and come to terms with social and personal crises. Listening could be used, for example, to imagine communities for the glorification of the nation, to stage war enthusiasm and other emotional reactions in public, or to construct the self through rituals of mourning. In this way, in the period between fin de siècle and Weimar Culture, the concert halls strengthened a close interdependency between the musical world and German society.[9] The frequency of social, political, and cultural changes—that started before the war with massive demographic change and continued after the war with the consequences of demobilization, inflation, and revolution—inspired a number of experiments in the concert hall in search of new social meanings.

The main protagonists of this discourse on listening were music journalists. As listening was a tacit and subtle activity often practiced without conscious or verbalized reflection, music journalists offer a unique record describing the listening experiences, and the meanings listeners heard. They relied on an established language of music listening as well as on their pre-war reputation as respected authorities on listening experiences. During the musical event, they relied on techniques resembling those of participant observers in anthropology, since they took part as listeners themselves, but also offered retrospective reflection and summary of the event, commenting, justifying, and explaining their own and others' listening experience.

In this chapter, I will focus on the reconstruction of three different social and political contexts that shaped listening in the concert hall during World War I. In the first part, I will reconstruct the intellectual and institutional context of the war society that influenced listening by intensifying music's relationship to the ubiquitous war discourse. After considering the changing definitions of music, concert organization, and behavioral styles, I will go on to ask how listeners used their interpretive flexibility to create social meaning. I will describe how listeners used symphonic music as a projection space through which the national community could be imagined. In the third part, I will show how this desire for national unity was countered by the plurality of interests in the audience, and how individuals turned to musical experiences in order to cope with the hardships of the war on the home front. Finally, I will conclude with an outlook on the impact of music listening during World War I for the further development of the contexts of listening during the inflationary period and the 1920s.

## Music Listening in Wartime: Ideas, Institutions, and Social Behavior

The outbreak of the war asked for a redefinition of music's social role in the emerging "war culture" that now began to govern public life in the German cities. This war culture has been described by historians as a "matrix and comprehensive framework" that helped German society at war to shape a broad consensus about the war aims and the commitment of the civilian sphere.[10] Music came to play a crucial part from the beginning in helping to build this broad public consensus. The so-called *Augusterlebnis* of 1914, for example, involved an unprecedented cultural mobilization of the masses in which choral groups and marching bands took part in staging the public's enthusiasm for the troops. Jointly singing a church hymn by Johann Sebastian Bach in Berlin's Potsdamer Platz after the victory at the Battle of Tannenberg on 30 August 1914 was seen as a musical experience of a new kind that could stand as a model for all other kinds of musical experiences.[11] Patriotic concerts (*vaterländische Konzerte*) were organized all over Germany until the end of the war, often in public spaces and attended by thousands of people. This public practice of instrumentalizing music for war purposes was justified by a long-held and now dramatically intensified belief in the social power of German music to bring people together.

Belief in the social power of German music provided the intellectual impetus for using music to activate support for the nation at war, and enabled an increasing politicization of music listening, not only in the streets but also in the concert halls. As Karen Painter has argued, from 1914 on music aesthetics could "no longer ignore physicality," and the idea of art for art's sake fell silent, being seen as "unpatriotic" in the light of the ascribed power of music to support the troops and to express the best values of the nation.[12] Music's role was now defined as part of the German *Kultur* concept that opposed other concepts of "civilization" from France and Great Britain. The Hamburg music journalist and conductor, Georg Göhler, for example, used Werner Sombart's influential wartime treatise on "Händler und Helden" (Businessmen and Heroes) as an example for his own "Händler und Künstler" in which he aggressively compared German musicians, responsible for the creation of musical culture, and English businessmen, whom he saw as responsible for the decline of musical culture. The English exemplified the new devastating trends of sports and commercialization that threatened German music. Göhler viewed the war not primarily as a conflict about political issues, but as a "war of world views" (*Krieg der Weltanschauungen*).[13]

In this attempt to create cultural, political, and social order by outlining music's special significance for German culture, Göhler established fundamental dichotomies by juxtaposing commercialization and art, superficiality and truth, fashion and values.[14]

One important function of this discourse was to help legitimate symphony concerts in the hometowns. At the beginning of war activities, there were strong doubts about the legitimacy of organized musical experiences; was not music listening an illegitimate distraction from more important concerns? Was it justified to invest resources in the organization of symphony concerts that could be used elsewhere? Questions such as these were asked by concert societies all over Germany. The editor of the *Frankfurter Zeitung*, Heinrich Simon, reported that Frankfurt had strong reservations about reopening the cultural season with operas, theaters, and concerts since they seemed inappropriate for the seriousness of the situation.[15] The leading local concert society, Frankfurt's Museums-Gesellschaft, set up a committee to assess the situation and to negotiate with Frankfurt's mayor, ultimately concluding in favor of concert organization. Although music, the committee agreed, might appear to be minor in the face of the "breakout of the gigantic struggle," they argued that making and listening to music were part of the war effort.[16] Yet, in their proposal to continue the concerts, there seem to have been other concerns as well. The committee observed a "nervousness" in the people who stayed at home and for whom music might provide a lifeline. In Frankfurt, they also feared that a possible interruption of subscription concerts would lead to a worsening of the already existing financial crises, since listeners would save their money, choral societies would not book the orchestras, and payments for soloists would increase even further.[17] Thus the discourse about music's role in wartime was instrumentalized to help concert societies survive the hardships of the war at a local level. The war brought the symphony concerts into a closer alliance with politics than ever before, both because of a belief in the nationalistic powers of music and also to secure institutional survival.

In practice, concert life resumed almost everywhere in Germany after the outbreak of war, even though not to the same extent as in the years preceding 1914. According to statistics of concert life in Berlin, Vienna, and Munich, the number of concerts decreased by 50 per cent in 1915.[18] Contemporaries explained this decline with the retreat of artists from Russia and France, and commentators argued that the war had a purifying effect on concert life since musicians from these nations were held responsible for the commercialization of concerts in Germany. In reality, the decline in the number of concerts probably had more to do with the conscription of German orchestra musicians for deployment to the front. Although we do not have any further quantitative evidence for the succeeding years of 1916, 1917, and 1918, journalistic accounts remarking on the number of concerts indicate that concert life slowly returned to pre-war levels. The organization of numerous patriotic and charity concerts marked the musical scene. It was possible for Beethoven's *Eroica* to be performed six times within twenty-four hours, as happened in Berlin in 1914.[19] But critics asked if these concerts had "a right to exist"—in other words, if they truly served the emotional needs of the public, or whether the proliferation of concerts was a symptom of an underlying crisis.[20] In 1916, one critic wrote that "our ears do not suffer" from neglect but that they were "oversaturated": "music and no end."[21]

These tensions between practical expectations of listeners, and political as well as cultural concerns, could be felt in the concert halls themselves. At first glance, concerts took place in their conventional ways despite the dramatic circumstances, and observers often noticed how seemingly unaffected the listeners were by the war. Of course, new practices that were fostered by the war, such as the audience singing along during a performance of "Heil Dir im Siegerkranz," could change the procedures of the performance.[22] But more often than not, the behavior of the listeners during the performance continued pre-war habits: listeners still showed up late for the beginning of the concert or left the concert hall before the end of it, they applauded during the performance of a work when they particularly liked it or they waved with their handkerchiefs. From the perspective of the behavior of the listeners, it seems that wartime listening did not rise to the high expectations that the political nature of these concerts were supposed to express. Max Marschalk, one of the leading Berlin music journalists and someone who understood himself as an advocate of the audience, praised the lively and festive atmosphere of the performances. Berlin's Philharmonic Hall had just been newly decorated in the summer of 1914, and the glimmering hall in white, golden, and purple colors contributed to the "ceremonial glamor" of the event. Marschalk took particular pleasure in the "glamorously dressed" listeners who were looking forward to a few hours of musical experiences.[23] Marschalk represented a group of listeners who saw concerts primarily as a social festivity, in spite of their political aims.

Even before 1914, such practices had become the target of a group of journalists, conductors, and musicians who attempted to reform the performance by changing the context of the listening experience.

They wanted to emphasize the artistic nature of the concert experience and hoped to establish reforms in listening behavior during the performance. Some had attempted to change behavior through programming politics; by, for example, putting more emphasis on the symphony or by a more careful composition of the individual concert programs. Others hoped to change listener behavior by building new music halls that would allow more focused listening and—often modeled on Wagner's *Festspielhaus* (Festival House)—elevate the musical experience to a quasi-religious status. Still others hoped to improve the symphony concert by dimming the lights and reducing noise during the performance. While most of these attempts were put on hold during the war, the issue of noise-making and the proper way to applaud during a concert were still publicly debated. The journalist Hans Fischer, for example, proposed to eliminate all sources of noise that disturbed focused listening.[24] He suggested ending the score-reading practice, which he identified as a major source of noise, and others suggested reducing the frequency of applause. Fischer observed that at the beginning of the war a certain "indifference" among the listeners had vanished, which he welcomed as a contribution to a new listening experience marked by a higher degree of concentration on the music. But by 1916 he noticed that indifference had returned. Reform efforts such as his were countered by arguments that the listener deserved freedom, especially in times of war. For listeners such as Marschalk, the noise of the performance was a sign of enjoyment; the more noise, the more people were enjoying themselves. Silence on the part of the listeners would be a sign of dissatisfaction and rejection, and most people's pleasure would be disturbed if they had to be silent. In his view, applause had "at all costs" to be part of this "true festivity of joy."[25]

While these controversies about the artistic nature of the concert experience drew on continuities with fin-de-siècle concerts, other tensions were introduced into the concert hall which were particular to the wartime culture. An important new aspect of wartime concert-going was a changed visual experience. Franz Calvelli-Adorno, Theodor W. Adorno's cousin and a regular concert-goer in Frankfurt, noticed that from 1916 onwards more and more soldiers in uniform, even wounded ones, attended the concerts and significantly changed the atmosphere. (And Calvelli-Adorno did not forget to mention the biographic changes in the listener's lives that were invisible and yet present.[26]) Almost everywhere, the presence of grey uniforms changed the visual impression of the audience and affected the audience's concert experience. Many observers noticed a change in the "physiognomy" of the audience. The longer the war took, the more the appearance of the listeners changed: women wore less jewelry and did not expose themselves as much as they used to, fashion styles changed and dark colors dominated the picture rather than the colorful dresses of the pre-war period.[27] Comments on the uniforms, changes in fashion, and the gaze of wounded soldiers in the concert halls illustrated how the performance of music was deeply influenced by the changing material culture. The dominance of the eye remained a crucial mediating factor between the sounds and the emotional responses, as Richard Leppert has pointed out.[28]

## Audience as Nation: Social Relationships in the Concert Hall

The symphonic concerts during wartime fostered in the audience an imagination of themselves as a national community, one that closely connected listeners with fellow listeners, listeners with composers and musicians, and listeners with soldiers on the front. Performances created social meaning by allowing listeners to assume a similarity of experience in the concert hall that could be used as a common emotional basis for the nation. Music listening seemed to be "where effectively the one and only thinking, the same yearning, the same angst and the same joy fill all hearts."[29] The concert hall was therefore a place where the listeners could go to experience the nation, and they employed the interpretative flexibility of symphonic music for this goal. Musical structures and thematic developments opened a screen onto which diverse cultural and political ideas could be projected.[30]

In the first half of the war in particular, the establishment of close social relationships among the audience members played a major role in creating an emotional community, and the feeling of close togetherness defined by national character differentiated the wartime concert hall experience from pre-war concerts.[31] The *Alpensinfonie* could, for example, be heard as a piece that offered "clarity, truthfulness, emotional unity, and Germaness of its language and its emotional content," and the musicians could be imagined as an "orchestra army."[32] Concerts in wartime, according to the journalist and conductor Rudolf Cahn-Speyer, enriched emotional life by "heightening the feelings that we are aware of in this moment."[33] He hoped that the war would end the inner fragmentation of the audiences that had begun before the war and that mirrored the disintegration of society. But now he observed a new need for an egalitarian and integrating concert that would allow music to unfold its powers. Music should not, he

contended, be understood only as intellectual pleasure or an individu-
alistic experience:

> All our current striving is aimed at emphasizing what is shared by all, we
> are ready to subordinate the individual under the grand general goals
> and needs ... As interesting as it is in normal times to get to know what is
> alien to us ... we now want to enjoy what everybody can enjoy. We do not
> want to know anything of currents and orientations ... Everybody strives
> to feel together with others as a great unity, and this is why the audience
> wants to listen to the works of older masters.[34]

The concert hall, as a microcosm of society, offered a unique opportunity
to allow the feeling of an emotional community and created a model for
how society in general should be perceived. As Michael Baxendall has
observed, a major function of art was to add something substantially
new to the lives of recipients.[35] Concert observers such as Cahn-Speyer
hoped to achieve the "new" in the projection of an emerging nationalized
unity onto the audience, and as a result viewed the "highest national
one-sidedness" and the exclusion of foreign music from the listeners'
experience as an "enrichment."[36] As much as this idea remained a
fiction and a utopia, it also illustrates how the concert hall could be
used to combine different strands of nationalism: the popular euphoria
on the streets and the official propaganda and policies. It provided
space to translate ideas into practice, which meant that nationalist ideas
could be experienced in concrete terms while listening together in an
enclosed space. While the nation was an abstract entity, the concert
hall could bring it to life, and it served as a stage for "enactment of the
identity of the nation."[37]

Contemporaries identified repertory programming as an effective
tool to steer the establishment of a national community, as a unity of
programming promised an emotional unity of the audience. Drawing
on nationalist stereotypes about German music, program organizers
used their power to radically change the nature of what was listened
to. More than ever before, performances were now determined by
the descent of composers and soloists and by their historical status in
the German musical tradition. While in the pre-war season nineteen
out of thirty-five composers performed by Frankfurt's municipal
orchestra came from German-speaking lands and sixteen from other
European countries (among them France, Italy, and England), in the
first war season twenty-two out of thirty-one performed composers
had a German-speaking background; the others came from Bohemia,
Hungary, Italy, and Norway. The more historical a work was, the more
likely was its performance. As a result of these two criteria, concert

programs were dominated by the music of Beethoven, Bach, Mozart, Brahms, Wagner, and Schubert.[38] Contemporary compositions were often limited to Reger, Strauss, and those composers who wrote works with a specific war theme. As Robin Lenman observed, "the war's first casualty was the cosmopolitanism of Germany's art centers."[39] The effort involved in creating nationalist wartime concerts only made clear how transnational the programs had been before the war.

Concert programs now focused on those composers who came from a seemingly homogenous geographical space. The magazine *Neue Zeitschrift für Musik* defined this space as consisting of those who "avow to Germanic-German culture, from the Swiss Alps to the Norwegian fjords and the Swedish plateau valleys and the Finnish lakes! ... What a glorious flock, which, with the feeling of interiority and simplicity of their popular sentiment, is much closer to us than the Russian or the Roman."[40] The musical map was not synonymous with the political map, and aimed at the *großdeutsch* (greater German) vision of a German cultural nation that extended beyond the borders of 1871.[41] But it was often difficult for the concert organizers to justify the identification of some composers as German, especially if they were born before the rise of the nation state. Fictional accounts that projected the nation's history back onto composers such as Bach, Mozart, Haydn, or Handel carefully avoided the multiple influences that different social and cultural contexts had on their lives and their music. Part of their construction as Germans was the ascription of certain racial attributes in order to make them fit the prevalent understanding of Germanness. A performance of Tchaikovsky, who had been hugely popular with the listeners before the war and was undoubtedly Russian, could be justified with "his light blond hair and his wonderful blue eyes," which were traits of his supposedly German heritage.[42]

The emotional unity of the audience could be achieved not only by creating a "purified" German performance, but also by establishing a closer relationship between listeners and composers in order to facilitate the identification of the audience with the composer and to enlist music history as proof of the superiority of the German nation. Listeners expected that the composers of the past had created something that was relevant to the present, and that contained unique insights on the hopes and needs of listeners and society more broadly. An artist was expected to be an "expert of the soul," as Adolf Weissmann wrote in 1914.[43] He had to sense the sentiment of his audience and had to take into account how the listeners' emotional state changed over time. While history had been gaining in importance in determining the role of music in public life, it became an ever-present feature of listening experiences in the wartime concerts. Reflections on historical events and on the historic lives of composers offered a tool to cope with the challenges of the day by projecting back into history a supposedly functioning emotional community. The history of music was used as a history of examples for the superiority of the nation. After a concert with works by Bach and Beethoven, for example, two listeners in Frankfurt claimed that they had had the opportunity to travel to the "crossroads" where Germanness, only too often "ravished by alien spirits," could assert and guarantee itself.[44] Historical comparisons offered examples of how to act and feel at decisive moments when the unity of the nation was at stake.

The most favored historical examples came from the Thirty Years' War, when baroque music was at its peak, and the wars of liberation, when the music of Beethoven could be used as a model for the nation, despite the fact that Beethoven himself did not represent a coherent political view. After attending concerts in Berlin in 1916, Leopold Schmidt wrote that one had felt the "glorious property of our German music" and noticed how much the sentiments of Mendelssohn's symphonies were in accordance with present emotions.[45] But this interpretation of Mendelssohn was by no means shared by all listeners, a fact which reveals the frictions in the audience and the difficulty in achieving unity, despite a common ambition for it. Much more successful was the attempt to establish Beethoven as an exemplary historical guide for how to deal with the present. Leopold Schmidt himself had claimed already in 1914 that Beethoven's symphonies were an "expression of our own sensations."[46] This comparison was particularly ripe given that the French occupation and the rise of German nationalism combined to provide the historical context for Beethoven's music. "The distress of the time after 1810 was not less than now," Meisterbernd wrote after a performance of the Third Symphony in 1918.[47] He reminded his readers that the present war was not the first occasion on which the "German fate" had hung in the balance. Reflecting on the performance of Beethoven's piano concerto in 1917, he told his readers that Beethoven was the most able leader, as a "true German musician," to represent the time in which music had given its listeners the chance to recover from hardship—the listeners of the piano concerto in 1917 were the counterparts of the listeners in 1805.[48] The advantage of such historicizations for the listeners consisted in the ascribed evidence of the unifying powers that music was supposed to have had in 1805. What had worked in 1805 could also work in 1917, and while listening to Beethoven in 1917, the wartime listeners could hope for a replication of that positive outcome because he offered them an immediate link between their experiences and the experiences of the past.

Finally, the ability of music to create a social idea of the audience as nation was not restricted to the concert hall. Music was considered to be an important part of the war effort on the front as well. "We need music for the army," one soldier wrote from the frontline in 1915, and he stated that music was essential for the soldiers and claimed that the power of music could be traced back to rhythms of the military marching bands.[49] For the Germans, war concerts in "enemy land" (*Feindesland*) were an "uplifting celebration," and some report that the sounds strengthened the soldier's trust in God and his "loyalty to the Fatherland."[50] Another soldier reported from a concert that had taken place in September of 1916 in Northern France and described how the soldiers became captivated by the music because in the "background there is always the Great and Terrifying of our times, the wild romp of the struggle."[51] These reports from the front allowed music at home to be seen as a national resource because the mystic powers of music helped the soldiers to cope with their everyday lives and to connect them to the nation. Journalistic accounts on the power of music at the front offered welcome opportunities to connect the readers in the cities with their "brothers in the field." The "enthusiasm" of the concerts would be transmitted through letters to those who could not take part on both sides.[52] Thus, the emotional power of music bound the listeners on the home front and on the war front together, through the joint emotional experiences that music could provide. The notion of the superiority of German music and its importance to the war effort legitimized the continuing practice of concert-going and music-making, even in times of war. Moreover, through the imagined connection between listeners on the battle lines of France and Belgium and listeners on the home front, the establishment of a German collective became a prime function of sharing musical listening experiences.

## Empowerment of the Listeners: Individualizations of Listening Experiences

Yet the search for national unity in the concert hall turned out to be in conflict with the listeners themselves. This became evident when the audience did not turn out to be the national community that it ought to have been. As Hans Fischer had to concede in 1916, the audience of symphony concerts remained a "miraculous multeity" that was "crystallized around a pole" and vanished as soon as it left the concert hall.[53] He noticed that the experience in the same space did not create a homogenous entity, rather the audience remained manifold and ever changing: "today nervous and conscious, tomorrow absent-minded and superficial." Fischer's observation does not go so far as to say that social meaning was absent from the performance experiences, but it points to the power and freedom of the listeners to make individual decisions about how they listened and the meaning they gave to the sounds they heard. Even during wartime, the plurality of "inner existences" and versatile subjectivities pointed to the fact that listeners felt empowered to actively use the concert hall for their private emotional needs that were sometimes in tune with the nationalistic tale and sometimes not.

The empowered listener could use a popular and recognized method of "musical hermeneutics" to listen, to explain the abstract sounds, and to affix the emotions evoked by the music to his or her own needs. Musical hermeneutics provided a shared vocabulary of music's effects on individual listeners that offered to explain inner reactions and to bestow on them a status of objectivity that served to legitimize the verbalization of the listener's inner feelings. As a concept, it was most famously formulated by the Berlin conductor and music historian, Hermann Kretzschmar. Kretzschmar developed a theory of the thematic effects of music in which he not only rejected the formalist thinking of "experts," but also the romantic-subjective and the enthusiastic-emotional exegesis of "dilettantes."[54] He referenced theological and philosophical traditions of hermeneutics that sought to understand musical experience not as accidental, but rather as based on rational deductions from the musical material itself onto which the listener then affixed terms derived from his or her own experiences, impressions, or memories, all of which could originate outside of the concert hall.[55] A hugely successful author of introductory concert guides, Kretzschmar's approach was popular and a widespread reference point during the war, as it picked up on common listening practices that had long been used in music journalism.[56]

Listeners used the method of musical hermeneutics by visualizing their experiences in the concert hall, even if the music, such as absolute music, was originally composed to eschew any concrete associations and images. The visualization of the musical experience was especially popular as it offered a freedom of imagination that could be connected to the everyday experiences and thus to wartime reality. In 1918 the Frankfurt critic, Max Meisterbernd, praised the program notes of one concert as "exemplary" because they "left the fantasy of the listener the biggest imaginable space."[57] He himself made use of this freedom to interpret the music when he, for example, listened to a performance of Beethoven's 7th Symphony, which had traditionally been interpreted, most famously by Richard Wagner, as a furious dance. Meisterbernd, by contrast, saw a whole different story unfolding before his inner eye: he heard military troops moving out of the cities, he imagined horses and trumpet signals and a cheering crowd, and he heard the end of the last movement as a soldier's pledge.[58] The critic retold his listening experience in the form of a narrative of soldiers who went to war, of their battles, and of their victory under the leadership of a hero. The Dionysian ecstasy that Wagner had heard fifty years earlier was transformed into a national celebration that could be used as a tool for individual identification and for providing hope in times of military crisis toward the end of the war.

As the war continued, the narratives and moments of concrete identification were increasingly used by the listeners to interpret their musical experiences. In particular, the themes of mourning, death transfiguration, and consolation seemed of special attraction to listeners who were searching for individual coping mechanisms. Concert hall experiences offered space for identification with war victims. In the first two years of the war this was often used to transfigure death as a service to the nation and to establish the concert hall as a location for ceremonies celebrating soldier deaths. One of the first pieces performed in Frankfurt during the war was Franz Liszt's *Heldenklage*, a symphonic poem that could be heard as a combination of history, victimhood, nation, and war. The journalist, Hans Pohl, explained to his readers that Liszt had written the piece "for all heroes" who had sacrificed their lives for a "grand idea" and who felt an "apotheosis of pain."[59] Pohl then described his own visualization of the listening experience: he saw a funeral procession marching through the concert hall, the woodwinds sounded like the "weeping and sobbing of the crowd" mourning the hero, and the music concealed the burial site of the hero in shimmering light. Pohl also transmitted his imagination into the present, and interpreted the performance as a ceremony "for all heroes who sacrificed their lives already for the German nature and the German land." Similarly, Pohl explained that while listening to the "Allegro maestoso" in Mahler's Resurrection Symphony, which had been performed twice within three months, he saw himself standing at the burial site of a dear friend whose struggles, sufferings, and sentiments were expressed in the music.[60] Pohl did not forget to point out to his readers that Mahler had allegedly conceived the idea for this symphony while attending the funeral of the conductor Hans von Bülow in Hamburg in 1897.

Such visualizations of mourning and the transfiguration of war deaths signified a shift on the home front in that, as Roger Chickering has stated, the differences between private and public spheres were diminished.[61] The concert hall was an ideal location to mark this shift in boundaries from the private to the public and back to the private, and to renegotiate the boundaries of the self. Almost like no other place in public urban life, the concert hall had already been established as a place for public staging of private emotions. During the war years, listeners went to symphony concerts in order to find a "self-assurance" that seemed to have been lost, the Frankfurt chronicler, Hans Drüner, observed.[62] For him, the armed struggles on the battlefields called for a "spiritual fight at home" that would support the "inner self assurance of our people's culture."[63] The war culture invaded private lives through personal and material hardships, from food shortage to the losses of family members. These personal "dramas" were too widespread and too significant to remain private.[64] The need to cope with crisis and hardships thus became a collective matter, and even the most private moments such as death took on a new public meaning. For Drüner, this presented an opportunity because, as he saw it, "the general sentiment of the time, the enragement about the fate of our people, the sorrow about our dead men created ever so much receptiveness" among the listeners.[65]

In some cases, however, the experience of war on the home front could foster a retreat into the personal self. Fischer observed how the facial expressions in the concert hall articulated a new kind of concentration, "the view focuses inside" and the listener "dives back into his most remote self" when the music began.[66] For Fischer, who was an advocate of introspective listening, the retreat into otherworldly realms was an attractive way to approach music. But there was a consensus among music journalists that symphony concerts did not serve as an escape or distraction for listeners, but were rather a way for listeners to confront and overcome grief.[67] Rather than a kind of aesthetic escapism, in their view, listening to music should be understood as a way to gaze into "deep human suffering" and a place where "we could see a people in weapons" and where "we see heroes die."[68] Max Marschalk praised Arthur Nikisch in one of the Berlin Philharmonic's Bruckner concerts in 1918 for transmitting to the listeners "sounds from a different world for our ears" that went right to their hearts.[69] The symphonies, another critic wrote, "transcribed our sentiments."[70] These reports emphasized the role of music in meeting the personal emotional needs of listeners as the changing context of the war culture required.[71]

But conflicts arose between socially desirable forms of listening imaginations that were in the service of the war and the needs of individual listeners who clung to traditions of listening other than musical hermeneutics or felt oppressed by the omnipresence of particular war associations. Especially toward the end of the war, some listeners started to challenge the intense nationalization and politicization of music, which they felt overpowered their own personal musical experiences. As the war dragged on, concern for the freedom of the individual listener grew; there was, for example, an increasing critique of the omnipresence of Beethoven's works in symphony concerts. Although by 1914 different interpretations existed about what Beethoven was a symbol for, during the war there was broad consensus about Beethoven's close association with military values, nationalist goals, and wartime experience; and his music was "ubiquitous in the political pageantry designed to give Germans a sense of national identity."[72] But the omnipresence of Beethoven made listeners feel uneasy. Open criticism of Beethoven was rare, but Max Marschalk remarked as early as 1914 that, although "we would like to continue to love our Beethoven," it was necessary to exercise a "dietetics of listening" in order to prevent the listener from "distressing reactions."[73] Ferdinand Scherber explained that at the beginning of the war Beethoven's greatness had offered "foothold" and that the war had provided an opportunity to recognize the real, modern, Beethoven. But, he continued, "you cannot always look into the sun." He complained about the "lethargy" that the listeners had fallen into by the repetition of the same musical works in the concert hall.[74]

Some listeners were criticized for not adhering to the dominant wartime interpretations. The influential Berlin critic, Oscar Bie, for example, was attacked by Richard Sternfeld for his "aestheticized style" and claimed that Bie was not able to see the ethical and moral values of music in times of national crisis.[75] At the same time, there was a growing controversy over how far one could go to publicly exploit musical experience for the construction of private emotionality. The young journalist, Karl Holl, a proponent of New Music at the *Frankfurter Zeitung* in the 1920s, expressed his doubts about listening's "too strong bond to the suffering of the day" that could inhibit the emotional perception of the transfiguration of sorrow that Brahms, for example, had implied in his music.[76] This was a call for more careful and judicious listening modes, and it illustrated the fragmentation of interests in the concert halls, where listening could fulfill different aesthetic needs for different listeners. But these reactions were made possible, in the first place, by the active role that listeners played in the concert halls during the war. Active listening, in turn, would eventually lead to increasing differentiation and pluralization—rather than unification—of listening tastes and listening styles in the 1920s.

## Conclusion: Toward Music Listening in the Weimar Republic

Before the war there had been a broad consensus among journalists that the musical world and listening had entered a fundamental crisis that could be perceived in all aspects of concert life. Although the omnipresence of this crisis perception was weakened during the war, when music was elevated to serve as a national resource by providing the emotional basis for unity, symptoms of crisis were still perceived when concert life resumed after 1914. But with the end of the war, the idea of the universal mission of German music began to crumble, and the fiction of a unified audience defined by certain Germanic characteristics lost its attraction for many concert-goers. From the end of the war and throughout the years of inflation and stability, the audience witnessed an increasing fragmentation and differentiation that allowed a period of experimentation and musical openness. Until the rise of National Socialism, when the role of the public sphere changed dramatically, the listener played an active role in the concert hall in search of solutions to contemporary perceptions of crisis.[77]

Music listening during the war relied on pre-war practices such as musical hermeneutics and romantic visions of musical power. By the end of the war, many were questioning hermeneutics, claiming that a depsychologization was badly needed. This reaction led to the search for new and seemingly objective ways to deal with emotional experiences in the concert hall. A growing professionalization of listening took place through analytic and phenomenological approaches, but also through the professionalization of music journalism. Concert reformers experimented with changing the listening conditions, such as light, noise, and applause regulations. In some cases, audiences rebelled against the changes that seemed to be too far removed from traditional listening practices.

The Weimar Republic opened a new period of conflicting listening experiences. Listening was praised as a tool to reform society or denigrated as a symptom of its deconstruction. Conceptions of music as a language of internationalism were as much represented as conceptions of music as a feature of racist ideology, which became, by 1933, the dominant paradigm, and changed future ideas and practices of listening. National Socialist ideas about the value of listening were not a simple continuation of the nationalistic discourse during World War I; but they used the rhetoric of nationalism and reapplied it to their utopia of a racially purified nation that radically excluded those who did not seem to belong to the German Reich. Their idea of listening fostered a retreat of the listener as an active player in the construction of social meaning.

## Notes

1. Paul Bekker, "Richard Strauß 'Eine Alpensinfonie,'" *Frankfurter Zeitung*, 3 November 1915.
2. Richard Specht, "Die Alpensinfonie," *Der Merker* 6, Nr. 23 (1915): 809–17, here 817.
3. Paul Bekker, "Nachklänge zur Alpensinfonie," *Frankfurter Zeitung*, 18 December 1915.
4. Roger Chickering, *The Great War and Urban Life in Germany: Freiburg, 1914–1918* (Cambridge, 2007); Benjamin Ziemann, "Germany 1914–1918: Total War as a Catalyst of Change," in *The Oxford Handbook of Modern Germany History*, ed. Helmut Walser Smith (Oxford, 2011), 378–400.
5. Peter Gay, *The Naked Heart* (New York, 1995), 13–35.
6. See for example: Christopher Small, *Musicking: The Meanings of Performing and Listening* (Hanover, NH, 1998), 13; Regula Burckhardt Qureshi, "Musical Sound and Contextual Input: A Performance Model for Musical Analysis," in *Soziale Horizonte von Musik: Ein kommentiertes Lesebuch zur Musiksoziologie*, eds. Christian Kaden and Karsten Mackensen (Kassel, 2006), 250–70; Steven Feld, "Sound Structure as Social Structure," in *Soziale Horizonte von Musik: Ein kommentiertes Lesebuch zur Musiksoziologie*, eds. Christian Kaden and Karsten Mackensen (Kassel, 2006), 179–200.
7. Judith Becker, "Exploring the Habitus of Listening: Anthropological Perspectives," in *Music and Emotion: Theory, Research, Applications*, eds. John Sloboda and Partik Juslin (Oxford, 2010), 127–57, here 128–29.
8. Ann Swidler, "Culture in Action: Symbols and Strategies," *American Sociological Review* 51, no. 2 (1986): 273–86, here 273.
9. Celia Applegate and Pamela Potter, "Germans as the 'People of Music,'" in *Music and German National Identity*, eds. Celia Applegate and Pamela Potter (Chicago, 2002), 1–35, here 21.
10. Martin Baumeister, "War Enacted: Popular Theater and Collective Identities in Berlin, 1914–1918," in *Endangered Cities: Military Power and Urban Societies in the Era of the World Wars*, eds. Roger Chickering and Marcus Funck (Boston, 2004), 113–26, here 113. See also: Chickering, *The Great War*, 1.
11. Karl Storck, "Krieg und Musikpflege," *Allgemeine Musik-Zeitung* 37, no. 81 (1914), 1127–29. See Daniel Morat's chapter in this volume on the role of sounds during the *Augusterlebnis*.
12. Karen Painter, *Symphonic Aspirations: German Music and Politics, 1900–1945* (Cambridge, 2007), 122.

13. Georg Göhler, *Händler und Künstler: Eine Kriegsbetrachtung* (Langensalza, 1915), 3–4.
14. For more examples of this discourse see: Moritz Bauer, "Krieg und Kunst," *Rheinische Musik- und Theaterzeitung* 16, no. 29–30 (1915): 174–75; Carl Krebs, *Krieg und Musik* (Berlin, 1917). See also: Christa Brüstle, Guido Heldt, and Eckhard Weber, eds. *Von Grenzen und Ländern, Zentren und Rändern: Der Erste Weltkrieg und die Verschiebungen der musikalischen Geographie Europas* (Schliengen im Markgräflerland, 2006).
15. Heinrich Simon, letter to Paul Bekker, 10 October 1914, Yale University, Paul Bekker Collection.
16. Board of the Museums-Gesellschaft to its Members and Subscribers, September 1914, University Library Frankfurt, Program Collection, Kaps. 57.
17. Friedrich Sieger, letter to Willem Mengelberg, 9 October 1914, Den Haag, Mengelberg Archief.
18. "Eine Statistik des deutschen Musiklebens," *Frankfurter Nachrichten*, 28 September 1916. [Number of concerts in Berlin: 1910/11–1096; 1911/12–1214; 1912/13–1210; 1913/14–1262; 1914/15–665; in Vienna: 1910/11–439; 1911/12–431; 1912/13–435; 1913/14–603; 1914/15–345; in Munich: 1910/11–374, 1911/12–347, 1912/13–430, 1913/14–413, 1914/15–197].
19. Max Marschalk, "Eroica," *Vossische Zeitung*, 20 October 1914.
20. Leopold Schmidt, "Konzert-Anfang," *Berliner Tageblatt*, 27 September, 1916; "Aus den Konzertsälen," *Berliner Börsen-Courier*, 30 November 1916.
21. Hans Baldrian, "Das Konzert, das uns fehlt." *Berliner Tageblatt*, 25 November 1916.
22. H. Pf., "Frankfurter Konzerte," *Frankfurter Zeitung*, 19 October 1915.
23. Max Marschalk, "'Künstlerisch' oder 'romantisch'?" *Vossische Zeitung*, 14 December 1916.
24. Hans Fischer, "Das Konzert-Publikum," *Neue Musik-Zeitung* 37, no. 9 (1916), 125–26.
25. Max Marschalk, "'Künstlerisch' oder 'romantisch'?" *Vossische Zeitung*, 14 December 1916.
26. Franz Calvelli-Adorno, "Im Museum—damals und heute: Erinnerungen eines alten Frankfurter Konzertbesuchers," in *Das Museum: Einhundertfünfzig Jahre Frankfurter Konzertleben, 1808–1958*, ed. Hildegard Weber (Frankfurt, 1958), 86–97, here 90.
27. A.E. Weirauch, "Musik …" *Berliner Tageblatt*, 9 December 1914.
28. Richard Leppert, "The Social Discipline of Listening," in *Le concert et son public: Mutations de la vie musicale en Europe de 1780 à 1914 (France, Allemagne, Angleterre)*, eds. Hans Erich Bödeker, Patrice Veit, and Michael Werner (Paris, 2002), 459–85, here 460–66.
29. Karl Storck, "Krieg und Musikpflege," *Allgemeine Musik-Zeitung* 37, no. 81 (1914): 1127–29, here 1127.
30. Painter, *Symphonic Aspirations*, 4.
31. Leopold Schmidt, "Konzert-Anfang," *Berliner Tageblatt*, 27 September 1916.
32. Paul Schwers, "Die 'Alpensinfonie' von Richard Strauß," *Frankfurter Zeitung*, 29 October 1915.

33. Rudolf Cahn-Speyer, "Der Krieg und die Konzertprogramme," *Allgemeine Musikzeitung* 43, no. 18 (1916), 249–51, here 250.
34. Ibid. ["Nun ist aber unser ganzes gegenwärtiges Streben gerichtet auf die Betonung des allen Gemeinsamen, wir sind eingestellt auf die Unterordnung des Einzelnen unter große allgemeine Zwecke und Notwendigkeiten. So interessant es in gewöhnlichen Zeiten für viele von uns sein mag, kennen zu lernen, was uns wesensfremd ist ... jetzt wollen wir genießen, was jeder genießen kann ... Wir wollen auch im Konzertsaal nichts von Strömungen und Richtungen wissen ... Jeder hat das Streben, sich mit allen anderen als eine große Einheit zu fühlen, und darum will das Publikum jetzt gerade die werke unserer älteren Meister hören."]
35. Quoted in Clifford Geertz, "Art as Cultural System," in *Local Knowledge*, ed. Clifford Geertz (New York, 1983), 94–120, here 104.
36. Karl Storck, "Ausländische Musik in Deutschland," *Allgemeine Musik-Zeitung* 43, no. 43 (1916), 587–88, here 588.
37. Michael Geyer, "The Stigma of Violence: Nationalism and War in Twentieth Century Germany," *German Studies Review: Special Issue German Identity* 15 (1992): 75–110, here 86.
38. Glenn Watkins, *Proof through the Night: Music and the Great War* (Berkeley, 2003), 219.
39. Robin Lenman, *Artists and Society in Germany, 1850–1914* (Manchester, 1997), 185.
40. Wilhelm Tapper, "Unsere Musikprogramme und Deutschlands Feinde: Eine Anregung," *Neue Zeitschrift für Musik* 81, no. 37–38 (1914): 487–88, here 487.
41. Applegate and Potter, "Germans as the 'People of Music,'" 17.
42. Max Meisterbernd, "Museumsgesellschaft," *Frankfurter Nachrichten*, 16 March 1918.
43. Adolf Weissmann, "Konzerte," *Berliner Tageblatt*, 14 December 1918.
44. Max Meisterbernd, "Museumsgesellschaft," *Frankfurter Nachrichten*, 14 August 1918.
45. Leopold Schmidt, "Aus den Konzerten," *Berliner Tageblatt*, 7 December 1916.
46. Ibid.
47. Max Meisterbernd, "Beethovenkonzert im Museum," *Frankfurter Nachrichten*, 14 October 1918.
48. Max Meisterbernd, "Museumsgesellschaft," *Frankfurter Nachrichten*, 15 January 1917.
49. "Die Musik im Krieg," *Kleine Presse*, 3 June 1915.
50. H.R., "Ein Kriegskonzert in der Kathedrale von Laon," *Frankfurter Zeitung*, 2 December 1914; Albert Freiherr v. Hacke, "Musik im Felde und in der Kriegszeit," *Neue Zeitschrift für Musik* 83, no.25 (1916): 208.
51. Adolf Kretzer, "Kammermusik in Feindesland. Einen Konzertreise des Klingler-Quartetts in Nordfrankreich," *Berliner Tageblatt*, 21 September 1916; Q.R., "Kammermusik hinter der Front," *Volksstimme*, 18 January 1916.

52. Quoted from "Jahresbericht 1914/1915 of the Sängerchor des Lehrervereins," Institut für Stadtgeschichte Frankfurt am Main, MAG S 1779/3, 13.

53. Hans Fischer, "Das Konzert-Publikum," *Neue Musik-Zeitung* 9 (1916): 125–26.

54. Hermann Kretzschmar, "Anregungen zur Förderung musikalischen Hermeneutik," *Jahrbuch der Musikbibliothek Peters* 9 (1902): 46–66, here 49–51.

55. Ibid., 52. For the philosophical background of Kretzschmar's approach at that time, see Lee Rothfarb, "Hermeneutics and Energetics: Analytical Alternatives in the early 1900s," *Journal of Music Theory* 1, no. 36 (1992): 43–68.

56. Robert Müller-Hartmann, "Musikalische Deutekunst," *Allgemeine Musikzeitung* 41, no. 51 (1914): 1295–96; Hans Mersmann, "Musikalische Hermeneutik und Musikunterricht," *Allgemeine Musikzeitung* 43, no. 38–39 (1916): 499–503, 531–34.

57. Max Meisterbernd, "Museumsgesellschaft," *Frankfurter Nachrichten*, 2 March 1918.

58. Max Meisterbernd, "Museumsgesellschaft," *Frankfurter Nachrichten*, 15 December 1917.

59. Hans Pohl, "*Heldenklage* von Franz Liszt. Zum 2. Freitagskonzert im Museum," *Frankfurter Nachrichten*, 14 November 1914.

60. Hans Pohl, "Rühlscher Gesangverein," *Frankfurter Nachrichten*, 1 February 1916; "Museumsgesellschaft," *Frankfurter Nachrichten*, 8 April 1916.

61. Chickering, *The Great War*, 262.

62. Hans Drüner, *Im Schatten des Weltkrieges: Zehn Jahre Frankfurter Geschichte von 1914–1924* (Frankfurt am Main, 1934), 104.

63. Ibid.

64. Chickering, *The Great War*, 318.

65. Drüner, *Im Schatten des Weltkrieges*, 104.

66. Hans Fischer, "Das Konzert-Publikum," *Neue Musik-Zeitung* 37, no. 9 (1916): 125–26.

67. Leopold Schmidt, "Unserer Helferin Musik," *Berliner Tageblatt*, 2 December 1914.

68. David Koch, "Musik im Krieg," *Neue Musik-Zeitung* 37, no. 3 (1916): 37–38.

69. Max Marschalk, "Konzerte," *Vossische Zeitung*, 7 December 1918.

70. Max Meisterbernd, "Rühlscher Gesangverein," *Frankfurter Nachrichten*, 29 January 1918.

71. Tia DeNora, *Music in Everday Life* (Cambridge, 2000), 53.

72. David B. Dennis, *Beethoven in German Politics, 1870–1989* (New Haven, CT, 1996), 36.

73. Max Marschalk, "Beethoven-Kultus," *Vossische Zeitung*, 24 October 1914.

74. Ferdinand Scherber, "Kriegskonzertprogramme," *Signale für die musikalische Welt* 17–18 (1916): 315–17.

75. Richard Sternfeld, "Musikkritischer Snobismus in deutscher Kriegszeit," *Allgemeine Musikzeitung* 83, no. 13 (1916): 179–81, here 180.

76. Karl Holl, "Frankfurter Konzerte," *Frankfurter Zeitung*, 29 January 1918.

77. See Hansjakob Ziemer, *Die Moderne hören: Das Konzert als urbanes Forum, 1890–1940* (Frankfurt, 2008), chapters 5 and 6.

# Bibliography

Applegate, Celia, and Pamela Potter. "Germans as the 'People of Music.'" In *Music and German National Identity*. Eds. Celia Applegate and Pamela Potter. Chicago, 2002, 1–35.

Bauer, Moritz. "Krieg und Kunst." *Rheinische Musik- und Theaterzeitung* 16, no. 29–30 (1915).

Baumeister, Martin. "War Enacted: Popular Theater and Collective Identities in Berlin, 1914–1918." In *Endangered Cities: Military Power and Urban Societies in the Era of the World Wars*. Eds. Roger Chickering and Marcus Funck. Boston, 2004, 113–26.

Becker, Judith. "Exploring the Habitus of Listening: Anthropological Perspectives." In *Music and Emotion: Theory, Research, Applications*. Eds. John Sloboda and Partik Juslin. Oxford, 2010, 127–57.

Brüstle, Christa, Guido Heldt, and Eckhard Weber, eds. *Von Grenzen und Ländern, Zentren und Rändern. Der Erste Weltkrieg und die Verschiebungen der musikalischen Geographie Europas*. Schliengen im Markgräflerland, 2006.

Cahn-Speyer, Rudolf. "Der Krieg und die Konzertprogramme." *Allgemeine Musikzeitung* 43, no. 18 (1916): 249–51.

Calvelli-Adorno, Franz. "Im Museum—damals und heute. Erinnerungen eines alten Frankfurter Konzertbesuchers." In *Das Museum: Einhundertfünfzig Jahre Frankfurter Konzertleben, 1808–1958*. Ed. Hildegard Weber. Frankfurt, 1958.

Chickering, Roger. *The Great War and Urban Life in Germany: Freiburg, 1914–1918*. Cambridge, 2007.

Dennis, David B. *Beethoven in German Politics, 1870–1989*. New Haven, CT, 1996.

DeNora, Tia. *Music in Everday Life*. Cambridge, 2000.

Drüner, Hans. *Im Schatten des Weltkrieges: Zehn Jahre Frankfurter Geschichte von 1914–1924*. Frankfurt am Main, 1934.

Feld, Steven. "Sound Structure as Social Structure." In *Soziale Horizonte von Musik: Ein kommentiertes Lesebuch zur Musiksoziologie*. Eds. Christian Kaden and Karsten Mackensen. Kassel, 2006, 179–200.

Fischer, Hans. "Das Konzert-Publikum." *Neue Musik-Zeitung* 37, vol. 9 (1916): 125–26.

Gay, Peter. *The Naked Heart*. New York, 1995.

Geertz, Clifford. "Art as Cultural System." In *Local Knowledge*. Ed. Clifford Geertz. New York, 1983.

Geyer, Michael. "The Stigma of Violence: Nationalism and War in Twentieth Century Germany." *German Studies Review: Special Issue German Identity* 15 (1992): 75–110.

Göhler, Georg. *Händler und Künstler: Eine Kriegsbetrachtung*. Langensalza, 1915.

Koch, David. "Musik im Krieg." *Neue Musik-Zeitung* 37, no. 3 (1916): 37–38.

Krebs, Carl. *Krieg und Musik*. Berlin, 1917.

Kretzschmar, Hermann. "Anregungen zur Förderung musikalischen Hermeneutik." *Jahrbuch der Musikbibliothek Peters* 9 (1902): 46–66.

Lenman, Robin. *Artists and Society in Germany, 1850–1914*. Manchester, 1997.

Leppert, Richard. "The Social Discipline of Listening." In *Le concert et son public: Mutations de la vie musicale en Europe de 1780 à 1914 (France, Allemagne, Angleterre)*. Eds. Hans Erich Bödeker, Patrice Veit, and Michael Werner. Paris, 2002.

Mersmann, Hans. "Musikalische Hermeneutik und Musikunterricht." *Allgemeine Musikzeitung* 43, no. 38–39 (1916): 499–503.

Müller-Hartmann, Robert. "Musikalische Deutekunst." *Allgemeine Musikzeitung* 41, no. 51 (1914): 1295–96.

Painter, Karen. *Symphonic Aspirations: German Music and Politics, 1900–1945*. Cambridge, 2007.

Qureshi, Regula Burckhardt. "Musical Sound and Contextual Input: A Performance Model for Musical Analysis." In *Soziale Horizonte von Musik: Ein kommentiertes Lesebuch zur Musiksoziologie*. Eds. Christian Kaden and Karsten Mackensen. Kassel, 2006, 250–70.

Rothfarb, Lee. "Hermeneutics and Energetics: Analytical Alternatives in the early 1900s." *Journal of Music Theory* 1, no. 36 (1992): 43–68.

Scherber, Ferdinand. "Kriegskonzertprogramme." *Signale für die musikalische Welt* 17–18 (1916): 315–17.

Small, Christopher. *Musicking: The Meanings of Performing and Listening*. Hanover, 1998.

Specht, Richard. "Die Alpensinfonie." *Der Merker* 6 (1915): 809–17.

Sternfeld, Richard. "Musikkritischer Snobismus in deutscher Kriegszeit." *Allgemeine Musikzeitung* 83, no. 13 (1916): 179–81.

Storck, Karl. "Krieg und Musikpflege." *Allgemeine Musik-Zeitung* 37, no. 81 (1914): 1127–29.

———. "Ausländische Musik in Deutschland." *Allgemeine Musik-Zeitung* 43, no. 43 (1916): 587–88.

Swidler, Ann. "Culture in Action: Symbols and Strategies." *American Sociological Review* 51, no. 2 (1986): 273–86.

Tapper, Wilhelm. "Unsere Musikprogramme und Deutschlands Feinde: Eine Anregung." *Neue Zeitschrift für Musik* 81, no. 37–38 (1914): 487–88.

Watkins, Glenn. *Proof through the Night: Music and the Great War*. Berkeley, 2003.

Ziemann, Benjamin. "Germany 1914–1918: Total War as a Catalyst of Change." In *The Oxford Handbook of Modern Germany History*. Ed. Helmut Walser Smith. Oxford, 2011, 378–400.

Ziemer, Hansjakob. *Die Moderne hören: Das Konzert als urbanes Forum 1890–1940*. Frankfurt, 2008.

# PART VI

# AUDITORY CULTURES IN
# THE INTERWAR PERIOD

**10**

# IN STORMS OF STEEL
## The Soundscape of World War I and its Impact on Auditory Media Culture during the Weimar Period
*Axel Volmar*

Research in the history of science and communication has emphasized a profound turning point in the auditory media culture of the Western world at the beginning of the twentieth century. This has mainly been characterized as the result of a process of mechanization and mediatization, which—as a consequence of industrialization and urbanization—mainly took place in towns and cities. Karin Bijsterveld has traced the joys and concerns of the technical age in a social and technological history of noise and noise control, while Emily Thompson has focused on the applied disciplines of architectural acoustics then emerging to explain the transformations of the urban soundscape.[1] In her study on the early history of radio in the United States, Susan Douglas has, in turn, pointed to the shift in the acoustic environment, as well as in practices of auditory perception, that occurred through the emergence of acoustic media technologies:

> [I]t is clear that with the introduction of the telephone, the phonograph, and then radio, there was a revolution in our aural environment that prompted a major perceptual and cognitive shift in the country, with a new emphasis on hearing.[2]

This dual process of mediatization represents without doubt an important factor for the shift in auditory culture around and after 1900. However, the usual focus on the urban space, and specifically on the city as the primary area of that shift, disregards another acoustic environment that also had an important impact on the auditory culture of the twentieth century: the battlefields of World War I. Due to the specific conditions of modern warfare, which had developed as a result of increasing mechanization, millions of combatants were forced to conceal themselves from the enemy. As a result, various listening practices evolved, many of which helped combatants to retrieve from the sounds of war information vital to their survival. Due to this "mobilization of the ear" as a military cognitive organ, the awareness of the auditory senses in general, and forms of active listening in particular, increased substantially among the soldiers. At the same time, the auditory violence of the constant battle noises caused mental trauma and physiological damage to hearing. Therefore, the soundscape of the war inscribed itself deeply into the bodies and the collective memory of frontline soldiers. The wholesale deployment of artillery was also the catalyst for putting all available resources into furthering research in the field of wireless communication—the technological forebear of later radio technology.

This chapter argues that the collective listening experiences on the battlefields of World War I profoundly affected the attitude to life of millions of war veterans. This led, first, to an increased awareness in the individual of their own faculty of hearing and, second, to an increased need for a larger discussion of hearing experiences in general, as well as for an acoustic presentation and re-staging of the war's soundscape in particular. Both the military technological developments and experiences on the battlefield were therefore responsible for the emergence of a trend toward auditory perception. Furthermore, both also had a decisive influence on the auditory culture of the Weimar Republic in Germany and prepared the cultural background for a large-scale distribution of acoustic media—especially radio and sound film. The fact that this was a decade characterized to a much greater degree than other decades by its auditory media culture is not least evidenced in its American label, the "Roaring Twenties."

In attempting to understand this auditory trend, it is not sufficient for historians to limit the scope of their research to the soundscape of urban environments. Attention must also be given to the soundscape of World War I as an important acoustic stage.[3] The first section will therefore set out to reconstruct the birth of various listening techniques during World War I, while emphasizing in particular the decisive influence of a listening mode I call "locating listening." The second section traces the impacts these listening techniques had on the media culture during the Weimar period. This section analyzes how soldiers returning home came to terms with their listening experiences, how they communicated them, and to what extent and in what way military listening techniques transformed into civilian practices such as amateur or "ham" radio, and other early radio cultures. This study mainly focuses on events in Germany, but reference is also made to developments in other European countries and the United States.

## Listening on All Fronts

In 1914, an entire male generation was confronted with a daily wartime situation in which—as the German field marshal and strategist von Schlieffen had predicted five years earlier—the customary methods of visual orientation proved to be of only limited use:

> However, while these battlefields may be large, they will offer little to the eye. Nothing is to be seen across the wide desert. When the thunder of cannon does not deafen the ears, the direction of the artillery will only be betrayed by weak flashes of fire. One would not know whence came the rolling infantry fire, if now and then a thin line of infantry did not make a momentary appearance while springing forward, only to disappear again quickly. No riders are to be seen ... No Napoleon stands upon a rise surrounded by his brilliant retinue. [Even with the best field glasses, he would not see much.] His white horse would be the easy target of countless batteries.[4]

Under the conditions of static warfare, *to see* also meant *to be seen*, and therefore to be at risk of becoming the "easy target" not only of batteries, but also of machine-gun fire and snipers. Thus, the development of concealment techniques became a tactical necessity, and consequently a feature, of World War I. According to the media historian, Stefan Kaufmann, three main techniques were applied to evade the gaze of the enemy: first, digging into the ground; second, using the nighttime darkness for movements; and, third, camouflaging soldiers and positions. This "loss of sight"[5] produced a void in the perception of soldiers and meant that hearing in particular was endowed with a new and vital importance as a cognitive sense. During a period of leave in 1915, the Italian Futurist, Luigi Russolo, described the change in the customary hierarchy of the senses due to the conditions of "modern" warfare:

> The ear had judged with greater certainty than the eye! In modern warfare, mechanical and metallic, the element of sight is almost zero. The sense, the significance, and the expressiven[e]ss of noises, however, are infinite. ... But noise, which conquers the blackest gloom and the densest fog, can betray as well as save. ... Marvelous and tragic symphony of the noises of war![6]

Above all, it was as a result of the artillery's greatly increased fire power that the soldiers at the front, who had withdrawn into the deeply furrowed earth, learned quickly to distinguish the sound of the different types and calibers of the various shells. This "qualitative sound recognition,"[7] as Bernhard Siegert called it, formed one of the most important survival techniques and was therefore also one of the first skills to be passed on to new arrivals. In 1920, the psychologist, Paul Plaut, outlined a *Psychographie des Kriegers* (Psychography of the Warrior) based on the results of numerous sources and questionnaires. Concerning the listening skills developed in the trenches, he writes: "The ability to discriminate sounds is the product of a relatively brief period spent in a gun position. After only one to two months the soldier can determine, with near total accuracy, which type of shells he can hear in the air."[8] The significance of the symphony of noises so acclaimed by Russolo differed substantively, however, from a concert situation in peace time. For instead of contemplative listening, it was now essential for the soldiers to be constantly vigilant and, with proverbially pricked ears, to extract from the noises of war a huge variety of information, as well as to undertake detailed mapping of the surrounding soundscape and to internalize it:

> The difference between his current living conditions and those of peacetime could not be greater than if, overnight, the earth were to change places with the moon. He knows everything. His ear instinctively checks the noises. He can skillfully discern the shot, the whining trajectory, and impact. He constructs the enemy from the position of the bursts of machine-gun fire. He senses what is going on to the right and to the left, even though he cannot see it. His nose knows all the smells of the battlefield, the smell of chlorine, the smell of gas, the smell of gunpowder, the smell of corpses, and all the variations between.[9]

Thus, new arrivals to the front had not only had to leave behind their home and daily life, but also the practices of perception and orientation to which they were accustomed. With entry into the danger zone of battle, the auditory perception of peacetime yields to a, in many respects, radicalized psychological experience—a shift that the Gestalt psychologist, Kurt Lewin, attempted to articulate with the term "warscape":[10] for the psychological subject, objects lost most of their peacetime characteristics during wartime because they were henceforth evaluated from a perspective of extreme pragmatism and exclusively in terms of their fitness for war. In correspondence with Lewin's reflections, the soundscape of World War I can therefore be understood as an "acoustic warscape," which not only featured numerous and previously unknown noise phenomena, but which also affected and shaped the individual's auditory perception in entirely new ways. In place of day-to-day auditory perception, which tended to be passive and unconscious, active listening techniques came to the fore: practices of sound analysis, which might be described as an "auscultation" of the acoustic warscape—the method physicians use to listen to their patients by the help of a stethoscope. In these processes, the question was no longer how the noises as such were structured (i.e. what they sounded like), but rather what they *meant*, and what consequences they would bring with them for the listeners in the trenches. The training of the ear was based on radically increased attentiveness.

The subject thrust to the front thus comprised the focal point of an auditory space in which locating and diagnostic listening practices became vital to survival. This gave rise to a completely new relationship between the listening subject and the objects for which they were listening: on the one hand, the latter were inherently a constant threat of death; on the other hand, through the information that the ear was able to extract from them, they were also closely associated with the hope of being able to make good decisions, thereby escaping injury or death.

The constant vigilance made imperative by the war situation meant that frontline soldiers lived intensely in the present. As both a result and an expression of this psychological situation, the new listening techniques were not only learned and used, but also consciously reflected on. This is supported by the fact that there are countless attempts in war diaries, letters, and other testimonials to describe the soundscape of the war. Among the best-known testimonials in the German context are, without doubt, the diaries of Ernst Jünger and Robert Musil, who later became renowned writers. However, the soundscape of the war also had a crucial significance for the general rank and file of the combatants.[11]

Noise has often been described as a characteristic phenomenon of the modern period, of industrialization, and not least of the metropolis. During World War I, however, these acoustic intrusions increased exponentially, and rose to an extreme level. In addition to the noises— the nuanced information bearing acoustic repertoire of the battlefields, which, according to the historian of science, Christoph Hoffmann, formed an "unmistakable sensory signature of World War I"[12]—the extreme volume levels associated with highly mechanized warfare in particular were also among the constant concomitant acoustic features of static warfare. These ranged from machine-gun barrage fire to the grinding drumfire of the artillery, and represented an enormous strain on combatants. The familiar way of listening to the acoustic environment, which is usually composed of distinct acoustic signs, was continually interrupted by phenomena that no longer engaged the faculty of hearing at a semantic level, but rather attacked as well as damaged it at both a psychological and a physiological one. Due to the extreme noise levels, and despite its beneficial information content, the acoustic landscape constituted a violent, inhospitable environment, such that blast traumas and ruptured eardrums were among the common cases of war pathology[13]—a dilemma for the frontline soldiers, who suffered under the heavy and continual impact of noise, and yet were dependent on active listening.

## Forms of Acoustic Reconnaissance

In his book, *The Audible Past*, Jonathan Sterne has shown that the prevalence of practices of diagnostic listening—for example, medical auscultation and other forms of "audile technique"—can be seen as indicators of an alternative, that is to say auditory, enlightenment, which he terms "ensoniment."[14] In this context, it seems worth noting that the German term for enlightenment, *Aufklärung*, has a second meaning, which denotes military reconnaissance. Interestingly, due to the revaluation of the faculty of hearing as a cognitive sense brought about by the war, new practices of acoustic reconnaissance emerged.[15] Some of the most significant will be discussed below. At this point, it is particularly revealing that the shift in the hierarchy of the senses not only influenced the individual experiences of the frontline soldiers in the trenches, but also affected nearly all sectors of the front in a variety of ways. Moreover, it introduced the science of acoustics to the battlefield, which thus became a kind of free field laboratory, and at the same time an environment for applied acoustic warfare technology.

In order to obtain information about the situation, the respective warring parties had already begun at an early stage in hostilities to install special listening posts on the forward lines—and even beyond these lines in the so-called "no man's land"—whose task was to listen to the opposing side or to tap into enemy telephone wires in order to gather information. However, auditory reconnaissance did not take place only in the trenches and in the direct vicinity of the enemy, but also between the artillery positions separated by great distances in the hinterland. While in previous wars the positions of enemy batteries could still in the main be ascertained through optical triangulation of the muzzle flashes as the guns fired (known as flash ranging), it soon became clear that, with the new ranges of which guns were capable, "the means which relied solely on the eye for reconnoitering enemy battery positions and for observation of our own fire were no longer adequate."[16] Thus, sound-ranging methods for locating enemy artillery were developed.

In spring 1915, Erich Moritz von Hornbostel and Max Wertheimer were instructed to improve the auditory methods used to determine the positions of batteries. At this time, there was no convincing theory of spatial hearing that could explain how the ear was actually capable of identifying the direction of sound sources. Thus, following on from the Duplex Theory on spatial hearing formulated by Lord Rayleigh in 1907, the two psychologists carried out a series of psycho-acoustic experiments. After ascertaining that volume and phase differences between the left and right ear could be ruled out as significant factors, they came to believe that the brain mainly used interaural time differences to determine the angle of approaching sound events. In experiments with length-adjustable pipes linked to the ears, they were able to produce changes in the subjective perception of the direction of a sound source solely through artificially generated time delays between the ears.

On the basis of their results, Hornbostel and Wertheimer developed the "time theory" of spatial hearing,[17] the results of which were directly applied for use at the front through the construction of a sound-locator device. This device was comprised of a frame to which acoustic tubes with funnel-shaped end pieces were attached; these artificially increased the auricular base (i.e. the distance between the ears). The instrument had the effect of an acoustic telescope, so sound direction could be determined with much more precision than with the unaided ear alone. Once again, the primary concerns in this listening technique were not the sound events per se or their auditory signature, but rather the ability to pinpoint specific information through listening: the angle of incidence as well as the estimated location of the sound source (through triangulation).

The German military authorities responded warmly, and the *Vorrichtung zur Bestimmung der Schallrichtung* (device for determining sound direction) was officially adopted by the sound ranging units over the course of the year in 1916.[18] This was a considerable development for German military sound measurement. In turn, the experimental conditions, which had been transferred from the acoustic laboratory to the front, transformed the battlefield into a laboratory for experimental psychology. For, as Curt Sachs wrote in his obituary for Hornbostel, "[he], together with his friend and co-inventor, Max Wertheimer, traveled from front to front, from fortress to submarine, until trained sound-ranging troops became a type of weapon in their own right."[19]

Although the sound-ranging device worked well in principle, limits to its military deployment in the field soon became apparent: in heavy barrage fire, or drumfire, the individual artillery shots merged into a constant roar, a wall of sound. Differentiating individual discharge sounds—the prerequisite for acoustic artillery locating—was made extremely difficult, or even rendered impossible, under these conditions. For in order to be able to determine the precise position of sound sources, individual shots had to be measured or triangulated—an endeavor that was doomed to failure, particularly on heavy battle days (*Großkampftagen*),[20] and thus severely limited the usefulness of the sound locator.

In other front sectors, however, the practice of subjective binaural sound location (i.e. executed by human listeners) was more successful, leading Max Wertheimer to adapt the technique to the demands of naval warfare. The result was the *Unterwasser-Richtungshörer* (UWRH, or "underwater sound locator"), which was deployed in U-boat battle.[21] Also, the German acoustician, Erich Waetzmann, developed a listening device for surveilling the airspace in 1916. To be able to recognize enemy aircraft at the earliest possible moment, huge listening trumpets were arranged in two pairs: one for determining the horizontal direction of the sound, one for its vertical angle. Similar instruments were also used by the other war parties.[22]

A further theater of war in which acoustic reconnaissance techniques were used prominently was the subterranean war—the underground excavation work beneath the trenches, which was also called *Minenkampf* (mine warfare) or *Maulwurfskrieg* (mole warfare).[23] While trench war raged close to the churned up earth's surface, squads of sappers on both sides would dig deep down into the earth with the aim of advancing as far as the enemy trenches and blowing them up at the right moment. Listening squads, which monitored sounds transmitted through the earth, were deployed as a counteragent:

> Listening is the miner's only reconnaissance method for detecting enemy subterranean activity. In mine warfare, everything depends on the results of the intercept service. To expand, to improve, and, wherever possible, to make it independent of the human ear by using all available means had to be the first and greatest endeavor of the mining specialists. The sound detector served this endeavor. However, it is also self-evident that without thorough training in subterranean listening … neither the human ear nor an ear equipped with the best instrument, or any other kind of instrument, is adequate for the task. The sound detector, a microphone fitted in a solid metal casing, transmits the sounds via cables to the telephone set, which connects several instruments, and

amplifies the recorded sounds in the telephone by means of station batteries.[24]

Initially, stethoscopes were used for this purpose, though systems based on telephone technology were developed later. Once again, it was Erich Waetzmann who worked in this frontline sector. In 1917, he introduced the "Geophon," an electro-acoustic version, with which much subtler reverberations could be made audible.[25]

As a result, functional, technical, and synthetic auditory spaces emerged on the battlefields of World War I, on land, in the sea, and in the air, which, in order to utilize them fully, required the development of specific listening practices performed by highly trained ears. These applied listening techniques for which diagnostic and locating listening were of central importance demonstrate that scientific listening practices had reappeared in altered form in the expanses of the open battlefield. Physicians, for instance, had long used medical listening methods to locate and identify physical legions inside the human body,[26] but the conditions on the battlefield had turned the ear into a tool for producing expedient knowledge.

## Telephone and Radio Communications

In addition to the various methods of acoustic reconnaissance, communications technology accompanied by the emergence of electro-acoustic auditory spaces also played an important role. Even before the outbreak of the war, telegraphic communication had largely been superseded by telephonic communication.[27] However, the telephonic transmission channel became an increasing problem, as the growing excess of artillery fire made maintaining the telephone network an almost unattainable logistical task. Ernst Jünger reports in his war diary:

> This dreadful array of artillery in this heaviest battle is altogether creating entirely new forms of war that in particular make any connection extremely difficult. Even the telephone wire is immediately destroyed. Communication with the artillery and the K.T.K. [*Kampftruppenkommandeur*, combat troops commander] is only possible with flares, and, in between, kilometer-wide zones in which only the explosives prevail.[28]

Wireless communication through radio technology therefore became an essential telecommunications method by 1915/16 at the latest, when, according to the "father of German radio," Hans Bredow, "the distress call came from Verdun saying that every square meter of ground had been churned up by shells, and the lines of communication between the troop elements could be kept open by neither messengers nor wire connections, [and hence] deploying small transportable radio stations became the last resort."[29] Extensive investment in developing and improving the transportable radio technology was the result.

Unlike telephonic communication, however, radio technology did not only open up a broad telemedial—in other words, electromagnetic— auditory space, but also called for the development of new, active listening practices. For, in contrast to tapping physical telephone lines, radio operators first had to detect the enemy's radio communication in the first place. To do this, they had to scour the great expanses of the electromagnetic spectrum meticulously for broadcasted messages. The acquisition of information no longer took place only in the real acoustic landscape of the battlefield, but was now also carried out in the electromagnetic ether, which had become the auditory space of seeking and exploratory listening.

## Communicating Listening Experiences after the War

As these examples show, the sense of hearing among soldiers in World War I underwent a transformational process: while auditory perception in everyday life was much more of a passive activity which—except by certain specialist groups such as musicians, physicians, or even telegraphists—was hardly ever used consciously, the conditions of static warfare led to "auricular training" and to the development of specific auditory reconnaissance techniques. In this process, listening was oriented toward very specific purposes—above all the *discrimination* and the *location* of sound sources. This utilitarian application of listening resulted in a revaluation of hearing, and eventually contributed to a reorganization of the "hierarchy of the senses."

But how did these listening experiences and auditory practices that had been developed during the course of the war affect the postwar period? The acoustic intrusions and the reeducation imposed upon the ear did not simply pass the combatants by without leaving their mark. On the contrary, the psychological conditioning, as well as physical damages, remained and spread into the postwar auditory culture. The active listening techniques learned during the war thus became the catalyst for intensive engagement with listening, which the literary scholar, Julia Encke, has termed a "new listening":

With the essential practice of listening there arose an interest in sound perception that did not abruptly cease with the end of the war. From then on, the ear played a new role. It was increasingly the subject of research and of a revaluation that, for a time, seemed to rank it ahead of the otherwise more highly rated sense of sight.[30]

The need of war veterans to share their listening experiences with those who had remained at home was great and was expressed in a variety of ways. Even during the war, the number of publications that focused on the war had risen into the thousands:[31] over and over again, the new listening experiences and practices were being discussed.

## Narrating the War

Attempts to describe in words how the ear was trained and how the characteristic noises of the war sounded are recurrent motifs in diaries, war reports, and literary efforts to reflect on World War I. The diaries of Robert Musil or Ernst Jünger seem to form a good starting point.[32] Jünger's diaries in particular are considered typical of the genre.[33] Dietrich Behrens and Magdalene Karstien's 1925 collection, *Geschütz- und Geschosslaute im Weltkrieg* (Noises of Shells and Projectiles in the World War),[34] appears to support this view. They typically include onomatopoeic descriptions, attempts to "transcribe the acoustics of war,"[35] for example, as a glance in Musil's diaries shows:

> Shelling: summary: the singing death (death sings here). Over our heads there is singing, deep, high. The batteries can be distinguished by their tone, *tschu i ruh oh—(pim) puimm.* If a shell lands close by: *tsch—sch—bam.* There're one, two short hisses and then it leaps at you.[36]

Similar descriptions can be found in Jünger's diary:

> The hail of shells continued. *Ssst—boom!* one landed in the dugout, lifted the back part of the roof off, and threw the earth into the air, as high as a house. Oh no! I thought, the poor chaps. Crash! Crash! Bam! *ssst! ssst! ssst!* We leapt about behind our tree like squirrels bombarded by stones, and just when we had jumped away from one side [characters struck out, illegible] there was a crash on the other. ... The trenches themselves were overflowing with the wounded and dying. One had an inverted triangle in the back of his head, continuously uttered a *Uh—ngn—Uhn—uh!* of pain.[37]

Under the title *Geräusche der Projektile* [Sounds of the Projectiles], Jünger also created an extensive acoustic chart of weapon noises, a kind of acoustic atlas of the sound events that occur on the battlefield.[38]

At the same time, however, a fundamental problem with attempting to depict complex sound phenomena in the form of symbolic descriptions becomes apparent. As an abstract information carrier comprised of arbitrary units, the usefulness of describing sounds with words is heavily dependent on the prior knowledge, experience, and imagination of the writer, as well as that of the reader. Therefore, the soundscape of the war is not conveyed; instead, merely memories of these are evoked. This means on the one hand that writing as a vehicle for communicating listening experiences can work well among those who share a similar bank of memories. On the other hand, the efficacy of this transcription method quickly reached its limits among those addressees who had not been combatants. The war literature of the Weimar Republic demonstrates the strategy of using narration in order to compensate for the shortcomings of writing in terms of notating acoustic events. The literary treatment of the diaries of Henri Barbusse (*Le Feu* [The Fire], 1916) and Ernst Jünger (*In Stahlgewittern* [Storm of Steel], 1920), and the antiwar novels of the 1920s, including Erich Maria Remarque's *Im Westen Nichts Neues* [All Quiet on the Western Front] (1929) and Ernest Hemingway's *A Farewell to Arms* (1929), all contain sections in which listening is described as an essential cognitive activity and underscored as one of the formative experiences in the war. In addition, they demonstrate the attempt to give an account of the unsettling soundscape of the war and, in the course of this account, to reenact it.[39]

In contrast, the Italian Futurists, who sought new aesthetic solutions to supersede writing as the primary medium of witness and narration, pursued different paths. In 1916, Luigi Russolo discussed the disparity between the acoustic world and writing as an information carrier in his article, *The Noises of War*, which he had appended to his text, *L'arte dei Rumori* [The Art of Noises], 1913:

> In modern warfare, mechanical and metallic, the element of sight is almost zero. The sense, the significance, and the expressiveness of noises, however, are infinite. And since traditional poetry lacks suitable means for rendering the reality and the value of noises, modern war cannot be expressed lyrically without the noise instrumentation of futurist *free words*. While the most illustrious poets continue to silence modern warfare in their medieval or Greco-Roman compositions, the futurist poets were and are since the beginning of the Libyan War the only ones who depict in noise with *free words* the essence of today's battles.[40]

The phrase "free words" is a reference to Filippo Tommaso Marinetti's *parole in libertà*, a typocallage technique that Marinetti had developed before World War I under the impression of the Libyan War and that represented the transfer of onomatopoetic descriptions into artistic practice.[41] Marinetti sought to overcome the difficulties of capturing the acoustic in writing by adding a visual plane to the character sequences of his sound poems. In order to evoke images of the war, the typocollages were arranged both as written text and as painting. Compared with the descriptions in the war reports, it becomes clear that Marinetti's *parole in libertá* is concerned with the artistic adaptation of the practice widespread among frontline veterans of recording the noises of the acoustic landscape of war in some kind of written form.

Russolo, being a Futurist more particularly interested in music, placed greater emphasis on the artistic presentation of the sounds and noise of the technical age in their original acoustic form. In 1913, together with Ugo Piatti, he constructed a variety of instruments that would produce sounds and noises mechanically—the so-called *intonarumori*. The following year in Milan, on 21 April 1914, the first public concert took place, which showcased some of Russolo's compositions for the noise orchestra. Contrary to many of his contemporaries, Russolo did not take a critical approach to the new soundscape of the machine age, but instead capitalized on the sublimity of acoustic violence through active aesthetic transformation. After suffering a severe battlefield injury in 1917, Russolo turned to the task of restaging the "Symphony of War Sounds" praised by him in the concert halls of Western art music. To some extent, this project was also doomed to failure, because even if Russolo had succeeded to a certain extent in simulating the acoustics of battle on stage, he would still not have been able to re-create the context, in which, for example, the enemy artillery's projectiles connoted sheer terror, while those from one's own side connoted retribution and hope. This required more than an acoustic similarity to those sounds, because the sounds of the battlefield remained—as with all other things and sensory impressions—constituent parts of the warscape described by Lewin. In the concert hall, by contrast, the sounds had lost their quality as "combat things" and therefore also the existential significance they yielded in battle. As a result, the attempt to reconstruct the soundscape of World War I within the context of Western art music was also ultimately an endeavor that was neither promising nor suitable for the general public. Even so, the aesthetic agenda of Futurism testifies to an experiential shift which was expressed through increased artistic reflection and thematization of mechanical sounds and excessive noise as phenomena of modern life. Furthermore, this shift contributed to the emergence of artistic forms, which not only focused on the sounds of the modern city, but also explicitly addressed the experiences of the ear trained on the battlefield.

## Demobilizing the Ear

The vital listening experiences and practices internalized by the trained ear also diffused from the context of the battlefield into everyday civilian culture. This development reverberates particularly in the literature of the time. The short novella *Die Amsel* [The Blackbird], written by the Austrian writer and experimental psychologist Robert Musil, may be considered typical for the revaluation of hearing in the 1920s.[42] In his story, Musil, who was a friend of both von Hornbostel and Wertheimer, translated the psycho-acoustic war research on spatial listening into prose. The central event is a near-death event during the war, described by the narrator, Aone, to his dialog partner, Atwo, in the form of three memories triggered by the sound of a slowly approaching flechette (a metal arrow cast off an aircraft). Although the flechette misses its target, the existential experience of the event has a lasting impact on the narrator. Musil based this story on one of his own war experiences in September 1915 in which he was nearly hit by a flechette dropped by an Italian plane. In every section of *Die Amsel*, Musil assigns sound events—the song of a blackbird, the sound of the flechette, and a hallucinated maternal voice—a portentous significance that the protagonist draws from his personal listening experience in wartime and transfers into the civilian situations framing his combat experience. Although the linking thread is the war experience, the "wartime ear" is, according to Encke, not Musil's primary concern: "Rather the Tyrolean mountains correspond to the 'stony mountains' of Berlin inner courtyards, the trench positions to bedrooms, the war to the city."[43] The frontline experiences are overlaid with quotidian perceptions and memories, which now, after the war, are experienced differently and assessed anew, meaning that past and present listening experiences only ever appear before a backdrop of war experiences, and auditory perception as a whole is imbued with existential significance.

This revaluation of the sense of hearing was not only evident among war veterans; it also entered into the cultural memory of the Weimar period and led to the general development of a new listening culture. An example that shows this is Kafka's uncompleted short story *Der Bau* [The Burrow]. The story, set down in winter 1923/24, concerns a mole-like creature that lives alone in an underground burrow it seeks to fortify against potential intruders. Sudden, but indeterminable, digging sounds signify that the creature, who is already paranoid, perceives an increasing threat to his existence. Exploratory listening, which the creature quickly uses to inspect the soil around its burrow, brings no explanation, but results only in growing uncertainty. *Der Bau* is, as literary scholar Wolf Kittler has convincingly argued, "no autonomous product of the imagination, but rather the contrafacture of a completely different story"[44]—the frontline report of the journalist and writer, Bernhard Kellermann, entitled *Der Krieg unter der Erde* [The War beneath the Ground].[45] The depiction of the situation, and in particular the "motif of listening within the earth,"[46] indeed corresponds in remarkable detail with the descriptions of the subterranean mine warfare conducted by sappers in World War I—even though Kafka had never taken part in it and only knew about the war through secondary accounts. "It rather appears," writes Kittler,

> as if Kafka was fascinated by the theme of mine warfare precisely because he had been spared taking part in it. This would mean his reference to Kellermann's *War beneath the Ground* was a symptom in the sense that Sigmund Freud defined for war neuroses in his work *Beyond the Pleasure Principle*. Just as it is precisely in those cases where the pain expected in terror did not occur that the traumatic event must be repeated compulsively, here Kafka, too, repeats the experience of mine warfare, which, according to his own testimony, was traumatic for him above all because he did not participate in it, had not been "there." Thus, the war discourse is particularly attractive for those who did not experience the war at first hand.[47]

The example of *Der Bau* therefore shows that the discourse of war experience in the 1920s increasingly affected those who had not come into immediate contact with the war themselves as well.

## DXing—Auscultating the Ether in Peacetime

The auditory knowledge produced by wartime experience not only found its way into the production of literature and art, but was also expressed in practices associated with new media technologies. For example, the first experiments in the field of stereophonic sound reproduction were carried out based on von Hornbostel and Wertheimer's theory of spatial hearing.[48]

For the emerging auditory media culture of the Weimar period, the development of a civil radio culture after the end of the war is of considerable significance. As historians of media technology have shown, the seepage of the audile techniques learned during the war into the culture of the Weimar Republic can be seen most clearly in the practices of wireless communication, which thousands of veterans brought back with them from the war. As Kate Lacey points out,

> [t]he potential for radio to develop as a multifaceted network of communication was all the greater given the return to civilian life of war veterans who had gained experience in radio transmission and reception and who represented a pool of technical expertise in the community.[49]

It is true that there had been amateur broadcasters or "radio hams" before the Great War (most prominently, in the United States), but it was above all the ever-growing numbers of signal troops that caused an equally significant increase of broadcasting experts over the course of the war. While, for example, at the outbreak of war the German signal units numbered 5,800 men, around 185,000 army radio operators were demobilized at the end of the war, most of them returning home with knowledge in wireless communication and equipment.[50] Moreover, the overextended electronics industries were now desperately seeking civilian consumer markets for the newly developed wireless technology.

As Susan Douglas has demonstrated in her book about American radio culture, the primarily male-dominated radio ham culture was heavily influenced by an investigative, seeking listening mode, which she terms *exploratory listening*: "The earliest mode, pioneered by 'ham' operators, but pursued by millions of others during the 1920s, was exploratory listening, in which people—mostly men—put on headphones to see how far they could listen and what they could pick up."[51] Years before the passive reception of professionally created radio programs became a common listening practice, the focus was on seeking out as many broadcasting stations as possible, which were, more particularly, located as far away as possible. This activity, which required some technical knowledge and above all a skillful touch when tuning the—usually self-built—receiver to particular broadcast frequencies, was known in the United States as *DXing* (DX is operator code for "distance" and means wireless broadcast or reception across large distances). For DXers, the fascination of their hobby lay in the possibility of being able to undertake virtual journeys into the unknown regions of electromagnetic space without having to leave their own home. These auditory adventures were also characterized by the joy of secret listening and eavesdropping, because the overwhelming majority of the channels in the early 1920s did not broadcast any public "programs," but messages intended for very specific, private addressees. DXing was additionally characterized by a pronounced curiosity about the nature of the electromagnetic terrain, which was expressed more tangibly in acoustic exploration and cartographies of the still largely unknown realms of the ether (which resulted, for example, in attempts to describe the various noises of atmospheric and technological interferences).[52]

For many amateurs, the content of those messages received by radio—and around 1920 these were still largely sent in the form of Morse code—was of only secondary importance. Instead, the locations from which the signals were broadcast, and the fact that a message could be received successfully at all, were considered much more important.[53] The initial enthusiasm for the technical possibility of wireless communication in the home also played a substantial role for early public radio broadcasting. This is also expressed by the German radio pioneer, Hans Flesch, when he states in retrospect that the listener was "grateful for every sound, every word he heard, regardless of what and how he heard it, so long as he only had reception."[54]

Both the trained ear of the frontline combatant and the practices of sound ranging with which enemy positions had been located through listening, as well as the radio communications and reconnaissance that had aimed to intercept messages in an acoustic background dominated by interference noises, lived on in the early radio ham culture. The characteristic mode of exploratory listening, which Douglas has claimed to be the earliest praxis of radio listening, stems from the military practices of listening and eavesdropping, and reappeared as a civilian listening practice in the form of DXing, the hunt for far away radio stations hidden in the static of the ether.[55]

## Reconstructing the Soundscape of War

Although early amateur radio was almost exclusively dominated by technophilic men, soon others also registered their interest in the new medium. In addition to the electronics industry, it was not least the radio amateurs themselves who spread enthusiasm for civilian use of radio technology and thus created a societal pressure, which led to the introduction of a state-run broadcasting system in Germany, and to a domestication of unregulated traffic on the ether:

> Indeed, it was precisely the very real prospect of radio developing into a potentially anarchic but influential form of communication that encouraged the nervous authorities to import the idea of entertainment

radio from America—for which there was very little public demand at the time—and set it within a tightly regulated framework.[56]

The potential for free radio communication was thus stifled at an early stage. However, institutionalized (as well as commercial) radio broadcasting offered listening enjoyment for audiences less fascinated with the technical aspects of the new medium. Hans Flesch recalls: "In the beginning, music of all kinds could be broadcast, books were read, dramas with different roles, textbooks imparted—in short, radio was regarded to be the perfect instrument for dissemination."[57]

The fact that there was "nothing to see" on the radio made the trained and sensitive ears of the war veterans particularly receptive to radio broadcasting because, at a technological level, it replicated the listening situation of the frontline: the separation of the visual from the acoustic perception. The conditions of total warfare had encouraged, even made essential, the development of effective listening tasks and the creation of new functional and media technological auditory spaces. The constructed—or "artificial realities," as Dominik Schrage termed it—were reflected in the discourse of early radio theory in the notion of "acoustic space." Schrage refers to a technically contrivable auditory space, which can be perceived subjectively by every listener, but which has to be developed by radio engineers with the appropriate aesthetic and technical means, as well as according to objective criteria.[58] Central to the debate in radio theory was the question of which aesthetic forms were genuinely "radiophonic," and hence how the radio drama (*Hörspiel*), oriented towards the technical and aesthetic opportunities of radio broadcasting, could accomplish this—in contrast to radio adaptations (*Sendespiele*), which were simply radio performances of existing material like books and stage plays that were read out or performed for radio broadcast.

The voices and music of this medium had a diverting and therefore also a beneficial, calming effect on its audiences. Douglas, for example, is convinced that the disembodied voices from the radio created a feeling of fellowship and generally amounted to self assurance.[59] Julia Encke comes to a similar conclusion when she presumes that the creature in Franz Kafka's *Bau* might have taken up its continuous monologue primarily as a reaction to the indeterminable hissing sounds that had begun to haunt it: "Thus it is the speaking and the hissing that compete with each other in Kafka's short story. The ever-present disturbance of the silence, the impossibility of a symbiosis of burrow and creature, produces the speaking creature."[60] If Kafka's story is understood as a metaphorical translation and psychological expression of mine warfare, then the creature's monologue may also be interpreted as metaphor for radio broadcasting as a cure for the indefinable "nervous anxiety" from which, according to Kafka, many traumatized veterans were suffering. It is precisely in the 1920s that the act of listening to the radio can be seen as a therapeutic activity—that is also how Bredow formulated it when he spoke of healing war wounds through the radio.[61] The elements of self-assurance and creating fellow feeling continue to be a characteristic of listening to the radio even today.

The trauma of the war also appears at the textual level. Surprisingly, disaster stories were a recurrent subject in the early years of the new radio drama genre. For example, Friedrich Kittler saw in the restaging or reenactment of the acoustic landscape of war an important aspect of Weimar audio culture: "Radio plays after World War I meant: hearing and staging the dangers to one's life again, as a comedy, a playback, or simulation."[62] In the audio dramas, the narrative dimension offered by the spoken word and the opportunity to create auditory worlds by introducing sound effects came together. Due to technical limitations, the use of sound effects in audio dramas remained rather marginal in the early years, at least insofar as they could not be produced directly in front of the microphone. Therefore during the 1920s, the audio drama remained primarily, though not exclusively, "speech radio." Nevertheless, radio became a prominent place for the reenactment of war experience. This spread even further, after the radio boom prevalent in Europe and the United States had also fueled the development of sound film. When switching to film sound technology, film producers quickly realized that the sound level could contribute significantly to heightening the cinematographic experience. Attempts to reenact the soundscape of the war can also be found in sound film. The Hollywood adaptation of Remarque's *Im Westen nichts Neues* in 1930 is not only a well-known, but also an especially impressive, example of this, since the experience of battle is greatly enhanced by the use of sound effects. At times, the noises of howling artillery, shell explosions, and machine-gun fire dominate the sound track for several minutes. *All Quiet on the Western Front* ultimately became the first sound film production not being a musical to win the Academy Award for the Best Picture—an accolade due not simply to the popularity of the novel on which it was based, but not least thanks to its impressive audio scenery. In conclusion, the process of coping with auditory war experiences found its culmination in audio drama, and in sound film in particular, precisely because the combination of narration and soundtrack produced a considerably heightened mediated experience.

## Conclusion: Media Soundscapes

As I have attempted to demonstrate in this chapter, the "loss of sight" caused by mechanized warfare fostered the development of specific listening techniques that helped soldiers in performing specific tasks for orientation and for gathering information. This "auricular training," which became a vital practice on the battlefields of World War I, heavily influenced the listening experience of an entire male generation. If we take the influence of these listening techniques into account, the acoustic environment of the war appears less as a concert or a "symphony of war noises," as the Futurists hyperbolically portrayed it, than a soundscape divided into several functionalized auditory spaces—a soundscape in which the usual manner of casual, and frequently unconscious, listening was largely replaced by active and target-oriented forms of locating and diagnostic listening. Due to listening's essential and lifesaving character in trench warfare, hundreds of thousands of frontline soldiers learned to use their ears in ways previously only performed by specialized groups of professionals, such as physicians or musicians. For this reason, the auscultating physician, who listens in to the acoustic world of the body for diagnostic purposes, seems to be a productive model for framing the "trained ear" in combat that produces insights and positive facts.

First, under the frontline conditions of constant mortal danger, the mode of diagnostic listening emerged as a vital technique for survival in trench warfare whose aim was to identify and categorize the many different types of shell by the sounds they made. Thus, diagnostic listening underwent what could be called a process of democratization. As a result, millions of soldiers consciously dealt with and reflected on phenomena of the acoustic world and the capabilities of their own auditory perception. Second, locating listening formed the basis for other frequent listening practices: both in the trenches and in the other frontline sectors, such as in artillery battle, the subterranean mine war, aerial defense, and the U-boat war, a specialized field of sound ranging developed, which, in addition to qualitative noise recognition, was intended to generate quantitative data. Acoustic reconnaissance methods point to the fact that locating listening represents a listening mode that has, until now, been neglected by scholars of sound.

As an examination of the literary and media treatments of war experiences produced in the Weimar Republic demonstrated, the auditory knowledge and the specialized listening modes obtained in the battlefields turned out to be a recurrent motif in cultural production.

Attempts to communicate the defining and often traumatic listening experiences also led to attempts to reenact the soundscape of the war in other artistic fields. In the culture of ham radio, the listening mode of exploratory listening even became a media-cultural practice. In the auditory culture of the Weimar period, military practices of listening merged into the mass culture of radio broadcasting and, later, of sound film, which, through the reenactment of media soundscapes, offered retrospective opportunities of *re-consuming* the experiences and traumas of the war. While technological advancements in electronic technology clearly formed a necessary prerequisite for fundamental changes in early twentieth-century media culture, it was undoubtedly the heightened auditory awareness of war veterans and their subsequent cultural enterprises after the war that rendered the Roaring Twenties a distinctively audiocentric decade.

## Notes

* Translation from German by Madeleine Brook. An earlier version of this chapter was published as "In Stahlgewittern: Mediale Rekonstruktionen der Klanglandschaft des Ersten Weltkriegs in der Weimarer Republik," in *Das Hörbuch: Audioliteralität und akustische Literatur*, eds. Natalie Binczek and Cornelia Epping-Jäger (Munich 2014), 47–64.
1. Karin Bijsterveld, *Mechanical Sound: Technology, Culture, and Public Problems of Noise in the Twentieth Century* (Cambridge, 2008); Emily Thompson, *The Soundscape of Modernity: Architectural Acoustics and the Culture of Listening in America, 1900–1933* (Cambridge, 2002).
2. Susan Jeanne Douglas, *Listening In: Radio and the American Imagination, from Amos 'n' Andy and Edward R. Murrow to Wolfman Jack and Howard Stern* (New York, 1999), 7.
3. A notable exception represents the work of Yaron Jean. See for instance Yaron Jean: "The Sonic Mindedness of the Great War: Viewing History through Auditory Lenses," in *Germany in the Loud Twentieth Century: An Introduction*, eds. Florence Feiereisen and Alexandra Merley Hill (New York, 2011), 51–62.
4. "So groß aber auch die Schlachtfelder sein mögen, so wenig werden sie dem Auge bieten. Nichts ist auf der weiten Öde zu sehen. Wenn der Donner der Geschütze nicht das Ohr betäubte, so würde nur schwaches Feuerblitzen die Anwesenheit von Artillerie verraten. Man wüßte nicht, woher das rollende Infanteriefeuer käme, wenn nicht ab und zu bald hier, bald dort eine dünne Linie für einen Augenblick einen Sprung nach vorwärts machte, um ebenso rasch wieder zu verschwinden. Kein Reiter ist zu erblicken. ... Kein Napoleon, umgeben von einem glänzenden Gefolge, hält auf einer Anhöhe. Auch mit dem besten Fernglas würde er nicht viel zu sehen bekommen. Sein Schimmel würde das leicht zu treffende

Ziel unzähliger Batterien sein." A. Graf von Schlieffen, "Der Krieg in der Gegenwart," in *Gesammelte Schriften*, vol. I, 1909, 15, as quoted in Christoph Hoffmann, "Wissenschaft und Militär. Das Berliner Psychologische Institut und der I. Weltkrieg," *Psychologie und Geschichte* 5, no. 3/4 (1994): 263; English translation from A. Graf von Schlieffen, *Alfred von Schlieffen's Military Writings*, ed. and trans. by Robert T. Foley (London, 2003), 198.

5. Stefan Kaufmann, *Kommunikationstechnik und Kriegführung 1815–1945: Stufen telemedialer Rüstung* (Munich, 1996), 184.

6. Luigi Russolo, *The Art of Noises*, trans. and introd. by Barclay Brown (New York, 1986), 49–50.

7. Bernhard Siegert, "Rauschfilterung als Hörspiel: Archäologie nachrichtentechnischen Wissens in Robert Musils Amsel," in *Robert Musil—Dichter, Essayist, Wissenschaftler*, ed. Hans-Georg Pott (Munich, 1993), 196.

8. "Die Unterscheidungsfähigkeit für Schälle ist das Produkt einer verhältnismäßig kurzen Zeit, die man in Feuerstellung zugebracht hat; schon nach ein bis zwei Monaten kann der Soldat mit fast absoluter Sicherheit feststellen, welcher Art die Geschosse sind, die er in der Luft hört." Paul Plaut, "Psychographie des Kriegers," *Zeitschrift für angewandte Psychologie* Beiheft 21, Beiträge zur Psychologie des Krieges (1920): 31; English trans. by M. Brook.

9. "Der Unterschied zwischen seinen jetzigen Existenzbedingungen und denen der Friedenszeit könnte nicht größer sein, wenn einer über Nacht die Erde mit dem Mond vertauschte. Er kennt alles. Sein Ohr prüft instinktiv die Geräusche. Er versteht sich auf Abschuß, Heranheulen und Einschlag. Aus der Lage der Maschinengewehrgarben konstruiert er sich den Feind. Er empfindet, was rechts und links los ist, obwohl er es doch nicht sehen kann. Seine Nase kennt alle Gerüche des Schlachtfeldes, den Chlorgeruch, den Gasgeruch, den Pulvergeruch, den Leichengeruch und alle Variationen dazwischen." Werner Beumelburg, *Sperrfeuer um Deutschland* (Oldenburg, 1929), 316, quoted in: Kaufmann, *Kommunikationstechnik*, 174; English trans. by M. Brook.

10. Kurt Lewin, "Kriegslandschaft," in *Kurt-Lewin-Werkausgabe*, ed. Carl-Friedrich Graumann, vol. 4 Feldtheorie oder 06 Psychol (Bern, 1917), 315.

11. This is illustrated, for example, by the fact that in 1925 a book was published with the title *Die Geschoss- und Geschützlaute des Weltkrieges* [The Shellers and Gunners of the World War], which had been compiled from a large number of personal war reports. Dietrich Behrens and Magdalene Karstien, *Geschütz- und Geschoslaute im Weltkrieg: Eine Materialsammlung aus deutschen und französischen Kriegsberichten* (Giessen, 1925).

12. Christoph Hoffmann, *Der Dichter am Apparat: Medientechnik, Experimentalpsychologie und Texte Robert Musils 1899–1942* (Munich, 1997), 114.

13. See Helmut Lethen, "Geräusche jenseits des Textarchivs: Ernst Jünger und die Umgehung des Traumas," in *Hörstürze: Akustik und Gewalt im 20. Jahrhundert*, eds. Nicola Gess, Florian Schreiner, and Manuela K. Schulz (Würzburg, 2005), 33–52.

14. See Jonathan Sterne, *The Audible Past: Cultural Origins of Sound Reproduction* (Durham, NC, 2003), 2 and 23.

15. In addition to acoustic reconnaissance practices, aerial reconnaissance using aircraft and moored balloons was particularly important. However, they had very little significance for the experiences of frontline soldiers.

16. Gretsch (Hauptmann), "Zielerkundung und Betrachtung durch Photographie, Ballon, Licht und Schallmeßtrupps," *Technik und Wehrmacht* 24 (1921): 114–15, as quoted in Kaufmann, *Kommunikationstechnik*, 185.

17. See Erich Moritz von Hornbostel and Max Wertheimer, "Über die Wahrnehmung der Schallrichtung," *Sitzungsberichte der Preussischen Akademie der Wissenschaften* (1920).

18. See Hoffmann, "Wissenschaft Und Militär," 268.

19. C. Sachs, Erich M. von Hornbostel (1875–1935) (obituary), in: Die Musikforschung I, 1948, 217, as quoted in Peter Berz, "Der Fliegerpfeil: Ein Kriegsexperiment Musils an den Grenzen des Hörraums," in *Armaturen der Sinne: Literarische und technische Medien 1870 Bis 1920*, ed. Jochen Hörisch and Michael Wetzel (Munich, 1989), 265–88.

20. Gretsch (Hauptmann), "Zielerkundung und Betrachtung," 114 ff.; as quoted in Kaufmann, *Kommunikationstechnik*, 186.

21. See Hoffmann, "Wissenschaft und Militär," 270.

22. Sound-ranging devices continued to be used in a modified form in World War II until they were eventually superseded by radar technology.

23. See Wilhelm Orschler, "Sieger im Minenkampf," in *Bayerische Pioniere im Weltkriege: Leistungen und Taten Speyerer Pioniere von Kriegsbeginn bis Frühjahr 1917*, ed. Karl Lehmann (Munich, 1918).

24. "Das Horchen ist das einzige Aufklärungsmittel des Mineurs über die feindliche unterirdische Tätigkeit. Von den Ergebnissen des Horchdienstes hängt im Minenkrieg alles ab. Ihn mit allen Mitteln auszubauen, zu verbessern und möglichst vom Menschen unabhängig zu machen, mußte das erste und große Streben der Minenfachleute sein. Diesem Streben diente und entsprach der Horchapparat. Es ist aber auch selbstverständlich, daß ohne gründliche Schulung im Horchen unter der Erde … weder das menschliche Ohr allein noch das mit dem besten Apparat bewaffnete Ohr noch sonst ein Apparat tauglich sind. Der Horchapparat, ein in fester Metallhülse eingebautes Mikrophon gibt durch das Kabel die Geräusche zur Telefonkassette weiter, die mehrere Apparate anschließt und durch Stationsbatterien die aufgenommenen Geräusche im Telefon verstärkt." See Uwe Nettelbeck, Der Dolomitenkrieg, in: Mainz wie es singt und lacht, Die Ballonfahrer, Briefe … Salzhausen-Luhmühlen 1976, XXXIII, 10; as quoted in Siegert, "Rauschfilterung als Hörspiel," 207; English trans. by M. Brook.

25. See Erich Waetzmann, "Zur Ausbreitung elastischer Wellen in der Erdoberfläche," *Die Naturwissenschaften* 15, no. 18 (1927), 401–3.

26. Sterne, *The Audible Past*, 87–136.

27. See Kaufmann, *Kommunikationstechnik*, 204ff.

28. "Dieses furchtbare Artillerieaufgebot dieser größten Schlacht schafft überhaupt ganz neue Formen des Krieges, die besonders jede Verbindung äußerst erschweren. Selbst der Telefondraht wir [sic!] sofort zerschossen. Verständigung mit der Artillerie und den K.T.K. (Kampftruppenkommandeur) erfolgt nur durch Leuchtkugeln, dazwischen kilometerbreite Zonen, in denen nur die Sprengstoffe herrschen." Ernst Jünger, *Kriegstagebuch 1914–1918*, ed. Helmuth Kiesel (Stuttgart 2010), 176; English trans. by M. Brook.

29. "… der Notruf aus Verdun kam, daß jeder Quadratmeter Boden durch Granaten zerpflügt würde und Verbindungen zwischen den Truppenteilen weder durch Meldegänger noch durch Drahtverbindungen aufrecht erhalten werden könnten, [und somit] der Einsatz von transportablen kleinen Funkstationen die letzte Rettung geworden [war]." Hans Bredow, *Im Banne der Ätherwellen*, vol. 2 (Stuttgart, 1956), 33; as quoted in Kaufmann, *Kommunikationstechnik*, 225.

30. "Mit der überlebensnotwendigen Einübung ins Hören kommt ein Interesse an der Schallwahrnehmung auf, das nach dem Krieg nicht plötzlich abbricht. Fortan spielt das Ohr eine neue Rolle. In zunehmendem Maße wird es erforscht und erfährt eine Aufwertung, die seine dem Sehen nachgeordnete Stellung vorübergehend außer Kraft zu setzen scheint." Julia Encke, *Augenblicke der Gefahr: Der Krieg und die Sinne 1914–1934* (Munich, 2006), 151; English trans. by M. Brook.

31. Plaut, "Psychographie Des Kriegers," 1–123.

32. See Robert Musil, *Tagebücher*, ed. Adolf Frise, 2 vols., 2nd edn. (Reinbek, 1983); Jünger, *Kriegstagebuch*.

33. "Vergleicht man nun Jüngers Tagebuchaufzeichnungen mit diesen [anderen Kriegstagebüchern] wie mit anderen Briefen und Tagebuchblättern, so zeigt sich, dass nichts an Jünger singulär war. Für seine Einstellung gegenüber dem Krieg, für seine Haltung in den verschiedenen Situationen des Dienstes und Kampfeinsatzes, für sein Draufgängertum und seine Todesverachtung, nicht zuletzt aber auch für seine rücksichtslos begeisterte Darstellung von Grabenkämpfen und Sturmangriffen gibt es in den Briefen der gefallenen Studenten Korrespondierendes, und dies nicht nur vereinzelt, sondern in Fülle." Helmuth Kiesel, "Ernst Jünger Im Ersten Weltkrieg. Übersicht Und Dokumentation," in *Kriegstagebuch 1914–1918*, by Ernst Jünger, ed. Helmuth Kiesel (Stuttgart, 2010), 628; "If Jünger's diary entries are now compared with these [other war diaries], or indeed with other letters and diary pages, it becomes evident that nothing about Jünger was unique. In the letters of other fallen students there can be found corresponding examples for his attitude to the war, for his demeanor in his various service and deployment situations, for his bravado and defiance of death, and, of course, not least for his uncompromisingly enthusiastic depiction of trench warfare and assaults—and this not only in isolated cases, but rather over and over again." English trans. by M. Brook.

34. Behrens and Karstien, *Geschütz- und Geschosslaute im Weltkrieg*.

35. Berz, "Der Fliegerpfeil," 272.

36. "Beschiessung: Zusammenfassung: Der singende Tod (Der Tod singt hier). Über unsern Köpfen singt es, tief, hoch. Man unterscheidet die Batterien am Klang, tschu i ruh oh—(pim) puimm. Wenn es in der Nähe einschlägt: tsch—sch—bam. Es pfaucht ein, zweimal kurz und springt dich an." Musil, *Tagebücher*, 324; as quoted in Berz, *Fliegerpfeil*, 272. For Musil's "Phonoskripten", see Hoffmann, *Der Dichter am Apparat*, 190f; English trans. by M. Brook.

37. "Der Granathagel dauerte an. Ssst–bum! saß eine in dem Unterstande, deckte den hinteren Teil des Daches ab und warf die Erde haushoch in die Lüfte. o weh! dachte ich, die armen Kerle. Krach! Krach! Bautz! ssst! ssst! ssst! Wir sprangen hinter unserm Baume herum, wie die Eichhörnchen, die mit Steinen geschmissen werden und grade, wenn wir von der einen Seite wegsprangen, [Buchstaben gestrichen, unlesbar] krachte es auf der andern. ... Der Graben selbst war überfüllt von Verwundeten und Sterbenden. Einer hatte ein nach innen gebogenes Dreieck am Hinterkopfe, stieß fortwährend den Schmerzlaut Üüh Ühühü! aus." Jünger, *Kriegstagebuch*, 36/37; English trans. by M. Brook.

38. "Wenn man längere Zeit im Felde steht, lernt man mancherlei seltsame Geräusche kennen. Erfahrung in dieser Hinsicht ist wichtigt [*sic!*], man lernt unterscheiden, wer geschossen hat, wohin es ging, was für ein Projektil es war u.s.w. Schon die Gewehrkugel, die man durch die Luft pfeifen hört und der Gewehrschuß, der aus der Ferne ans Ohr dröhnt, erzählen viel." Ibid., 75–78, here 75; "When you have been in the field long enough, then you get to know all kinds of strange noises. Experience is important in this respect; you learn to distinguish who has fired, where it went, what sort of projectile it was, etc. Even the rifle bullets that can be heard whistling through the air and the artillery shot that thunders into the ear from a long way away tell a lot."

39. For example, using the literature of the Weimar Republic, this is how the literary critic Wolf Kittler described the effect of a traumatic discourse expressed through the collective need for replication: "Literary production no longer appears as being able to choose freely from among certain experiences that can be reproduced in a generally intelligible sign system or, respectively, in a newly created sign system. Instead, it proves to be a repetition of the kind that S. Freud defined in his text *Jenseits des Lustprinzips* [Beyond the Pleasure Principle] with, not incidentally, reference to war neuroses. It is, however, not the repetition of an individual, but rather a collective history, and, moreover, not in the sense of reflecting social reality through a literary fiction, nor in the sense of a collective unconscious, but rather in the much narrower sense of reproduction—not of reality, but rather of a very particular discourse linked with a specific event." ("Die literarische Produktion erscheint nicht mehr als freies Verfügen über bestimmte Erfahrungen, die in einem allgemeinverständlichen oder jeweils neu geschaffenen Zeichensystem wiedergegeben werden können, sie erweist sich vielmehr als Wiederholung von der Art, wie sie S. Freud nicht zufällig mit Bezug auf die Kriegsneurosen in seiner Schrift *Jenseits des Lustprinzips* definierte. Es ist aber nicht die Wiederholung einer

individuellen, sondern die einer kollektiven Geschichte, und zwar nicht im Sinn der Widerspiegelung gesellschaftlicher Wirklichkeit durch die literarische Fiktion oder im Sinn eines kollektiven Unbewußten, sondern in dem sehr viel strengeren Sinn der Reproduktion—nicht von Wirklichkeit, sondern eines ganz bestimmten, an ein bestimmtes Ereignis gekoppelten Diskurses." Wolf Kittler, "Grabenkrieg—Nervenkrieg—Medienkrieg. Franz Kafka und der 1. Weltkrieg," in *Armaturen der Sinne: Literarische und technische Medien 1870 bis 1920*, eds. Jochen Hörisch and Michael Wetzel (Munich, 1989), 300; English trans. by M. Brook.

40. Russolo, *The Art of Noises*, 49–50.
41. See Filippo Tommaso Marinetti, *Zang Tumb Tuuum: Adrianopoli Ottobre 1912 / Parole in libertà* (Milan 1914). See also Horst Albert Glaser, "Der Große Krieg: Techniken seiner Schilderung bei Marinetti und Jünger," in *Literatur im Wandel: Festschrift für Viktor Zmegac*, ed. Marijan Bobinac (Zagreb, 1999), 253–67; Ulrich Schulz-Buschhaus, "Die Geburt einer Avantgarde aus der Apotheose des Kriegs: Zu Marinettis Poetik der 'Parole in libertà,'" *Romanische Forschungen* 104 (1992): 132–51.
42. Musil wrote his dissertation on Ernst Mach under the supervision of Carl Stumpf.
43. "Vielmehr korrespondiert das Tiroler Gebirge mit dem 'steinernen Gebirge' der Berliner Hinterhöfe, die Grabenstellung mit den Schlafzimmern, der Krieg mit der Großstadt." Encke, *Augenblicke der Gefahr*, 171; English trans. by M. Brook.
44. "kein autonomes Phantasieprodukt, sondern die Kontrafaktur einer ganz anderen Geschichte" Kittler, "Grabenkrieg," 294; English trans. by M. Brook.
45. Bernhard Kellermann, "Der Krieg unter der Erde," in *Das Große Jahr 1914–1915* (Berlin, 1915), 125–30.
46. "Motiv des Lauschens im Inneren der Erde": Kittler, "Grabenkrieg," 296; English trans. M. Brook.
47. "Es scheint vielmehr als sei Kafka vom Thema des Grabenkrieges gerade deshalb fasziniert, weil er ihm erspart geblieben war. Dann wäre sein Rückgriff auf Kellermanns Krieg unter der Erde ein Symptom in dem Sinne, wie es Sigmund Freud in seiner Schrift Jenseits des Lustprinzips für die Kiegsneurosen definierte. Wie dabei das traumatische Ereignis gerade in den Fällen zwanghaft wiederholt werden muß, in denen der im Schreck erwartete Schmerz ausgeblieben ist, so wiederholt auch Kafka jetzt die Erfahrung des Grabenkrieges, die nach seiner eigenen Aussage vor allem deshalb schrecklich für ihn war, weil er nicht an ihr teilgehabt, ›dort‹ gewesen war. So drängt sich der Diskurs des Krieges gerade demjenigen auf, der den Krieg nicht am eigenen Leib erfahren hat." Ibid., 297; English trans. by M. Brook.
48. Hoffmann, "Wissenschaft und Militär," 279–80.
49. Kate Lacey, "The Invention of a Listening Public: Radio and Its Audiences," in *Mass Media, Culture and Society in Twentieth-Century Germany*, eds. Karl Christian Führer and Corey Ross (Houndsmills, UK, 2006), 69.

50. Winfried Bernhard Lerg, *Rundfunkpolitik in der Weimarer Republik*, vol. 1, Rundfunk in Deutschland, ed. Hans Bausch 3183 (Munich, 1980), 43; see Friedrich A. Kittler, *Grammophon, Film, Typewriter* (Berlin, 1986), 148.
51. Douglas, *Listening In*, 33–34.
52. Ibid., 71–77.
53. Dieter Daniels, *Kunst als Sendung. Von der Telegrafie zum Internet* (Munich, 2002), 131–52.
54. "dankbar für jeden Ton, für jedes Wort, das er vernahm, gleichgültig, was und wie er es vernahm, wenn er nur Empfang hatte." Hans Flesch, as quoted in Hans Bredow, *Aus meinem Archiv: Probleme des Rundfunks* (Heidelberg, 1950), 94–95; English trans. M. Brook; see also Dominik Schrage, *Psychotechnik und Radiophonie: Subjektkonstruktionen in artifiziellen Wirklichkeiten 1918–1932* (Munich, 2001), 226.
55. Interestingly, however, and in contrast to Lacey, Douglas does not make this link explicit.
56. Lacey, "The Invention of a Listening Public," 69.
57. "Im Anfang ließ sich Musik in jeder Form senden, Bücher wurden vorgelesen, Schauspiele mit verteilten Rollen, Lehrbücher vermittelt, kurz, man sah im Rundfunk das ausgezeichnete Verbreitungsinstrument." Hans Flesch in Bredow, *Aus meinem Archiv*, 121; English trans. by M. Brook.
58. See Schrage, *Psychotechnik und Radiophonie*, esp. chapter "Der akustische Raum," 221–65.
59. Douglas, *Listening In*, 40.
60. "Das Sprechen und das Zischen sind es demnach, die in Kafkas Erzählung miteinander konkurrieren. Die immer schon vorhandene Störung der Stille, die Unmöglichkeit einer Symbiose von Bau und Tier, bringt das Tier als Sprechendes hervor." Encke, *Augenblicke der Gefahr*, 133; English trans. by M. Brook.
61. Lacey, "The Invention of a Listening Public," 66.
62. "Hörspiel nach dem Ersten Weltkrieg hieß: seine Todesgefahren wiederhören und inszenieren, als Komödie, als Playback oder Simulation." Friedrich Kittler, as quoted in Encke, *Augenblicke der Gefahr*, 190; English trans. by M. Brook.

# Bibliography

Behrens, Dietrich, and Magdalene Karstien. *Geschütz- und Geschosslaute im Weltkrieg. Eine Materialsammlung aus deutschen und französischen Kriegsberichten*. Giessen, 1925.
Berz, Peter. "Der Fliegerpfeil: Ein Kriegsexperiment Musils an den Grenzen des Hörraums." In *Armaturen der Sinne: Literarische und technische Medien 1870 bis 1920*. Eds. Jochen Hörisch and Michael Wetzel. Munich, 1989, 265–88.
Beumelburg, Werner. *Sperrfeuer um Deutschland*. Oldenburg, 1929.
Bijsterveld, Karin. *Mechanical Sound: Technology, Culture, and Public Problems of Noise in the Twentieth Century*. Cambridge, 2008.

Bredow, Hans. *Aus meinem Archiv: Probleme des Rundfunks*. Heidelberg, 1950.

———. *Im Banne der Ätherwellen*. Vol. 2. Stuttgart, 1956.

Daniels, Dieter. *Kunst als Sendung: Von der Telegrafie zum Internet*. Munich, 2002.

Douglas, Susan Jeanne. *Listening In: Radio and the American Imagination, from Amos 'n' Andy and Edward R. Murrow to Wolfman Jack and Howard Stern*. New York, 1999.

Encke, Julia. *Augenblicke der Gefahr: Der Krieg und die Sinne 1914–1934*. Munich, 2006.

Glaser, Horst Albert. "Der Große Krieg: Techniken seiner Schilderung bei Marinetti und Jünger." In *Literatur im Wandel: Festschrift für Viktor Zmegac*. Ed. Marijan Bobinac. Zagreb, 1999, 253–67.

Gretsch (Hauptmann). "Zielerkundung und Betrachtung durch Photographie, Ballon, Licht und Schallmeßtrupps." *Technik und Wehrmacht* 24 (1921): 65–71, 114–25.

Hoffmann, Christoph. "Wissenschaft und Militär. Das Berliner Psychologische Institut und der I. Weltkrieg." *Psychologie und Geschichte* 5, no. 3/4 (1994).

———. *Der Dichter am Apparat: Medientechnik, Experimentalpsychologie und Texte Robert Musils 1899–1942*. Munich, 1997.

Hornbostel, Erich Moritz von, and Max Wertheimer. "Über die Wahrnehmung der Schallrichtung." *Sitzungsberichte der Preussischen Akademie der Wissenschaften* (1920).

Jean, Yaron. "The Sonic Mindedness of the Great War: Viewing History through Auditory Lenses." In *Germany in the Loud Twentieth Century: An Introduction*. Eds. Florence Feiereisen and Alexandra Merley Hill. New York, 2011, 51–62.

Jünger, Ernst. *Kriegstagebuch 1914–1918*. Ed. Helmuth Kiesel. Stuttgart, 2010.

Kaufmann, Stefan. *Kommunikationstechnik und Kriegführung 1815–1945: Stufen telemedialer Rüstung*. Munich, 1996.

Kellermann, Bernhard. "Der Krieg unter der Erde." In *Das große Jahr 1914–1915*. Berlin, 1915, 125–30.

Kiesel, Helmuth. "Ernst Jünger im Ersten Weltkrieg: Übersicht und Dokumentation." In Jünger. *Kriegstagebuch*. Stuttgart, 2010, 596–617.

Kittler, Friedrich A. *Grammophon, Film, Typewriter*. Berlin, 1986.

Kittler, Wolf. "Grabenkrieg—Nervenkrieg—Medienkrieg: Franz Kafka und der 1. Weltkrieg." In *Armaturen der Sinne: Literarische und technische Medien 1870 bis 1920*. Eds. Jochen Hörisch and Michael Wetzel. Munich, 1989, 289–309.

Lacey, Kate. "The Invention of a Listening Public: Radio and Its Audiences." In *Mass Media, Culture and Society in Twentieth-Century Germany*. Eds. Karl Christian Führer and Corey Ross. Houndsmills, UK, 2006, 61–79.

Lerg, Winfried Bernhard. *Rundfunkpolitik in der Weimarer Republik*. Vol. 1. Rundfunk in Deutschland, ed. Hans Bausch. Munich, 1980.

Lethen, Helmut. "Geräusche jenseits des Textarchivs: Ernst Jünger und die Umgehung des Traumas." In *Hörstürze: Akustik und Gewalt im 20. Jahrhundert*. Eds. Nicola Gess, Florian Schreiner, and Manuela K. Schulz. Würzburg, 2005, 33–52.

Lewin, Kurt. "Kriegslandschaft." In *Kurt-Lewin-Werkausgabe*. Ed. Carl-Friedrich Graumann, 04 Feldtheorie oder 06 Psychol: 315. Bern, 1917.

Marinetti, Filippo Tommaso: *Zang Tumb Tuuum*: *Adrianopoli Ottobre 1912 / Parole in liberta*. Milan, 1914.

Musil, Robert. *Tagebücher*. Ed. Adolf Frise. 2 vols. 2nd edn. Reinbek, 1983.

Orschler, Wilhelm. "Sieger im Minenkampf." In *Bayerische Pioniere im Weltkriege: Leistungen und Taten Speyerer Pioniere von Kriegsbeginn bis Frühjahr 1917*. Ed. Karl Lehmann. Munich, 1918.

Plaut, Paul. "Psychographie des Kriegers." *Zeitschrift für angewandte Psychologie* Beiheft 21. Beiträge zur Psychologie des Krieges (1920): 1–123.

Russolo, Luigi. *The Art of Noises*, trans. and introd. by Barclay Brown. New York, 1986.

Schlieffen, A. Graf von. "Der Krieg in der Gegenwart." In *Gesammelte Schriften*, vol. I (1909): 11–24.

Schrage, Dominik. *Psychotechnik und Radiophonie: Subjektkonstruktionen in artifiziellen Wirklichkeiten 1918–1932*. Munich, 2001.

Schulz-Buschhaus, Ulrich. "Die Geburt einer Avantgarde aus der Apotheose des Kriegs: Zu Marinettis Poetik der 'Parole in liberta.'" *Romanische Forschungen* 104 (1992): 132–51.

Siegert, Bernhard. "Rauschfilterung als Hörspiel: Archäologie nachrichtentechnischen Wissens in Robert Musils Amsel." In *Robert Musil—Dichter, Essayist, Wissenschaftler*. Ed. Hans-Georg Pott. Munich, 1993, 193–207.

Sterne, Jonathan. *The Audible Past: Cultural Origins of Sound Reproduction*. Durham, NC, 2003.

Thompson, Emily. *The Soundscape of Modernity: Architectural Acoustics and the Culture of Listening in America, 1900–1933*. Cambridge, 2002.

Waetzmann, Erich. "Zur Ausbreitung elastischer Wellen in der Erdoberfläche." *Die Naturwissenschaften* 15, no. 18 (1927): 401–3.

# 11

## SOUND AESTHETICS AND THE GLOBAL IMAGINATION IN GERMAN MEDIA CULTURE AROUND 1930

*Carolyn Birdsall*

> *Mein Arm ist schon Antenne, fühlt das Weben,*
> *Wunderwellen, fühlt das Wollen jener Welt…*
> — Karl August Düppengießer (1928)

> *Wenn man an diesem schwarzen Knopf hier dreht –*
> *Man hört die Welt … der ganze Raum hängt voll Melodien.*
> — Johannes R. Becher (1929)

This chapter takes up Kate Lacey's call for radio scholars to conduct medium-specific analyses that draw on cultural historical insights and reflect on sound culture at large. In the contemporary field of radio studies, she argues, the efforts to establish a scholarly community and institutional settings for radio studies may, ten years later, run the risk of fixing definitions too narrowly, separating radio from other medial forms, and disconnecting it from broader debates in studies of media and communication. According to Lacey, there is a certain danger in "continuing to isolate radio, to separate it off from its rightful connections with the more established currents in media and cultural studies."[1] In other words, it is vitally important to historicize our use of terminology (like "radio") and acknowledge shifts in listening patterns, ways of describing that experience, and the cultural practices and attitudes toward the medium. Such insights have a direct import for the broader field of sound studies. In sound studies, too, there has been a certain uneasiness toward the field's formal institutionalization due to the perceived need for scholars of sound to pursue interdisciplinary reflections, and acknowledge exchange between the senses and between sound and image.[2]

If we take our cue from soundscape studies, there has been an unambiguous call for the interdisciplinary study of sound. R. Murray Schafer's 1977 study of localized soundscapes, urban and otherwise, ultimately seeks to approach soundscapes from a global perspective that responds to change over time and deals with contextual and comparative issues. Schafer's work in establishing the World Soundscape Project—motivated by environmental concerns about noise pollution—was part of an overall attempt to restore the "tuning of the world."[3] This project may also be historicized around four decades later, but it remains a key departure point for studies of soundscapes and auditory cultures, and yet it begins with a fundamental tension. Schafer, himself a composer, urges for an openness to all sounds. He cites the influence of John Cage in helping to open up music composition and performance to the "sonic universe" as all sounds and panaurality.[4] However, the universe also needs aesthetic improvement, and Schafer treats the world as a "macrocosmic musical composition," positing composers and performers as being "responsible for giving it beauty and form".[5] For this, he takes as his model the interdisciplinary Bauhaus School, which, in Weimar Germany, "brought aesthetics to machinery and mass production."[6] Schafer, himself a child of the interwar period, echoes a common trope to unite man and machine, head and heart, in this case by reinvesting the modern industrial world (and city) with spirituality, quiet, and a sense of authentic community.[7]

A second marked tension concerns the position of technology in Schafer's taxonomy. Schafer calls on scholars to employ sound technologies as aids for analyzing soundscapes. And yet he pursues an overwhelmingly negative interpretation of the "schizophonic" effects of sound technologies on modern auditory perception and listening attention.[8] Schafer gives an unsatisfactory reading of the past, with a pathology of modern listening as schizophonic and nervous that dwells on problems of hearing loss and desensitization.[9] From the present-day perspective, this reading seems like a missed opportunity to do justice to the historicity of modern listening perception, and to trace out more carefully the specific cultural imaginaries, generic forms, and practices developed for and with modern sound technologies.

In this chapter, I will primarily pursue questions concerned with how modern (urban) sound and auditory experience were imagined and creatively rendered in the interwar period in Germany, in particular how the multidirectionality and immersive nature of auditory experience was identified as representative of modern urban life. My broader aim is to reevaluate the cultural fascination with worldly sound as an aesthetic response (if not strategy) to the restrictions and censorship on Weimar era cultural production, particularly within radio. I will start by reflecting on the notion of the auditory imagination and how it may be adapted to address a longer periodization of mediated sound in terms of its imagination and technological realization in the early twentieth century in Germany. Earlier discourses around wireless transmission in terms of imaginative travel and gaining access to world sounds through the "ether" were reworked in later experimental radio works and early sound cinema. Walther Ruttmann's film *Melodie der Welt* (1929) and Fritz Walter Bischoff's sound experiment *Hallo! Hier Welle Erdball!* (1928) will provide case studies of how a global soundscape was conceived in relation to montage aesthetics, sound (on) film techniques, and technological tropes about modern urban perception. In particular, I will map out the political and technological restraints on those seeking to represent sounds related to the tense socio-political reality of German cities in the period around 1930.

## Modern Sound and the Imagination

In order to map out the auditory imagination, it is important to delimit what is meant by modern sound, and reflect on its periodization. My emphasis on modern sound involves, on the one hand, recognition of the increased sounds of daily life due to industrialization and urbanization. On the other hand, there is the technologized mediation achieved by sound technologies. To take a larger periodization of modern sound, we can draw attention to a broader framing of modern sound and modes of listening. For instance, in *The Audible Past* (2003), Jonathan Sterne outlines several professional fields where new "techniques of audition" revealed sound as a key source of professional knowledge.[10] This account traces out a historical framing of modern listening, which can be delineated in modern medicine (1760s–1900s) and sound telegraphy (1840s–1900s). By theorizing longer patterns of change (or *longue durée*), media historians can see how certain patterns may "exceed the lifespan of any particular concrete media form."[11] In the work of Douglas Kahn, too, we can find a broader periodization for the examination of the audio arts across the twentieth century. When dealing with phonography, Kahn defines a broad interest in:

> All mechanical, optical, electrical, digital, genetic, psychotechnic, mnemonic and conceptual means of sound recording as both technological means, empirical fact, and metaphorical incorporation, including nineteenth-century machines prior to the invention of the phonograph.[12]

The significance of such a broad scope is that it allows for attention to the cultural imagination and inventions that predate Thomas Edison's phonograph in 1877. This conception thus makes room for implied and imagined mediated sound as well as its material realization. As Kahn's work demonstrates, phonography mechanically inscribed sound and created new concepts of its storage, temporal delay, and transmission. In this account, the paradigm of *inscription* led to an interest in a wider tonality of noise and "all sounds."[13] Nonetheless, the difficulties involved in making wax disc recording frustrated early phonographic investigations of these "all sounds" or worldly sounds. Dziga Vertov, for instance, attempted such a documentary project in 1916, seeking out various tonalities in the sounds of waterfalls and a lumber mill, but was disappointed by the restrictions posed by phonographic recording.[14]

For the case of wireless technologies, Kahn sees a distinct paradigm of *transmission*, which encompasses wireless telegraphy and radio. In Italian Futurist experiments with noise in the 1910s, F.T. Marinetti also conceived of a "wireless imagination," which has been compared to a mode of listening practiced by wireless operators that translated noisy signals and static into inscription.[15] The cultural imagination with wireless not only comprised the earlier interest in all sounds but their spatial distribution: "Wirelessness immediately meant great distances, thus all the references to the expanses of the oceans, to crowds, to other lands, and to the otherness of the unexplored globe."[16] Whether taking the form of supersensitive ears, keyboard effects, or global broadcasts, a number of literary and avant-garde projects pursued such oceanic metaphors and the notion of taking an aural tour of the globe, imaginatively visiting its various urban settings through hearing their characteristic sounds.[17]

There is clearly a key trope of world sounds in early radio, yet I would also like to acknowledge a broader periodization for the "auditory imagination" of this period. As I have emphasized, it is not necessary to restrict this concept to radio alone or to the "wireless imagination." Radio broadcasting emerged as part of a network of existing sound technologies, including gramophone, telegraphy, and telephony, and situated within the context of a noisy industrialized work environment and urban everyday. In what follows, I will pick up on emergent documentary sound aesthetics and (wireless-influenced) auditory imagination in post-World War I Germany. This will require an initial elaboration on the specific institutional context of Weimar radio, but also on how sound was imagined and rendered in advertising, silent film, and audio-visual experimentation of the 1920s.

Radio as a state-administered institution emerged directly out of German military uses of wireless during World War I, primarily for point-to-point communication for naval ships and, later, in trench warfare. The subsequent development of broadcasting was influenced by the involvement of state postal (and military) authorities in telegraphy, and the close relationship between state and industry in developing communications technologies.[18] Telegraphy pioneer and postal services director, Hans Bredow, was placed in charge of developing a radio network from 1919. Following the establishment of the licensing system and regular programming in 1923, Bredow maintained the assertion that radio should be a public trust that would be above party politics. He also pursued a bourgeois concept of radio in terms of cultural and educational improvement (*Bildungsideal*).[19] We might say that not only the political sphere was rendered absent by the Weimar concept of non-partisanship (and ensured by its censorship system) from 1923, but that with it the sounds of the urban social realm were silenced too.

While there may have been restrictions on representing the political, a new generation of advocates for new music and radio-specific composition emerged during the 1920s. Many of these composers were influenced by Futurist aesthetics, their own experiences of war, and the sound of the modern city (usually typified by whistles, sirens, bells, engines, and transport vehicles).[20] In terms of creating new sounds or musicalizing urban tonalities, avant-garde composition and radio performance provides a rich field of inquiry. Composer Ernst Krenek observed in 1930 that radio's "deviations from reality" (*Abweichungen von der Wirklichkeit*) allowed for the creation of "new material, which present[s] certain features found nowhere else."[21] However, such efforts focused on an aesthetic interpretation or approximation of urban sound phenomena, with only perhaps implicit references to the experience of social and political instability. Radio's facilitation of broadcast sounds was also impeded by broadcasting range and signal interference, often due to nearby frequencies or urban phenomena like trams and electrical works. While such disturbances or distortions were not literal sounds of society, poor signal quality did involve an "intensification and thickening of the transactions between foreground and background, signal and noise, hearing and listening."[22]

In more general terms, Weimar radio did not really constitute a public sphere since there was still too little news and political information.[23] Indeed, there was a clear separation of news and commentary, with centralized news service Dradag dictating the agenda and indirect style of news programming. In the first few years after 1923, politicians occasionally appeared on radio, but then only in their representative function, with their party name left unmentioned. From May 1924, election night reporting was broadcast for regional and national elections. These programs initially involved a somewhat monotonous reading out of results, but they were increasingly given event status, alternating between information and musical entertainment. With the liberalization within national politics in 1928 and 1929, there was new license for politicians (particularly for social democrats) to speak on radio, along with the broadcast of Republican commemorations.[24] Some attempts were also made to broadcast parliamentary debates and speeches, although numerous radio stations and politicians were reluctant to allow radio to be used for "advertising purposes" by parties.[25]

## The "Global Ether"

German radio, from its inception, referred to forms of visualization, with the technology as a "magic eye," and programming described as providing a "sound portrait" or "acoustical film" (*akustischer Film*), particularly of urban phenomena like the street or harbor.[26] The importance of visualization was conceded by radio makers like the Berlin program director, Hans Flesch, who has been credited with creating the first medium-specific radio play in 1924. Flesch acknowledged the importance of developing radio as an art of both reproduction and approximation, and the potential for using radio's visual deprivation for sparking the listener's imagination. Involved in setting up the Rundfunkversuchstelle (music and radio lab) at the Berlin Hochschule, Flesch was primarily engaged in the exploration of the possible range of tonalities for radio. In late 1929, Flesch took advantage of gramophone recording techniques for reporting current affairs, launching a program titled "Akustische Weltgeschichte," (Acoustic World History) which led to a new series the following year "Rückblick auf Schallplatten" (Retrospective on Record).[27] This monthly program included a sound collage of the most important events of the previous month, with sound bites from public speeches, sporting events, and other newsworthy items.

While numerous critics praised new techniques for giving "acoustic portraits" (*Hörbilder*), others were concerned that montage techniques undermined a faithful, chronological rendering of public events.[28] However, this impulse to employ wax recordings to record world events (for later broadcast) sometimes took more personal or impressionistic forms. In September 1931, the Cologne radio station broadcast a report by journalist Hellmut H. Hellmut as part of the series "Die Welt auf der Schallplatte" (The World on Record). For this program, Hellmut traveled through the streets of New York in a recording van, with a microphone to record ambient sounds and his description of what he saw and heard.[29] This recording, which seems to prefigure the subjective style of soundscape walks, was recorded onto wax records and reworked for the Cologne broadcast.

Such attempts reflect an interest in investigating cityscapes and the public sphere on the basis of their characteristic sounds. Nonetheless, discourses about radio transmission as having magical or metaphysical qualities remained. An interesting illustration of how this "ether" discourse figured in the promotion of radio is suggested by Walther Ruttmann's advertising short film *Spiel der Wellen* [Play on the Waves] (1926). This animation film promoted AEG radio equipment with the central motif of radio allowing sound waves and melodies to travel through the ether.[30] Radio waves, shown moving across a German city street, cannot even be stopped by a traffic policeman, who signals for the waves to halt but is engulfed in sonic excess. To some degree, this motif might suggest a lack of control over sound. Indeed, as Jeffrey Sconce points out,

> Whereas the "live" qualities of electronic transmission in telegraphy and telephony had put the listener in immediate, fairly intimate, and ultimately physical contact via a wire with another interlocutor across time and space, wireless offered the potentially more unsettling phenomenon of distant yet instantaneous communication through open air. Abstract electricity in the "ether" made for messages and audiences that were once vast and communal yet diffuse, isolated, and atomized.[31]

The persistent associations with radio sound in terms of "waves" and the "ether" reflect the cultural fascination with what Sconce terms "oceanic metaphors." However, these earlier associations with wireless also reflected cultural anxieties about the atmosphere as mysterious, boundless, and uncanny.

More generally, Ruttmann's *Spiel der Wellen* reflects AEG's commercial interest in recuperating radio as a pleasurable listening experience. The visual depiction of transmission waves in the ether enable the (male) German radio listener to enjoy music broadcast from Africa, with the implication that radio broadcasting could overcome national, cultural, and linguistic borders. The film begins with a striking scene, in which an animated black figure in the African desert (stereotyped with large lips) strikes a drum, from which expanding circles emanate outwards as implied sound waves. The man, shown in close up, begins to open his lips as if singing, before strumming on a guitar. Waves also emanate from the man's head, along with musical notes spelling out the company's name: A – E – G. This scene is consistent with a broader interwar media culture in which the emphasis on technological modernity drew on comparisons with people thought to be premodern or from the past. In reference to 1920s radio, musicologist Timothy Taylor has argued that "the West's conception of itself as technological and modern is highlighted and reinforced by juxtaposing itself and its technologies against people without those technologies."[32] The AEG advertising film, moreover, is consistent with David Ciarlo's *Advertising Empire*, which observes the ongoing circulation of "imagery of colonial mastery and racialised stereotypes of blackness" in Weimar-era culture.[33] Examples such as this necessitate further analysis of the relationship between sound technologies, race and consumer culture. What is clear, however, is how the regularity in the film's depiction of parallel waves emanating around the globe imparts the idea that radio transmission and reception occurs without interference, and is thus reliable.

The notion of a "world sound" or global ether was not, as Wolfgang Hagen points out, subscribed to by those who were superstitious or naïve.[34] Radio managers like Fritz Walter Bischoff (in Breslau) also pursued this notion. This is illustrated by Bischoff's sound montage with Werner Milch titled *Hallo! Hier Welle Erdball! Eine Hörspielsinfonie* [Hello! You're Tuned In to Radio Earth! A Sound Symphony] (1928/1929). This radio play was created with sound strips of optical film celluloid, and partially recorded onto gramophone for playback.[35] The notion of a musicalized world soundscape appears in the opening sequence with a text in rhyming couplets referring to a "symphony of the world" that held the promise of providing worldly sounds to the listener, whether from a football match in London, from Japan, America, of machines and telephones.

> The day of sensations! The day of sensations!
> Fred and Erna place first in the championship for the 66-hour dance.
> Fred Groggi runs around the world in sixteen months, two days, three hours, twenty-one minutes, and seventeen and one half seconds.
> The renowned coloratura singer Maria Polodi shoots her husband in the coatroom of the theatre and poisons herself with lipstick.
> Sensations! Sensations!
> The world consists of nothing, only of sensations!
>
> The day of catastrophes! The day of catastrophes!
> Immense earthquake in Japan! Twenty thousand people homeless!
> A blizzard destroys the prosperous city Georgia in New Mexico!
> At the bobsled championship in St. Moritz in an accident one, two, three, four, five, six, seven, ten heads, crack apart.
> Catastrophes! The world consists of catastrophes!
> The world consists of nothing, only of catastrophes![36]

In this first part, a cacophony of voices are presented, reflecting competing news agendas, and reminiscent of the street cries of newspaper sellers. In other words, rather than actually providing the sounds of the world to the listener, Bischoff's radio play approximates the aural experience of hearing headlines and news from around the world, alluding to the sometimes ridiculous facts circulated by emergent global news-gathering and news bureaus. In doing so, it subtly critiques the dominance of sensation and trivia over socially relevant content and political discussion.

We might characterize the exploration of world sounds on the basis of two main trends. The first can be identified in direct relation to the cultural imagination bound up with audio technologies, and in their potential for long-distance transmission and communication. The second was a direct response to the restrictions on news and reportage on Weimar radio, which led to a focus on "sensation and calamities" rather than "ministerial crises" or the "noise and stamping" on the streets (as Bischoff's script implies).[37] Appearing during the brief liberal period following the Young Plan in 1929, this intermedial radio broadcast offered an expanded concept for the production of radio art.

During this period, some circumvention of restrictions on radio content is evidenced by the cautious development of discussion formats and programs based on newspaper summaries, where different political positions on issues could be articulated.[38] In the case of the Cologne Werag station, a new series began in 1928 that eventually appeared on weekdays under the title "Vom Tage." This was a short and accessible presentation of current political affairs, yet it had all but disappeared in 1931 and was finally discontinued in autumn 1932. The longevity of this program, presented by Hermann Tolle, has since been attributed to its avoidance of domestic politics and a favorable reading of economic forecasts.[39] With the onset of the Depression, this and other programs devoted to economic questions, world politics, and news were put under pressure from the right (particularly the National Socialist Rundfunkteilnehmer radio lobby group). Due to political fragility in 1930–31, state intervention became more prevalent, and state monitoring boards (*Überwachungsschüsse*) were more prone to censoring or refusing station programs in advance.[40] In July 1932, Chancellor Franz von Papen approved extensive radio reforms that resulted in increased state ownership and unprecedented control over regional stations. These reforms meant that only government-issued reports were aired, and there was more policing of the ban on political discussion.

Against this background, one of the most distinct changes in radio sounds in the crisis years prior to 1933 was that new music and jazz featured less in programming, unless it could be disguised with the pretext of, for instance, a historical overview of popular music. The remaining "worldly" or on-location sounds on radio primarily comprised sport and *Heimat* programming, which dealt with supposedly inoffensive and popular topics such as dialect, songs, customs, and cultural traditions.[41] During this period, the few experimental programs with "topical" sounds were all but replaced by a more sanitized and often culturally conservative field of *Heimat* content. I will now further probe this connection between a fascination with worldly sounds and the amplified role of *Heimat* culture and nationalist thinking by examining Germany's first feature-length sound film, *Melodie der Welt* [Melody of the World].

## The Sounds of the World

*Melodie der Welt* (1929), directed by Walther Ruttmann, is an advertising film that served both the interests of its main investors, Hapag and Tobis. The shipping company Hapag had their cruise ships promoted, while for Tobis the motivation was primarily to promote their sound systems in a period with substantial resistance in Germany.[42] It is primarily a silent feature with synchronized orchestral accompaniment, except for a few key scenes with dialogue, diegetic sound, or sound effects. The film is framed by a loose narrative of a Hamburg sailor bidding farewell to his wife and going to sea on a Hapag liner. The sailor is seen several times, sometimes in posed shot-reverse-shot situations, and the film closes with the return of the ship, supposedly after one year traveling around the world. The compiled scenes emphasize the exoticism of far-flung places and cultures, although this "otherness" was partially defused by stressing similarities to European customs.

Ruttmann's work offers a useful case for considering the function of a "global ether" discourse, also due to his previous attempts to render the immersive and multidirectional experience of modern urban sound. For the premiere of Ruttmann's 1927 film *Berlin: Die Sinfonie der Großstadt* [Berlin: Symphony of a Large City], Edmund Meisel wrote a film-specific composition for a full orchestra with sound-effect machines. Since Meisel's main priority was to address "the city dweller and their environment," he listened to the noisy sounds of the city and tried to feed this experience into the musical score.[43] Meisel's composition thus attempted to find some continuum between the audience's prior knowledge of the urban soundscape and the aesthetic reinterpretation of its sounds in the cinema. In fact, Meisel emphasized that these sounds should be heightened during screenings: "In the moments when a total impression is absolutely necessary, parts of the orchestra will be positioned around the auditorium."[44] This use of *surround sound* in the cinema precisely suggests the staging of the multidirectional urban soundscape.

Whereas the silent Berlin film involved an aesthetic composition of urban activity as a "symphony," *Melodie der Welt* extended this premise to the whole world. *Melodie der Welt* reflects Ruttmann's attempt to develop rhythm as both an auditory and visual principle, to some degree limited by the techniques of sound and film editing in this early part of the transition era.[45] This compilation film, created primarily through a selection of material made by other cameramen, used a composed score to provide overall consistency between the intermittent sequences with synchronized sound. Nonetheless, as the composer Wolfgang Zeller pointed out, his goal was:

> To give a musical playing against [*Gegenspiel*] of the film [images], so that these naturalistically filmed sounds are prepared for and sustained … Due to the complexity of the film, it could never be my task to merely complement the images with any kind of illustrative sounds. It had to be created—running parallel with the main line of the film—as a completely well-composed acoustic line.[46]

In other words, Zeller argued that his music was not merely illustrative, and his task was to establish a sense of structural unity on the level of sound, as the synchronized diegetic sounds in this film were limited due to technical restrictions on vocal audibility.[47]

There are several vignettes that suggest how sonic immersion and multidirectionality figure in *Melodie der Welt*. In two scenes, the spectator is privy to the thrill of ambient noise in the city, of being on the street, and in the midst of the crowd at a horse, bike, or car race, with giddy spirals, sounds, and cheers. In a third key sequence, various activities of women in public are showcased, before the narrative shifts to men's speech in public. Political speeches on the street eventually lead to overlaid images and a growing cacophony of layered voices— Indian, Chinese, German, and other muffled languages—resembling a Babylonian babble that seems to resemble radio interference. This scene makes a similar allusion to the multiple voices comprising world events and news that I noted in Bischoff's radio play. The scene implicitly refers to the noise of domestic street politics in Germany, and in a move not unlike Schafer's blueprint for a "tuning of the world," this noise (as societal chaos) is given significance within a global perspective (or global melody).[48] The activities of people from across the world are reorganized according to thematic groups, which emphasize the similarities between their various cultural practices. These vignettes are introduced with onscreen titles, which announce anthropological-like categories, such as buildings, streets, worship, war sounds, children, farming, sport, racing, language and music, cuisine, dance, theater, and work.

In his 1936 commentary on the film, Kurt London argued that the soundtrack was clever in resisting an "exoticist" trend in composition. Nonetheless, the principle of creating a "melody" does suggest a process of aestheticization and narrative organization whereby musical sound (and sense) is created out of noise. This universalist gesture to seek out the correspondence in sound, language, music, and customs across cultures has a faint subtext of seeking control. While the portrayal of ethnic cultures seems to suggest a discourse of primitivism, it is implied that the ritual sounds of music making retain their symbolic meaning as opposed to the noisy clamor of European cities. The sponsorship of the film by Hapag Lloyd cruise ship company was a form of promotion, with one purpose being to activate a "tourist" gaze and listening mode.[49]

There is one scene in *Melodie der Welt* that seems to offer a counter-discourse to the imperialist undercurrent in this film (and its institutional framing as a film sound advertisement). The sequence begins with scenes of mobilization, with marching armies and tanks, which draws attention to the (potentially traumatic) experience of explosions and gunfire in modern warfare. It ends with the expressionist-style screams of a presumably German mother, and a closing image of rows of white wooden crosses. Indeed, as Douglas Kahn has pointed out, the historical narrative of immersive and amplified sound should also take note of "[w]ar as a model for an 'all-encompassing sound'... but it was conditioned by the ever-expanding machinations of imperialist exploits, mass culture, global militarism, scientific incursions, ideas of an infinite nature, the other world of spiritism, communications technologies, and the like."[50] In other words, we should pay attention to the personal experience of World War I (and experience of overwhelming sound) that informs Ruttmann's portrayal, himself a returned soldier. The overpowering sounds of modern warfare—with shells, guns, and artillery— were produced at an intensity that was unlike anything experienced or imagined before. This soundscape, dominated by the "technologized sonority" of warfare, was the basis for distress, and often lasting trauma, for those subjected to its relentless noise and overwhelming of the self.[51] Nonetheless, as Kahn suggests, this model for "all sound" should not be separated from a broader set of imaginaries and fields of modern culture. This example, moreover, illustrates how the immersive soundscape of warfare has an "afterlife" in Weimar-era culture, as Axel Volmar also demonstrates in this volume.

Even though I am wont to read a critical position in relation to warfare—and it is possible to recall scenes of social critique in Ruttmann's Berlin film—such potentially critical moments would seem to be defused in *Melodie der Welt*'s concluding scenes. This final vignette of the film, titled "work and homecoming," creates a sound mix, although this time drawing on the noisy sounds of work (electric saws and hammering). The film closes with the end of the workday, with factory sirens intercut with anchor and horn sounds as the Hapag ship returns to Germany, followed by the non-diegetic sounds of a choral. This final scene allows for a reincorporation of the foreign and strange elements of world sounds in the form of the imposing cruise ship, which returns safely to domestic waters. In Malte Hagener's analysis of Hapag Lloyd film production for their passenger ships, he notes that the production of *Melodie der Welt* is representative of the overlap of national and commercial interests governing the interaction between Weimar politicians, big business, and entertainment industries in the 1920s, particularly as a response to the perceived threat of American sound film systems.[52] Similar to the repeated horns of Hapag Lloyd's ships, Hamburg's harbor sounds also figured in radio as positive national symbols for the resurgence of German industry and technological advancement after World War I. Radio programs like "Das Hamburger Hafenkonzert" (Hamburg Harbor Concert), which was hosted by Karl Esmarch from 1929 onward, also offered listeners a similar national celebration of German maritime culture. These cultural expressions coincided with the expansion of Hamburg harbor activity; by 1929 it had outstripped its competitors of Rotterdam and Antwerp for the first time since before 1914.[53]

To conclude, we might say that in many cases the exploration of world sounds represented a compulsory alternative or euphemism for local events and sounds in the 1920s. In some cases, program makers sought to explore "America" as a cultural model, with syncopated and dissonant jazz sounds operating as sonic metaphors for the rhythm and tempo of modern life. For others, the internationalization of the world (and onset of American forms of mass culture and modernism) appeared to be threatening, with repeated emphasis on the need for Germanization. Such anxieties about national and cultural identity can be traced to the emphasis on *Heimat* and *Volk* culture on radio. Cultural artifacts like *Melodie der Welt* should thus not only be explored in terms of their technological innovation or montage aesthetics, but also situated within a socio-political context that is informed by cultural insecurities about American influence and colonialist-style imaginaries that employed exotic sounds as replacements for domestic politics.

This chapter has sought to trace several trajectories for the "auditory imagination" that marked the emergence of sound as a discursive field and fledgling artistic practice. This narrative requires some contextualization of the modern sounds produced by the broader impact of the industrialization and technologization of sounds (including those of war) and the emergence of various sound technologies (phonograph, wireless, sound film). I have argued for the necessity of having broader categories of periodization for modern sound and the auditory imagination, and that the analysis of radio and film texts should be situated in terms of the cultural landscape (and soundscape) of their production and distribution. When dealing with the specific case of Weimar Germany, and the particular situation of radio's emergence, organization, and content regulation, I have traced two particular trajectories. The first concerns the persistence of the "global ether" concept and the oceanic metaphors associated with radio, and how the restrictions on portraying local sounds and current affairs may be directly connected to a fascination for (exotic) world sounds. This, in turn, appears to be intertwined with post-World War I anxieties about national and cultural identity after the loss of imperial assets and military power, and vis-à-vis the perceived threat of American mass cultural forms. The case of *Melodie der Welt* precisely reveals such tensions, with a sound aesthetic that is reliant both on local, on-location recordings and on the persistent imaginary of a global soundscape.[54]

The second major aim of this chapter was to investigate the possibilities for representing or approximating urban sounds and the modern experience of sonic immersion. My understanding of emergent documentary aesthetics has comprised both attempts to literally portray the sounds of daily life and the public sphere, and to narrativize or creatively render these sounds, whether heard or imagined, with the means of radio or silent film. As these case studies have shown, a fledgling practice of "documentary sound" was established in a variety of media in the late 1920s, and its scope extends beyond the current examination of Weimar Germany.[55] I have drawn attention to both visual and audio artefacts, to multisensoriality, and exchanges between radio and cinema practices (and industries) in the interwar period. This ultimately points to one of the main rewards and challenges in writing about past auditory cultures: the task of achieving both close analysis and "thick" description, and thereby addressing specific phenomena and their relation to broader social, cultural, and political patterns.

## Notes

1. Kate Lacey, "Ten Years of Radio Studies: The Very Idea," *The Radio Journal* 6, no. 1 (2009): 22.
2. Michele Hilmes, "Is There A Field Called Sound Culture Studies? And Does It Matter?," *American Quarterly* 57, no. 1 (March 2005): 249–59. Idem, "Foregrounding Sound: New (and Old) Directions in Sound Studies," *Cinema Journal* 48, no. 1 (Fall 2008): 115–17.
3. R. Murray Schafer, *The Soundscape: Our Sonic Environment and the Tuning of the World* (Rochester, [1977] 1994).
4. Ibid., 5.
5. Ibid.
6. Ibid., 4.
7. For a perceptive account of similar themes in Weimar-era cinema, see Anton Kaes, "*Metropolis* (1927): City, Cinema, Modernity," in *Weimar Cinema*, ed. Noah Isenberg (New York, 2009), 173–91.
8. Significantly, Schafer does not date the advent of schizophonia with telegraphy from the 1840s, but several decades later with the popular dissemination of telephone, radio, and gramophone. He thus pinpoints the "era of schizophonia" as starting with the invention of Alexander Graham Bell's telephone in 1876, and the invention of gramophone in 1877 by Charles Cross and Thomas Edison. See Schafer, *The Soundscape*, 90.
9. For a critical evaluation of the contributions (and shortcomings) of soundscape theory and its conception of the modern city, see Sophie Arkette, "Sounds Like City," *Theory, Culture & Society* 21, no.1 (2004): 159–68. For an extended discussion of soundscape theory and the value of phenomenological approaches to auditory experience, see Carolyn Birdsall, *Nazi Soundscapes: Sound, Technology and Urban Space in Germany, 1933–1945* (Amsterdam, 2012).
10. Jonathan Sterne. *The Audible Past: Cultural Origins of Sound Production* (Durham, 2003), 3.
11. Lacey, "Ten Years," 30. For an elaboration on *longue durée*, which, in his understanding, goes beyond the individual or social measurement of long-term change, see Fernand Braudel, *The Mediterranean and the Mediterranean World in the Age of Philip II* (New York, [1949] 1972). In Braudel's account, this change is that of geological or climactic change, but I employ it here for a more general sense of periodization and gradual change over time.
12. Douglas Kahn, *Noise, Water, Meat: A History of Sound in the Arts* (Cambridge, 1999), 16.

13. Douglas Kahn, "Introduction: Histories of Sound Once Removed," in *Wireless Imagination: Sound, Radio, and the Avant-Garde*, eds. Douglas Kahn and Gregory Whitehead (Cambridge, 1994), 18.
14. Ibid., 10. Nonetheless, Vertov, along with Joris Ivens and members of John Grierson's GPO Film Unit, have been described as the first filmmakers to fully explore the possibility of "soundscapes" within non-fiction filmmaking. See Michael Chanan, *The Politics of Documentary* (London, 2007), 116, 125.
15. Timothy C. Campbell, *Wireless Writing in the Age of Marconi* (Minneapolis, 2006).
16. Kahn, *Noise, Water, Meat*, 21.
17. Ibid., 22–26. For the broader appeal of radio to various modernist figures and intellectuals, see Debra Rae Cohen et al., eds., *Broadcasting Modernism* (Gainesville, FL, 2009).
18. Michael Friedewald, *Die "Tönenden Funken": Geschichte eines frühen drahtlosen Kommunikationssystems 1905–1914*. Berlin, 1999. Idem, "The Beginnings of Radio Communication in Germany, 1897–1918," *Journal of Radio and Audio Media* 7, no. 2 (2000): 441–63.
19. Bredow joined in the widespread articulation of fears about the urban masses, citing radio as a domestic medium that would help to unite families and keep children away from the corrupting influences of urban streets. This institutional context involved a gradual domestication of the medium, shifting from the early male tinkers (*Bastlern*) with crystal detectors to licensed (vacuum tube) sets in the domestic environment, which remained predominantly for the consumption of the middle classes in the 1920s. See Kate Lacey, "From *Plauderei* to Propaganda: On Women's Radio in Germany 1924–1935," in *Women and Radio: Airing Differences*, ed. Caroline Mitchell (London, 2000), 49; Inge Marßolek, "Radio in Deutschland, 1923–1960: Zur Sozialgeschichte eines Mediums," *Geschichte und Gesellschaft* 27 (2001): 214; Wolfgang Hagen, *Das Radio: Zur Geschichte und Theorie des Hörfunks—Deutschland/USA* (Munich, 2005), 75–78.
20. These composers included Franz Schreker, Paul Hindemith, Max Butting, and Kurt Weill, alongside those working in North America such as Georges Antheil and Edgar Varèse. See Christopher Hailey, "Rethinking Sound: Music and Radio in Weimar Germany," in *Music and Performance during the Weimar Republic*, ed. Bryan R. Gilliam (Cambridge, 1994), 14–16.
21. Ibid., 32.
22. Ibid., 11.
23. Ibid., 79.
24. Marßolek, "Radio in Deutschland," 213.
25. Renate Schumacher, "Radio als Medium und Faktor des aktuellen Geschehens," in *Programmgeschichte des Hörfunks in der Weimarer Republik*, ed. Joachim-Felix Leonhard (Munich, 1997), 568.
26. The term acoustical film was also employed by Alfred Braun (Berlin) to describe the radio experimentation pieces created there, such as Walther Ruttmann's *Weekend*. See Klaus Schöning, "The Contours of Acoustic Art," *Theatre Journal* 43 (1991): 307–24; Mark E. Cory, "Soundplay:

The Polyphonous Tradition of German Radio Art," in *Wireless Imagination: Sound, Radio, and the Avant-Garde*, eds. Douglas Kahn and Gregory Whitehead (Cambridge, 1994), 339; Virginia Madsen, "Radio and the Documentary Imagination: Thirty Years of Experiment, Innovation, and Revelation," *The Radio Journal* 3, no. 3 (November 2005): 195–96.

27. For a more detailed discussion and typology of these programs, see Carolyn Birdsall, "Sonic Artefacts: Reality Codes of Urbanity in Early German Radio Documentary," in *Soundscapes of the Urban Past: Staged Sound as Mediated Cultural Heritage*, ed. Karin Bijsterveld (Bielefeld, 2013), 129–68.

28. See Renate Mohl, "Wie der Rundfunk die Befreiung der Rheinlande feierte," in *Jahrtausendfeiern und Befreiungsfeiern im Rheinland: Zur politischen Festkultur, 1925 und 1930*, ed. Gertrude Cepl-Kaufmann (Essen, 2009), 398.

29. Schumacher, "Radio als Medium," 567.

30. Another advertising short by Ruttmann that made appeals to the auditory imagination was *Dort wo der Rhein…* (1927), commissioned by the national-liberal newspaper *Kölnische Zeitung*. The film title, which refers to the Rhine River, is the first line of a traditional folk song. However, this six-minute animated silent also stresses the imagined sounds of voice, music, and newspaper printing. The newspaper seller, a characteristic figure in the early twentieth-century cityscape, is shown calling out the headlines to passersby. The voice, which cannot be heard on the soundtrack, is filled in by the audience watching the visual depiction of facial movements of the mouth.

31. Jeffrey Sconce, *Haunted Media: Electronic Presence from Telegraphy to Television* (Durham, NC, 2000), 62.

32. See Timothy D. Taylor, "Music and the Rise of Radio in Twenties America: Technological Imeprialism, Socialization and the Transformation of Intimacy," in *Wired for Sound: Engineering and Technologies in Sonic Cultures*, eds. Paul D. Greene and Thomas Porcello (Middleton, CT, 2005), 249.

33. David Ciarlo, *Advertising Empire: Race and Visual Culture in Imperial Germany* (Cambridge, MA, 2011), 320.

34. Hagen, *Das Radio*, 87–89.

35. Prior to this broadcast, all radio plays were broadcast live and were not recorded for archiving purposes. There appears to have been two versions of Bischoff's radio play. The original version was aired in February 1928. The remaining recording fragment in the German Radio Archive (Frankfurt) appears to be derived from a second airing in November 1929; see Daniel Gilfillan, *Pieces of Sound: German Experimental Radio* (Minneapolis, 2009), 75–76.

36. For an analysis and the English translation of the script, see ibid., 75–81; Dieter Daniels, *Kunst als Sendung: Von der Telegrafie zum Internet* (Munich, 2002), 150–52.

37. Ibid., 100–101, for a transcript of the opening sequence of *"Hallo! Hier Welle Erdball!"*

38. Such programs had a predominantly bourgeois-democratic tone, but a number of conservative positions could be found in other programming,

such as Karl Haushofer's geopolitical analyses in "Weltpolitischen Monatsberichte," which appeared regularly on Bavarian radio from 1925 to 1932 (Schumacher, "Radio als Medium," 446, 486).

39. See Ulrich Heitger, *Vom Zeitzeichen zum politischen Führungsmittel: Entwicklungstendenzen und Strukturen der Nachrichtenprogramme des Rundfunks in der Weimarer Republik, 1923–1932* (Münster, 2003), 401.

40. Marßolek, "Radio in Deutschland," 213.

41. For further discussion of *Heimat* and *Volk* programming in Weimar-era radio, see Birdsall, "Sonic Artefacts," 129–68.

42. For more on the industrial development of sound film in Germany, see Wolfgang Mühl-Benninghaus, *Das Ringen um den Tonfilm: Strategien der Elektro- und der Filmindustrie in den 20er und 30er Jahren* (Düsseldorf, 1999).

43. See Edmund Meisel, "Wie schreibt man Filmmusik?," *Licht-Bild-Bühne* (4 July 1927): n. pag.; "Edmund Meisel über seine BERLIN-Musik," *Film-Kurier* (20 Sept. 1927): n. pag.; *Berlin: Die Sinfonie der Großstadt, Musik zu dem gleichnamigen Fox-Film von Walther Ruttmann* (Berlin, 1927); Anthony McElligott, "Walter Ruttmann's Berlin: Symphony of a City: Traffic-mindedness and the City in Interwar Germany," in *The City in Central Europe: Culture and Society from 1800 to the Present*, eds. Malcolm Gee, Tim Kirk and Jill Stewart (Aldershot, 1999), 209–30. A similar desire to incorporate the sounds of the city for film scores is suggested by composer Georges Antheil, who employed sirens and phonographs in his 1927 performance of the score for *Ballet Mécanique* (1924); see Kahn, *Noise, Water, Meat*, 124–26.

44. "*Für die Momente, in denen der Totalitätseindruck unbedingt erforderlich ist, werden Teile des Orchesters in den Zuschauerraum postiert*" (Meisel, "Edmund Meisel über seine BERLIN-Musik"). The film was released with a complete score for seventy-five musicians dictating the music and acoustic effect to be played simultaneously to the image track. Meisel also prepared a version for a smaller instrumentation. Due to budgeting reasons, the premiere in Berlin only featured eighteen musicians; Friedrich P. Kahlenberg, "Der wirtschaftliche Faktor 'Musik' im Theaterbetrieb der Ufa in den Jahren 1927 bis 1930," in *Stummfilmmusik gestern und heute*, ed. Walther Seidler (Berlin, 1979), 61. For an extended discussion of metaphors of symphony and rhythm in Ruttmann's films of the interwar period, and the depiction of the urban soundscape, see Birdsall, *Nazi Soundscapes*.

45. For the most part, the agency of the people depicted is through their gestures or movements rather than speech or dialogue. It is important to note that the soundtrack had to be recorded simultaneous to the sounds due to difficulties in recording sound onto optical film. Only in 1932 did it become possible to feed a separate sound mix into optical film.

46. "*ein musikalisches Gegenspiel des Films zu geben, das die naturalistisch fotografierten Geräusche vorbereitet und fortsetzt … Bei dem Umfang des Werkes konnte es nicht meine Aufgabe sein, die Bilder einfach mit irgendwelchen illustrierenden Klängen auszufüllen. Es musste—parallel laufend mit der*

*filmischen Linie—eine vollkommen durchkomponierte akustische Linie geschaffen werden"*; Wolfgang Zeller, "Die musikalische Originalkomposition zur Weltmelodie," in *Melodie der Welt* (Berlin, 1929), n.p.

47. This poor quality of vocal sound in early sound film, as a *Film-Kurier* critic later recalled, led to short dialogue and a preference for songs, because "melodies are always easy to understand"; "Wandlung des Musikfilms," *Film-Kurier* (2 May 1933): 3.

48. The act of normalizing the Oriental "other" for the Western viewer might also be reinscribed as an effort to normalize Germany's cultural similarities to Europe and the world in the aftermath of World War I. Nonetheless, the question of "internationalism" was also a key theme for European film industries in the sound transition era, where sound film posed a challenge to the earlier international appeal and lower costs of silent film. On this broader process, see Tim Bergfelder, "Negotiating Exoticism: Hollywood, Film Europe and the Cultural Reception of Anna May Wong," in *Stars: The Film Reader*, eds. Lucy Fischer and Marci Landy (London, 2004), 59–75.

49. See Malte Hagener, "Propaganda auf hoher See: Bordkinos und Reisebilder Deutscher Reedereien, 1919–1939," in *Fasten Your Seatbelt! Bewegtbilder vom Fliegen*, eds. Judith Keilbach and Alexandra Schneider (Münster, 2009), 187–99, for a media-theoretical reflection on the development of film programming for Hapag-Lloyd passenger ships, and the overlap of national and commercial interests governing the interaction between Weimar politicians, big business, and entertainment industries (as demonstrated in the case of Ruttmann's *Melodie der Welt*).

50. Kahn, *Noise, Water, Meat*, 9.

51. Bruce Johnson, "Technologized Sonority," in *Dark Side of the Tune: Popular Music and Violence*, by Bruce Johnson and Martin Cloonan (Aldershot, 2008), 50–54.

52. Hagener, "Propaganda," 187–99.

53. See Stefan Kiekel, "Kurt Esmarch und das Hamburger Hafenkonzert: Über das Selbstverständnis eines Rundfunk Pioniers und die Gründe für ein erfolgreiches Format," *Rundfunk und Geschichte* 37, No. 1/2 (2011), 14. For further discussion of how local radio programming was given national significance, see Birdsall, "Sonic Artefacts," 129–68.

54. A number of recent publications have emphasized such links between modern(ist) aesthetics and a fascination with the exotic, primitive or colonial in the 1920s. See, for instance, Oksana Sarkisova, "Across One Sixth of the World: Dziga Vertov, Travel Cinema and Soviet Patriotism," in *October* 121 (2007), 19–40; Laura Doyle, "Colonial Encounters," in *The Oxford Handbook of Modernisms*, eds. Andrzej Gasiorek, et al. (Oxford, 2010), 249–66.

55. For a broader overview of early sound documentary practice in different European contexts, see Carolyn Birdsall, "Die Orchestrierung urbaner Akustik: Dokumentarische Form, akustische Medien und die moderne Stadt," in *Ton: Texte zur Akustik im Dokumentarfilm*, eds. Volko Kamensky and Julian Rohrhuber (Berlin, 2013), 76–97.

# Bibliography

Anon. "Wandlung des Musikfilms." *Film-Kurier* (2 May 1933): 3.

Arkette, Sophie. "Sounds Like City." *Theory, Culture & Society* 21, no.1 (2004): 159–68.

Bergfelder, Tim. "Negotiating Exoticism: Hollywood, Film Europe and the Cultural Reception of Anna May Wong." In *Stars: The Film Reader*. Eds. Lucy Fischer and Marci Landy. London, 2004, 59–75.

Birdsall, Carolyn. *Nazi Soundscapes: Sound, Technology and Urban Space in Germany, 1933–1945*. Amsterdam, 2012.

———. "Sonic Artefacts: Reality Codes of Urbanity in Early German Radio Documentary." In *Soundscapes of the Urban Past: Staged Sound as Mediated Cultural Heritage*. Ed. Karin Bijsterveld. Bielefeld, 2013, 129–68.

———. "Die Orchestrierung urbaner Akustik: Dokumentarische Form, akustische Medien und die moderne Stadt." In *Ton: Texte zur Akustik im Dokumentarfilm*. Eds. Volko Kamensky and Julian Rohrhuber. Berlin, 2013, 76–97.

Braudel, Fernand. *The Mediterranean and the Mediterranean World in the Age of Philip II*. New York, (1949) 1972.

Campbell, Timothy C. *Wireless Writing in the Age of Marconi*. Minneapolis, 2006.

Chanan, Michael. *The Politics of Documentary*. London, 2007.

Ciarlo, David. *Advertising Empire: Race and Visual Culture in Imperial Germany*. Cambridge, MA, 2011.

Cohen, Debra Rae, et al., eds. *Broadcasting Modernism*. Gainesville, FL, 2009.

Cory, Mark E. "Soundplay: The Polyphonous Tradition of German Radio Art." In *Wireless Imagination: Sound, Radio, and the Avant-Garde*. Eds. Douglas Kahn and Gregory Whitehead. Cambridge, 1994, 331–71.

Daniels, Dieter. *Kunst als Sendung: Von der Telegrafie zum Internet*. Munich, 2002.

Doyle, Laura. "Colonial Encounters." In *The Oxford Handbook of Modernisms*. Eds. Andrzej Gasiorek, et al. Oxford, 2010, 249–66.

Friedewald, Michael. *Die "Tönenden Funken": Geschichte eines frühen drahtlosen Kommunikationssystems 1905–1914*. Berlin, 1999.

———. "The Beginnings of Radio Communication in Germany, 1897–1918." *Journal of Radio and Audio Media* 7, no. 2 (2000): 441–63.

Gilfillan, Daniel. *Pieces of Sound: German Experimental Radio*. Minneapolis, 2009.

Hagen, Wolfgang. *Das Radio: Zur Geschichte und Theorie des Hörfunks – Deutschland/USA*. Munich, 2005.

Hagener, Malte. "Propaganda auf hoher See: Bordkinos und Reisebilder Deutscher Reedereien, 1919–1939." In *Fasten Your Seatbelt! Bewegtbilder vom Fliegen*. Eds. Judith Keilbach and Alexandra Schneider. Münster, 2009, 187–99.

Hailey, Christopher. "Rethinking Sound: Music and Radio in Weimar Germany." In *Music and Performance during the Weimar Republic*. Ed. Bryan R. Gilliam. Cambridge, 1994, 13–36.

Heitger, Ulrich. *Vom Zeitzeichen zum politischen Führungsmittel: Entwicklungstendenzen und Strukturen der Nachrichtenprogramme des Rundfunks in der Weimarer Republik, 1923–1932.* Münster, 2003.

Hilmes, Michele. "Is There A Field Called Sound Culture Studies? And Does It Matter?," *American Quarterly* 57, no. 1 (March 2005): 249–59.

———. "Foregrounding Sound: New (and Old) Directions in Sound Studies." *Cinema Journal* 48, no. 1 (Fall 2008): 115–17.

Johnson, Bruce. "Technologized Sonority." In *Dark Side of the Tune: Popular Music and Violence.* By Bruce Johnson and Martin Cloonan. Aldershot, 2008, 49–63.

Kaes, Anton. "*Metropolis* (1927): City, Cinema, Modernity." In *Weimar Cinema.* Ed. Noah Isenberg. New York, 2009, 173–91.

Kahlenberg, Friedrich P. "Der wirtschaftliche Faktor 'Musik' im Theaterbetrieb der Ufa in den Jahren 1927 bis 1930." In *Stummfilmmusik gestern und heute.* Ed. Walther Seidler. Berlin, 1979, 51–71.

Kahn, Douglas. "Introduction: Histories of Sound Once Removed." In *Wireless Imagination: Sound, Radio, and the Avant-Garde.* Eds. Douglas Kahn and Gregory Whitehead. Cambridge, 1994, 1–29.

———. *Noise, Water, Meat: A History of Sound in the Arts.* Cambridge, 1999.

Kiekel, Stefan "Kurt Esmarch und das Hamburger Hafenkonzert: Über das Selbstverständnis eines Rundfunk Pioniers und die Gründe für ein erfolgreiches Format," *Rundfunk und Geschichte* 37, no. 1/2 (2011): 3–17.

Lacey, Kate. "From *Plauderei* to Propaganda: On Women's Radio in Germany 1924–1935." In *Women and Radio: Airing Differences.* Ed. Caroline Mitchell. London, 2000, 48–63.

———. "Ten Years of Radio Studies: The Very Idea." *The Radio Journal* 6, no. 1 (2009): 21–32.

Madsen, Virginia. "Radio and the Documentary Imagination: Thirty Years of Experiment, Innovation, and Revelation." *The Radio Journal* 3, no. 3 (November 2005): 189–98.

Marßolek, Inge. "Radio in Deutschland, 1923–1960: Zur Sozialgeschichte eines Mediums." *Geschichte und Gesellschaft* 27 (2001): 207–39.

McElligott, Anthony. "Walter Ruttmann's Berlin: Symphony of a City: Traffic-mindedness and the City in Interwar Germany." In *The City in Central Europe: Culture and Society from 1800 to the Present.* Eds. Malcolm Gee, Tim Kirk, and Jill Stewart. Aldershot, 1999, 209–30.

Meisel, Edmund. "Wie schreibt man Filmmusik?," *Licht-Bild-Bühne* (4 July 1927): n. pag.

———. "Edmund Meisel über seine BERLIN-Musik." *Film-Kurier* (20 Sept. 1927): n. pag.

———. *Berlin: Die Sinfonie der Großstadt, Musik zu dem gleichnamigen Fox-Film von Walther Ruttmann.* Berlin, 1927.

Mohl, Renate. "Wie der Rundfunk die Befreiung der Rheinlande feierte." In *Jahrtausendfeiern und Befreiungsfeiern im Rheinland: Zur politischen Festkultur, 1925 und 1930.* Ed. Gertrude Cepl-Kaufmann. Essen, 2009, 329–99.

Mühl-Benninghaus, Wolfgang. *Das Ringen um den Tonfilm: Strategien der Elektro- und der Filmindustrie in den 20er und 30er Jahren.* Düsseldorf, 1999.

Sarkisova, Oksana. "Across One Sixth of the World: Dziga Vertov, Travel Cinema and Soviet Patriotism." *October* 121 (2007): 19–40.

Schafer, R. Murray. *The Soundscape: Our Sonic Environment and the Tuning of the World*. Rochester, [1977] 1994.

Schöning, Klaus. "The Contours of Acoustic Art." *Theatre Journal* 43 (1991): 307–24.

Schumacher, Renate. "Radio als Medium und Faktor des aktuellen Geschehens." In *Programmgeschichte des Hörfunks in der Weimarer Republik*. Ed. Joachim-Felix Leonhard. Munich, 1997, 423–621.

Sconce, Jeffrey. *Haunted Media: Electronic Presence from Telegraphy to Television*. Durham, NC, 2000.

Sterne, Jonathan. *The Audible Past: Cultural Origins of Sound Production*. Durham, 2003.

Taylor, Timothy D. "Music and the Rise of Radio in Twenties America: Technological Imperialism, Socialization and the Transformation of Intimacy." In *Wired for Sound: Engineering and Technologies in Sonic Cultures*. Eds. Paul D. Greene and Thomas Porcello. Middletown, CT, 2005, 245–68.

Zeller, Wolfgang. "Die musikalische Originalkomposition zur Weltmelodie." In *Melodie der Welt*. Berlin, 1929, n.p.

12

## NEURASTHENIA, CIVILIZATION, AND THE SOUNDS OF MODERN LIFE
### Narratives of Nervous Illness in the Interwar Campaign against Noise

*James G. Mansell*

In 1907, Marcel Proust sealed himself in a cork-lined room to free himself from the noises of the Boulevard Haussmann which passed outside. He later wrote *In Search of Lost Time* (1913–1927), a series of novels resonating with the city sounds which echoed in his mind.[1] He was not the only writer of the period to require refuge from the metropolitan din. Joris-Karl Huysmans, author of the infamous decadent novel, *Against Nature* (1884), was also hyper-sensitive to Paris's street sounds.[2] Fifty years earlier in London, writer Thomas Carlyle had soundproofed his attic and retreated there to think.[3] Along with Charles Dickens and other Victorian intellectuals, he sent a letter to parliament in 1864 urging action over the rising noise level of London streets.[4] Indeed, over the course of the late nineteenth and early twentieth century, a feeling gathered pace that the conditions necessary for "brain work" were being eroded by modern urban cacophony.[5] The desire to protect spaces for quiet contemplation in the modern city was widely shared. A fully blown noise abatement campaign took shape after 1900 in which a chorus of public figures joined writers and intellectuals in their call for tranquility.[6] The crisis of quiet intellectuality identified by the leaders of this campaign became a commonly debated problem after World War I. By the 1930s, national anti-noise associations had formed across Europe and were increasingly successful in their call for new noise control legislation. Combating urban noise was now a priority of urban governance. Even the League of Nations saw fit to devote a conference to the problem in 1937.[7]

The course of early anti-noise campaigns has been amply detailed by historians.[8] It is the purpose of this chapter, instead, to outline the cultural origins of noise abatement in the interwar period and, in particular, to argue that its discourse relied upon a medicalized critique of modernity in which narratives of nervous overstimulation played a central role.

This discourse, I will argue, emerged at the intersection of medicine, literature, and cultural criticism, an intellectual territory in which scientific and cultural representations of nervous illness, and in turn of noise suffering, cannot easily be disentangled. The argument that urban sounds might cause an epidemic of "nervousness"—a term instantly understood at the time to denote jumpy and anxious urbanites—carried a good deal of weight.[9] This argument was promoted by doctors and medical writers under the heading of "neurasthenia," but its popularity also benefited from the intervention of novelists like Proust and Huysmans, famous for experiencing and writing about nervousness. Doctors and writers, this chapter will argue, self-consciously borrowed from one another's narratives in order to construct "the noise problem."

Debates about noise grew alongside a deepening sense of unease about the future of European "civilization" around the turn of the twentieth century. Although "modern civilization" was acknowledged to have provided the means for great material development over the course of the nineteenth century, its ceaseless technological and cultural development was now seen to pose a physical threat to health. Ideals of limitless progress had been all but forgotten by a generation who saw in the conditions of industrial modernity only degradation and intoxication. Cultural critics Max Nordau and Georg Simmel, for example, suggested that the human body could no longer keep pace with the enormous strain put on it by the experience of living in modern times.[10] "Its own new discoveries and progress have taken civilized humanity by surprise," exclaimed Nordau in *Degeneration* (1895).[11] A source of illness and misery, the environmental conditions of the modern age, and of the modern city in particular, made it all the less likely that civilized Europe would survive. Christopher E. Forth has identified this medical critique of "modern civilization" as a central component of elite male intellectual culture at the beginning of the twentieth century. Locating the period's cultural criticism in the politics not only of health but also of gender, Forth argues that early twentieth-century medical discourses leveled "their gaze on the interplay between the body and its conditions of life, and thus turned a critical eye upon the environment that created and was created by civilized manhood."[12] Modern urban life, it was thought, corrupted civilized men through the temptations of alcohol, sexual immorality, and more generally by the sedentary nature of the life it imposed. It also brought about sensory degradation.

Writers and intellectuals who criticized noise emphasized the incompatibility of intellectual leadership with modern, technological civilization. The paradox of a civilization which threatened to decapitate its supporting social structure was increasingly seen to be encapsulated in the noise problem in early twentieth-century culture.[13] Noise became thoroughly entwined with the masculine critique of civilization identified by Forth. It was invested with political significance, becoming an urban battleground for the survival of civilized men under the conditions of mechanized modernity. While interwar noise abatement supporters acknowledged that noise suffering was not an exclusively male problem, they tended to emphasize that, in an age of economic and military crisis, the damage done by noise to the nerves of educated men was the most urgent reason for action to be taken.[14] Leader of Britain's interwar noise abatement campaign, the eminent physician Thomas Horder, argued that his crusade for "acoustic-civilization" found support mostly with the "intelligent" section of society, because it was more often than not people of this class, he thought, who suffered from the sounds caused by the unruly users of motor vehicles and by those who indulged in "louder forms of amusement."[15] There was, therefore, a class politics inherent in noise abatement discourse. The professional, usually middle class, men who led noise abatement campaigns often hinted that the noise problem was caused by the thoughtlessness of those whose work did not require silence. Without the quiet conditions necessary for their intellectual superiority, "intelligent" men feared that they would descend into the culture of the noisy urban masses.[16]

Highlighting the continuity between late nineteenth- and early twentieth-century theories of nervousness, this chapter argues that the case of interwar noise abatement should cause us to question whether World War I represents as sharp a break in attitudes towards modernity as scholars usually suppose.[17] In its intermingling of medical and literary accounts of nervousness, interwar noise abatement built discursive bridges between the late nineteenth-century's fin-de-siècle moment and the renewed cultural pessimism of the 1930s. The gloomy intellectual atmosphere of that decade gave impetus to the noise abatement movement, causing it to take institutional shape where it had earlier been the cause of individual complainants. The French and British supporters of noise abatement upon whom this chapter focuses argued that in an increasingly uncertain age, the nervous drain caused by noise could be ill afforded.

## Noise as Public Health Crisis

Formal noise abatement organizations took shape and began to exercise significant influence from the late 1920s onward. The common factor in many of these organizations was the leadership of medical experts.

While politicians, town planners, and engineers all had a role to play in the solution to the noise problem, it was doctors who formed the shape of the problem itself. Horder, for instance, was a well-known and influential physician in Britain. He headed London's Anti-Noise League, formed in 1933. The league published a journal, entitled *Quiet*, in which leading medical writers put the case against noise. It staged educational exhibitions such as that held at London's Science Museum in 1935. It also lobbied government departments, with some success, about the need to control noise. In Paris, it was an organization for the promotion of tourism, the Touring Club de France (TCF), which played the leading role in promoting anti-noise intervention led by the city's police authorities. The president of the TCF's noise abatement commission was the engineer Léon Auscher. He explained that the TCF had taken upon itself to seek, in the first instance, existing laws and administrative channels through which noise could be reduced.[18] However, in order to do so, it relied upon the close collaboration of the National Academy of Medicine whose experts were closely involved in presenting the case against noise.[19] In New York, to give a third example, it was the Commissioner of Health's office which published an influential report on city noise in 1930 following several years of fieldwork.[20] When local and national governments took action against noise in the 1930s, it was more often than not on the basis of medical advice about the effects of noise on health.

Despite the existence of a relatively plentiful historiography on noise, comparatively little has been written about the importance of medical expertise.[21] It is not especially surprising that anti-noise campaigners sought medical evidence in support of their crusade. Historians such as Emily Thompson have tended to see it as having only a supporting role, preferring to characterize early twentieth-century noise abatement campaigns as part of a wider capitalist culture of efficiency led by commercial interests and architectural acousticians.[22] Yet it was the backing of prominent doctors which meant that "the noise problem" could be transformed from the complaint of individual cranks into a question of mass public health. Doctors argued that although "brain-workers" were more likely than others to notice the effects of noise, nervous overstimulation caused by urban sound affected all those living in big towns and cities. They argued that even if people were not aware of it, noise causes a chronic drain of nervous energy. Doctors' intervention also allowed the noise abatement campaign to be situated within the medicalized critique of modern civilization identified by Forth, lending it, crucially, a ready-made narrative through which to communicate its aims.

Neurasthenia—the lack of nerve force seen as a key characteristic of cultural modernity—was identified by interwar doctors as the condition most likely to result from overexposure to the discordant sounds of city life. A counterpart to female hysteria, neurasthenia, first popularized as a diagnosis in the 1880s by American neurologist George M. Beard, was often reserved for middle- and upper-class male patients in the nineteenth century.[23] Since "modern civilization" was seen by Beard and other nerve doctors to be at the root of the "nervous condition," it was the bourgeois male, creator and principal beneficiary of civilization, who was thought to suffer the most from this condition.[24] Others, as Mark S. Micale puts it, "were too primitive in their emotional and nervous apparatus to suffer from the 'diseases of civilization.'"[25] A distinction should be made, for example, between neurasthenia and the nervous disorders, such as railway spine, which resulted from specific traumas, such as railway accidents. The celebrated French doctor, Jean-Martin Charcot, diagnosed these specific disorders, instead of neurasthenia, in working-class men. Neurasthenia, on the other hand, was reserved by Charcot for bourgeois male patients. Described by Michael R. Finn as a "quasi-clinical state of hypersensitivity coupled with nervous exhaustion," neurasthenia (or *maladie de Beard*, as it was sometimes known in France) was not caused by any specific trauma, but was simply a side effect of modern life.[26] The link between modernity and the increasing prevalence of nervous disease was widely propagated in late nineteenth-century medical literature, and this connection was enthusiastically championed by cultural critics such as Nordau. In an 1880 lecture delivered to the Chicago Philosophical Society, for example, J.S. Jewell supported Beard by stating that he was "firmly convinced" that civilization "carries with it the causes or conditions of decay, or even of its final destruction." He identified the nervous system as the "chief theater" of this "ruin."[27] Nordau added in *Degeneration* that, "[m]any affections of the nervous system already bear a name which implies that they are a direct consequence of certain influences of modern civilization."[28] Ironically, this included not only the environmental conditions of the modern city, but also the high cultivation of the senses demanded of the civilized classes by the arts. "The more a part of the nervous system is used the more extended its development," explained Jewell. For this reason, nervous disorders were thought to be most common in those who devoted themselves more than others to "the study and practice of art in its various forms."[29]

Although noise was not originally a prominent feature in the theory of neurasthenia, it became so in the 1930s as a result of the increasing association made between it and technological progress. For the doctors who supported noise abatement campaigns, neurasthenia, a disease bound up with modern civilization, was the best paradigm in which to explain the effects of noise, increasingly a symbol of modernity's dysfunctionality. Neurasthenic theory was premised on the notion that the human body has a limited amount of nervous energy at its disposal. When people experience nervous breakdowns that have no obviously organic cause, it is because they have exhausted this reserve of energy by putting their nervous system under intolerable strain.[30] The cause might be overwork or lack of sleep, but neurasthenia could also come about as a consequence of over exposure to the environmental conditions of the modern city. When doctors began to make the connection between noise and neurasthenia, they emphasized that disturbing urban noises cause arrhythmic and unnatural vibrations to pass from the ear through the body's nervous system to the brain. They argued, in other words, that noise leads to nervous illness because of its *physical* effects on the nervous system. This took the noise problem out of the realm of mere irritation and turned it into a question of physiological well-being. It allowed noise to be cast as a pathogen and as a drain on nervous energy. Noise's pathological characteristics were often contrasted with music's positive effects on the body. Albert Deschamps and Jean Vinchon's *Les maladies de l'energie* (1927), for example, suggested that "[m]usic is not only an art, it is also a therapeutic agent." If noise has a negative impact on the nervous system then music, in contrast, causes our nerves to vibrate as if it were "the bow on the strings of a violin."[31] Dedicating oneself too extensively to music and the arts was thought to contribute to increased nerve sensitiveness; but, in moderation, and as a therapeutic agent, music promised to undo some of the damage done by noise. The sounds of the countryside were also thought to be a positive influence on the nervous system. The city and its soundscape were cast, in contrast to music and rural sounds, as unnatural.

The argument that noise causes neurasthenia was the fundamental basis on which the 1930s noise abatement campaign was waged. By the interwar period the neurasthenic diagnosis had lost some of its earlier class and gender specificity, but the emphasis on civilized men was retained in noise abatement discourse. *Quiet*, to give a typical example, quoted the evidence of psychiatrist James Purves-Stewart in 1939, who wrote that "[t]he rush of civilised life becomes ever faster and noisier. This involves a breakdown of one sort or another. Such breakdowns are popularly and loosely known as 'nerves.'"[32] "Some individuals possess brains," he continued, sufficiently robust to withstand excessive nervous strains. Thus, for example, stolid, "stodgy" people do not suffer from "nerves" so often as those with a more sensitive and finely-organised nervous system. We should remember, however, that even the stoutest nervous systems may break down if the strain becomes excessive. On the other hand many sensitive people adapt themselves successfully to noxious stimuli and are able to remain active and efficient. Those who fail to cope with the prolonged strain develop nervous breakdowns ... Amongst the various factors which impose an increased burden upon our nervous system, noise is one of the commonest.[33]

Here Purves-Stewart explicitly appealed to the "intelligent" readership of *Quiet*, whose "finely-organised" nervous systems were particularly vulnerable to noise. He was also careful to emphasize that, if it was allowed to continue getting louder, noise would eventually strike down even those with "stout," implicitly less civilized, nervous constitutions.

It was not only in Britain that the link between noise and neurasthenia was made. New York's report on city noise stated that "the continual pressure of strident sound to which New Yorkers are subjected tends to produce impairment of hearing, to induce harmful strain upon the nervous system" and leads ultimately to "neurasthenic" states.[34] "[N]oise pervades the city and undoubtedly does increase the nervous tension of our daily life," concluded the report.[35] In France, too, the argument that noise causes nervousness was to the fore. The French government commissioned a report in 1928 that pointed to the "physiological effects on the nervous system of individuals subject to sound stimulations."[36] In response to the TCF's lobbying, the National Academy of Medicine published a report in 1930 by Paul Portier, also a member of the TCF's noise abatement committee. For him, the case against noise was certain: "The damaging effects of noise in terms of public health are not in doubt. It is important, therefore, to alleviate wherever possible, those effects that cannot be completely suppressed."[37] The progress of modern civilization and the damage it was causing to the nerves were at the forefront of Portier's analysis: "[M]otorised machines," he wrote, "have taken on an ever increasing role in our civilisation, and this has resulted in a series of noises, the number and amplitude of which are one of the characteristics of our time." For bodies already weakened by the strains of modern life, noise "creates a state of intolerance favourable to the development of psycho-neuropathic conditions."[38] Noise disturbs "the most simple of intellectual operations." It disturbs "cerebral work" and "increases fatigue."[39] Portier suggested, as per the recommendations of the TCF, that the police should do everything in their power to reduce the noises of central Paris, particularly those of tramways, buses, and all forms of alarms and sirens. Since the center of the city was likely to remain noisy, he argued, silent zones should be planned in the suburbs in which city residents could recuperate.

Following Portier's interest, several medical theses on noise were published in France over the course of the 1930s, each emphasizing familiar links between the modernity of the noise problem and the proliferation of nervous illness. Alberte Leconte's *Noise and its Effects in Urban Life* (1930) claimed: "The question of noise in towns is, one might say, a decidedly modern question."[40] Specifically, he explained, the new products of technological civilization such as gramophone loudspeakers have been "invented and put to use for the greatest pleasure of our ears," but, as a result, "all large towns become centers of noise for which our organism has not been prepared but to which it must nevertheless accommodate itself."[41] Noise-abating doctors such as Leconte pointed to the damaging impact of the urban environment on the body. "It is the role of the doctor, the hygienist, and the urbanist, to ensure in some way that life becomes less tense, less tiring, [more] bearable."[42] Pierre Petit stated in *Noise and its Effects in Modern Life* (1936) that for the medical community of Paris, "[t]he battle against noise is increasingly becoming the order of the day."[43] For people of a normal nervous state, Petit claimed that noise "results in a feeling of fatigue, a particular tension of the mind," while for others, "a truly nervous disequilibrium" may ensue. Petit proposed the restorative qualities of the natural soundscape as one solution to noise. "One of the reasons for the beneficial effects of holidays taken in the countryside," he explained, "is the quality of sleep afforded in the absence of any disruptive noise, so different from that which awaits us in noisy cities."[44] Portier, Leconte, and Petit's focus on Paris was extended to Toulouse by Charles Bernadin's study, which sought to extend lessons learned in the capital city to another big city.[45]

The language of neurasthenia and nervousness allowed interwar doctors to cast the noise problem as an urgent public health crisis, but neurasthenia had in fact lost much of its credibility as a psychiatric diagnosis by the 1930s. The theory that "modern civilization" caused a physical disturbance to the nervous system was the product of a distinctly late nineteenth-century form of neurology. It posited a somatic explanation of functional nervous illness. Those who were uncontrollably anxious, jumpy, or indeed hypersensitive to noise, had come to be so due to physical strain on the nerves. Such explanations of nervous breakdown had been widely rejected in professional psychiatric circles by the 1930s, with psychological explanations for nervousness largely replacing the earlier somatic paradigm.[46] Indeed, if Marijke Gijswijt-Hofstra's argument that World War I "marked the more or less final retreat of neurasthenia" as a serious psychiatric category, then its prominence in interwar noise abatement campaigns is all the more noteworthy.[47] Neurasthenia was a relic of the pre-psychological age, but it remained rhetorically useful to those who sought to provide medical justification, and narrative coherence, for the campaign against noise. In order to understand how and why "nervousness" continued to have such a prominent place in the discourse of interwar noise abatement, it is necessary to set the medical writings discussed above alongside the literary life of neurasthenia, which, as the next section will argue, played an important role in the medical justification for noise abatement in the 1930s.

## Literary Echoes from the Fin de Siècle

Neurasthenia's endurance into the language of interwar noise abatement owed much to a literary tradition in which nervousness and modern subjectivity were bound together. Beard's formulation of neurasthenia was, from the beginning, an amalgam of medical and cultural critique, tied up as it was with nineteenth-century discourses about racial degeneration and civilized manhood.[48] This social aesthetics of medicine was mirrored at the fin de siècle by a contemporaneous medicalization of fiction. In a parody of literary naturalism, the decadent writing of the 1880s and 1890s, typified by the work of Huysmans and Proust, incorporated medical case studies into its narratives of overstimulated and degenerate men.[49] Monique Bablon-Dubreuil argues that the late nineteenth century in fact witnessed a dual process in which creative writers such as Huysmans took an increasing interest in medicine at the same time as medical men were newly fascinated by the pathologies of creative artists. She demonstrates that a shared fascination with neurasthenia, a disease of civilized nerves, characterized the relationship between creative writers and doctors at the fin de siècle.[50] Michael R. Finn goes further, and argues that "[n]ot only was the novel taking its documentation from medical cases, it was to some extent occupying a limelight that medico-psychiatric research would have preferred for itself."[51]

The significance of this fin-de-siècle interplay of medical and literary discourse to interwar noise abatement is revealed by the frequent references made by noise-abating doctors of the 1930s, particularly in

France, to the likes of Proust, Huysmans, and other fin-de-siècle writers, including in particular Octave Mirbeau and the Goncourt brothers, all of whose novels featured noise-sensitive neurasthenics. The process identified by Finn was reversed in the 1930s, a decade in which medicine reappropriated the case studies found on the pages of decadent novels. Since decadent authors themselves often suffered from the same nervous conditions as their characters, medical men of the 1930s referred to their novels as realistic accounts of bodily suffering in their critiques of noise in order to lend popular appeal to their cause. Although neurasthenia was a more or less discarded psychiatric category, the medical experts who lined up in support of noise abatement (often, as in Horder's case, physicians rather than full-time psychiatrists) found its *cultural* appeal useful in outlining the threat posed by noise. These medical men also made a deliberate attempt to draw parallels between the culture of their time and the crisis of the fin de siècle. Both the 1890s and the 1930s were characterized by an intensely pessimistic outlook for the future of civilization. In the case of interwar noise abatement, at least, it is evident that the cultural pessimism of the 1930s drew explicitly on models of cultural critique developed in the 1880s and 1890s.

Recent work in literary studies has proved to be a fertile ground for understanding noise, forming an indispensable counterpart to a growing historiography.[52] Literature offers the cultural historian an account of how noise was experienced, albeit by the elite group of individuals who wrote novels. Melba Cuddy-Keane's work on Virginia Woolf, for example, has identified a "new aural sensitivity" in the literary culture of the early twentieth century.[53] A systematized approach to literary acoustics has also been proposed by Philip Schweighauser, who suggests that literature is not simply a means of representing noise, but also, as a disruptive voice in the channels of cultural communication, "negotiates, affirms, critiques, *and* becomes an integral part of the acoustics of modernity/postmodernity."[54] This was the case for the medical supporters of noise abatement in the 1930s. They drew upon fictional accounts of noise in order to illustrate their attack on the painful and disturbing effects of modern urban sounds.

Despite growing attention to noise in literature, no study has yet accounted for the close interaction between fiction writers and medical writers in the period between the 1890s and the 1930s. The paradigm of neurasthenia was central to this interaction. Far from being a category of the pre-1914 period only, neurasthenia was a common feature of 1890s and 1930s fiction. In both decades, noise was invested with cultural significance as an appendage to anxiety about urbanization, mechanization, and the place of intellectual men in modernity. Since it played a crucial role in establishing the meaning of noise in the 1930s, therefore, literature is an essential source for those who wish to understand why noise featured so prominently in critiques of modern urban life at this time.

One of the most striking features of the medical texts published in support of interwar noise abatement, particularly in France, is the extent to which they made reference to the decadent fiction of the fin de siècle. The medical journal *Les cahiers médicaux français* made the link clear in its 1946 account of noise abatement. The special edition of this journal carried articles on Proust's cork-lined room on the Boulevard Haussmann alongside an article on the soundproofing of hospitals, an article on noise in the work of the Goncourts alongside a medical text entitled "The Noises of Paris," as well as articles on the bell-ringing torture in Mirbeau's novel *Torture Garden*, and on Huysmans's hypersensitive life. "Poor Marcel Proust had many other enemies, daylight, the scent of flowers, but noise was also for him one of the greatest torments," explained the journal.[55] This citation of decadent literature in medical writings on noise was not a unique feature of the *Cahiers médicaux*. Both Leconte's and Petit's books on noise had established this trend, containing exactly the same references as *Les cahiers médicaux*. "Literature is very much occupied with noise," explained Petit. "The example of Marcel Proust, whose bedroom was entirely lined with cork, is well known."[56]

Paris's interwar doctors mined the decadent fiction of the 1890s for evidence that supported their animosity to noise and that would allow them to present their campaign against noise in an immediately intelligible way. The novel that they most consistently quoted was Mirbeau's *Torture Garden*, first published in 1899. In each of the French medical writings on noise cited above, a passage from this novel is quoted in full. The section in question is the bell-ringing torture scene, in which a man's body is torn apart by the powerful vibrations of a bell tolling directly above his bonded limbs. This passage is used by Petit as evidence for the physical damage that sound waves can cause to the human body.[57] The bell-ringing scene is the climax of the novel, but taken as a whole, the book can be read as a commentary on neurasthenia and masculinity, and more generally on the nature of European civilization at the end of the nineteenth century. Its prominence in interwar French medical writings on noise is suggestive of the continuities between 1890s and 1930s cultural critique.

Situated in the context of the Dreyfus Affair, Mirbeau, a Dreyfusard, ironically dedicated his novel to "priests, soldiers, judges—to men who rear, lead or govern men."[58] He mocked the idea of civilized Europe, parodying in the same breath its decadent masculinity and its colonial violence. The first four chapters of *Torture Garden* are set in the decadent Paris of the early Third Republic. They follow the nervous decline of the anonymous male narrator, a politician. "I had burned my candle at both ends," he explains, "and I was weary of these perilous and precarious adventures which had led me—whither? I was experiencing mental fatigue, a paralysis of my energies, and all my faculties were diminishing while still in their prime, sapped by neurasthenia."[59] Mirbeau was fascinated by the neurasthenic character of Third Republic France, dedicating another novel, *The Twenty-One Days of a Neurasthenic* (1901), to the topic.[60] Mirbeau associated nervousness with the political culture of the new Republic: "Today, in our cramped, sickly democracy, nervousness is the symbol of power: not the calm, full, impassive power of the male, but a worried, troubled face, a slave to its passions, like that of women."[61]

Forced out of politics and told to leave the country, the main character of *Torture Garden* is offered an "embryological" expedition to Ceylon by the Republican government, despite having no qualifications as an embryologist. Unsure at first, he accepts the offer. "'Bravo!' applauded the Minister; 'seeing that embryology, my boy, Darwin, Haeckel ... Carl Vogt, after all—it must be a great joke!'"[62] However, on the boat to Ceylon, the narrator meets a beautiful and mysterious Englishwoman called Clara. She is bound for China, and on discovering a deep affection between them, he agrees to stay on the boat and accompany her to her final destination, abandoning his bogus scientific mission. Her attraction is based on the exotic charm she attaches to life as a European in China. In a voice which is evidently that of the author himself, she presents China's freedom from Europe's hypocritical civilization as the cure to his neurasthenic malaise:

> "You're a child," Clara repeated, "and talk like they do in Europe, darling. And you have stupid scruples, like in Europe. In China life is free, joyous, complete, unconventional, unprejudiced, lawless ... at least for us. No other limits to liberty than yourself ... or to love, than the triumphant variety of your desire. Europe and its hypocritical, barbaric civilization is a lie ... You're obliged to pretend respect for people and institutions you think absurd. You live attached in a cowardly fashion to moral and social conventions you despise, condemn, and know lack all foundation. It is that permanent contradiction between your ideas and desires and all the dead formalities and vain pretenses of your civilization which makes you troubled and unbalanced.[63]

The promise of reinvigoration by extra-European and extra-masculine influences is doubly ironic. Far from being a civilizing influence, imperialism features prominently in the novel as an outlet for the violent desires of the French bourgeois man. This reveals Mirbeau's skepticism about the future of Parisian civil society. If murder is the only catharsis available to the neurasthenic bourgeois, then European civilization was ultimately teetering on the brink of its own mortality. In China, Clara's greater bodily resistance to the chaotic crowds is contrasted to the over sensitiveness of the main character:

> She was unrestrained and delighted in the midst of this crowd whose odour she inhaled, and to whose repugnant embraces she submitted with a sort of swooning lust. She offered her body—all her lithe and vibrant body—to the brutality, the blows, and the clawing.[64]

Her exuberance is brought to the fore in contrast to the weakness of the neurasthenic man. She taunts him with jibes about his ailing masculinity: "Once more she said to me: 'Ah, little woman! [L]ittle woman … little woman! You'll never be anything but a little, insignificant woman!'"[65] Her cultivation of traditional male attributes and her aggressive energy is mirrored by her healthy interest in torture, an art honestly preserved by the Chinese in contrast to Europe whose lust for violence is practiced only in the colonies at arm's length of polite society.

"What does that bell mean? Where does it come from?" asks the narrator as Clara escorts him through the torture garden. "What? Don't you know?" She replies, "Why, it's the bell in the Torture Garden! Imagine… They bind a victim, and they lay him under the bell. Then they ring it wildly until the vibration kills him!"[66] The sound of the bell guides Clara and her companion through the torture garden, where they witness the effects of the torture bell. The main character's exclamation that the sound of the bell tortured its victim by "infuriating all the sensitive and thinking parts of an individual at the same time" was cited by Leconte and Petit as evidence that the physical impact of noise on the nervous system is a malicious influence on the body and its mental well-being, even in small doses. Petit argued that "the direct reason" for the bell-ringing torture scene in *Torture Garden* was to draw attention to the damaging effects of noise in everyday life.[67]

The fascination of doctors such as Leconte and Petit with Mirbeau's novel, an infamous book in French debates about moral decency, requires some contextualization. In particular, the prevalence of Chinese torture has been shown to be a feature of French literary-philosophical culture from Mirbeau to Bataille.[68] Claire Margat has argued that *Supplice Chinois* mixed "real and fictitious elements within a discourse of horror that originates in the evolution of French literature itself rather than in early-twentieth-century China."[69] Chinese torture nonetheless remained real in France through a process of popularization which included, for example, the dramatization of *Torture Garden* at Paris's Grand-Guignol Theater in 1922. Margat explains that the image of Chinese torture persisted into the interwar period because of the need to offer objective proof of the barbarity of non-civilized races in order to justify continuing colonial intervention. The popular currency of Chinese torture as a cultural image in interwar France may help to explain why noise-abating doctors placed such great emphasis on Mirbeau's *Torture Garden*.

While doctors' use of fin-de-siècle fiction was especially prominent in French noise abatement, it also had a role to play elsewhere. In Britain, Thomas Horder and his Anti-Noise League relied upon the support of science-fiction writer, H.G. Wells, whose best-known works were dystopian visions of the future, such as *The Time Machine* (1895), produced at the fin de siècle. New York's report on city noise made reference to the folly of decadent writers who broke down due to over-exposure to noise. "Back in the first decade of this century, when the great development of noise was just beginning," wrote the authors of the report, "O. Henry sang praises of the hum."[70] Short-story writer Henry was among those who decadently embraced neurasthenia and rejected the need to protect oneself from noise.[71] His story "Let Me Feel Your Pulse," for example, tells the story of a neurasthenic aesthete and the doctors who seek to cure him. "What I need," the neurasthenic main character recounts to a hotel clerk, "is absolute rest and exercise. Can you give me a room with one of those tall folding beds in it, and a relay of bellboys to work it up and down while I rest?"[72] New York's report castigated Henry for expressing "his love of city noise" in the 1911 story "Adventures in Neurasthenia," and noted that he

> complained of the quiet of the country where his friends had invited him in the hope that he would regain his health. But noise is not a lullaby— and never has been. It was the chief danger warning for primitive man— and for people during all the ages up to our own strident present. The more discordant the noise, the more menacing the danger as a rule! Today we hear hundreds of noises a day that would have struck terror to the hearts of our ancestors. And they strike terror to our hearts too— almost literally—whether we are conscious of it or not.[73]

In the face of the renewed threat to civilization that technology was perceived to pose in the 1930s, doctors' anxiety about noise was fuelled by the evidence they found in decadent literature and in the lives of decadent writers. Yet doctors did not have to rely upon their knowledge of 1890s fiction to be reminded of the link between noise and nervousness. Writers of the 1930s were often all too willing to renew the literary association. The reference point for this cultural pessimism was often the sonic experience of the Great War. The *Manifeste auditiviste* (1920), published in Paris under the pen name "de Maxange," explained why this should be the case. Subtitled *L'auditivité en literature, rehabilitation du bruit*, it argued that as a result of the traumatic soundscape of World War I, writers such as Maxim Gorky and Gabriele D'Annunzio began to incorporate noise as a major component of their descriptive repertoire. Significantly, this renewal of interest in noise, according to de Maxange, resulted in sound replacing vision as the predominant mode of perceiving the world in literature.[74]

It was in the context of this perceptual shift that Paris's interwar doctors turned to decadent fiction in search of a framework in which to understand urban noise. If shellshock, in essence a neurasthenic disorder stimulated by noise, could have such devastating effects on fit young men, then it stood to reason that the cacophony of Paris's streets might become a public health crisis of the highest order. The connection between the Great War and urban noise suffering was made explicit by the novelist, Georges Duhamel.[75] He had trained as a doctor before turning to full-time writing, and spent the war as an army surgeon—an experience which formed the basis of his first two novels, *Vie des Martyrs* (1917) and *Civilization* (1918), the latter of which won the 1918 Prix Goncourt.[76] This book marked the return to a profound pessimism about civilization in French culture, the same pessimism which underpinned noise abatement campaigns in the 1930s. Duhamel confessed in *Civilization*, through the autobiographical main character, that "I hate the twentieth century, as I hate rotten Europe and the whole world on which this wretched Europe is spread out like a great spot of axle-grease."[77] Describing European colonialism through this machine metaphor updated Mirbeau's critique of civilization for the interwar period, an era in which the impact of technology replaced inherited degeneracy as a source of anxiety for intellectuals.

Technology, and the noises which it made, are thoroughly integrated into Duhamel's *Civilization*. "Before the war I was an assistant in an industrial laboratory," recalls his main character.

> It was a good enough little place; but I assure you, if I have the melancholy luck to come out of this catastrophe [the war] alive, I shall never enter it again. The open country! Some spot where I shall never hear the whirring of your aeroplanes or any of those machines of yours that used to amuse me once, when I knew nothing about anything, but that now fill me with horror, because they are the very soul of this war, the principle and reason of this war![78]

This is one of many sound-sensitive references in Duhamel's description of trench warfare. By attributing the very cause of the Great War to machines, and in turn identifying machines with noise, Duhamel made a direct link between the savagery of trench warfare and its noisy soundscape.

Later in the same chapter of *Civilization*, the main character, who, like Duhamel himself, is an army surgeon, is about to perform an operation in the mobile hospital that attended to the trench's wounded. In the hospital, realization of civilization's folly is brought about by the surrounding mechanical sounds:

> Fatigue, the noise of the cannonade, the dazzling lights, the hum of industry about me, all contributed to give me a sort of lucid intoxication. I remained motionless, carried away in a turmoil of thoughts. All these things that surrounded me were made for a good purpose. It was civilization's reply to itself, the correction it was giving to its own destructive eruptions; it took all this complexity to efface a little of the immense harm engendered by the age of the machine.[79]

Duhamel maintained a pessimistic outlook on technological modernity into the 1930s, and became a leading voice in Paris's noise abatement movement. His most important work of this period was *Scènes de la vie future* (1930), a satiric critique of contemporary America, which was translated into English as *America the Menace: Scenes from the Life of the Future* (1931).[80] The book was a warning to the French about what would happen to their civilization if they continued to follow the path of America's noisy industrialization and urbanization. The noise of Chicago's elevated railway is singled out for particularly painful analysis in Duhamel's prose. He also described jazz, which exploded in popularity in 1920s Paris, as the musical expression of the age of noise. "The music suddenly burst forth from a corner," wrote Duhamel in *America the Menace*. "It was the falsest, the shrillest, the most explosive of jazz—that breathless uproar which for many years now has staggered to the same syncopation, that shrieks through its nose, weeps, grinds its teeth, and caterwauls throughout the world."[81] Through his fiction, and through his association with the interwar noise abatement campaign, Duhamel was among those who updated a pre–World War I critique of "modern civilization" to meet the needs of the 1930s. Other writers played a similar role in different national contexts. In Britain, for example, Aldous Huxley, another writer of dystopian stories set in the future, wrote about the connection between urban noise and the crisis of modern civilization.[82]

## Conclusion

Despite Amelia Jones's suggestion that "the corporealized neurotic symptoms of the neurasthenic were seen as responses to the noise and crowds of urban modernity," very little has been written by cultural or medical historians about the link between noise and nervousness.[83] This chapter has argued that neurasthenia, although it had fallen out of favor as a serious psychiatric category by the 1930s, remained a useful paradigm through which interwar doctors could narrate their campaign against noise, lending it an instantly recognizable urgency. Creative writers played a pivotal role in preserving and updating neurasthenic discourse, and its associated critique of modern civilization, for the interwar period. Doctors made direct reference to fin-de-siècle novels and novelists in their writings on noise in the 1930s, and in turn, writers such as Duhamel took a direct role in shaping interwar noise abatement. The intellectual male body was central to the interaction of late nineteenth- and early twentieth-century cultural criticism. The cultural moment in which noise and neurasthenia were intertwined was also one in which intellectual masculinity mutated in response to the challenges of modern warfare, industrial production, and cultural life. An aural signifier for the mechanization of these spheres, noise was both symbol and agent of the damaging impact of technological progress on the civilized male body. Noise abatement discourse evidences clear continuities between fin-de-siècle and interwar critiques of modern civilization. While it is often proposed that World War I caused new ways of thinking and writing about modernity to evolve, noise abatement narratives suggest that fin-de-siècle modes of cultural criticism remained useful and relevant to those wishing to articulate the anxieties of life in the interwar city.

## Notes

* This research was funded by an Arts and Humanities Research Council (U.K.) doctoral studentship held at the University of Manchester between 2005 and 2008. I am grateful to my supervisors Bertrand Taithe, Laura Tunbridge, and Frank Mort, and to my examiners Stuart Jones and Daniel Pick for all their helpful comments and suggestions. My thanks are also due to Katherine Davies and Lucinda Matthews-Jones for their generous assistance.

1. Marcel Proust, *In Search of Lost Time, Volume I: Swann's Way*, trans. Charles Kenneth Scott Moncrieff and Terence Kilmar ([Paris, 1914], New York,

1992). On sounds in Proust's writing, see Hiromi Masuo, *Les bruits dans 'A la recherche du temps perdu'* (Tokyo, 1994).

2. Joris-Karl Huysmans, *Against Nature*, trans. Robert Baldick ([Paris, 1884] Harmondsworth, 1959). The aural sensitivity of both Proust and Huysmans is outlined from a medical point of view in a special edition of the journal *Les cahiers médicaux français* 7 (1946): 1–23.

3. John M. Picker, *Victorian Soundscapes* (Oxford, 2003), 41–81.

4. Ibid., 60–61.

5. The argument that anti-noise discourse was developed by a "brain-working" middle class is proposed by Picker in *ibid.*, 41–81.

6. See Lawrence Baron, "Noise and Degeneration: Theodor Lessing's Crusade for Quiet," *Journal of Contemporary History* 17, no. 1 (1982): 165–78; and Michael Cowan, "Imagining Modernity through the Ear: Rilke's *Aufzeichnungen des Malte Laurids Brigge* and the Noise of Modern Life," *Arcadia* 41, no. 1 (2006): 124–46.

7. The League of Nations conference on noise was held in Geneva in 1937 and was chaired by the British physicist George William Clarkson Kaye. See George William Clarkson Kaye, "Sound and Noise Insulation," *Journal of Scientific Instruments* 15 (1938): 185–90; and Anonymous, "La lutte contre le bruit," *Les Cahiers Médicaux Français* 7 (1946): 4.

8. The key work in this respect is Karin Bijsterveld, *Mechanical Sound: Technology, Culture and Public Problems of Noise in the Twentieth Century* (Cambridge, MA, 2008). See also Peter Payer, "The Age of Noise: Early Reactions in Vienna, 1870–1914," *Journal of Urban History* 33, no. 5 (2007): 773–93; Emily Thompson, *The Soundscape of Modernity: Architectural Acoustics and the Culture of Listening in America, 1900–39* (Cambridge, MA, 2002); and Michael Toyka-Seid, "Noise Abatement and the Search for Quiet Space in the Modern City," in *Resources of the City: Contributions to an Environmental History of Modern Europe*, eds. Dieter Schott, Bill Luckin, and Geneviève Massard-Guilbaud (Aldershot, 2005), 216–28.

9. On the cultural history of nervousness, see, in particular, Andreas Killen, *Berlin Electropolis: Shock, Nerves and German Modernity* (Berkeley, 2006); and Tom Lutz, *American Nervousness, 1903: An Anecdotal History* (Ithaca, NY, 1991).

10. See Max Nordau, *Degeneration* (London, 1895); Georg Simmel, "The Metropolis and Mental Life," [1903] in *The Urban Sociology Reader*, eds. Jan Lin and Christopher Mele (London, 2005), 23–32.

11. Nordau, *Degeneration*, 40.

12. Christopher E. Forth, "*La Civilisation* and its Discontents: Modernity, Manhood and the Body in the Early Third Republic," in *French Masculinities: History, Culture and Politics*, eds. Christopher E. Forth and Bertrand Taithe (London, 2007), 87.

13. Intellectuals' critique of modern civilization is discussed in Christopher E. Forth, *Masculinity in the Modern West: Gender, Civilization and the Body* (London, 2008).

14. Medical writer Edwin L. Ash first made this point about noise during World War I in *Nerve in Wartime* (London, 1914).

15. Lord Horder papers, Wellcome Library, GP/31/B.4/4; GP/31/B2/23.
16. For an example of an early twentieth-century intellectual who made this argument, see James G. Mansell, "Sound and the Cultural Politics of Time in the Avant-Garde: Wyndham Lewis's Critique of Bergsonism," in *Wyndham Lewis and the Cultures of Modernity*, eds. Andrzej Gasiorek, Nathan Waddell, and Alice Reeve-Tucker (Aldershot, 2011), 111–26. On critiques of the mass and mass culture, see in particular Gustave Le Bon, *The Crowd: A Study in the Popular Mind* ([Paris, 1895] London, 1896).
17. The classic exposition of this theory is Paul Fussell, *The Great War and Modern Memory* (London, 1975).
18. Léon Auscher, "Introduction," in André Defert, *Le bruit au point de vue juridique* (Paris, 1930), 3–4.
19. The importance of collaboration between the TCF and the National Academy of Medicine to the course of noise abatement in France is proposed by Anonymous, "La lutte," 6. On the Touring-Club de France see Patrick Young, "*La Vieille France* as Object of Bourgeois Desire: The Touring-Club de France and the French Regions, 1890–1918," in *Histories of Leisure*, ed. Rudy Koshar (Oxford, 2002), 169–89. The history of French noise abatement is recounted in Jean-Pierre Gutton, *Bruits et sons dans notre histoire: Essai sur la reconstitution du paysage sonore* (Paris, 2000).
20. Edward F. Brown et al., eds., *City Noise: The Report of the Commission Appointed by Dr. Shirley W. Wynne, Commissioner of Health, to Study Noise in New York City and to Develop Means of Abating It* (New York, 1930).
21. The exception is Jon Agar, "Bodies, Machines and Noise," in *Bodies/Machines*, ed. Iwan Rhys Morus (Oxford, 2002), 197–220.
22. Thompson, *Soundscape of Modernity*.
23. Christopher E. Forth, "Neurasthenia and Manhood in *fin-de-siècle* France," in *Cultures of Neurasthenia from Beard to the First World War*, eds. Marijke Gijswijt-Hofstra and Roy Porter (Amsterdam, 2001), 329. George M. Beard's key writings on neurasthenia are *A Practical Treatise on Nervous Exhaustion (Neurasthenia)* (New York, 1880); *American Nervousness: Its Causes and Consequences* (New York, 1881); and *Sexual Neurasthenia [Nervous Exhaustion]: Its Hygiene, Causes, Symptoms, and Treatment, with a Chapter on Diet for the Nervous*, ed. Alphonso David Rockwell (New York, 1884). Beard's earliest use of the term "neurasthenia" was in his article "Neurasthenia, or Nervous Exhaustion," *The Boston Medical and Surgical Journal* 3 (1869): 217–21.
24. Forth, '*La Civilisation*', 85–102.
25. Mark S. Micale, "Jean-Martin Charcot and *les névroses traumatiques*: From Medicine to Culture in French Trauma Theory of the Late Nineteenth Century," in *Traumatic Pasts: History, Psychiatry, and Trauma in the Modern Age, 1870–1930*, eds. Mark S. Micale and Paul Lerner (Cambridge, 2001), 117.
26. Michael R. Finn, *Proust, the Body and Literary Form* (Cambridge, 1999), 10. On *maladie de Beard*, see Fernand Levillain, *La neurasthénie: maladie de Beard* (Paris, 1891).

27. James Stewart Jewell, "Influence of Our Present Civilization in the Production of Nervous and Mental Diseases," *Journal of Nervous and Mental Disease* 8 (1881): 3–4.

28. Nordau, *Degeneration*, 41.

29. Jewell, "Influence of Our Present Civilization," 5.

30. Albert Deschamps and Jean Vinchon, *Les maladies de l'énergie: Les asthénies et la neurasthénie* (Paris, 1927).

31. Deschamps and Vinchon, *Les maladies de l'énergie*, 369–71. This and all future translations are the author's own.

32. James Purves-Stewart, "Noise and 'Nerves,'" *Quiet* 2 (1939): 10.

33. Ibid.

34. Brown et al., *City Noise*, 17.

35. Ibid., 217.

36. "Effets physiologiques sur le système nerveux des individus soumis à des excitations sonores." Pierre Bordas, *Le bruit et la fumée dans les stations thermales climatiques et de tourisme. Rapport présenté au conseil supérieur du tourisme (session de décembre 1928)* (Paris, 1929), 5.

37. "Les méfaits du bruit au point de vue de la santé publique ne sont donc pas douteux. Il importe donc d'atténuer, dans la mesure du possible, ceux qu'on ne peut pas supprimer complètement." Paul Portier, "Sur les méfaits du bruit," *Bulletin de l'Académie National de Médecine* 104 (1930), reprinted in Gutton, *Bruits et sons*, 178–79.

38. "Les machines motrices ont pris dans notre civilisation un développement toujours croissant, entrainant comme conséquence une série de bruits dont le nombre et l'amplitude sont une des caractéristiques de notre époque." "[Le bruit] crée un état d'intolérance propice au développement des conditions psycho-névropathiques." Ibid.

39. "les operations intellectuelles les plus simples." "[Il] apporte une extrave marquée au travail cérébral, il exagère donc la fatigue, déjà grande du fonctionnement de nos centres d'élaboration." Ibid.

40. "La question du bruit dans les villes est, peut-on dire, une question des plus moderne." Alberte Leconte, *Du bruit et de ses effets dans la vie urbaine* (Paris, 1930), 13.

41. "est inventé et mis en action pour le plus grand plaisir de nos oreilles et le plus grand repos de notre esprit"; "toutes les grandes villes deviennent des centres de bruits pour lesquels notre organisme n'a pas été préparé et auxquels il doit cependant s'accommoder." Ibid., 13.

42. "C'est le rôle du médecin, de l'hygiéniste, de l'urbaniste, de faire en sorte que celle-ci devienne moins tendue, moins fatigante, supportable." Ibid., 15.

43. "La lutte contre le bruit devient de plus en plus à l'ordre du jour." Pierre Petit, *Le bruit et ses effets dans la vie moderne* (Paris, 1936), 13.

44. "détermine une sensation de fatigue, une tension d'esprit particulière"; "un véritable déséquilibre nerveux." "Une des raisons de l'effet bienfaisant des vacances prises à la campagne est la qualité du sommeil effectue dans l'absence de tout bruit perturbateur, si différent de celui que nous réservent les cités bruyants." Ibid., 28.

45. Charles Bernadin, *Le bruit danger social: Le bruit à Toulouse* (Toulouse, 1938).

46. The difference between somatic and psychosomatic explanations of nervous illness is outlined in Tim Armstrong, "Two Types of Shock in Modernity," *Critical Quarterly* 42, no. 1 (2000): 60–73.

47. Marijke Gijswijt-Hofstra, "Introduction: Cultures of Neurasthenia from Beard to the First World War," in *Cultures of Neurasthenia from Beard to the First World War*, 1.

48. Brad Campbell, "The Making of 'American': Race and Nation in Neurasthenic Discourse," *History of Psychiatry* 18, no. 2 (2007): 157–78.

49. Finn, *Proust, the Body and Literary Form*.

50. Monique Bablon-Dubreuil, "Une fin de siècle neurasthénique: le cas Mirbeau," *Romantisme : Revue du dix-neuvième siècle* 94 (1996): 7. See also Michael R. Finn, "Neurasthenia, Hysteria, Androgyny: The Goncourts and Marcel Proust," *French Studies* 51, no. 3 (1997): 293–304.

51. Finn, *Proust, the Body and Literary Form*, 10.

52. On the relationship between history and the novel see Lynn Hunt, "'No Longer an Evenly Flowing River': Time, History, and the Novel," *The American Historical Review* 103, no. 5 (1998): 1517–21.

53. See Melba Cuddy-Keane, "Modernist Soundscapes and the Intelligent Ear: An Approach to Narrative through Auditory Perception," in *A Companion to Narrative Theory*, eds. James Phelan and Peter J. Rabinowitz (Oxford, 2005), 382–98; and Melba Cuddy-Keane, "Virginia Woolf, Sound Technologies, and the New Aurality," in *Virginia Woolf in the Age of Mechanical Reproduction: Music, Cinema, Photography, and Popular Culture*, ed. Pamela Caughie (New York, 2000), 69–96.

54. Philipp Schweighauser, *The Noises of American Literature, 1890–1985: Toward a History of Literary Acoustics* (Gainesville, FL, 2006), 3. On noise in literature, see also Picker, *Victorian Soundscapes*.

55. "Le pauvre Marcel Proust eut bien d'autres ennemis, la lumière du jour, le parfum des fleurs, mais le bruit était aussi pour lui un des plus grands supplices." "Marcel Proust dans sa chambre de liège," *Les cahiers médicaux français* 7 (1946): 8.

56. "La littérature s'est fort occupée du bruit." "L'exemple de Marcel Proust dont la chambre était entièrement tapissée de liège est bien connu." Petit, *Le bruit et ses effets*, 23.

57. Petit, *Le bruit et ses effets*, 25–26.

58. Octave Mirbeau, *Torture Garden*, trans. A.C. Bessie ([Paris, 1899] New York, 1931), frontispiece.

59. Ibid., 60.

60. Octave Mirbeau, *Les vingt-et-un jours d'un neurasthénique* (Paris, 1901).

61. Octave Mirbeau, "Les Nerveux," quoted in Sharif Gemie, "Octave Mirbeau and the Changing Nature of Right-Wing Political Culture: France, 1870–1914," *International Review of Social History* 43, no. 1 (1998), 119.

62. Mirbeau, *Torture Garden*, 71.

63. Ibid., 116–17.

64. Ibid., 160.

65. Ibid., 161.

66. Ibid., 172–73.

67. "[L]e bruit aurait été la raison directe du drame," Petit, *Le bruit et ses effets*, 26.

68. Claire Margat, "Supplice Chinois in French Literature: From Octave Mirbeau's *Le Jardin des Supplices* to Georges Bataille's *Les larmes d'Éros*," *Chinese Torture-Supplice Chinois* [an online resource of the University of Lyon, 2005]. Accessed 15 April 2014 at <http://turandot.chineselegalculture.org/Essay.php?ID=38>.

69. Ibid.

70. Brown et al., eds., *City Noise*, 212.

71. Neurasthenia was embraced by some artists and writers around the turn of the century as a sign of their acceptance of modernity. For a wide-ranging discussion of neurasthenia in literary culture, see Lutz, *American Nervousness, 1903*.

72. O. Henry, "Let Me Feel Your Pulse," in O. Henry, *The Complete Works of O. Henry* (Garden City, 1927), 883.

73. Brown et al., eds., *City Noise*, 212.

74. De Maxange, *Manifeste auditiviste: auditivité en littérature, réhabilitation du bruit* (Paris, 1920), 3.

75. Duhamel is little discussed in Anglophone literary criticism and history. Reference works in French include Arlette Lafay, *Duhamel revisité* (Paris, 1998).

76. Duhamel's account of World War I is discussed in Michael Adas, *Machines as the Measure of Men: Science, Technology, and Ideologies of Western Dominance* (Ithaca, NY, 1989), 367–69.

77. Georges Duhamel, *Civilization*, trans. Elbridge Streeter Brooks ([Paris, 1918] New York, 1919), 271.

78. Ibid.

79. Ibid., 284.

80. Georges Duhamel, *America the Menace: Scenes from the Life of the Future*, trans. Charles Miner Thompson (London, 1931). This novel was originally published in French as *Scènes de la vie future* (Paris, 1930).

81. Duhamel, *America the Menace*, quoted in Jeffrey H. Jackson, "Making Jazz French: The Reception of Jazz Music in Paris, 1927–1934," *French Historical Studies* 25, no. 1 (2002): 155. On the noise–jazz association in interwar Paris, see also Jeffrey H. Jackson, *Making Jazz French: Music and Modern Life in Interwar Paris* (Durham, NC, 2003).

82. See, for example, Aldous Huxley, "Preface," in Maurice Alderton Pink, *A Realist Looks at Democracy* (London, 1930).

83. Amelia Jones, *Irrational Modernism: A Neurasthenic History of New York Dada* (Cambridge, 2004), 29.

# Bibliography

Adas, Michael. *Machines as the Measure of Men: Science, Technology, and Ideologies of Western Dominance*. Ithaca, NY, 1989.

Agar, Jon. "Bodies, Machines and Noise." In *Bodies/Machines*. Ed. Iwan Rhys Morus. Oxford, 2002, 197–220.

Anonymous. "La lutte contre le bruit." *Les Cahiers Médicaux Français* 7 (1946): 4–6.

Armstrong, Tim. "Two Types of Shock in Modernity." *Critical Quarterly* 42, no. 1 (2000): 60–73.

Ash, Edwin L. *Nerve in Wartime*. London, 1914.

Auscher, Léon. "Introduction." In André Defert, *Le bruit au point de vue juridique*. Paris, 1930, 3–4.

Bablon-Dubreuil, Monique. "Une fin de siècle neurasthénique: le cas Mirbeau." *Romantisme: Revue du dix-neuvième siècle* 94 (1996): 7–47.

Baron, Lawrence. "Noise and Degeneration: Theodor Lessing's Crusade for Quiet." *Journal of Contemporary History* 17, no. 1 (1982): 165–78.

Beard, George M. "Neurasthenia, or nervous exhaustion." *The Boston Medical and Surgical Journal* 3 (1869): 217–21.

———. *A Practical Treatise on Nervous Exhaustion (Neurasthenia)*. New York, 1880.

———. *American Nervousness: Its Causes and Consequences*. New York, 1881.

———. *Sexual Neurasthenia [Nervous Exhaustion]: Its Hygiene, Causes, Symptoms, and Treatment, with a Chapter on Diet for the Nervous*. Ed. Alphonso David Rockwell. New York, 1884.

Bernadin, Charles. *Le bruit danger social: Le bruit à Toulouse*. Toulouse, 1938.

Bijsterveld, Karin. *Mechanical Sound: Technology, Culture and Public Problems of Noise in the Twentieth Century*. Cambridge, 2008.

Bordas, Pierre. *Le bruit et la fumée dans les stations thermales climatiques et de tourisme. Rapport présenté au conseil supérieur du tourisme (session de décembre 1928)*. Paris, 1929.

Brown, Edward F., et al., eds., *City Noise: The Report of the Commission Appointed by Dr. Shirley W. Wynne, Commissioner of Health, to Study Noise in New York City and to Develop Means of Abating It*. New York, 1930.

Campbell, Brad. "The Making of 'American': Race and Nation in Neurasthenic Discourse." *History of Psychiatry* 18, no. 2, (2007): 157–78.

Cowan, Michael. "Imagining Modernity through the Ear: Rilke's *Aufzeichnungen des Malte Laurids Brigge* and the Noise of Modern Life." *Arcadia* 41, no. 1 (2006): 124–46.

Cuddy-Keane, Melba. "Virginia Woolf, Sound Technologies, and the New Aurality." In *Virginia Woolf in the Age of Mechanical Reproduction: Music, Cinema, Photography, and Popular Culture*. Ed. Pamela Caughie. New York, 2000, 69–96.

———. "Modernist Soundscapes and the Intelligent Ear: An Approach to Narrative through Auditory Perception." In *A Companion to Narrative Theory*. Eds. James Phelan and Peter J. Rabinowitz. Oxford, 2005, 382–98.

Deschamps, Albert, and Jean Vinchon. *Les maladies de l'énergie: Les asthénies et la neurasthénie*. Paris, 1927.

Duhamel, Georges. *Civilization*, trans. Elbridge Streeter Brooks. [Paris, 1918] New York, 1919.

———. *Scènes de la vie future*. Paris, 1930.

———. *America the Menace: Scenes from the Life of the Future*, trans. Charles Miner Thompson. London, 1931.

Finn, Michael R. "Neurasthenia, Hysteria, Androgyny: The Goncourts and Marcel Proust." *French Studies* 51, no. 3 (1997): 293–304.

———. *Proust, the Body and Literary Form*. Cambridge, 1999.

Forth, Christopher E. "Neurasthenia and Manhood in *fin-de-siècle* France." In *Cultures of Neurasthenia from Beard to the First World War*. Eds. Marijke Gijswijt-Hofstra and Roy Porter. Amsterdam, 2001, 329–61.

———. "*La Civilisation* and its Discontents: Modernity, Manhood and the Body in the Early Third Republic." In *French Masculinities: History, Culture and Politics*. Eds. Christopher E. Forth and Bertrand Taithe. London, 2007, 85–102.

———. *Masculinity in the Modern West: Gender, Civilization and the Body*. London, 2008.

Fussell, Paul. *The Great War and Modern Memory*. London, 1975.

Gemie, Sharif. "Octave Mirbeau and the Changing Nature of Right-Wing Political Culture: France, 1870–1914." *International Review of Social History* 43, no. 1 (1998): 111–35.

Gijswijt-Hofstra, Marijke. "Introduction: Cultures of Neurasthenia from Beard to the First World War." In *Cultures of Neurasthenia from Beard to the First World War*. Eds. Marijke Gijswijt-Hofstra and Roy Porter. Amsterdam, 2001, 1–30.

Gutton, Jean-Pierre. *Bruits et sons dans notre histoire: Essai sur la reconstitution du paysage sonore*. Paris, 2000.

Henry, O. [William Sidney Porter]. "Let Me Feel Your Pulse." In O. Henry, *The Complete Works of O. Henry*. Garden City, NY, 1927.

Hunt, Lynn. "'No Longer an Evenly Flowing River': Time, History, and the Novel." *The American Historical Review* 103, no. 5 (1998): 1517–21.

Huxley, Aldous. "Preface." In Maurice Alderton Pink, *A Realist Looks at Democracy*. London, 1930.

Huysmans, Joris-Karl. *Against Nature*. Trans. Robert Baldick. (Paris, 1884) Harmondsworth, 1959.

Jackson, Jeffrey H. "Making Jazz French: The Reception of Jazz Music in Paris, 1927–1934." *French Historical Studies* 25, no. 1 (2002): 149–70.

Jewell, James Stewart. "Influence of Our Present Civilization in the Production of Nervous and Mental Diseases." *Journal of Nervous and Mental Disease* 8 (1881): 1–24.

Jones, Amelia. *Irrational Modernism: A Neurasthenic History of New York Dada*. Cambridge, 2004.

Kaye, George William Clarkson. "Sound and Noise Insulation." *Journal of Scientific Instruments* 15 (1938): 185–90.

Killen, Andreas. *Berlin Electropolis: Shock, Nerves and German Modernity*. Berkeley, 2006.

Lafay, Arlette. *Duhamel revisité*. Paris, 1998.

Le Bon, Gustave. *The Crowd: A Study in the Popular Mind*. (Paris, 1895) London, 1896.

Leconte, Alberte. *Du bruit et de ses effets dans la vie urbaine*. Paris, 1930.

Levillain, Fernand. *La neurasthénie: maladie de Beard*. Paris, 1891.

Lutz, Tom. *American Nervousness, 1903: An Anecdotal History*. Ithaca, NY, 1991.

Mansell, James G. "Sound and the Cultural Politics of Time in the Avant-Garde: Wyndham Lewis's Critique of Bergsonism." In *Wyndham Lewis and the Cultures of Modernity*. Eds. Andrzej Gasiorek, Nathan Waddell, and Alice Reeve-Tucker. Aldershot, 2011, 111–26.

Margat, Claire. "Supplice Chinois in French Literature: From Octave Mirbeau's *Le Jardin des Supplices* to Georges Bataille's *Les larmes d'Éros*," *Chinese Torture-Supplice chinois* [an online resource of the University of Lyon, 2005]. Accessed 15 April 2014 at http://turandot.chineselegalculture.org/Essay.php?ID=38.

Masuo, Hiromi. *Les bruits dans 'A la recherche du temps perdu.'* Tokyo, 1994.

Maxange, de. *Manifeste auditiviste: auditivité en littérature, réhabilitation du bruit*. Paris, 1920.

Micale, Mark S. "Jean-Martin Charcot and *les névroses traumatiques*: From Medicine to Culture in French Trauma Theory of the Late Nineteenth Century." In *Traumatic Pasts: History, Psychiatry, and Trauma in the Modern Age, 1870–1930*. Eds. Mark S. Micale and Paul Lerner. Cambridge, 2001, 115–39.

Mirbeau, Octave. *Les vingt-et-un jours d'un neurasthénique*. Paris, 1901.

———. *Torture Garden*, trans. A.C. Bessie. (Paris, 1899) New York, 1931.

Nordau, Max. *Degeneration*. London, 1895.

Payer, Peter. "The Age of Noise: Early Reactions in Vienna, 1870–1914." *Journal of Urban History* 33, no. 5 (2007): 773–93.

Petit, Pierre. *Le bruit et ses effets dans la vie moderne*. Paris, 1936.

Picker, John M. *Victorian Soundscapes*. Oxford, 2003.

Portier, Paul. "Sur les méfaits du bruit." *Bulletin de l'Académie National de Médecine* 104 (1930), Reprinted in Jean-Pierre Gutton. *Bruits et sons dans notre histoire: Essai sur la reconstitution du paysage sonore*. Paris, 2000, 178–79.

Proust, Marcel. *In Search of Lost Time, Volume I: Swann's Way*. Trans. Charles Kenneth Scott Moncrieff and Terence Kilmar. [Paris, 1914] New York, 1992.

Purves-Stewart, James. "Noise and 'Nerves.'" *Quiet* 2 (1939): 10–12.

Schweighauser, Philipp. *The Noises of American Literature, 1890–1985: Toward a History of Literary Acoustics*. Gainesville, FL, 2006.

Simmel, Georg. "The Metropolis and Mental Life" [1903]. In *The Urban Sociology Reader*. Eds. Jan Lin and Christopher Mele. London, 2005, 23–32.

Thompson, Emily. *The Soundscape of Modernity: Architectural Acoustics and the Culture of Listening in America, 1900–39*. Cambridge, 2002.

Toyka-Seid, Michael. "Noise Abatement and the Search for Quiet Space in the Modern City." In *Resources of the City: Contributions to an Environmental History of Modern Europe*. Eds. Dieter Schott, Bill Luckin, and Geneviève Massard-Guilbaud. Aldershot, 2005, 216–28.

Young, Patrick. "*La Vieille France* as Object of Bourgeois Desire: The Touring-Club de France and the French Regions, 1890–1918." In *Histories of Leisure*. Ed. Rudy Koshar. Oxford, 2002, 169–89.

# PART VII

# THE SOUNDS OF WORLD WAR II

13

# The Silence of Amsterdam before and during World War II
## Ecology, Semiotics, and Politics of Urban Sound
*Annelies Jacobs*

> A profound silence sinks over the houses. The din of the busy working week has died down hours ago. Now, the loud cheerfulness of family life also falls silent.[1]

> The night was dreadfully silent: no flying machines, no anti-aircraft gunfire, no bullets, no cars driving on the roads, no trams or transport of troops.[2]

These quotes, telling us about Amsterdam before and during World War II, depict within a few short sentences two very different types of silence. Peaceful silence is evoked by the fading sounds of daily life, whereas the unexpected absence of the sounds of war and traffic conjure up an eerie hush. In the first place, these examples show that in this chapter on the silence of Amsterdam, the focus will be on its sounds since it is impossible to write about the first without mentioning the latter. Second, both quotes illustrate how intricately the meaning and impact of sound and silence are related to a listener's knowledge about their origin and context.

In line with this last point, this chapter builds on Emily Thompson's view that "like a landscape, a soundscape is simultaneously a physical environment and a way of perceiving that environment; it is both a world and a culture constructed to make sense of that world."[3] This particular definition of a soundscape is an extension of the original concept coined by Murray Schafer in *The Soundscape: Our Sonic Environment and the Tuning of the World.* Moreover, it fits in with the view that sensory perception and interpretation are highly influenced by culture.[4] I will return to this later, but for now it is important to stress that this sort of "cultural framing" of perception implies that historical sound recordings alone will not suffice to understand how soundscapes of the past were perceived and valued by contemporaries. We also need text or other media used by them to express the perception and appraisal of these sounds.

In this chapter, the focus is on texts, mostly short pieces that mention or allude to sounds, sound sources, hearing, or listening.[5] For the section that covers the period between the two world wars, the texts are mainly selected from articles in newspapers and from memoirs by Amsterdam citizens. For the section on the sounds and silences of World War II, the texts come from thirty diaries written in Amsterdam in that period. Not all diarists were Dutch, but all of them were residents, who, from the outset, longed to be freed from the occupation. The texts were scrutinized for sounds mentioned or implied, and for the relative frequency of their occurrence. Moreover, attention was paid to the choice of words used to describe a particular sound, to a possible value judgment of this sound, and to the way this judgment was expressed. Finally, for both periods of time, I have used a variety of historical publications on activities going on in Amsterdam in order to be able to extrapolate the related production of sound.

The aim of the chapter is twofold. Before touching upon the silences and sounds of Amsterdam from 1918 until 1945, I want to argue for the adoption of three different perspectives to study soundscapes of the past. First, the sounds that contemporaries could reasonably have heard need to be ascertained. This is the "ecology of sound" perspective, and it focuses on sources of sound in the environment of the observer. The second perspective bears the label "semiotics of sound" and studies the meaning attributed to sounds at a specific place and moment in time. The third perspective concentrates on the judgments of and debates on sounds, and the role they may play in power relations. This is the "politics of sound" perspective.

After a brief overview of the field of soundscape studies that stimulated me to conduct my research on the sounds of the past in this particular way, I will elaborate on the three perspectives by referring to well-known publications in the field. Finally, in order to illustrate the advantages of studying soundscapes this way, I will show the results of my own research on the silences and sounds of Amsterdam in the two time periods mentioned.

## The Landscape of Urban Soundscape Studies

In the 1970s, composer and environmentalist Raymond Murray Schafer opened up the historiography of sound by documenting the changes in the Western soundscape resulting from the Industrial Revolution.[6] The environmentalists, now known for their World Soundscape Project,[7] aimed to document these changes by collecting recordings. "I honestly believe we were the first people to take the microphone out of the studio to make phenomenological recordings, that is to record phenomena in their native environment without trying to mediate or manipulate the material for other purposes," said Schafer in a lecture presented during the fall of 2005 at the Canadian Centre for Architecture.[8]

Just like the environmentalists, historians interested in sound started out in a descriptive vein: they simply cataloged all the sounds citizens could hear at particular moments in time.[9] Alain Corbin, however, stressed that such work wrongly implied that the past habitus of citizens did not condition their listening. Modalities of attention, thresholds of perception, and configurations of the (in)tolerable should be taken into account.[10] His own work on bells in the nineteenth-century French countryside showed how these bells not only structured the villagers' days and mediated news in ways we would not be able to understand today, but also how they contributed to villagers' spatial orientation and expressed the symbolic power of towns.[11]

Other more recent publications in auditory studies give ample attention to the cultural meaning of sound and shifting modes of listening.[12] From these studies we also know that conflicts about sound always involved issues of power and the right to dominate the environment with, or free it from, specific sounds.[13]

Most of the earlier works in soundscape studies address vast regions like the French countryside or the southern United States.[14] Recently published works, however, often focus on urban areas or a specific city.[15] These publications on urban sound approach their field of inquiry from perspectives related to both the successive stages in the history of soundscape studies as sketched before, and the academic background of the authors. The perspectives boil down to three approaches. Most of the analyzed works apply two of the three approaches at the same time, yet often without being explicit about switching from one approach to the other during the article, chapter, or book. However, in any research on soundscapes it is helpful to apply all three approaches very consciously.

## The Ecology, Semiotics, and Politics of Urban Sound

In the first approach or perspective, sound is perceived as an environmental and given quality: an "ecology of sound" affecting human life and human conduct in an unmediated way. The second approach understands a soundscape as a kind of information system operational within a specific time period and location, and is implicitly or explicitly based on semiotics. The third approach narrows down from sound to noise as a political and societal issue, and considers noise as the carrier or expression of contested situations. In doing so, this last approach explicitly addresses power struggles. Moreover, both the second and the third approaches start from the assumption that the perception of sound is dependent on time and place, and that it is mediated. This implies that there is no direct relation between the physical sound and the perception of that sound, but some sort of (unconscious) "translation" based on social, cultural, and sometimes even individual codes. Both the second and third approaches are in line with Emily Thompson's definition of a soundscape quoted in the introduction.

The works in the following overview of literature are categorized according to the differences between these three approaches. In addition, I also distinguish between works with a historical perspective and those with a more contemporary focus that express the desire to be able to intervene in present or prospective urban environments.

The first approach, which perceives sound as an environmental and given quality that affects human life in an unmediated way, can be recognized clearly in the works by Murray Schafer and Thuillier.[16] As Schafer aimed to preserve soundscapes by recording them, and Thuillier cataloged sounds that could be heard, it is obvious that both authors neglect the mediated aspect of perception. To a certain extent this is also the case with the articles on urban sound by Sophie Arkette, Rowland Atkinson, Peter Payer, and Michael Toyka-Seid.[17]

Rowland Atkinson stimulated me to use the term "ecology of sound" for this first approach. He explicitly argues for the development of the idea of a "sonic ecology," and emphasizes the "resonant metropolitan fabric, which may exclude or subtly guide us in our experience of the city."[18] This author is active in the field of Urban Studies and ultimately wants to be able to intervene in the urban soundscape. He implicitly distinguishes between two different levels of activity. The first is the level of the sounds "out there" that directly affect human beings. These sounds are either caused by technologies like machines, traffic, factories, and musical instruments, or influenced by things like buildings, pavements, or amplifiers. The second level of activity is the application or modification of these technologies in order to influence the character of the sounds "out there." For Atkinson, being able to interfere in the urban soundscape implies that one has access to the aforementioned technologies. This access is regulated by some kind of "social system" or "power-system." A shop owner, for instance, has the power to play muzak in his store, and a city council can decide to have a noise barrier built to shield a particular area from traffic noise. But in the end the crucial thing is the sound "out there," and its perception is but a marginal aspect.

This can also be said of an article by Michael Toyka-Seid that addresses "the effect of noise and acoustic pollution on urban societies, and the reactions of individuals and of society as a whole to this environmental problem."[19] Although the author stresses the problems regarding the definition of noise, there is a strong "environmental" thrust in his paper. Finally, Sophie Arkette, who is a sound designer and theorist, criticizes Murray Schafer for his "romantic bias towards antiquarian or rural soundscapes," but is nevertheless also primarily interested in the "urban sonic fabric" or "acoustic territory" that acts upon the listener.[20]

The "ecology of sound" approach can be contested for not being aware of the conditioning of listening by place, time, and culture, as stated by Corbin.[21] Nevertheless, what should be adopted from this approach is the idea that sound is more than a construct, and that some of its effects on human beings cannot be related to a semiotic system, a discourse, or a social practice. To a certain extent, sound really is something "out there" that influences people precisely because of its physical properties. That is why Steve Goodman in his recent publication *Sonic Warfare: Sound, Affect, and the Ecology of Fear* explicitly addresses the physical properties of sound, and argues for research on the politics of frequency.[22] However, "[l]ike a landscape, a soundscape is simultaneously a physical environment and a way of perceiving that environment; it is both a world and a culture constructed to make sense of that world."[23] The problem that we have to face is that we do not know at which point the construct starts to dominate the physical, or the other way around. We can therefore neither do without the construct nor the physical. The ecology of sound approach helps to focus on the latter.

Applying this approach means scrutinizing texts or other media for hints about both the sounds produced at the time and changes in these sounds. When studying changes, it is important both to analyze changes in the material settings that emit sound and those that influence its propagation, such as buildings and pavement structures. Peter Payer's work, which I will discuss later, offers numerous examples of the kind of material settings that should be analyzed, like types of buildings, pavement, carts and carriages, streetcars (horse-drawn, steam-powered, and electrified), cars, motorcycles, and cycles. Another important feature the "ecology of sound" approach offers, especially the work of Murray Schafer, is notions like "keynote sounds" and "sound marks," which help to analyze a soundscape.[24]

Corbin's work on bells in the nineteenth-century French countryside made clear how these bells structured the villagers' days, mediated news, contributed to their spatial orientation, and expressed the symbolic power of towns.[25] This work is probably the first work where a semiotic approach can be discerned so explicitly. Notions like Murray Schafer's "soundmark" and "sound signal" suggest that, right from the start, soundscape studies recognized that sound can convey meaning. Yet, in the environmental historical research focusing on changes in the soundscape, tracing variations in cultural meaning was not priority number one.

Among the works on urban sound, *Sounds of the City: The Soundscape of Early Modern European Towns* by Garrioch[26] is the most illustrative example of the semiotic approach. It not only describes all kinds of sounds that could be heard in early modern European towns, but also clarifies how this auditory environment constituted a semiotic system. Bells, for example, could signal the beginning of the day, the opening of the gates, or a fire alarm, while drums or the night watchman's call were used to indicate the curfew. Although the author acknowledges that sound also played a vital role in the daily life in the countryside, he suggests that sound as a semiotic system was most thoroughly exploited in cities. Sound was not only a vital element of an urban information system, but it also "formed part of people's way of navigating in time, space and in the social world of the city."[27] Garrioch then argues that, due to changing political and social practices, the auditory information system of the towns and cities gradually lost its usefulness for a significant and growing segment of the population. This is not to say that sound suddenly lost all of its meaning. But the specific information system constituted by sound that Garrioch considered to be so central to early modern European towns gradually disappeared.

Because of its historical perspective, Garrioch's article offers a very useful "checklist" of urban sounds from the past. His conclusions suggest that searching for auditory semiotic systems in modern cities is useless. However, even if sounds have disappeared and new ones have emerged, this might have happened in a pattern typical to each city or town.

Moreover, early auditory semiotic systems may not have collapsed completely. It is arguable that because of the sheer increase in the quantity of sound sources (for example, car horns and bicycle bells in

Amsterdam in the 1930s), the signaling function of specific sounds may have disappeared as the inhabitants were no longer able to distinguish the direction from which such sounds came. Besides, a rising sound level may mask all kinds of sounds and thus erase parts of the semiotic system. But this does not imply the complete disappearance of the system. In addition, new sounds with new meanings may emerge in (certain parts of) the city. It therefore makes sense to keep listening for meaning within the urban soundscape. These can be meanings intentionally communicated through sound, like the tolling of bells—or unintentionally, like the sounds produced by a gathering crowd.[28]

The third and last approach is termed the "politics of sound." This approach focuses on the evaluation of sound and its relation to political and societal issues. It considers complaints about sounds as carriers or expressions of contested situations, and acknowledges that disputes on sound always involve issues of power and often fulfill a role in processes of social distinction. This may imply that complaints about noise are linked to the repudiation of situations one cannot easily or justifiably contest in a more direct sense.

This third approach can be discerned in many publications on twentieth-century debates on noise. As Bijsterveld has stated: "Western elites continually thought of noise as a sign of a deliberate disruption of societal order, often by those lower in the hierarchy."[29] When the focus is on a very specific debate, the "politics of sound" approach is best exemplified by Picker's article "The Soundproof Study: Victorian Professionals, Work Space, and Urban Noise." In this article, the author convincingly unravels how in mid and late nineteenth-century London, attacks on street music were linked to "economic and social divisions between the lower and middle classes" or even more particularly to the complainers' "fledgling and curious status as housebound profession-als."[30] By contrast, Peter Payer addresses the debate on a more general level by relating the noise abatement to anti-urban or even anti-modern sentiments. He also describes the changes in the soundscape of Vienna between 1870 and 1914 as a result of alterations in "the way that mate-rial structures are arranged and the types of sound produced." So he both elaborates on the ecology *and* the politics of sound.[31]

So far, I have discussed three approaches to the investigation of urban sound. I have also argued that it is necessary to acknowledge that sound has both physical and constructed dimensions, and that for this reason these approaches should be applied alongside one another. Moreover, systematic application of these approaches helps to contextualize each one. When researching the "ecology of sound," awareness of the constructed aspects can be necessary to judge the value or completeness of the information on sound in specific sources; and a profound knowledge of the variety of sounds that were audible will help to gain a better understanding of the contested sounds.

## Amsterdam's Sound and Silence in the Interwar Period

In order to understand the Amsterdam "ecology of sound" in the interwar period, it is important to know that long before World War I the city was bursting at the seams. Eventually, in 1921, Amsterdam was able to increase its domain fourfold by incorporating neighboring municipalities. This was followed by two decades of building activity on the outskirts of the old town to provide much needed housing facilities.[32] Consequently, workers and clerks living in these suburbs started to commute by streetcar or bicycle. In 1921, one in eight residents owned a bicycle and one in three hundred a car. In 1930, these numbers had increased to one in three having a bicycle and one in one hundred driving a car.[33]

> The traffic has increased tremendously, especially in the old city. Countless are the motorcars, taxis, motorcycles, delivery vans, and lorries traversing the town from dawn till dusk—not to mention the even greater number of barrows and delivery bicycles. In addition, there are the cyclists moving in hordes of tens of thousands through the city in the early morning and afternoon, creating a spectacle one might not encounter anywhere else in the world, Copenhagen included.[34]

However, traffic changed in more ways than merely quantitatively. After World War I, the combustion engine gradually started to take over from the horse-drawn carts, and in the course of the 1920s Amsterdam was at the forefront in the Netherlands in asphalting its streets.[35] So, little by little, the sound of "farmers' carts without springs and rattling lorries, which thundered on the rough round cobblestones, their sounds reverberating down the streets at two hundred meters' distance" disappeared from the city.[36] This sound was replaced by "cars rustling over a shining wet road with hoarsely coughing, nasty claxons."[37]

Although there was definitely an increase of traffic in the streets of Amsterdam, it is not certain that this also implied more noise. In the early thirties, residents of Groningen noticed that, in comparison with their hometown with its cobbled streets, in Amsterdam there was more silence.[38] Moreover, looking back in 1938, the Dutch classicist and literary scholar, Aegidius Willem Timmerman, claimed that

Amsterdam had been noisier at the end of the nineteenth century than it was in the present. According to him, this was not only due to tarmac streets and rubber tires, but also to a decrease in hawkers, street musicians, and yelling drunks swarming the streets.[39]

But even if we put aside the question of whether one had to cope with more or less traffic noise in Amsterdam, it is obvious that from a "semiotics of sound" perspective there was a profound change in the sound of traffic during the interwar period. The sound of the aforementioned carts rattling over the cobblestones had always been a clear and far-reaching sign for road users that prudence was called for. However, a car with rubber tires moving swiftly over the asphalt did not automatically generate such a warning sound. That is why hooting became so important, especially in a city like Amsterdam with its narrow streets and many crossings. In 1928 a road safety motto issued by the Amsterdam police stated: "Signal well! Do you think we can look round a corner?"[40]

One also has to bear in mind that in the 1920s the zoning of the streets in Amsterdam and the traffic rules had not yet adjusted to the rapidly increasing number of cyclists and car drivers, nor had the behavior of most road users. Cyclists did not feel obliged to stay to the side of the street, and pedestrians were accustomed to taking the shortest route, crossing a street whenever and wherever it suited them best.[41] Consequently, the number of traffic accidents increased, and every car driver involved could be sure that the police would ask whether he or she had hooted properly.

> Some people honk out of bravura and others out of anxiety. An anxiety found in drivers who feel insecure at the steering wheel. Others just hoot out of habit. If only we would all just hoot when it is necessary, we would be making good headway already.
> Unnecessary hooting is caused, I would almost say is increased, by the question: "Did you hoot properly?" A question not only asked by every police officer and resident, but also regularly heard at court meetings.
> So, to insure themselves, hundreds hoot their horns at night. Even the public demands to be startled at street corners. That is why motorists often hear: "Hey, aren't you able to honk?"[42]

Obviously, many car drivers did honk regularly. This of course diminished the effect of the signal as it was often unclear who was hooting at whom. That is why the aforementioned safety motto also stated: "However, hooting continually is unnecessary and annoying."

It may come as no surprise that hooting figured prominently in the noise abatement campaigns of the interwar period. This does not only hold for Amsterdam, but also for many other European cities, where big campaigns were organized in the late 1920s and early 1930s.[43] In Amsterdam the debate was closely related to traffic safety and the question of whether the street belonged to motorized traffic or to cyclists and pedestrians. The narrow streets, many crossings, and huge numbers of cyclists and barrows may have fueled this debate in Amsterdam in a specific way. Car drivers complained that they did not want to hoot but were forced to do so, as barrows regularly obstructed roads, pedestrians did not pay attention when rushing over a street, and cyclists swarmed over the full width of the road or flocked annoyingly in front of cars at every crossing. Conversely, pedestrians and cyclists accused car drivers of arrogantly and noisily monopolizing the road.[44]

Evaluated by means of the "ecology," "semiotics," and "politics" perspectives on sound, a neat sequence of developments can be seen. The changes in pavement structures and in the construction of vehicles resulted in changing sounds and also in considerably less sound on the streets of Amsterdam. However, this tendency was at least partially undone by the considerable increase in traffic. Next, it became apparent that the speed of the relatively silent motorized vehicles necessitated the use of warning signals in order to avoid accidents, especially because of the increase in traffic volume, and because Amsterdam residents still had to adjust to the changing situation. In consequence, motorists felt obliged to hoot regularly in order to avoid accidents and legal liability. This had a detrimental effect on the meaning of this sound as it was no longer clear whether it was really intended to be a warning. So hooting became part of the debate on the behavior of the different traffic participants. Pedestrians and cyclists contested this sound as a symbol of the arrogance of car drivers trying to monopolize the road, while motorists, agreeing that all this hooting was a nuisance, put the blame on the irresponsible behavior of cyclists and pedestrians.

In addition to hooting, there were other contested sounds in Amsterdam. As in other debates throughout Europe and the Netherlands, the noise of neighbors also became an issue.[45] It is known that several housing blocks built in the 1920s in Amsterdam were anything but soundproof; complaints could certainly be expected here. On a more general level, there is also the assumption that a rise in population density plays a role in the origin of complaints.[46] However, in Amsterdam quite a different development can be seen.

One of the residents who had lived in the slums of the inner city recalls that, as people could not afford to have carpets on the floor, it was far from uncommon to see (and hear) the downstairs neighbors through gaps between the floorboards. Moreover, an incredibly high number of people used to live in these slums and it was common for an entire family to live in just one room.[47] In the course of the 1920s, part of the population living in these slums moved to the newly constructed suburbs. After a while, they started to complain about noise. "Talking about noise nuisance in these 'airy' new dwellings shows how fast ideas on living comfort can change," wrote another resident.[48] This suggests that the sounds of the neighbors only started to be a nuisance after residents had adjusted to less crowded living quarters and to more silence. Indeed, apart from parts of the inner city, most of the residents now lived in quarters with far more silence then before.

> Is the noise really too much? The answer to this question depends on one's whereabouts. Large areas to the south, west, east, and north of Amsterdam, and many canals, can already be excluded as the silence that can be found here is almost that of a village. Even if this silence is occasionally interrupted by the shrill signal of a car, or a hawker yelling too loudly. The inner city is busy and noisy, of course, at least between 8 a.m. and 8 p.m. Is there the desire for this to change? It is the area of offices and stores, and few people live here.[49]

The expansion of Amsterdam, starting in the middle of the nineteenth century, continued during the interwar period. There is no mistaking that the growth of the population and the related process of urbanization resulted in an increase in traffic. So far, the situation in Amsterdam corresponds to the common notion of city life growing ever noisier from the late nineteenth into the first half of the twentieth century. The rise of the noise abatement movement in the interwar period only seems to reinforce this idea. Researching this period solely from a "politics of sound" perspective will therefore easily lead to the conclusion that the situation in Amsterdam is the equivalent of that in other European capitals during this period.

However, a closer investigation of the ecology of sound reveals that the sound qualities of traffic also profoundly changed. These changes from horse-drawn carts to combustion-engine cars, from iron-rimmed wheels to rubber tires, and from cobbled streets to asphalted roads, took place in other capitals too, but not necessarily in the same period. Moreover, it is possible that within the typical acoustic environment of Amsterdam, with its many narrow and curving streets, the changing sound of the traffic produced a greater effect. The sound of traffic did change indeed, but it is far from certain that it also increased. And finally, there is no doubt that in the course of the interwar period, many residents moved to living quarters with more silence than they had ever experienced before.

## Sound and Silence during World War II

It will come as no surprise that the war brought considerable changes to the city's sounds and silences, as it affected the soundscape on two levels. Residents not only had to cope with the sounds of war, but also with changes in the soundscape resulting from the disruptions to everyday city life. Researching this period in the history of Amsterdam from the "semiotics of sound" perspective makes clear how heavily the context affects the meaning of a specific sound. At the outbreak of the war, it gradually dawned upon the residents of Amsterdam that the resounding explosions no longer referred to peacetime military exercises. "Nearly every war diary starts the same. In the early morning of 10 May 1940, the diarist wakes up to explosions, airplanes coming over, or frightened relatives. He goes out onto the street in pajamas, talks to neighbors, suggests the possibility of a military exercise, and then realizes what is going on: the Netherlands is at war."[50]

Even if the sound of explosions or airplanes overhead seemed familiar, the awareness that this was not a military exercise made a world of difference. The gunfire now took on a new meaning and was listened to differently. This dramatic shift can be compared, in some respects, with the experience of moving to another house: on the very first day, all sounds and noises heard are new, and are therefore much more noticeable. In fact, this was the situation in which the residents of Amsterdam found themselves on the morning that World War II reached their city. It was as if, overnight, all residents had moved to another house.

Five days later, after the surrender, the situation changed again. Now, for example, the anti-aircraft guns no longer targeted the enemy but potential liberators. This influenced the way of listening, even if the potential risk of gunfire to urban residents did not alter. Prior to the capitulation the sound of flak indicated that the enemy was near—afterwards it signaled both danger and the presence of friendly forces. As one diarist observed: "Wednesday, 6 November 1940. Last night at eight the anti-aircraft artillery started pounding, also in the night at around one we were jolted awake by the guns. I always enjoy hearing it."[51]

Applying the "politics of sound" approach revealed the importance of music as a relatively easy, accessible, and subtle means to boost one's own spirits and express disrespect, disobedience, or disdain for the enemy. On 4 January 1942, one diarist wrote:

Yesterday I heard it was a mess in town on New Year's Eve. No permission was given to be out on the street after midnight, so people could not celebrate the N[ew] Year with their friends. Still, at 1.40, our actual N[ew] Year, there was a lot of noise: loudspeakers from the windows, shivaree, loud singing of the national anthem, etc. Shots were fired as well. They will not bring our people down.[52]

Conversely, on 6 July 1940, the Nazis ordered the erection of a "bandstand on Dam Square for concerts by the German Brass Band."[53] In the period 1940–43, they also organized several parades and marches in the city. However, these kinds of events hardly ever appear in the diaries. Just one diarist mentions one occasion, and then only to say that none of her acquaintances attended such events.

So, in Amsterdam, both the residents and the occupying forces made music and at the same time tried to ignore or hinder the music of "the other." The diaries almost completely ignore even the proximity of, or contact with, German soldiers. It is as if they were neither heard nor seen, unless they shouted or were violent.

This insight gained from the politics of sound perspective also makes clear that diaries do not provide sufficient information for the ecology of sound approach. Therefore, additional sources have been used to investigate the sounds that were probably produced and heard. Surprisingly, the results showed two contrasting developments in Amsterdam's ecology of sound.

The diarists paid most attention to the sounds of gunfire, air-raid alarms, and airplanes. Understandably so, since these sounds forced the residents to adjust to changing situations all the time: "It was another old fashioned bad night. We are never secure here, but after a few quiet nights you get the feeling that 'now they will finally leave us alone.' Now we have lost that confidence again."[54]

Parallel to this ongoing rhythm of warfare, the familiar sounds of motorized traffic, people, street music, bells, and carillons disappeared. The changed sounds of the city, its residents, and its traffic triggered memories of bygone days. After a visit to the Leidsche Plein Theater, "to forget our worries," one author writes: "When we came out of it … it was pitch dark under the trees of the Leidsche Plein. With the silhouettes of people, horses, and carriages (that now replace the taxis), the weak lights of arc lamps, bicycles, and trams, the scene had an old-fashioned air to it—previous century or so."[55]

So, by the sound of airplanes, anti-aircraft guns, and explosions, Amsterdam was drawn into the twenty-four-hour rhythm of international warfare. At the same time, however, the city grew increasingly silent due to the deportation of residents and vanishing city life. But this was not the quiet many residents may have longed for before the outbreak of the war. The silence was now called "gloomy" and "dreadful," and its meaning had profoundly changed.

## Conclusion

As this chapter has shown, a deeper understanding of the complexity of sound and soundscapes begs for a combination of approaches. For the interwar period, the ecology of sound approach makes clear that changes in the traffic sounds of Amsterdam do not necessarily match those of other European capitals. There are even reasons to assume that many residents were confronted with more silence in their daily lives than ever before. This kind of information is crucial for the politics of sound perspective, as it shows that emerging debates on the noise of neighbors cannot simply be related to the common idea that cities grew noisier from the nineteenth century onward. In Amsterdam, many people only began to complain about the noise of the neighbors after they had become used to more silence in daily life.

The semiotics of sound perspective shows how the reduction of the sound of approaching vehicles required new and specific warning signals. Subsequently, it became apparent that in Amsterdam there was a perceived obligation to hoot excessively, and, in doing so, this not only diminished the meaning of this sound, but also turned it into a symbol of the debate on proper behavior for road users.

For the war period, the ecology perspective makes clear that both noise and silence were prominent in Amsterdam. However, as the semiotics of sound perspective shows, the meaning of sounds had profoundly changed as silence was now frightening, and the noise of a potentially dangerous bomber was met with joy. Finally, the politics of sound approach reveals the importance of music to boost individual morale and express disdain for the enemy. It also shows the subtle link between the perception of a sound and its source—as in the observation that German airplanes were making a "puffing drone," while the English planes "were buzzing smoothly like blowflies."[56]

## Notes

* I would like to thank Karin Bijsterveld and Andreas Fickers for their support during my research and their valuable comments on this chapter. I am also very grateful to the Dutch Foundation for Scientific Research

(NWO) for funding the Soundscapes of the Urban Past project, from which this chapter originated.

1. This quote stems from a text about a Friday evening in the Jewish quarter of Amsterdam before World War II. "At eleven, behind the curtains of all houses, the lights dim down. A profound silence sinks over the houses. The din of the busy working week has died down hours ago. Now, the loud cheerfulness of family life also falls silent. The whole neighborhood seems to be covered by a gigantic glass bell, shutting off every sound." M. Sluyser and W. Drees, *Voordat ik het vergeet* (Amsterdam, 1957), 63.

2. Dutch Institute for War, Holocaust and Genocide Studies (NIOD), Diary Collection, nr. 1187, Diary Verwey, 9 September 1940.

3. Emily Thompson, *The Soundscape of Modernity: Architectural Acoustics and the Culture of Listening in America, 1900–1933* (Cambridge, 2002), 1.

4. Constance Classen, "The Senses," *Encyclopedia of European Social History from 1350 to 2000*, ed. Peter N. Stearns (Detroit, 2001); Martin Jay, "In the Realm of the Senses: An Introduction," *The American Historical Review* 116, no. 2 (2011): 307–16; Sophia Rosenfeld, "On Being Heard: A Case for Paying Attention to the Historical Ear," *The American Historical Review* 116, no. 2 (2011): 316–35; Mark M. Smith, *Sensing the Past: Seeing, Hearing, Smelling, Tasting, and Touching in History* (Berkeley, 2007), 2–4.

5. My research is part of the program *Soundscapes of the Urban Past: Staged Sound as Mediated Cultural Heritage* funded by the Dutch Foundation for Scientific Research NWO. *Soundscapes of the Urban Past* explicitly concentrates on the dramatization or staging of sound in media like text, film, and radio play.

6. R. Murray Schafer, *The Soundscape: Our Sonic Environment and the Tuning of the World* (Rochester, [1977] 1994).

7. See the website http://www.sfu.ca/~truax/wsp.html; accessed 8 August 2013.

8. See the website http://alcor.concordia.ca/~senses/sensing-the-city-index.htm; accessed 8 August 2013.

9. Guy Thuillier, *Pour une histoire du quotidien au XIXe siècle en Nivernais* (Paris, 1977).

10. Alain Corbin and Jean Birrell, *Time, Desire and Horror: Towards a History of the Senses* (Cambridge, 1995).

11. Alain Corbin, *Village Bells: Sound and Meaning in the Nineteenth-century French Countryside* (New York, 1998).

12. Karin Bijsterveld, "'The City Of Din': Decibels, Noise, and Neighbors in the Netherlands, 1910–1980," *Science and the City*, eds. S. Dierig, J. Lachmund and J.A. Mendelsohn (Chicago, 2003), 173–93; Michael Bull and Les Back, *The Auditory Culture Reader* (Oxford, 2003); Jonathan Sterne, *The Audible Past: Cultural Origins of Sound Reproduction* (Durham, NC, 2003); Thompson, *The Soundscape of Modernity*.

13. Bijsterveld, "The City Of Din"; Peter A. Coates, "The Strange Stillness of the Past: Toward an Environmental History of Sound and Noise," *Environmental History* 10, no. 4 (2005): 636–66; John M. Picker, "The Soundproof Study: Victorian Professionals, Work Space, and Urban

Noise," *Victorian Studies: A Quarterly Journal of the Humanities, Arts and Sciences* 42, no. 3 (2000): 427–53; Mark M. Smith, *Listening to Nineteenth-Century America* (Chapel Hill, 2001).

14. Corbin, *Village Bells*; Bruce R. Smith, *The Acoustic World of Early Modern England: Attending to the O-Factor* (Chicago, 1999); Smith, *Listening to Nineteenth-Century America*.

15. Sophie Arkette, "Sounds Like City," *Theory, Culture & Society* 21, no. 1 (2004): 159–68; Rowland Atkinson, "Ecology of Sound: The Sonic Order of Urban Space," *Urban Studies* 44, no. 10 (2007): 1905–17; David Garrioch, "Sounds of the City: The Soundscape of Early Modern European Towns," *Urban History* 30, no. 1 (2003): 5–25, here 21; Picker, "The Soundproof Study"; Michael Toyka-Seid, "Noise Abatement and the Search for Quiet Space in the Modern City," in *Resources of the City: Contributions to an Environmental History of Modern Europe*, eds. D. Schott, B. Luckin, and G. Massard Guilbaud (Aldershot, 2005), 215–29; Rosemary Wakeman, "Street Noises: Celebrating the Liberation of Paris in Music and Dance," in *The City and the Senses: Urban Culture since 1500*, eds. A. Cowan and J. Steward (Aldershot, 2007), 219–37.

16. Schafer, *Soundscape*; Thuillier, *Pour une histoire du quotidien*.

17. Arkette, "Sounds Like City"; Atkinson, "Ecology of Sound"; Peter Payer, "The Age of Noise: Early Reactions in Vienna, 1870–1914," *Journal of Urban History* 33, no. 5 (2007): 773–93; Toyka-Seid, "Noise Abatement."

18. Atkinson, "Ecology of Sound," 1905.

19. Toyka-Seid, "Noise Abatement," 216.

20. Arkette, "Sounds Like City," 167.

21. Corbin and Birrell, *Time, Desire and Horror*.

22. Steve Goodman, *Sonic Warfare: Sound, Affect, and the Ecology of Fear* (Cambridge, 2010).

23. Thompson, *Soundscape of Modernity*, 1.

24. "In soundscape studies, keynote sounds are those which are heard by a particular society continuously or frequently enough to form a background against which other sounds are perceived." Whereas the term "soundmark" refers to "a community sound which is unique or possesses qualities which make it specially regarded or noticed by the people in that community." Schafer, *Soundscape*, 272, 274.

25. Corbin, *Village Bells*.

26. Garrioch, "Sounds of the City," 21.

27. Ibid., 6.

28. The articles by both Arkette, "Sounds Like City," and Toyka-Seid, "Noise Abatement," acknowledge this as they argue for an approach that recognizes the functions sound can have in the social and cultural domain. Thus, to a certain extent these authors also pay attention to the meaning of sound.

29. Bijsterveld, "The City Of Din," 60.

30. Picker, "The Soundproof Study," 428, 431.

31. Payer, "The Age of Noise."

32. Piet de Rooy, "De donkerte der tijden 1920–1940," *Geschiedenis van Amsterdam: tweestrijd om de hoofdstad 1900–2000*, ed. Piet de Rooy

(Amsterdam, 2007), 127–234; Michael Wagenaar, "Kantoren, hotels en warenhuizen. Functie-veranderingen in de Amsterdamse binnenstad 1870–1940," *Ons Amsterdam / maandblad van de Gemeentelijke Commissie Heemkennis*, no. 33 (1981): 194–99.

33. In 1930 in Amsterdam, having a population of almost 750,000, the traffic consisted of: 6,300 cars, 3,361 lorries, 220,000 bicycles, 2,368 motorcycles, 142 buses, 12,000 barrows, 2,350 horse-drawn carts, and 2,475 carriages. Sources: *Algemeen Handelsblad*, 12 March 1930, 28 March 1930, and 27 August 1930; *De Telegraaf*, 27 February 1930.

34. Henri Polak and Willem de Vlugt, *Amsterdam die groote stad …: een bijdrage tot de kennis van het Amsterdamsche volksleven in de XIXe en XXe eeuw*, 2nd edn. (Amsterdam, 1936), 140–41.

35. Hans Buiter, *Riool, rails en asfalt: 80 jaar straatrumoer in 4 Nederlandse steden* (Zutphen, 2005), 145, 176.

36. Aegidius W. Timmerman, *Tim's herinneringen* (Amsterdam, 1938), 257.

37. Michiel de Jong, A., *Amsterdam bij nacht: snelkieken van de "Leven"-redacteuren en teekeningen van Jordaan*. Amsterdam, ca. 1920, 5.

38. Archives *Anti-lawaai comité Groningen* (ALCG, Noise Abatement Committee Groningen), File *"Brieven op Persberichten"* (Letters in response to Press Reports), 1935–1937; courtesy Hero Wit, now stored at Maastricht University, Faculty of Arts & Social Sciences. The committee itself numbered the letters. ALCG: 9, 66.

39. Timmerman, *Tim's herinneringen*, 257–58.

40. *Algemeen Handelsblad*, 18 April 1928.

41. Municipal Archives (MA) Amsterdam. Collection of newspaper clippings, access code 30486, inventory 718, pages 86581–87595; 86599.

42. *De Telegraaf*, 17 November 1930.

43. Bijsterveld, "The City Of Din," 110, 117.

44. *Algemeen Handelsblad*, 28 February 1926, 07 November 1927, 18 August 1928, 10 January 1929; *De Telegraaf*, 17 November 1930, 31 December 1930, 19 November 1931, 21 June 1933, 22 October 1933; *De Groene Amsterdammer*, 24 October 1925, 25 October 1930.

45. Bijsterveld, "The City Of Din," 159–91.

46. Ibid., 63.

47. Philo Bregstein and Salvador Bloemgarten, *Herinneringen aan Joods Amsterdam*, 3rd edn. (Amsterdam, 2004), 125.

48. Jacques Presser, *Autobiografische schets 1899–1919* (Bergen, 1974), 47–51.

49. *Algemeen Handelsblad*, 14 April 1934.

50. Bart Eric van der Boom, *"We leven nog": de stemming in bezet Nederland* (Amsterdam, 2003), 17.

51. NIOD, nr. 1179, Diary van der Does.

52. NIOD, nr. 1151, Diary Bruijn—Barends, 4 January 1942.

53. Joh. Franc. Maria de Boer and Sophie Duparc, *Kroniek van Amsterdam over de jaren 1940–1945* (Amsterdam, 1948).

54. NIOD, nr. 1151. Diary Bruijn—Barends, 30 October 1940.

55. NIOD, nr. 1187, Diary Verwey, 5 September 1940.

56. NIOD, nr. 1092, Diary Lans—Van der Wal, 30 August 1940.

# Bibliography

Arkette, Sophie. "Sounds Like City." *Theory, Culture & Society* 21, no. 1 (2004): 159–68.

Atkinson, Rowland. "Ecology of Sound: The Sonic Order of Urban Space." *Urban Studies* 44, no. 10 (2007): 1905–17.

Bijsterveld, Karin. "'The City of Din': Decibels, Noise, and Neighbors in the Netherlands, 1910–1980." In *Science and the City*. Eds. S. Dierig, J. Lachmund and J.A. Mendelsohn. Chicago, 2003, 173–93.

Boer, Joh. Franc. Maria de, and Sophie Duparc. *Kroniek van Amsterdam over de jaren 1940–1945*. Amsterdam, 1948.

Boom, Bart Eric van der. *"We leven nog": de stemming in bezet Nederland*. Amsterdam, 2003.

Bregstein, Philo, and Salvador Bloemgarten. *Herinneringen aan Joods Amsterdam*, 3rd edn. Amsterdam, 2004.

Buiter, Hans. *Riool, rails en asfalt: 80 jaar straatrumoer in 4 Nederlandse steden*. Zutphen, 2005.

Bull, Michael, and Les Back. *The Auditory Culture Reader*. Oxford, 2003.

Classen, Constance. "The Senses." In *Encyclopedia of European Social History from 1350 to 2000*, Vol. IV. Ed. Peter N. Stearns. Detroit, 2001, 356–57.

Coates, Peter A. "The Strange Stillness of the Past: Toward an Environmental History of Sound and Noise." *Environmental History* 10, no. 4 (2005): 636–66.

Corbin, Alain. *Village Bells: Sound and Meaning in the Nineteenth-century French Countryside*. New York, 1998.

Corbin, Alain, and Jean Birrell. *Time, Desire and Horror: Towards a History of the Senses*. Cambridge, 1995.

Garrioch, David. "Sounds of the City: The Soundscape of Early Modern European Towns." *Urban History* 30, no. 1 (2003): 5–25.

Goodman, Steve. *Sonic Warfare: Sound, Affect, and the Ecology of Fear*. Cambridge, 2010.

Jay, Martin. "In the Realm of the Senses: An Introduction." *The American Historical Review* 116, no. 2 (2011): 307–16.

Jong, A., Michiel de. *Amsterdam bij nacht: snelkieken van de "Leven"-redacteuren en teekeningen van Jordaan*. Amsterdam, ca. 1920.

Payer, Peter. "The Age of Noise: Early Reactions in Vienna, 1870–1914." *Journal of Urban History* 33, no. 5 (2007): 773–93.

Picker, John M. "The Soundproof Study: Victorian Professionals, Work Space, and Urban Noise." *Victorian Studies: A Quarterly Journal of the Humanities, Arts and Sciences* 42, no. 3 (2000): 427–53.

Polak, Henri, and Willem de Vlugt. *Amsterdam die groote stad …: een bijdrage tot de kennis van het Amsterdamsche volksleven in de XIXe en XXe eeuw*, 2nd edn. Amsterdam, 1936.

Presser, Jacques. *Autobiografische schets 1899–1919*. Bergen, 1974.

Rooy, Piet de (2007). "De donkerte der tijden 1920–1940." In *Geschiedenis van Amsterdam: tweestrijd om de hoofdstad 1900–2000*. Ed. Piet de Rooy. Amsterdam, 2007, 127–234.

Rosenfeld, Sophia. "On Being Heard: A Case for Paying Attention to the Historical Ear." *The American Historical Review* 116, no. 2 (2011): 316–35.

Schafer, R. Murray *The Soundscape: Our Sonic Environment and the Tuning of the World*. Rochester, VA, (1977) 1994.

Sluyser, Meyer, and Wilhelm Drees. *Voordat ik het vergeet*, 2nd edn. Amsterdam, 1957.

Smith, Bruce R. *The Acoustic World of Early Modern England: Attending to the O-factor*. Chicago, 1999.

Smith, Mark M. *Listening to Nineteenth-Century America*. Chapel Hill, 2001.

———. *Sensing the Past: Seeing, Hearing, Smelling, Tasting, and Touching in History*. Berkeley, 2007.

Sterne, Jonathan. *The Audible Past: Cultural Origins of Sound Reproduction*. Durham, NC, 2003.

Thompson, Emily. *The Soundscape of Modernity: Architectural Acoustics and the Culture of Listening in America, 1900–1933*. Cambridge, 2002.

Thuillier, Guy. *Pour une histoire du quotidien au XIXe siècle en Nivernais*. Paris, 1977.

Timmerman, Aegidius W. *Tim's herinneringen*. Amsterdam, 1938.

Toyka-Seid, Michael. "Noise Abatement and the Search for Quiet Space in the Modern City." In *Resources of the City: Contributions to an Environmental History of Modern Europe*. Eds. D. Schott, B. Luckin, and G. Massard-Guilbaud. Aldershot, 2005, 215–29.

Wagenaar, Michael. "Kantoren, hotels en warenhuizen. Functie-veranderingen in de Amsterdamse binnenstad 1870–1940." *Ons Amsterdam / maandblad van de Gemeentelijke Commissie Heemkennis*, no. 33 (1981): 194–99.

Wakeman, Rosemary. "Street Noises: Celebrating the Liberation of Paris in Music and Dance." In *The City and the Senses: Urban Culture since 1500*. Eds. A. Cowan and J. Steward. Aldershot, 2007, 219–37.

# 𝕏 Notes on Contributors

**Carolyn Birdsall** is Assistant Professor at the Media Studies department, University of Amsterdam. She received her Ph.D. in 2010, with a dissertation since published as *Nazi Soundscapes: Sound, Technology and Urban Space in Germany, 1933–1945* (Amsterdam University Press, 2012). Latest publication: "Die Orchestrierung urbaner Akustik: Dokumentarische Form, akustische Medien und die moderne Stadt," in *Ton: Texte zur Akustik im Dokumentarfilm*, eds. Volko Kamensky and Julian Rohrhuber (Berlin, 2013), 74–97.

**Christine Ehardt** is Lecturer in Theater, Film, and Media Studies at the University of Vienna. She is currently working on a dissertation about the cultural impact of radio in Austria. Latest publication: "Wie klingt Kluge? Eine akustische Spurensuche," in *Die Frage des Zusammenhangs. Alexander Kluge im Kontext*, ed. Christian Schulte (Berlin, 2012), 217–27.

**Anthony Enns** is Associate Professor in the Department of English at Dalhousie University in Halifax, Nova Scotia. He received his Ph.D. from the University of Iowa in 2005, and has held positions at the University of Iowa and Cornell College. Latest publication: *Vibratory Modernism*, eds. Anthony Enns and Shelley Trower (New York, 2013).

**Stefan Gauß** is a cultural historian. He earned his Ph.D. at the Berlin University of the Arts in 2009. He is the author of *Nadel, Rille, Trichter: Kulturgeschichte des Phonographen und des Grammophons in Deutschland (1900–1940)* (Cologne, 2009). Latest publication: "Der Sound aus dem Trichter. Kulturgeschichte des Phonographen und des Grammophons," in *Sound des Jahrhunderts: Geräusche, Töne, Stimmen, 1889 bis heute*, eds. Gerhard Paul and Ralph Schock (Bonn, 2013), 30–35.

**Alexandra E. Hui** is Associate Professor of History at Mississippi State University. She received her Ph.D. in History from the University of California, Los Angeles in 2008. She is currently working on a history of the co-development of new listening practices, conceptions of the environment, and the science of functional music. In addition to her monograph, *The Psychophysical Ear: Musical Experiments, Experimental Sounds, 1840–1910* (Cambridge, 2013), she has published several articles and book chapters.

**Annelies Jacobs** is Lecturer at the Faculty of Arts and Social Sciences of Maastricht University. She received her Ph.D. in Science, Technology and Society Studies at Maastricht University and has also been trained as an architect at Eindhoven Technical University. Latest publication (with Karin Bijsterveld, Jasper Aalbers, and Andreas Fickers): "Shifting Sounds: Textualization and Dramatization of Urban Soundscapes," in *Soundscapes of the Urban Past: Staged Sound as Mediated Cultural Heritage*, ed. Karin Bijsterveld (Bielefeld, 2013), 31–66.

**James G. Mansell** is Assistant Professor of Cultural Studies at the University of Nottingham, U.K., and a graduate of the Ph.D. programme in History at the University of Manchester. His research to date has been concerned with cultural histories of sound and hearing in twentieth-century Britain and Europe. He is currently finishing a book manuscript on the topic of sound and selfhood in early twentieth-century Britain. He co-edited *The Projection of Britain: A History of the GPO Film Unit* (Basingstoke, 2011).

**Daniel Morat** is Research Fellow and Lecturer at the History Department of the Free University Berlin. He received his Ph.D. at the University of Göttingen in 2006. He is currently working on a research project on "The Soundscape of the Metropolis: Auditory Cultures in Berlin and New York, 1880–1930" and directing the international research network "Auditory Knowledge in Transition", funded by the German Research Foundation. Latest publication: "Urban Soundscapes and Acoustic Innervation around 1900," in *Les cinq sens de la ville: Du Moyen Age à nos jours*, eds. Robert Beck, Ulrike Krampl, and Emmanuelle Retaillaud-Bajac (Tours, 2013), 71–83.

**Sven Oliver Müller** is Research Group Leader at the Max Planck Institute for Human Development in Berlin. He received his Ph.D. from the University of Bielefeld in 2001. His major fields of research are European Cultural History, theories of Nationalism and the War

Crimes of the "Wehrmacht" in Eastern Europe. Latest publication: *Das Publikum macht die Musik: Musikleben in Berlin, London und Wien im 19. Jahrhundert* (Göttingen, 2014).

**John M. Picker** is Lecturer in Literature and Comparative Media Studies at the Massachusetts Institute of Technology. He previously taught at Harvard University and the University of Virginia. He is the author of *Victorian Soundscapes* (Oxford and New York, 2003). Latest publication: "Aural Anxieties and the Advent of Modernity," in *The Victorian World*, ed. Martin Hewitt (London and New York, 2012), 603–18.

**Mark M. Smith** is Carolina Distinguished Professor of History at the University of South Carolina, Columbia. His published work includes *Mastered by the Clock: Time, Slavery, and Freedom in the American South* (Chapel Hill, 1997), *Listening to Nineteenth-Century America* (Chapel Hill, 2001), *How Race Is Made: Slavery, Segregation, and the Senses* (Chapel Hill, 2006) and *Sensing the Past: Seeing, Hearing, Smelling, Tasting and Touching in History* (Berkeley, 2008). He is currently working on a book manuscript entitled *When War Makes Sense: A Sensory History of the American Civil War* (under contract at Oxford University Press).

**Axel Volmar** is Teaching Fellow in Media Studies at the University of Siegen, Germany. He is also a member of the international research network "Auditory Knowledge in Transition", funded by the German Research Foundation. In his doctoral dissertation, "Sound Experiments" (forthcoming), he has studied the auditory culture of science since 1800. He has co-edited collected volumes on auditory media cultures: *Auditive Medienkulturen*, with Jens Schröter (Bielefeld, 2013); and on the cultural history of data sonification: *Das geschulte Ohr*, with Andi Schoon (Bielefeld, 2012).

**Hansjakob Ziemer** is Research Fellow at the Max Planck Institute for the History of Science in Berlin. He received his Ph.D. in Modern History at Humboldt University in Berlin in 2007 after studying at the universities of Berlin, Oxford and Stanford. His dissertation was published as *Die Moderne hören: Das Konzert als urbanes Forum, 1890–1940* (Campus Verlag, 2008), and received the Bethmann Prize of the City of Frankfurt am Main. In addition, he has published several articles on the cultural history of music and the public sphere. He is also a member of the international research network "Auditory Knowledge in Transition", funded by the German Research Foundation.

 Index

Note: page numbers in *italics* refer to illustrations; n = note

Leopoldi, Hermann: "Lovely Adrienne
has a radio antenna", 112–13
Leppert, Richard, 209
Lessing, Theodor, 92; *Pamphlet for the
Battle against Noise*, 93–95
Levine, Lawrence, 163–64
Lewes, George Henry, 29
Lewin, Kurt, 230, 239
Lewis, Wyndham, 296n16
Libyan War (1911–12), 238–39
"Lied der Deutschen", 186
Lindenberger, Thomas, 184–85
Lind, Jenny, 160–61
listening: active, 217–18, 228, 230–31,
236, 246; aesthetic, 132–33, 136,
141; close, 26–30, 37, 41; collective,
116–17; contextuality, 202; as cultural
process, 83; democratization of,
144–45; diagnostic, 229–31, 232, 246;
effect of recording technology on,
83–86, 87, 141; emotional, 203–204;
exploratory, 242–43; as heightened
skill on World War I battlefields,
227–36; hermeneutical, 214–16,
218; as historically determined
process, 71, 83; inner, 201–202;
introspective, 84, 89, 216; as method
of location, 228, 236, 246; and musical
expertise, 130–31; "new", 236–37;
observant, 132; pathological, 132;
post-World War I reevaluations of,
236–47; professionalization of, 218;
"schizophonic", 257; secret, 242,
243; selective deafness, 141, 144, 145;
silent, 154, 157–58, 159–68, 202–203,
208; and social meaning, 202–203;
as social tool, 218; structural 147n9;
subjectivity of, 88; utilitarian, 236. *See
also* auditory perception
listening posts, 232
Liszt, Franz, 131, 133; *Heldenklage*, 215;
"The Ideal", 161
Literarische Anstalt A.G., 112
literature: decadent, 287, 288, 291, 292;
neurasthenia as theme of, 286–93;
references to stethoscope and close
listening, 27–31
liveness, 101, 105, 107, 109–10
London: Anti-Noise League, 281,
291; audience behavior and silent
listening, 154, 162–67; class-based
attacks on street music, 311;

Gouraud's "phonogram" from,
40–41; Great Exhibition, 35; influence
of German attitudes to music, 167–68;
labor dispute, 163; noise, 30–31, 278;
opera, 156–57, 162, 163, 164, 165;
performance of *The Merry Widow*,
109; Royal Academy Exhibition
(1844), 33–34
London, Kurt, 267
*longue durée*, 258, 270n11
Lorenz, Carl, 134–36, 137
Lothar, Rudolf, 88
loudspeaker, 116, 117
"Lovely Adrienne has a radio antenna",
112–13

Mach, Ernst, 134
machines, 292–93
Mahler, Gustav: Symphony No. 2
(*Resurrection*), 215
*Manifeste auditiviste* (de Maxange), 292
Mann, Thomas, 75, 88; *The Magic
Mountain*, 84, 89
manometric flame, 54
Mansell, James, 17
manuscript culture, 179
Marconi Company, 112
Margat, Claire, 290–91
Marinetti, Filippo Tommaso, 238–39,
259
Marks, Stephan, 178–79
Marschalk, Max, 207, 208, 216, 217
masculinity: linked with imperialism
288–90; linked with sensitivity to
noise 30–31, 278, 279–80, 282, 283,
284, 287–88, 294
Mason, James, 33
Massachusetts Charitable Eye and Ear
Infirmary, 55
Massachusetts Institute of Technology,
55
mass culture: industrial, 72–80;
Lessing's contempt for, 93–95;
radio and, 116; role of recordings,
109; social anxiety about, 150n53;
telephone and, 107
mass mobilization. See *Augusterlebnis*
Mayer, Alfred, 52
McLuhan, Marshall, 47, 64, 179–80
media theory, 179–80
mediation, 258–59, 308
mediatization, 227

Lightning Source UK Ltd.
Milton Keynes UK
UKHW02f2136211117
313106UK00005B/321/P

9 781785 333491